Varieties of Personal Theology
Charting the Beliefs and Values of
American Young Adults

DAVID T. GORTNER
Virginia Theological Seminary, USA

Routledge
Taylor & Francis Group

LONDON AND NEW YORK

First published 2013 by Ashgate Publishing

Published 2016 by Routledge
2 Park Square, Milton Park, Abingdon, Oxfordshire OX14 4RN
711 Third Avenue, New York, NY 10017, USA

First issued in paperback 2016

Routledge is an imprint of the Taylor & Francis Group, an informa business

British Library Cataloguing in Publication Data
Gortner, David.
  Varieties of personal theology: charting the beliefs and values of American young adults.
  1. Young adults–Religious life–United States. 2. Young adults–United States–Psychology.
I. Title
200.8'42'0973-dc23

The Library of Congress has cataloged the printed edition as follows:
Gortner, David.
  Varieties of personal theology : charting the beliefs and values of American young adults / by David T. Gortner.
     p. cm.
  Includes bibliographical references and index.
  ISBN 978-1-4094-2552-6 (hardcover : alk. paper)
1. Young adults–United States–Religious life. 2. United States–Religion. I. Title.
  BL2525.G67 2014
  202.084'20973–dc23

                                                                    2012038192

ISBN 13: 978-1-138-27719-9 (pbk)
ISBN 13: 978-1-4094-2552-6 (hbk)

Contents

List of Figures

Varieties of Personal Theology

List of Tables

Acknowledgements

As both a psychologist and a priest, it is natural for me to move between two worlds of thought. Additionally, in both domains of work, while I draw distinctions between my pastoral concern for and my scholarly interest in situations, these different perspectives also frequently overlap and inform each other. Young adults' personal theologies are for me not only the lively subject of scholarly inquiry; they are also the subject of prayer. I have held in prayer the young adults about whom I have written and whose narratives I have meticulously explored, because their lives have become important to me. I hope for them lives of joy, wisdom and continuing discovery.

The variety found in young adults' personal theologies related to worldview, theodicy, life purpose and ultimate values resonates with the variety of theological perspectives both within and across the great scriptural texts and commentaries of the world's major religions. To illustrate this wide range of theological perspectives, I have quoted a series of excerpts from religious texts at the beginning of Chapters 4 through 7. These scriptural quotations are mostly drawn from the fine compendium of thematically related religious texts in *World Scripture: A Comparative Anthology of Sacred Texts*, compiled in 1991 by the International Religious Foundation. Other religious texts are drawn directly from English translations of scriptures (such as the New Revised Standard Version of the Bible), commentaries, or classic theological or philosophical texts. We are all indebted to the many scholars who have over the centuries committed themselves to careful transmission, translation and interpretation of these texts.

I want to express my deep gratitude to the University of Chicago and the National Opinion Research Center for the opportunities provided to me for such rich, interdisciplinary research and analysis. I am particularly grateful to Barbara Schneider for her invitation to me to join the research team for the *Making the Transition* study of emerging adults (the source of this book), for her analytical insights, and for her support and generosity in providing a young researcher a place to thrive. *Making the Transition* was funded by the US Department of Education (Principal Investigator, Barbara Schneider), as a longitudinal extension of the Sloan Study of Youth and Social Development (Principal Investigators, Charles Bidwell, Mihaly Csikszentmihalyi, Larry Hedges and Barbara Schneider), funded by the Alfred P. Sloan Foundation. I am immensely grateful to Don Browning for his assistance in bringing sound practical theological analysis to bear on the interview responses of these young adults; Don has left a significant mark on the emerging field of practical theology and has been one of the great interdisciplinary scholars bridging theology, ethics and the social sciences. Other scholars such as Mihaly Czikszentmihalyi, Richard Taub, Dan McAdams, Nancy Stein, Andrew

Greeley, Mark Leary and John Driebelbis enriched this endeavour through their consultations that have provided new insights, theoretical perspectives and methodological clarification.

Research such as that undertaken in *Making the Transition* requires many hands and minds to collect, organize, manage and analyse the rich array of quantitative and qualitative data gathered. And it requires strong interpersonal skills and a readiness to connect deeply with the young adults we encountered. I am grateful for the assistance and collegial partnership of Lisa Hoogstra, Laura Lewellyn, Joe Miller, Charles Hooker, Phaedra Daipha and others who together conducted hundreds of interviews, helped manage complex datasets and analyse qualitative responses. Their skill in interviewing ensured high-quality responses from young adults.

Coming forward several years, I wish to express my gratitude to Virginia Theological Seminary for providing me the scholarly professional space and time to bring this book to completion. I am especially grateful to Ian Markham for his encouragement to seek publication of this volume with Ashgate, and to my colleagues Timothy Sedgwick, Joyce Mercer, Elisabeth Kimball, Jonathan Gray, and Jessicah Duckworth for their thoughtful critiques and recommendations. I am indebted to Vicki Black, who assisted me in editing and bringing the project to fruition.

I am immensely grateful to my family for their constant support, challenge, and space for discussion – parents Robert and Jane, in-laws James, Joan and Stewart, wife Heather and daughters Cassie and Miriam.

Chapter 1

Introduction

It was early spring, it was dark, and I was lost. I had driven two hours to meet Jason, a young man who had agreed to meet me for a face-to-face interview at his home. I had the address, I had my printout from MapQuest (no GPS yet available for mere mortals like me). But I could not find the road where Jason lived. There were no stores nearby. I was on the outskirts of a small Midwestern city, in a shutter-and-shack part of town, on the edge of farms and country and a lot of nowhere.

I was on a quest to hear a young man's personal theology – the beliefs and values contributing to how he made sense of the world, humanity, and life. Jason was one more among 82 emerging adults across the United States whom I and others visited in their homes or local settings to talk about meaning and purpose in their lives.

I stopped at a building where there were cars and pickup trucks. It was lit, but there were no windows – a small, semi-industrial-looking building surrounded by a gravel parking lot. I walked in, determined to ask for directions, and found myself in a 'gentlemen's' strip club, complete with bar, tables, stage with poles, and nearly naked women doing lap dances for beer-bellied men dressed in their workday flannel shirts and jeans. This was not part of the evening's planned research activities.

I quickly asked for directions and exited. I learned I was within three blocks of Jason's house. Once back on the road, I turned into a trailer park neighbourhood. I stopped at the right trailer home and went to the door. Jason, who at that time was 20 years old, lived with his father, who opened the door. I explained why I was there. Jason's father said that his son was not yet home from the steakhouse where he worked. He invited me to sit at the kitchen table where we sat and chatted a bit awkwardly for about ten minutes until Jason arrived. He greeted me and we went to his room.

I found myself in a dimly lit room, lit with crisscrossed strings of blood-red lights. An impressive stereo system came on, playing a driving kind of hard rock I had not heard before. There was little furniture, but there were some cushions on the floor for seating. In the corner was a walk-in closet, its doorway lined with yellow police crime-scene tape and its floor covered by a bed mattress – where Jason slept. This was not exactly what I expected as the space for our conversation about beliefs and values. I said something about the music, and Jason explained that it was Scandinavian death-metal music: 'The words are really dark. The music, it's intense, like acid rock or heavy metal – comes out of punk rock, really. But the words are completely dark, and they're nihilists. Their voices – I mean, can you believe how low they growl? It's great stuff.'

What was I going to hear from Jason in the next hour? What would he have to say about the nature of the world, human purpose, life's uncertainties and the best of human ideals?

I found myself compelled to listen in this unfamiliar space, this inner sanctum that Jason had constructed in his world to give expression to what he believed and saw about the world beyond his doors. A soft-spoken young man in his early twenties, living with his divorced dad just down the road from a strip club, who saw the dirty underside of the restaurant industry and mucked through its thick, fatty residuals of food consumption, listened to Scandinavian death-metal music and slept on a mattress on the floor of a closet behind strands of police crime-scene tape ... . What would this young man have to say? What kind of personal theology was taking shape in him?

Discovering the Beliefs and Values of Emerging Adults

The 82 interviews that make up the core of the study documented in this book were all conducted in the two years prior to September 11, 2001, a date of tragedy and trauma for the nation of the United States. These 82 emerging adults (ages 18–25) were part of a national study of 314 young adults transitioning to work after high school, themselves originally part of a national longitudinal study of over 1,200 teenagers and their social development – a study running in tandem with the National Education Longitudinal Study, which followed 25,000 eighth-grade students starting in 1988. The 82 young women and men came from a wide spectrum of American life, across social classes, races and family backgrounds, from rural and suburban and urban contexts.

We brought our questions to these 82 emerging adults at the end of a period of remarkable prosperity in American society, during a time when jobs were still plentiful, when young people were being sought out explicitly for their ingenuity and unorthodox approaches to building organizations, when entrepreneurs commanded keen interest, when cigars were back and yachts were getting bigger, and people were buying homes in the ongoing housing boom – and when spirituality seemed to have awakened with new force among youth and young adults.

The questions we asked were about the world, one's purpose in life, causes of and coping with tragic and traumatic events, and the highest values by which to live. It seemed reasonable to expect that the answers coming out of such a time of prosperity would be markedly different from those heard after 9/11, when the world for Americans changed – or from the answers that would have been given during the more challenging economic and political times of the 1960s and 1970s.

I discovered, however, that many of the patterns in responses seem to hold, across years and periods and events. Evidence from these surveys and studies, which will be presented in later chapters, suggests a deep consistency of overall patterns in the beliefs and values comprising personal theologies across the decades of the last 40–50 years. In my own work, I had already asked these questions among sixty religious young adults in a separate study I had conducted over the decade from 1995 to 2005, documenting religious communities and programs formed by young adults who sought to reinvent and revitalize shared religious life.[1] I have continued to ask these questions in my work as a professor, a priest, a psychologist. And in all these years, I have not found significant differences in the pattern of answers given to these questions across time, before or after 9/11, inside or outside of religious contexts. I have, however, found marked differences among individuals. These young adults as individuals were makers of meaning, constructors of world and cosmos, philosophical theologians. Each voice offered unique insight into the variety of ways young adults were attempting to make sense of the world in which they found themselves. Even when most of them held strong beliefs that everything happened for a reason or stressed the importance of good relationships and the development of personal strengths as their primary organizing values, these patterns were far from universal.

Over half of the emerging adults we interviewed during this time of relative prosperity and peace nonetheless tended to view the world through a dark, pessimistic filter. Jason described the world as 'very hectic, chaotic, unorganized, with a whole hell of a lot of evil', full of dark forces and twisted motivations:. 'People are looking out for themselves. And they usually don't even know their own darkest, secret motivations.' Regarding his purpose or place in the world, Jason saw himself as a small bit player in the world:

> I prefer to leave the world alone, except when I have to get involved. You know, every once in a while at the steakhouse, I have to clean out the 'fat vat.' It's out back behind the building, it's got all the leftover grease and fat and stuff from the kitchen. It is the grossest job I have. I don't do it but once a month. But it's gotta be done. That's what it's like, trying to get involved in the world.

None the less, his negative worldview and propensity for withdrawal from the world did not leave him with a completely bleak, nihilistic and cruel outlook that would simply mimic the death-metal lyrics to which he listened and the tomb-like setting of his bed. Jason attempted to make sense of unexpected tragedies or traumas by trying to find the good in a situation and move forward. His core organizing values were individuality and a strong will:

---

[1]   Jacqueline Schmitt and David Gortner, 'The Challenges of Evangelism with Students and Young Adults', in *Disorganized Religion: The Evangelization of Youth and Young Adults in the Episcopal Church*, ed. Sheryl Kujawa (Cambridge, MA: Cowley Press, 1997); David Gortner, 'Terminal Values of Young Adults: Evidence of a New Values Structure', presented at the American Psychological Association Annual Meeting, Toronto, Ontario, August 2003; David Gortner, 'Young Adult Worldviews and Life Purpose – Shaped by Social Capital, Education, and Self-Efficacy, but not Religion', presented at the American Academy of Religion Annual Meeting, Philadelphia, PA, November 2005.

People who are strong-willed, who don't take 'no' for an answer, who can stand on their own, keep pushing – those are the ones I admire. People who know who they are and don't apologize for it. They don't get sucked in by everything around them. I can't stand the people who are just a bunch of dumb followers, y'know, the people who just line up behind some cause without thinking for themselves. And drug addicts. I've got no patience for drug addicts. There were plenty around in high school, and there are some around in this neighbourhood. I've got no time for them. Wasting their lives.

In the chapters that follow, the voices of emerging adults will help map some of the patterns and variances in the beliefs and values that comprise personal theologies. It is their voices that I hope will bring together social scientists and theologians in greater curiosity and more disciplined mutual inquiry into the wide variations and combinations of beliefs and values that comprise people's personal theologies, the social and developmental factors that help shape those varied beliefs and values, and the ways in which personal theologies interact with and shape people's choices and perceptions in daily life.

Beliefs and values are fundamental to human behaviour, attitudes and experiences – and are formed in the crucible of life experiences. What we believe and value directs our attention, shapes our perception and interpretation of things, and channels our choices, plans and actions. Yes, as social psychologists like John Bargh have noted, human beings also have marked tendencies toward automaticity in their thoughts and actions.[2] We can be fickle and can find ourselves changing course without realizing the simple external cues that have swayed us. But we are still shaped and directed in no small measure by beliefs and values we have learned, absorbed, or inherited – and our beliefs and values can themselves become part of our 'automatic' manner of responding, thinking and acting – and the way we explain ourselves and the world.

We learn, internalize and construct beliefs and values in relation to all areas of living – sometimes in tension or contradiction with each other, for example:

> 'It is good / it is bad to be assertive.'
> 'Poverty is self-induced / is the result of cultural and political forces.'
> 'I must strive to be honest / to win.'
> 'A good parent controls her child in public / gives her child freedom to express himself.'
> 'Money is the root of all evil / makes the world go around.'

---

[2]   In his 1999 seminal article, Bargh argued that as little as 5 per cent of human behaviour is attributable to choice, thus raising questions about the importance of beliefs and values in guiding human behaviour: John Bargh and Tanya Chartrand, 'The Unbearable Automaticity of Being', *American Psychologist* 54: 462–79.

From the cognitive-behavioural perspective of automaticity in human life, these beliefs and values may begin simply as cognitive reinforcements and *post hoc* permissions for our own and others' thoughts, choices, or actions. But even if this is the case, in time, beliefs and values take on a life of their own, focusing our attention and actions in particular ways so that we begin to experience and engage life according to those beliefs and values.

Social scientists and theologians alike will affirm the importance of beliefs and values. But theologians have not typically applied disciplined methods to hear and understand first-hand the theologies of people 'on the street', nor have they resisted the temptation to leap quickly to prescriptive judgements of those beliefs and values in the light of platonic universal ideals. Social scientists, conversely, have developed and used a variety of disciplined methods for the study of daily life, and personal attitudes and thoughts, but have only rarely focused these methods on the study of personal theologies. They have concentrated significant effort on understanding beliefs and values *about the self* (that is, matters of identity, self-concept and person-perception), but have neglected inquiry into people's values and beliefs *about the world* (that is, the overarching assumptions, expectancies and ideals that deal with matters of being, purpose, ultimate causes and the good). It is these types of values and beliefs that comprise a 'personal theology' – a 'world-concept' that, like a 'self-concept', is an amalgamation of perceptions, expectations and goals. Unlike self-concept, which is an operating personal theory of personality or identity (and unlike other-concept, which is a personal theory of other people's location *vis-à-vis* oneself), the world-concept of personal theology is an operating personal theory of the entirety of the world or cosmos in which one finds oneself. This book enters the hidden world of personal theologies by beginning to describe and map a terrain of the beliefs and values having to do with people's conceptions of the broadest external realities: the field of being.

The few social scientists who have explored more theological beliefs and values (for instance, Max Weber, Rodney Stark, Florence Kluckhohn, James Fowler and Robert Wuthnow) have typically relied on a priori broad-brush categories such as religious affiliation (and the distinctive dogmatic assertions of each religious body), stages of moral and faith development, and large-scale socio-historical typologies to frame the research methods they employed and the choices they defined for people in survey and interview questions. Theologians as diverse as Karl Barth, Karl Rahner, Gustavo Gutiérrez and Grace Jantzen have tended to leap to universalizing generalizations about beliefs and values among people – either as the whole of humanity or as whole groups juxtaposed in rough contradistinctions, usually without sufficient field research or conversations to justify such descriptive claims.

While these broad-brush generalizing and universalizing approaches may be somewhat useful in describing some simple patterns and providing basic heuristics, they paint an overly uniform picture, neglecting the subtleties of individual differences and, as a result, miss important nuances in how people construct and use personal theology. In today's increasingly multicultural and individualized society, people's deepest beliefs and values about existence, purpose, cause and the good are more variable and less clearly derived from any singular religious or socio-political perspective. As a result, personal theologies, or broad conceptions of the world and the nature of reality, become as varied as the variations in personality, personal and group identity, and identifications of the other – and as important in their impact on people's thoughts, motivations, choices and actions.

Picking up William James's mapping of diverse religious phenomena in his classic lectures, *Varieties of Religious Experience*, this book begins to chart the variations and patterns found in the personal theologies of young adults in contemporary America – without investment in any specific theological perspectives being 'right'. This book starts from Paul Tillich's daring assertion that all human beings engage in theological thinking, and puts that assertion to the test. It treats theological categories as accessible and of interest to people in everyday life – especially some of the most central and fundamental questions of being, purpose, ultimate cause and the good.

Young, emerging adults (ages 18–25) are a particularly interesting age-group to engage around questions of personal theology. Their continuing work on identity formation and on conceptions of the other is not without regard for the larger world in which they exist. Increasing cognitive complexity, education and exposure to broader contexts and more significant stakes in living all contribute to late adolescence and early adulthood as significant periods in the formation of personal theologies. It is not just the self that matters. It is the world that matters. Jason was not simply engaged in the process of coming to know himself. More intently, Jason was coming to know and frame the world, the field of being in which he as a self needed to navigate and function. And his experiences, like the multiple experiences of his emerging adult peers in domains of work, relationships and leisure, contributed to the intensity with which some of these questions are engaged.

Personal Theologies: Defining the Terms

> Our species has been designed to actively create *theories* about one's world, to make *meaning* of one's experiences, including the construction of a theory of self.
>
> Susan Harter[3]

> Ordinary people are not religious professionals who approach spirituality the way an engineer might construct a building. They are amateurs who make do with what they can. Hardly anybody comes up with a truly innovative approach to life's

---

[3]   Susan Harter, *The Construction of the Self: A Developmental Perspective* (New York: Guilford, 1999), p. 8.

enduring spiritual questions, but hardly anybody simply mimics the path someone else has taken either.

Robert Wuthnow[4]

Admittedly, 'personal theology' is a complicated and potentially controversial term to introduce into the discourses of theology and the social sciences – almost as controversial as 'spirituality'. For scholars and practitioners in the social sciences, the word 'theology' may conjure images of beliefs that cannot be proved, conceptions of deity, and idealistic and prescriptive assertions that supposedly do not enter pure social scientific discourse and research. Theology also gets conflated with dogma and doctrine, those institutionally defended statements of absolutes to which religious members are expected to adhere. The effect of these assumptions on various fields has been profound. For example, psychology as a discipline carries a history of abreaction to theological or religious beliefs, having long regarded such thoughts as reinforcements for overactive superegos, systems used by people to sustain neuroses and avoid the anxieties of true freedom and responsibility. The past twenty-five years have marked a shift within psychology, making space for greater appreciation of spirituality and a growing acknowledgement of the positive influences of religion, as well as an increasing interest in ultimate concerns and meaning-making.[5] But the term 'theology' still seems *verboten*.

Even the word 'personal' raises problems for some anthropologists and sociologists in particular, who may find little value in a focus on individual differences and may question the legitimacy of 'personal' concepts such as individual identity and self-construction. Social psychologist Daryl Bem and sociologist John Elder have each raised eyebrows among personality researchers, pointing out the ways in which individual 'personality' itself is mediated and sustained by social contexts and communication patterns,[6] even pressing the question of whether or not 'personality' is something truly intrinsic to individuals. Recent studies that reveal significant geographic variations in 'personality' in

---

[4]   Robert Wuthnow, *After the Baby Boomers: How Twenty- and Thirty-Somethings Are Shaping the Future of American Religion* (Princeton, NJ: Princeton University Press, 2007), p. 14.

[5]   See Raymond Paloutzian and Crystal Park, *Handbook of the Psychology of Religion and Spirituality* (New York: Guilford, 2005).

[6]   See Avshalom Caspi, Daryl Bem and Glen Elder, 'Continuities and Consequences of Interactional Styles across the Life Course', *Journal of Personality* 57(2) (June 1989): 375–406. Bem and Elder discussed self-perception and other-perception (the primary means of assessing 'personality') not as tags for intrinsic traits but as indicators of negotiated and practiced patterns of interaction. They saw identity in terms of cumulative continuity, 'when a person's interactional style channels him or her into environments that themselves reinforce that style', and interactional continuity, 'when an individual's style evokes reciprocal, sustaining responses from others' (375). For them, the social context encountered shapes, supports and sustains self-concept and 'personality'.

the United States, related directly to socio-economic, political and health-related differences, are bringing this debate to light again,[7] resurrecting questions of what is regarded as truly personal, that is, intrinsic or unique to the individual.

Theologians and religious scholars and leaders may also react negatively to the term 'personal theology'. While theologians might welcome interdisciplinary discourse as expansive to the field, it can be unsettling for them to consider theology as a matter of social scientific investigation; as medieval scholasticism has imprinted on the field, theology is to be regarded as the queen of the sciences rather than their subject. It is far preferable to be the examiner and make prescriptive statements based on a bit of interdisciplinary insight than it is to be the examined and described as an object of study. Furthermore, the notion of 'personal' theology may for some be synonymous with theological error. Theology, some will argue, is not a matter of personal construction or choice, but a matter of collective wisdom and insight by those who have been exposed to a community of revelation. Resistance to the 'personal' in the Christian religion can be traced back through the negative reactions of many institutional religious leaders to the First and Second Great Awakenings, in the attempts to silence or eliminate voices of reform in Europe during the Age of Reform, and in the prescribed musical forms that kept local or unique musical expressions from public worship in late medieval Catholicism, and in Eastern Orthodoxy to the current day.[8]

But why shouldn't theologians take a greater interest in the wide range of beliefs and values among individuals and the ways that personal theologies are shaped and used? Why shouldn't social scientists attend more closely to the ways in which people construct 'world-concepts'?

I have chosen the term 'personal theology' intentionally, to characterize how individuals are agents in collecting and constructing ways of making sense of existence in the broadest sense. Individuals contribute actively to the formation of their own ideas and theories about the nature of place and the purpose of being, drawing from their varied perceptions, experiences and interpretations about the

---

[7]   Peter Jason Rentfrow, 'Statewide Differences in Personality: Toward a Psychological Geography of the United States', *American Psychologist* 65(6) (September 2010): 548–58.

[8]   Clergy in England and America alike reviled 'enthusiasm' and public displays of individual emotion (see eighteenth century sermons against Enthusiasm, for example by Charles Chauncy and Edmund Gibson). George Fox, founder of the Quakers, recorded how he was 'beaten about the head' and driven from the church when he stood to speak as he was moved by the Spirit. John Hus, an early reformer hailed by Moravians as their founder, brought John Wycliffe's ideas back to Belgium, including the use of the common language in worship and the reading of scripture. He was tried as a heretic and burned at the stake – with copies of Wycliffe's bible used as kindling. Resistance to cultural and personal expression or innovation in musical style has been a common formula for religious leadership. In the Catholic Church, new forms of polyphony and harmony, as well as public musical forms using rhythm and instruments, were at first banned and then only slowly accepted. Music in Eastern Orthodox traditions must adhere to clearly established patterns – Sergei Rachmaninoff's setting of the Divine Liturgy is not permitted for church services.

world. People are not only passive recipients of the organizing philosophies, theologies and mythologies of their cultures, religions, or economic or socio-political locations in a given place and time in history. Even if this were true, the wide variations of settings and experiences in subcultures, clans and households would warrant an examination of individual differences in beliefs and values. But people are active: they observe, internalize, interpret and reformulate the broadest theological, mythological and philosophical constructs they learn or encounter – in unique, individualized ways. People construct worlds.

'Personal theology' need not imply an explicit belief in a deity.[9] I recognize, especially as an ordained priest, that this is a brazen claim. From its Greek linguistic roots, the word 'theology' itself literally means speech, accounts, thoughts, or principles about a deity. But, following Aristotle's suggestion,[10] we may consider theology as more than beliefs and assertions about a God, gods, or no god. Preceding, surrounding and proceeding from assertions or denials of deity are a set of more experientially fundamental questions, perceptions and beliefs about the world, humanity and existence, combined with ultimate values about ideal ways to live, that provide an interpretive framework for experience in relation to these ultimate questions, and shape motivations, goals and behaviours. These questions reside at the overlapping spaces of philosophy and theology.

In this sense, I do not mean theology as dogma or doctrine, or 'right belief'. That implies a normative or prescriptive lens that is not appropriate for descriptive research. It is not the task of description – the task I have undertaken as a social scientist – to determine whether or not individuals' personal theologies are right or wrong. It is the task of description to reveal the content of individuals' personal theologies and to examine how they relate to their lives. People may hold varying theologies, and those beliefs and values may differ in their origins and effects. In addition, I do not use the term 'personal' to imply a purely intrinsic or solipsistic source of meaning, emerging from a self that has no relation to its surrounding. Personal theologies are informed by the socio-cultural, religious, ethnic and familial realities each person experiences.

Existential psychologists and pastoral theologians have long given consideration to individuals' perceptions, explanations, expectancies and ultimate concerns about the broadest environmental contexts into which they find themselves 'thrown'. It is these types of values and beliefs that comprise a personal theology – a 'world-

---

9   Even Fritz Oser, though heavily influenced by constructivist and progressive theorists (for example, Lawrence Kohlberg and Richard Hersch, 'Theory into Practice', *Moral Development* 16(2) (April 1977): 53–9) and a Judeo-Christian bias, recognized the importance of understanding the 'personal theologies', that is, the beliefs and values held with conviction, among atheists and agnostics. See Fritz Oser, 'The Development of Religious Judgment', in *Fundamental Research in Moral Development*, ed. B. Puka, vol. 2 (New York: Garland, 1994), pp. 375–96.

10   See Aristotle, *Metaphysics*, Book VI, trans. W.D. Ross <classics.mit.edu/Aristotle/metaphysics.6.vi.html>.

concept' or *umwelt* that, like a 'self-concept', is an amalgamation of perceptions, expectations and goals, transmitted through cultural and developmental forces such as family, education and religion, and then filtered and interpreted by each individual.

The fundamental questions that I have explored with young adults arise from philosophical theology. But they are not confined within theological discourse: they recur among the writings of different social scientists, philosophers and poets as well. They are some of the 'big questions' about nature and quality of being, causation and justice in the face of harmful and seemingly irrational events, human purpose and destiny, and ultimate values and ideals for human life. While other core questions are doubtless worthy of similar study in the mapping of personal theologies, I have limited the exploratory analyses of this study to these four facets of personal theology, through specific focus on the following questions:

1. the overall quality and nature of the world as a place of existence;
2. a human being's place and purpose *vis-à-vis* the world;
3. causes and meanings behind traumatic and tragic life events, and
4. human qualities and values most constitutive of (or most contrary to) a good life.

These are the questions that brought me to Jason's home.

So how does one begin to learn and understand the personal theologies held by different individuals? We start by asking people questions and listening to their responses. It is actually a relatively simple matter – on the surface. But, as we shall see, it is particularly challenging to stay in the listening mode and not move too quickly to interpretation, using the various theories we bring to bear upon the project. In Jason's dark bedroom, it would have been very easy to jump to conclusions about his personal theology and label him a nihilist, without ever listening to a word he might say. It was tempting to filter Jason's responses to questions through the surrounding visual and audible signals of police crime-scene tape and death-metal music that were part of his environment. But then I would not be allowing Jason to express himself directly. I would not be taking his own theological thinking seriously, and I would be robbing him of his own capacity to articulate his own 'world-concept', because I would be too busy layering my own artful interpretations onto what he was saying. It is essential to remain curious and open: 'I wonder how this young man will describe the world, humanity, and the good?'

An Interdisciplinary Approach

The term 'personal theology' is intended to convey the interdisciplinary sweep of this project. It is essential for scholars and practitioners in the social sciences and religion to develop more than a cursory understanding of each others' discourses, assumptions and methods. Both the social sciences and the theological and religious disciplines can illuminate for each other new questions, different approaches, and unsearched or untested presumptions. Let me illustrate why such an interdisciplinary approach is important by pointing out some presumptions and missing elements in the social sciences and in the theological disciplines.

The Content Gap in the Social Sciences

For decades, social scientists have committed themselves to the study and exploration of human identities. Psychologists have invested resources and effort in understanding identity through studies on personality, identity development, self-image and self-esteem. Sociologists and anthropologists have studied identity through an examination of societal attitudes and beliefs, racial and gender identities, group identity, cultural images, political identities and patriotism. Recently, organizational behaviour scholars have focused on corporate or organizational identity and the degree to which individuals align themselves with the identity of their employing organization. Postmodern and postcolonial perspectives have added further focus on local or indigenous identity that stands in contrast to, or in dialogical or dialectic tension with, assumptions about identity imposed by the dominant cultural, political and economic forces. Alongside this work on self and identity, there has been an important body of research and theory about the other: also an identity, a perceptual framework to define a person or group not the same as oneself.

Social scientists have become scientists of the figure – the individual or the collective body. Their commitment to the study and exploration of both self-identities and social identities is rooted in a deeper fundamental assumption that human beings commit significant mental, emotional and motivational effort – as individuals and as groups – to answering the question, '*Who / what* am I?',[11] and that this is the primary orienting question in human life. It is a worthy pursuit, But it is limited in what it can reveal. Jason's room décor and the words he said revealed far more than what Jason thought about himself; they revealed what Jason thought about the world as he knew and perceived it.

What is missing in the social sciences is a similarly focused study of how human beings form enduring and organizing concepts not only about identity (self and other), but also about the ground of identity, the ground of being. Few have committed themselves to studying the ways in which people perceive and interpret the broadest external environments they encounter – the 'world,' the 'cosmos' and the nature and spectrum of human life.[12] While some may affirm the importance of a *Weltanschauung* or world-concept in the lives of individuals and groups,

---

[11]   Whether this fundamental question of identity or 'self-image' is presented in the singular or in the plural clearly depends on collectivist or individualist assumptions of both cultures and researchers.

[12]   A simple review of publications in psychology and other social sciences, compared to publications in theology, reveals the relative paucity of publications dealing with terms

social scientists tend in their writing to conflate world-concept with self-concept, simply shifting the focus to self-concept or reducing world-concept to political or religious opinion.[13]

In contrast, philosophers and theologians repeatedly have pointed to beliefs about the nature of the world, causation, the purpose of human existence, and values of ultimate good in human behaviour as some of the most basic questions around which individuals and groups organize their lives. For them, the fundamental organizing question for human cognition and motivation is 'What is *this place*?', or, as the point of connection with individual and group identity, '*Where* am I?' It is a question of location, without which an identity lacks form and distinction. From a painter's perspective, it is the ground without which a figure is flat and lacking the definition that a surrounding provides. From a novelist's or playwright's perspective, it is the setting without which a character cannot be developed.

Just as '*Who* am I?' is the basic question being pursued in the construction of personal and collective *identities*, '*Where* am I?' or 'What is *this place* in which I find myself?' is the question people pursue in the process of constructing personal *theologies*. As people pay attention to their environments and interpret the bits of information they receive, they begin to formulate answers to these theological questions of location. Cultures and groups help collect and convey their answers to individual members, and provide mental frameworks through which the world and humanity are perceived. Nonetheless, each individual arrives at a personally internalized convergence of beliefs and values about the world, causality, human purpose, and the good that is worthy of human pursuit. These themes are familiar concepts in existential and ontological philosophy as well as in systematic and fundamental theology. Together, the convergence of these beliefs and values for each person yields a distinct personal theology. This personal theology may be as important and basic a construct for understanding the convergence of human thought, motivation and behaviour as are the constructs of personal and group identities. A *self* (individual or collective) may only be defined and constructed within a definite *world* – itself a set of conceptions, projections and construals regarding one's broadest setting, one's cosmic location.

Max Weber, one of the great figures in sociology, understood this. He used the term 'theology' freely to describe what he regarded as publicly or culturally

---

like 'theology', 'worldview', '*Weltanschauung*', 'cosmology', 'axiology', 'moral/morality' 'theodicy', and 'ultimate' or 'terminal' values or concerns.

[13]   For instance, developmental psychologist Susan Harter, in *The Construction of the Self* (New York: Guildford Press, 1999), recognizes the importance of perceptions and beliefs about the world and the nature of being in the development of identity – but then her work focuses solely (as needed) on the development of a sense of self, without a deeper exploration of how world-concept contributes to and shapes self-concept. Alternatively, sociologist Robert Wuthnow, in *After the Baby Boomers*, makes broad distinctions between contrasting 'worldviews' that are extrapolated from contrasting patterns of responses to national opinion research questions about political or religious ideological statements.

held beliefs about the ground of being.[14] Similarly, Peter Berger has spoken of the overarching influence and protective field provided by a culture's commonly held beliefs and values about the world and its nature.[15] In their times, these sociologists have described culturally generalized theologies emerging from initial folk psychologies and folk-religious practices intended to have an impact on the specific needs and problems of the local society at the moment. For Weber particularly, but also more recently for Berger, a core cultural theological construct was *theodicy* – the way in which a people sought to explain and understand evil, trauma and tragic events in some frame of cosmic justice. In Weber's formulation, cosmology (beliefs about the source, formation and nature of the world and the cosmos) begets theodicy, which then makes way for formulations about human destiny or purpose, which then helps shape codes of morality and values.

More recently, Roy Baumeister, a social psychologist, has argued that *cultural theology* and *ideology* are insufficient in accounting for individual variation. In his argument for a focus on individual variations, he makes a case for what I am calling 'personal theology' – and he builds his case using what has since become a commonplace assertion among postmodern sociologists, religionists and theologians:

> The culture and society toss fragments of meaning at the individual, who somehow manages to choose among them to create a more or less unique set. By choosing consciously, the individual *might* be able to make the set of meanings fairly consistent and coherent. By simply going along with the social pressures in the press of immediate circumstances, the person may end up with a hodgepodge of fragments.[16]

In his writing, Baumeister, along with Canadian sociologist Reginald Bibby and American sociologist Robert Wuthnow, describes what Claude Levi-Strauss (and now a host of postmodernists) called the practice of *bricolage*,[17] or tinkering: the construction of a useful or meaningful thing (or, in this case, a personalized belief system) out of remainders and fragments from various segments of a fractured landscape. There is growing evidence that people in America are doing this with religious and spiritual practices, so that individuals may claim dual or primary and secondary religious affiliations (described by Janet Bennion as 'double-dippers'),

---

[14]   M. Weber, *The Sociology of Religion*, trans. E. Fischoff (Boston, MA: Beacon Press, 1963). Original work published in 1922 under the title *Wirtschaft und Gesellschaft*.

[15]   Peter L. Berger, *The Sacred Canopy: Elements of a Sociological Theory of Religion* (Garden City, NY: Doubleday, 1967).

[16]   Roy Baumeister, *Meanings of Life* (New York: Guilford, 1991), p. 7.

[17]   See Claude Levi-Strauss, *The Savage Mind* (Chicago, IL: University of Chicago Press, 1968).

or, increasingly, hold no religious affiliation commanding their loyalty.[18] But they are not only engaging in *bricolage* with religious and spiritual practices. They are also engaging in the individualized construction of theologies. This is particularly true of contemporary young adults in America, who have over the last decade progressively increased in their frequency of claiming no religious affiliation.[19] In fact, there is no better age-group with whom to explore this phenomenon of personal theology construction than with emerging adults, who dwell in the awkward societal borderlands between the end of high school and the early first investments in adult careers and roles, and who are in the process of what James Marcia has called 'ideological identity' construction.[20]

The Methodological Gap in Theological Disciplines

The content gap in social scientific research and discourse is not a problem in theology and religious studies: the very nature of theological work and religious life is to focus on fundamental questions of being, ultimate causes, purpose and the good. Religions provide people with stories, images, ideals and assertions that are the building-blocks for theologies. Theologians and religious scholars offer, outline and exhaustively discuss systems of beliefs and values as they reflect on core religious texts, central religious stories, commonly held religious practices and broadly understood experiences of religious people. In the past several decades, there has even been increasing attention to particular theologies of different subgroups of people – and an increasing number of publications dealing with concepts of 'identity' and the ways in which cultural identities have shaped theological perspectives and the crafting of scriptures, religious practices and theological texts.

What has been missing in theological and religious scholarship is attention to disciplined research methods in descriptive work, particularly as it pertains to the documenting of theologies of individuals. Theologians often drift into speaking in generalizations and typologies about what humans believe and value – even amid the significant eye-opening contributions of African-American, feminist, womanist, Asian, liberationist and postcolonial contributions to theology.

---

[18]   See Wuthnow, *After the Baby Boomers*; J. Bennion, 'Double-dippers: An Exploration of Alternative Mormon Activities' (lecture, Society for the Scientific Study of Religion, Salt Lake City, UT, November, 2002); Barry A. Kosmin and Ariela Keysar, *American Religious Identification Survey (ARIS) Summary Report, 2008*, (Hartford, CT: Institute for the Study of Secularism in Society & Culture, 2009) <http://commons.trincoll. edu/aris/files/2011/08/ARIS_Report_2008.pdf>.

[19]   See The Pew Forum on Religion & Public Life, '"Nones" on the Rise: One in Five Adults Have No Religious Affiliation', posted 9 October 2012, <http://www.pewforum. org/unaffiliated/nones-on-the-rise.aspx>.

[20]   James Marcia, 'Development and Validation of Ego Identity Status', *Journal of Personality and Social Psychology* 3(5) (May 1966): 551–8.

Variations in beliefs and values related to social class, race or ethnicity, gender, life experiences and age are now being considered more thoroughly in theologians' discussions of beliefs and values. But the inherited pattern of universalizing and generalizing can be seen even among those theologians who have focused on particular groups, communities and shared identities of people to help explore and expose the range of theological beliefs and the circumstances that create problems for 'universal' assertions. African-American womanist theologians have taken early feminist theologians to task for assumptions of middle-class white culture perpetuated in their explorations of women's theological beliefs and values and the challenges *all* women face. Liberationist and Korean *minjung* theologians have been critiqued for their assumptions about what the poor would embrace as theologically liberating, without spending enough time asking the poor directly about the beliefs and values that help them make sense of and navigate the world they inhabit.

The fundamental problem is in theological methodology that presses toward universal or generalized descriptions and prescriptions without sufficient attention to and intentional investigation of individual variances. Theology still resides methodologically close to philosophy in its primary focus on analysis of inherited texts and its penchant for armchair introspective self-inquiry and extrapolation from a few cases. These methods certainly have their place. Close examination of one's own experiences, thoughts and actions can lead to intriguing new insights and connections worthy of further research. Extrapolation from patterns of experience, thought and action in other individuals or groups can likewise bring attention to themes and patterns previously unrecognized. But the problem comes in the temptation to universalize or overgeneralize – a temptation not unfamiliar in the history of the social sciences, which over time have developed a watchfulness for overstating claims and making generalizations from limited samples or undisciplined methods. The question, 'What do we *really* know so far?' is regularly revisited.

There are movements within theology that attempt to address the tendencies to make untested claims. A small group of theologians and religious scholars have joined Dutch theologian Johannes van der Ven in creating a subdiscipline of 'empirical theology', devoting energy to examining people's beliefs and values through the use of social scientific methods.[21] A variety of practical theologians or applied theologians – such as Paul Ballard, Don Browning, Bonnie Miller-MacLemore and Joyce Mercer – have focused on articulating folk beliefs, values, practices and experiences of religion and spirituality in relation to the prescriptive claims of inherited theological texts and traditions.[22] Ellen Clark-King and Mary

---

[21]   See Johannes van der Ven, 'God Reinvented? A Theological Search in Texts and Tables', *Empirical Studies in Theology*, vol. 1(Boston, MA: Brill, 1998).

[22]   See Paul Ballard and John Pritchard, *Practical Theology in Action: Christian Thinking in the Service of Church and Society* (London: Society for Promoting Christian Knowledge, 1996/2006); Don Browning, *A Fundamental Practical Theology: Descriptive*

McClintock Fulkerson have attempted to correct the temptation that has beset feminist and liberationist theologians to drift back to armchair extrapolations and 'speaking for the other', by engaging in direct interviews with women not of their own social class and allowing their voices to speak for themselves.[23] Prior to these, ethicist James Gustafson articulated the radical shift leading up to and following the Second Vatican Council in Roman Catholic theology from a Platonic commitment to universalisms to a more Aristotelian commitment to take into account historical and cultural realities.[24] Resulting from challenges noted by Christian missionaries and missiologists, debates continue in regard to appropriate indigenization and adaptation of 'standard' religious ideals and claims as they come into contact with local theologies. Catholic theologian and missiologist Robert Schreiter, who first used the term 'local theologies', set out some methods for mapping local theologies (including the generation of what anthropologist Clifford Geertz called 'thick description'), but then focused extensively on how to evaluate, shape and direct local theologies so that they fit under the umbrella of more universally accepted teachings of the religious tradition.[25] In a similar vein, Paul Tillich earlier proposed what he termed a *theology of culture*, and called for expanded study, research and theological and philosophical analysis of how each culture's peculiar and *autonomous* ways of looking at life 'expresses the ultimacy of meaning even in the most limited vehicles of meaning – a painted flower, a family habit, a technical tool, a form of social intercourse, the vision of a historical figure, an epistemological theory, a political document, and so on'.[26] But neither he nor Schreiter extended his focus to the level of examination of *individual* differences.

The theological disciplines are indeed beginning to learn and articulate methods for how to attend to, analyse and interpret the perspectives of people 'on the ground'. The problem remains one of rigour and consistency. Brian Castle, a bishop in the Church of England, noted that the discipline of applied theology 'can be the most difficult and challenging of subjects', since it requires a 'stringent

---

and Strategic Proposals (Minneapolis, MN: Fortress Press, 1991); Joyce Mercer and Bonnie Miller-McLemore, *Welcoming Children: A Practical Theology of Childhood* (St. Louis, MO: Chalice, 2005); Bonnie Miller-McLemore, *Christian Theology in Practice: Discovering a Discipline* (Grand Rapids, MI: Wm. B. Eerdmans, 2012).

[23]   See Ellen Clark-King, *Theology by Heart: Women, the Church and God* (Peterborough, UK: Epworth, 2004), and Mary McClintock Fulkerson, *Changing the Subject: Women's Discourses and Feminist Interpretation of the Bible* (Minneapolis, MN: Fortress Press, 1994).

[24]   See James Gustafson, *Protestant and Roman Catholic Ethics: Prospects for Rapprochement* (Chicago, IL: University of Chicago Press, 1978).

[25]   See Robert Schreiter, *Constructing Local Theologies* (Maryknoll, NY: Orbis, 1985).

[26]   Paul Tillich, *Systematic Theology, Vol. III: Life and the Spirit, History and the Kingdom of God* (Chicago, IL: University of Chicago Press, 1963), p. 250; Van Harvey, *A Handbook of Theological Terms* (New York: Touchstone, 1997), p. 64.

examination of the experiences of a person or group or culture', as well as the necessary tools in the fields of psychology, sociology, philosophy and politics. 'It can also be the easiest and most insipid,' Castle warned, 'if the applied theologian is not committed to making these explorations at the level required.'[27]

Ellen Clark-King, in her seminal study of the theologies of urban poor and working class women in eastern England, exercised a discipline of giving direct voice to the women she interviewed through a generous use of quotations and limiting her own impulse to interpret their statements through the prescribed lenses of feminist and postcolonial ideals. She raised a critique for her colleagues in feminist theology, pointing to the necessity of attending to the uniqueness of varied voices – especially those not adhering to beliefs or values that might be regarded as normative or judged as most beneficial. Her critique can apply as easily to theologians of any stripe: some of the easiest and most insipid of errors are to universalize from a small and socio-culturally similar group, or to engage in a process of inquiry with a group as yet unexplored but then to apply standards and prescriptive ideals to that group from another context. Clark-King lamented that, in her experience, the poor and working class women she interviewed in eastern England were more open to learning about some academic feminist perspectives of theology than her academic colleagues were to the distinctly different theological beliefs and values of urban poor and working class women.[28]

Castle's warning and Clark-King's critique may seem heavy-handed when directed at practical theologians and feminist and liberationist theologians, some of the very theologians who have made the best attempts to conduct descriptive work and listen directly to the folk theologies of ordinary people. Many theologians and religious scholars do not even make this effort, instead relying for contemporary 'real world' references on impressionistic perspectives drawn together from observations of popular culture, opinion research polls, broad sociological trends and personal experiences. These habits support theology's methodological temptations to overinterpret and overapply a limited amount of data, without an awareness of methods that can at least help safeguard against some tendencies to jump too quickly from description to prescription.

Mapping the Terrain

This book is uniquely positioned to speak to social scientists on one hand and theologians on the other. While the methodology is primarily from the social sciences, the principal research questions are rooted in philosophical and fundamental theology. Rather than attempting to document normative patterns or offer uniform descriptions of personal theologies, I point out the wide variations

---

[27]   Brian Castle, *Unofficial God? Voices from Beyond the Walls* (London: Society for Promoting Christian Knowledge, 2004), p. 30.

[28]   Clark-King, *Theology by Heart*, pp. 206–9.

possible. Variety is what we are continuing to grasp and to chart. What is the range of variation? What general patterns emerge from an examination of these variations that can provide at least a basic roadmap of the terrain in people's varying personal theologies?

Inductive questions exploring variability rather than normativity are not unfamiliar or unusual in the social sciences. Howard Gardner's idea of 'multiple intelligences' emerged from a combination of dissatisfaction with the overly normative and limiting notion of generalized intelligence (GI) and a curiosity about cases and situations that revealed startling variations.[29] His subsequent works on leadership and change have used case-based methods of inquiry to pursue questions – and to uncover new patterns – that these cases elicit.[30] Likewise, Dan McAdams has revolutionized research in personality and personal identity through a disciplined but open inquiry into the varieties of people's responses and stories told during interviews. From the many voices heard, McAdams came to recognize four general types of personal identity narratives, as well as four distinct forms of what he calls 'redemptive narratives'.[31] Lewis Rambo, Bob Altemeyer and Bruce Hunsberger, Jon Alexander, and others have documented a variety of types of religious and ideological conversion – as both entrances to and exits from systems of beliefs.[32] Rarely is it possible to place the variations these scholars have documented neatly along a continuum with measured gradations moving from one type to the next. Instead, their varieties help to map a terrain, a field of possibilities, with the varied types uncovering hidden dimensions of difference. We may aim for the same approach to the exploration and mapping of personal theologies.

Limitations of 'Broad-brush' Contrasts

Broad-brush theological and religious categories, recognized and touted by the media as well as by social scientists and theologians, provide quick-and-dirty clusters of variations in personal theology. Such categories include the obvious, well-articulated and oft-debated differences of religious affiliation, as

---

[29]   See Howard Gardner, *Frames of Mind: The Theory of Multiple Intelligences* (New York: Basic Books, 1993). This seminal work has had a profound effect upon educational theory and practices, and is the foundational touchstone for what has emerged in Daniel Golman's and Richard Boyatzis' work on emotional intelligence.

[30]   See Howard Gardner's *Leading Minds* (New York: Basic Books, 1995, 2001) and *Changing Minds* (Boston, MA: Harvard Business School Press, 2006).

[31]   See Dan McAdams, *The Stories We Live by* (New York: Guilford Press, 1993), and *The Redemptive Self* (New York: Oxford University Press, 2006).

[32]   See Lewis Rambo, *Understanding Religious Conversion* (New Haven, CT: Yale University Press, 1995); Bob Altermeyer and Bruce Hunsberger, *Amazing Conversions: Why Some Turn to Faith and Others Abandon Religion* (Amherst, NY: Prometheus Press, 1997); Jon Alexander (ed.), *American Personal Religious Accounts, 1600–1980: Toward an Inner History of America's Faiths* (Lewiston, NY: Edwin Mellen, 1983).

well as the variations within and between religions and religious denominations. Theological differences have also been examined in relation to people's self-reported religiosity. Broad theological contrasts have been documented according to political parties, ethnic backgrounds, geographic regions and historical periods. As will be discussed in Chapter 2, these sweeping distinctions provide some useful insights but at the cost of masking meaningful individual variations.

It is tempting to seek simplistic dichotomies when attempting to describe variations in beliefs and values. But dichotomous categories are overly reductionistic, especially when applied at the outset of inquiry and designing questions that have only binary responses. Consider the following di-polar categories:

Theistic	Atheistic
Nature-focused	Mind-focused
Dualistic	Monistic
Eastern	Western
Achievement-ethic	Honour-ethic
Harmony	Contest
Science and reason	Faith and feeling.

None of these dichotomies is very satisfying. They overly reduce a range of diverse alternatives to a simplistic binary universe, limiting a multidimensional question to a two-dimensional choice or continuum. Such categories fail to describe or chart the wide varieties of beliefs and values within each type. Not all theists hold similar beliefs and values, nor do all atheists. People may intermingle values of harmony and contest in unique ways—and may also hold other values that either compete or comingle with this pair in ways that significantly alter their fundamental meaning.

This simple exercise, I hope, illustrates the limitations of broad-brush contrasts between groups or types of theologies. It is rare to find a significantly coherent group of people whose personal theologies align with some supposed ideal type (or antitype) of theology – especially when we press beneath the surface of simplistic dichotomies. In an increasingly globalized world with broadened cultural interactions and exchanges of ideas, it is even less likely that people align themselves with these broad-brush categories. Jason was not simply a nihilist or neo-Nietzschean individualist.

As education and multicultural interaction have increased in America, so has the level of religious non-affiliation, 'double-dipping' and blending of religious ideas and systems, and autonomy in meaning-making. The pattern of slow drift away from religious heritage that Wade Roof began to document among the 'Baby Boom generation'[33] has had an effect on subsequent generations, with religious non-adherence increasing steadily, and with more and more people coming to

---

[33]   See Wade Clark Roof, *A Generation of Seekers: The Spiritual Journeys of the Baby Boom Generation* (New York: HarperCollins, 1993).

adulthood without any significant exposure to the stories, ideals, texts, or images that have shaped common cultural theologies in America. We cannot afford to continue using categories derived within an assumed cultural religious hegemony and established range of doctrines, creeds and stories. This knowledge has not been passed on; it has eroded,[34] and it may not have ever been as well-defined as supposed.

Furthermore, some categories constructed by social scientists and theologians belie a clear theological bias. Take, for instance, the wide range of instruments in use to explore and document spirituality, religiosity, or spiritual beliefs.[35] Many instruments include items or scales created around broad Judeo-Christian or more narrow Evangelical Christian theological assumptions – for instance, belief in a personal God. Scholars conducting research with these instruments unintentionally (or intentionally) impose the underlying assumptions upon the people in their studies, forcing them to make choices in responses to closed-ended, scaled, or multiple-choice questions that are not natural to their own way of thinking and believing.

Categories used in developmental research on beliefs and values can be similarly problematic. With a few notable exceptions, such as the breakthrough studies by Christian Smith, not much attention has been given to young adults' theological frameworks or 'world-concepts'.[36] Indeed, there has been limited research on these topics in developmental literature in general, given the minimal attention paid to early adulthood in developmental literature, the difficulty of studying the content of belief and value systems with sufficient depth and rigour, and biases among researchers that have resulted in beliefs and values being either ignored as epiphenomenal or summarized in overgeneralized or religiously skewed categories. In the limited research that exists on young adults' beliefs and values, scholars have tended to impose constructivist theories based on rationalistic ideals and assumptions of stage-like, progressive development on their research methods and data.[37] Many of these theorists, in an attempt to present organizing constructs for the emergence and convergence of beliefs and values over the lifespan, tend

---

[34]   Pew Forum on Religion & Public Life, 'U.S. Religious Knowledge Survey', posted 28 September 2010 <http://www.pewforum.org/U-S-Religious-Knowledge-Survey-Who-Knows-What-About-Religion.aspx>.

[35]   See, for instance, Peter Hill and Ralph Hood, Jr. (eds), *Measures of Religiosity* (Birmingham, AL: Religious Education Press, 1999).

[36]   James Marcia, Gerald Adams and others have explored the process of ideological commitment from an Eriksonian perspective, but these researchers have not examined the content of young adults' emerging ideological frameworks or 'personal theologies': James Marcia, 'Ego Identity Status: Relationship to Change in Self-Esteem, "General Maladjustment," and Authoritarianism', *Journal of Personality* 35(1) (March 1967): 118–33; Gerald Adams, *Adolescent Identity Formation* (London, UK: Sage, 1992).

[37]   Some of the classic constructivists in moral and faith development include Lawrence Kohlberg (1977), James Fowler (1981), Carol Gilligan (1982), and Fritz Oser (1991).

to frame 'faith development' or 'moral development' as an almost solipsistic stepwise venture, void of cultural context or influence.

It is time to revisit – and perhaps to abandon – the assumption that broad-brush categorizations capture some kind of perceived 'central tendencies' of people to gather their beliefs and values around a commonly shared and well-defined set of theologies. The time is ripe to engage in primary research on personal theologies, and to do so in a way that offers some direction for the development of common methods and categories that are not theory-driven but are theory-generating. And it is time to examine and begin to document the varieties of personal theology in American society by asking those adults who are most likely to be influenced by the cultural changes that have loosened ties to organized religions and political ideologies: emerging adults, whose preliminary adult choices and decisions are still being formulated and tested in the crucibles of adult transitions.

Why Young Adults?

It is precisely the volatile formative nature of this period of life that may be most interesting for the study of personal theologies. Young Jason was facing into the wind, struggling to make sense of the world he had known through his adolescence and the expanded world he was coming to know as a working adult. He was experimenting with different ways to express what he was coming to believe about the nature of the world, human society, existence and purpose. Young adulthood can be an intense crucible of meaning-making.

Developmental and social theorists have pointed to early adulthood as a decisive period in which various aspects of ideology are formed, tested, internalized and crystallized. In the period of early adult development (age 18–35),[38] young men and women are faced with increasing responsibility and consequences for their actions, in terms of financial, legal, social and emotional costs. At the same time, they are expected to embark on a journey toward independence that embraces such costs. As Barbara Maughan and Lorna Champion state:

> More than at any earlier stage, there is the potential, and often the requirement, for the individual to play *a consciously perceived role* in shaping his or her development, determining long-term goals and more immediate courses of action, and selecting the environments … in which those plans will be played out. Decisions taken during this period lay the foundations for much of adult development.[39]

For a review, see Lawrence Walker and Russell Pitts, 'Naturalistic Conceptions of Moral Maturity', *Developmental Psychology* 34(3) (May 1998): 403–19.

[38] This is the timeline of early adulthood outlined by Daniel Levinson and his colleagues in *The Seasons of a Man's Life* (New York: Ballantine, 1978).

[39] Barbara Maughan and Lorna Champion, 'Risk and Protective Factors in the Transition to Young Adulthood', in Paul Baltes and Margaret Baltes (eds), *Successful*

During these years, foundational decisions are framed and guided by a variety of internal and external forces – for instance, personal interests, career availability, financial necessity, political events, convenience, and motivations for personal success and happiness. But in the background of these competing personal and societal motivations and interests are young adults' emerging ideological frameworks, or 'personal theologies' – foundational beliefs and values about the world and the nature of being which provide an orienting perspective to life – that are still in the process of being formed, with or without the direct help of religious affiliation, parental interaction, or educational experiences.

This book illuminates and explores dominant and variant types of young adults' beliefs and values about 'the world' and humanity that frame the basis of personal theologies, addressing the following questions about young adult personal theologies:

- What are signs of culturally dominant and variant patterns of beliefs and values of young adults at the turn of the twenty-first century?
- For American young adults, is there a typical pattern of convergence among the various aspects of personal theology?
- Are the patterns of beliefs and values of American young adults at the turn of the century historically unique, or are they similar to other generational cohorts?
- How are young adults' beliefs and values shaped developmentally, and what social and developmental forces are most influential on different beliefs and values?
- Do these beliefs and values have an impact on young adults' daily lives?
- Do these beliefs and values have implications for the trajectory of psychosocial maturation?

Benefits of a Grounded-theory Approach

Addressing these questions requires a mixture of qualitative and quantitative methods, in order to reveal and tag the variations in young adults' personal theologies, and to illuminate the developmental and social factors that influenced young adults' construction of their personal theologies.

I have employed a grounded-theory approach to the study of personal theologies, with an emphasis on the thematic content of each person's stated beliefs and values. 'Grounded theory' is an approach to research in sociology first proposed and pursued by Glaser and Strauss,[40] as a corrective to the overemphasis on deductive research. Glaser and Strauss proposed coming to a place or group of

Aging: Perspectives from the Behavioral Sciences (Cambridge, UK: Cambridge University Press, 1990), italics added.

[40]   Barney Glaser and Anselm Strauss, *The Discovery of Grounded Theory: Strategies for Qualitative Research* (Chicago, IL: Aldine, 1967).

people without a preconceived theory, but with a set of open-ended questions that allowed for a disciplined process of listening, followed by a close examination of thematic content in order to discern similarities and differences, map connections and uncover the latent beliefs, ideals, values, or theories held by a group of people. Theory emerges from the voices of the people, carefully heard and compared.

An emphasis on content is integral to a grounded-theory approach to research. *What* people say is of primary interest. Encounter with raw content in beliefs and values can be daunting, even off-putting, to scholars who seek to use preconceived concepts and previously used structures in order to make sense of variation. There are scholars who have claimed an attempt to analyse presumed underlying structure rather than surface content,[41] or have thrown up their hands in the face of seemingly unpredictable diversity of content and claimed that further analysis would be fruitless. But these approaches fail to chart the rich depth and variation found through attention to themes emerging from a simple semiotic analysis of people's responses.[42]

In this book, readers will find an approach to mapping the range of young adults' personal theologies and the relationships of these personal theologies to various experiences in their lives. This first requires an exploration of the thematic content and patterns of ideas in each aspect of personal theologies. Once again, these include individuals' fundamental beliefs about the nature of 'the world' (worldview), their sense of place or purpose in the world (life purpose), their ideas about causation and justice in the face of negative life events (theodicy), and the moral and ethical values that shape their ideas of the good person (ultimate values). Thematic content analysis leads to descriptive analyses of patterns that begin to be revealed across different groups of young adults. A clearer understanding of common patterns in beliefs and values then allows for categories to be constructed, emerging directly from the patterns found in young adults' responses. Using these emergent categories, it becomes possible to look at relationships, convergences and divergences among different types of beliefs and values.

But simply charting variations and patterns in personal theology leaves unanswered questions. What influences and shapes personal theology? What impact does personal theology then have? One of the primary advantages to a longitudinal study and a nested design is the possibility of pursuing such questions of influence and correlation. *Making the Transition* is just such a nested-design longitudinal study – a study of young adults in their first seven years following graduation from high school, nested within its longitudinal antecedent, the Sloan Study of Youth and Social Development and the even larger National Education

---

[41] This was James Fowler's primary claim in his initial work on faith development: James Fowler, *Stages of Faith: The Psychology of Human Development and the Quest for Meaning* (New York: HarperCollins, 1981).

[42] Martha Feldman, *Qualitative Research Methods Series*, vol. 33, *Strategies for Interpreting Qualitative Data* (Thousand Oaks, CA: Sage, 1995).

Longitudinal Study.[43] Additionally, I have drawn on comparative data from studies conducted by the National Opinion Research Center from 1960 to the present. These data sources allowed for a unique mixed-methodological approach to longitudinal analysis, and a series of historical cohort comparisons. They also provided a larger contextual frame for the core 82 young adults interviewed about their worldviews, life purpose, theodicies and ultimate values. A full discussion of data sources and research methods follows in Chapter 4.

Drawing from the grounded-theory content analysis of interviews, I used the categories of beliefs and values to statistically investigate relationships between different aspects of personal theology and the following:

- demographic and class-related differences, including race, parent education and parental marital status;
- adolescent experiences of family, school, work, peer relationships, leisure and religion;
- adolescent attitudes and dispositions, including self-esteem and locus of control;
- educational and vocational experiences in young adulthood;
- career-related motivations and behaviours, including career investment, post-secondary school performance, job satisfaction and career-related values, and
- young adult experiences of relationships, leisure and religion.

Through this exploratory study, intriguing patterns emerged, revealing dominant and variant patterns in worldview, theodicy, life purpose and ultimate values (Chapters 4–7). I was able to uncover deeper themes and patterns of meaning-making from interview transcripts, and to show consistency and change in beliefs and values across generations. I also found wide variations in the relationships among beliefs and values and the cultural and religious imprints that contribute to dominant patterns, and surprising developmental and social factors from adolescence that influence personal theologies – with education, social capital and intrinsic motivation taking the lead, but religion in a weaker influential role (Chapter 8). We were also able to discern some of the relationships between personal theology and the concurrent experiences and life plans in emerging adulthood – including continuing strong connections with education and social capital. This book concludes with a grounded theory of personal theology that

―――――――――――

[43]   Barbara Schneider, *Making the Transition: Work Experiences After High School*, funded 1997–2001 by the US Department of Education, Office of Education Research and Improvement (FIS Grant #R309F70069); Barbara Schneider, *Sloan Study of Youth and Social Development*, funded 1992–97 by the Alfred P. Sloan Foundation (Chicago, IL: University of Chicago, National Opinion Research Center); United States Department of Education, National Center for Education Statistics, *National Education Longitudinal Study, 1988*, Inter-university Consortium for Political and Social Research.

opens an avenue for further research and maps over a hundred possible variations in personal theology based on the emerging general patterns of three worldviews, three theodicies, three types of life purpose, and two pairs of contrasting sets of ultimate values. I propose some elements of a developmental theory of personal theology, accounting for the relatively weak influences of family, friends and religion and the robust effects of education, social capital and dispositional factors such as intrinsic motivation – and the ubiquitous influence of cultural scripts – in shaping what young adults believe about the world, ultimate causation, life purpose and ultimate values.

Before turning to the results of the study, we need to lay the foundations for studying the beliefs and values comprising what I am calling 'personal theologies', describe the larger research context for this study of young adults, and provide a roadmap for the methods and approaches used in studying personal theology in its many varieties.

Chapter 2
Mapping Personal Theologies

What is this place in which I find myself alive? What kind of place is the
world?
Why do things happen as they do?
Where is all of this headed? What is the world becoming?
Is there any purpose, really, for being? What makes the most sense as a way
of being in the world?
What is good? What, really, makes life good and is worth pursuing?
How do I ever know something is really true?

People ask questions about more than themselves and their identity. They
ask questions about the world they inhabit. The questions arise in late-night
conversations, during quiet play or reflection, in the midst and wake of encounters
with stories and histories, and through times of challenge and transition. In my work
as a therapist, researcher, professor, pastor, father and friend, I have heard people
wrestle with these questions, right alongside their questions about themselves.
These are some of the fundamental questions of philosophy and theology, and
of what I am calling personal theologies. They give voice to people's search for
meaning and understanding about the world in which they find themselves.

Meaning-making is a perceptual and interpretive act. Identities and personal
theologies alike are the children of a basic human quest for *meaning*. 'Quest' may
sound a bit grandiose, but at the very least, people develop and repeatedly use a
propensity to construct explanations, goals and heuristic expectations about all
they experience. Human beings seek to make sense – not only of themselves and
others, but of the whole world of being that is the ground upon which figures live
their lives.

The construction of meaning about the world of being is, by very nature
of being, rooted in local personal and interpersonal experience. It begins, as
psychologist Roy Baumeister has stated, with 'recognizing signals and patterns
in the environment',[1] and expands through the activities of thought and language
that weave ideas and conceptions about the environment together into a fabric of
meaning. Such development of sense-making of the world at the very least runs
parallel to and coincides with the development of conceptions about the self. And
some social scientists, such as George Herbert Mead and Kurt Lewin, for many
years previously argued that perception and understanding of one's *field* or broad
environmental context (that is, 'world') not only precede but shape each person's

---

[1]   Roy Baumeister, *Meanings of Life* (New York: Guilford, 1991), p. 18.

self-perception and self-understanding.[2] In narrative terms, setting precedes (or at least coincides with) character. As developmental psychologist Dan McAdams asserted, 'To understand myself fully, I must come to believe that the universe works in a certain way, and that certain things about the world, about society, about God, about the ultimate reality of life, are true. Identity is built upon ideology.'[3]

The Building-blocks: Beliefs and Values

Beliefs and values are both outcomes and tools of meaning-making. They become heuristics for interpreting and setting goals in the environment, and thus structure and streamline further processes of meaning-making. Beliefs and values are thus primary building-blocks in personal theologies. Social scientists, philosophers and religious scholars alike assume that beliefs and values are fundamentally intertwined with perceptions, attitudes, behavioural choices and experiences. Beliefs and values help people orient and express their expectations, motivations and explanations for events and situations encountered in their own lives and the lives of others. Both beliefs and values are more than mere detached factual assertions. They carry a basic level of conviction, a sense of importance and implication for further choices in perception, interpretation and behaviour.[4] In this way, beliefs and values become the internal *lingua franca* of an interpretive framework from which goals, attitudes and behaviours emerge.

There are important distinctions between beliefs and values.[5] Beliefs allow people to give definition not only to themselves but to their world. They include schemas, or heuristic definitions of groups, situations, or ideas that help people

---

[2]   See George Mead, *Mind, Self and Society* (Chicago, IL: University of Chicago, 1934), and Kurt Lewin, *A Dynamic Theory of Personality* (New York: McGraw-Hill, 1935).

[3]   Dan McAdams, *The Stories We Live by: Personal Myths and the Making of the Self* (New York: Guilford, 1993), p. 81.

[4]   For full discussions, see David Wulff, 'Beyond Belief and Unbelief', in Joanne Greer and David Moberg (eds), *Research in the Social Scientific Study of Religion 10*, pp. 1–15 (Stanford, CT: JAI, 1999); Rodney Needham, *Belief, Language, and Experience* (Oxford: Blackwell, 1972), and Robert Emmons, *The Psychology of Ultimate Concerns: Motivation and Spirituality in Personality* (New York: Guilford, 1999).

[5]   A number of key social and cognitive psychologists have illustrated this: Susan Folkman and Richard Lazarus, 'Coping and Emotion ,' in Alan Monat and Richard Lazarus (eds), *Stress and Coping: An Anthology*, 3rd edn, pp. 207–27 (New York: Columbia University Press, 1991); Nancy Stein, Susan Folkman, Tom Trabasso and T. Anne Richards, 'Appraisal and Goal Processes as Predictors of Psychological Well-Being in Bereaved Caregivers', *Journal of Personality & Social Psychology* 72(4) (April 1997): 872–84; George Mandler, 'Approaches to a Psychology of Value', in Michael Hechter, Lynn Nadel and Richard Michod (eds), *The Origin of Values* (New York: Aldine de Gruyter, 1993), pp. 229–58; Milton Rokeach, *The Nature of Human Values* (New York: The Free Press, 1973), and Emmons, *Ultimate Concerns*.

organize their perceptions (for instance, 'I am a kind person', or 'people in power are not trustworthy'). They also include attributions, or assignments of cause to events that have happened or are happening (for instance, 'you get what's coming to you'). We recognize beliefs when stated as equivalences or contrasts: 'The world is full of opportunity', or 'Fundamentalists are extremists.' But beliefs are also stated in other ways. Practical theologian John Dreibelbis made the case that faith statements (like beliefs) extend beyond mere factual assertions because they carry implications for potential action.[6] For instance, 'This bridge is constructed of steel and follows formulas for suspension bridges' is a statement of facts, but does not carry the same potential for action as 'This bridge will hold my car.' Everyday examples of such beliefs are 'My company will continue to provide steady employment', or 'The sun will rise tomorrow.' These kind of beliefs implicitly elicit assent and participatory action.

In contrast, values are motivational, or *conative,* statements. Not simply construals or judgements of existing situations, they are concerns marked by their imperative quality[7] and, like all goals, by their aspirational orientation toward the future.[8] These concerns, grasped as mental images and conceptions of 'desired states', help orient and direct people's behaviour.[9] We recognize values most easily when stated with use of the verbal infinitive,[10] for example, 'I want *to provide* for my children', or 'It is important *to tell the truth*' (or, with an adjective, '*to be honest*'). Values point directly toward desired action, and necessitate a verb-state of activity in order to achieve the ideal being sought. Values as goals or motivations thus communicate both ideal-but-not-yet-attained aims (products) and guidelines for selection of current actions (processes). As Alasdair MacIntyre and Eric Klinger each have asserted, values are inherently *telic* in focus[11] – rather than static explanations, assumptions, or probabilities, they are intentions for action toward a desired end.

---

6   See John Dreibelbis, 'Scientific, Normative and Faith Statements in the Work of Heinz Kohut' (unpublished dissertation, University of Chicago, 1990).

7   See Richard Kilby, *The Study of Human Values* (Lanham, MD: University Press of America, 1993).

8   See Emmons, *Ultimate Concerns*, Chapter 2.

9   See James Austin and Jeffrey Vancouver, 'Goal Constructs in Psychology: Structure, Process and Content', *Psychological Bulletin* 120(3) (November 1996): 338–75.

10   See an analytic example of this basic goal expression by a 5-year-old in Nancy Stein, Tom Trabasso and Maria Liwag, 'A Goal Appraisal Theory of Emotional Understanding: Implications for Development and Learning', in Michael Lewis and Jeannette Haviland-Jones (eds), *Handbook of Emotions*, 2nd edn, p. 443 (New York: Guilford, 2000).

11   See Alisdair MacIntyre, *After Virtue* (Notre Dame, IN: University of Notre Dame, 1981), and Eric Klinger, 'On Living Tomorrow Today: The Quality of Inner Life as a Function of Goal Expectations', in Z. Zaleski (ed.), *Psychology of Future Orientation* (Lublin: Towarzystwo Naukowe KUL, 1994), pp. 97–106.

Both beliefs and values are organized in ascending levels of abstraction, from very concrete explanations or goals to more general and encompassing assertions or aims.[12] For instance, 'I want to wash the car' is a concrete goal, while 'I want to live in a clean and orderly world' is a more abstract aim that takes the shape of a value. More concrete goals can be intermediary steps toward more abstract values – or introduce necessary adjustments to higher-order values. More concrete or basic beliefs may provide building-blocks of evidence leading to more abstract beliefs – or as ways to refute higher-order beliefs. Higher-order abstractions emerge as resources to coordinate and connect between simpler, more concrete abstract beliefs and values,[13] and as such provide a deep background structure to the overall life course – even if on a day-to-day or moment-to-moment basis it seems that more immediate and concrete beliefs and goals have a more direct influence on what people say and do.

Higher-order beliefs and values are the building-blocks of self-concepts – and of world-concepts. Discussing the development of personal identity, Susan Harter stated that 'such higher-order abstractions provide self-labels that bring meaning and therefore legitimacy to what formerly appeared to be troublesome contradictions within the self.'[14] Similarly, higher-order beliefs and values provide heuristic labels for the world, humanity and the nature of existence – the stuff of personal theologies.

The higher-order beliefs and values comprising personal theologies are at some of the broadest levels of abstraction. They may not be accessed frequently or directly by individuals in their everyday lives. Rather, they form a deep structure that serves to organize individuals' more immediate perceptions, beliefs and goals in their environments. Whether they are called 'faith statements', 'ultimate values', or 'ultimate concerns', these higher-order beliefs and values comprising personal theologies operate like deep subscripts or subroutines in people's everyday lives.

---

[12]   See, for instance, the semantic learning theory of Eleanor Rosch and the action identification theory of Robin Vallacher and Daniel Wegner: Eleanor Rosch, 'Human Categorization', in N. Warren (ed.), *Advances in Cross-Cultural Psychology* vol. 1 (London, UK: Academic, 1977), and Robin Vallacher and Daniel Wegner, 'What Do People Think They're Doing? Action Identification and Human Behavior', *Psychological Review* 94(1) (1987): 3–15.

[13]   Kurt Fischer and Richard Canfield, 'The Ambiguity of Stage and Structure in Behavior: Person and Environment in the Development of Psychological Structure', in Iris Levin (ed.), *Stage and Structure: Reopening the Debate* (New York: Plenum, 1986), pp. 246–67.

[14]   Susan Harter, *The Construction of the Self: A Developmental Perspective* (New York: Guilford, 1999), p. 80.

The Individuality of Personal Theologies

> The world view is something more elaborate than a religious story. But it is also less elaborate than a doctrinal proposition. Doctrinal propositions and world views need not correlate.
>
> Andrew Greeley[15]

Personal theologies are sets of beliefs and values regarding the broadest contexts of the world, existence and humanity, encountered and learned *by individuals* within various cultural contexts but *individually* internalized and interpreted. Hence, they can never be a simple recitation of religious or political dogma or creeds as received from authoritative social systems. Images and narratives provided by organized religion and political systems *inform* individuals' beliefs and values and likely provide some general frameworks within which individuals think – but they do not prescribe the shape and content of personal theologies.

Erikson's description of young adults' ideological formation is helpful in portraying how individuals mould and shape their personal theologies:

> At the most it is a militant system with uniformed members and uniform goals; at the least, it is a 'way of life,' or what the Germans call, *Weltanschauung*, a world view which is consonant with existing theory, available knowledge, and common sense, and yet is significantly more: an utopian [or dystopian] outlook, a cosmic mood, or a doctrinal logic, all shared as self-evident beyond any need for demonstration.[16]

Individuals are active as well as receptive in this process of meaning-making about the world and being – and, as Erikson suggested, the beliefs and values that help form personal theologies will vary in their degree of coherence and internal consistency, but will nonetheless be taken as true and directive.

From an existential as well as psychodynamic viewpoint – and from the perspective of pastoral and constructive theology – the world is not a uniform experience or stable mental construct across groups and individuals. As psychiatrist Clemens Benda said, 'Since each individual is confronted with the world from a different stand in space and time... no two human beings perceive the world in the same way.'[17] Humans need and actively construct a map of the natural and social world. Without such a map, Erich Fromm observed, one 'would be confused and unable to act purposefully and consistently ... [and] would have no way of

---

[15] Andrew Greeley, *Religion: A Secular Theory* (New York: Free Press, 1982), p. 98.

[16] Erik Erikson, *Young Man Luther* (New York: Norton, 1958), p. 41 (brackets added).

[17] Clemens Benda, 'The Existential Approach to Religion,' in E. Mansell Pattison (ed.),*Clinical Psychiatry and Religion* (Boston, MA: Little, Brown and Company, 1969), p. 42.

orienting himself.'[18] Active construction of a philosophy and a set of overarching goals, according to Fromm, is not only essential for functioning, it is natural and unconscious, leading each person to take her own personal theology for granted. The more people draw on explicit or widely shared ideologies, the less they are apt to question beliefs and values that seem like common sense. But in current pluralistic societies that value and give primary voice to academic and journalistic scepticism, resulting in a tendency to question everything, 'each one of us is forced to do deliberately for oneself what in previous ages was done by family, custom, church, and state, namely, form the myths in terms of which we can make some sense of experience.'[19]

The *personal* nature of personal theologies should not be underestimated. Indeed, the work of the individual in constructing personal theologies is not unique to what is currently called a pluralistic postmodern world. Scriptures of varied religious traditions are full of accounts of subcultural and individual difference – and of the importance of individual efforts in meaning-making. In the *Bhagavad-Gita*, Prince Arjuna gazes upon the world of battle and grapples with questions of cosmic justice, life purpose and ideas of the good before he gains new perspective from Krishna that releases him into action.[20] One of the reprises in the Book of Judges in the Hebrew Scriptures paints a picture not unfamiliar to postmodern theorists: 'In those days there was no king in Israel; all the people did what was right in their own eyes.'[21] Biblical books like Judges, Ruth, Jonah and Esther provide rich accounts of individual leaders who wrestled with their beliefs and values and how to live in relation to the worlds in which they found themselves called to action. As such, they offer a glimpse into how varied the personal theologies of people 'on the ground', outside of the tabernacle or temple square, might have been in an ancient and supposedly more uniform culture.

Experiences, assertions of the public square, and political and religious ideologies do not really become beliefs until the individual internalizes and incorporates them, evidenced by times when the individual accesses, states, or acts upon them. The Muslim concept of *tasdiq* (assent or acceptance), or the individual's affirmation and embracing of the beliefs and values of Islam, stresses the action both implicit and necessary for beliefs to become personal: 'By living them out, one proves them and finds out that they do indeed become true, both for oneself and for the society and world in which one lives.'[22]

---

[18]   Erich Fromm, *The Anatomy of Human Destructiveness* (New York: Holt, Rinehart, and Winston, 1973), p. 230.

[19]   Rollo May, *The Cry for Myth* (New York: W.W. Norton & Company, 1991), p. 29.

[20]   See *Baghavad Gita*, Chapter 1, 'Arjun-Vishad' and Chapter 2, 'Sankyha-Yog'.

[21]   Judges 17:6 and 21:25 (NRSV).

[22]   Wilfred Cantwell Smith, 'Faith as *Tasdiq*', in Parviz Morewedge (ed.), *Islamic Philosophical Theology* (Albany, NY: State University of New York, 1979), p. 106. See also Abbas Yazdani, 'An Internalist Model of Immediate Awareness of God from an Islamic Philosophy Perspective', in Anna-Theresa Tymieniecka and Nazif Muhtaroglu

This has long been the operating assumption in pastoral theology and in the work of religious sages or guides. Major writers in pastoral theology, pastoral counselling and pastoral ministry have attempted to map some paradigms for assessment of the expressed and implicit theologies of individuals, families, religious communities and societies.[23] The primary assumption of many pastoral theologians is that individuals indeed have and use personal theologies. A further assumption, not always shared by other theologians and at times contested among pastoral theologians, is that personal theologies should first be understood and assessed in terms of their existential functionality rather than in terms of their adherence to a particular religious ideology. The first question is not 'How does this person's beliefs and values align with a recognized or dogmatically acclaimed theological system?' but rather, 'How does this person's beliefs and values function in her life?' To answer either question requires listening, with a starting aim of learning what comprises an individual's personal theology. But primary curiosity about function keeps the pastoral theologian listening longer and engaging in more 'thick description', without leaping to prescriptive analysis of how someone measures up to an assumed system.

Four Facets of Personal Theology

What, then, are the types of beliefs and values that might comprise personal theologies? It will be helpful to consider some fundamental questions in philosophy and theology as a starting-point.

- What is human nature, the human will and humanity's origin, place and destiny in the cosmos? (*Anthropology*: Greek roots – 'knowledge about the human')
- How do we come to know anything, and to know if it is true? (*Epistemology*: 'knowledge about knowing')
- What does it mean to exist, and what is the nature of being? (*Ontology*: 'knowledge about that which is')
- What are the world and the cosmos? What is their structure? How did they come to be? (*Cosmology*: 'knowledge about the universe/world/totality')

(eds), *Classic Issues in Islamic Philosophy and Theology Today: Islamic Philosophy and Occidental Phenomenology in Dialogue* vol. 4 (New York: Springer, 2010), pp. 5–8.

[23] These include Paul Pruyser, *The Pastor as Diagnostician* (Philadelphia, PA: Westminster, 1967); George Fitchett, *Assessing Spiritual Needs: A Guide for Caregivers* (Minneapolis, MN: Augsburg, 1993); Margaret Kornfeld, *Cultivating Wholeness: A Guide to Care and Counseling in Faith Communities* (Harrisburg, PA: Continuum, 2000); Nancy Ramsay, *Pastoral Diagnosis: A Resource for Ministries of Care and Counseling* (Minneapolis, MN: Augsburg, 1998), and Gary Ahlskog and Harry Sands, *The Guide to Pastoral Counseling and Care* (Madison, CT: Psychosocial Press, 2000).

- What are the ultimate ends, purposes, or destinies of things? (*Teleology*: 'knowledge about the end')
- Why do evil, chaos, destruction, or other unanticipated negative events exist? (*Theodicy:* Latin roots – 'judgement about God')
- What change or destiny will make human life better? (*Soteriology*: 'knowledge about salvation/preservation/restoration')
- How do time and history move? What ultimately will become of humanity and current reality? (*Eschatology*: 'knowledge about furthest/final things')
- What is ultimately worthy, virtuous, valuable? (*Axiology*: 'knowledge of worthy things')
- How should human beings live and what ideals should be followed? (*Ethics*: 'character')

This is only one list of possible classifications of what we might call 'the great questions', and the questions themselves have been asked and explored in varied ways. For any scholar, the questions chosen as most central naturally shape the research and discourse that follows. In her seminal study in the 1950s of five subcultures (Zuni Pueblo, Mormon, Spanish-American, Navajo and Texas-Oklahoma 'immigrants') in New Mexico, cultural anthropologist Florence Kluckhohn worked with five core questions that she considered universal concerns 'for which all peoples at all times and in all places must find some solution':[24]

1. What core, innate predispositions shape human behaviour?
2. How does humanity fit into the scheme of the natural order?
3. How does humanity orient itself to time – past, present and future?
4. What is the dominant motivation for activity?
5. What is the dominant relational ethic in human exchange?

Kluckhohn asserted that the number of fundamental questions of humanity are limited, and that variations in beliefs and values are patterned and limited in range, existing in all cultures in differing frequencies. Within every culture, there are dominant, 'required variant', and 'permitted variant' solutions to each of these questions.[25] Thus, both culturally and individually, human behaviour emerges only after being filtered through the cultural and individual solutions to these questions.

There are a variety of core questions considered by scholars as fundamental to what I am calling personal theology – Kluckhohn's set of fundamental questions represents only one perspective. And yet, I have found a notable convergence around four recurring questions. These include the questions of *cosmology* and

---

[24]   Florence Kluckhohn, 'Dominant and Variant Value Orientations', in Clyde Kluckhohn and Henry Murray (eds), *Personality in Nature, Society, and Culture* (New York: Alfred A. Knopf, 1956), pp. 342–57.

[25]   See Florence Kluckhohn and Fred Strodtbeck, *Variations in Value Orientations* (Evanston, IL: Row, Peterson and Company, 1961).

ontology (the nature and quality of the world and of being), *theodicy* (causation of seemingly irrational and harmful events), *teleology* (human purpose and destiny), and *axiology* and *ethics* (ultimate values and ideals of human behaviour). These four facets are not exhaustive of the beliefs and values comprising personal theologies, but they provide a starting-point for exploring the range of ideas, themes and perspectives people hold, and the degree to which these different facets of personal theology are interrelated. In our study, they were identified as follows:

1. *Worldview*, or one's evaluative sense of the world and the reasons for that evaluation;
2. *Theodicy*, or the meaning or lack of meaning, agency and causation in traumatic or tragic events in life;
3. Sense of *life purpose*, or one's place *vis-à-vis* the world, and
4. *Ultimate values* and ideals (and 'anti-ideals') about the good that is worthy of pursuit, principles by which to live, and human qualities worth emulating or rejecting.

Worldview

To invite young adults' worldviews, we asked three open-ended questions, together:

Think for a minute about the world as you know it.

1. How do you make sense of the world?
2. What do you do to make sense of the world?
3. What kind of a place is the world, in general?

How someone perceives and conceives of 'the world' taps into their beliefs about the nature, origin and trajectory of this vast place of habitation and of the human beings and other beings that inhabit it. A worldview is where cosmological, anthropological and ontological beliefs meet. It includes views of the natural order, of human nature, of human relation to the rest of nature. People can have widely varied and richly textured beliefs about the world, from which they form general qualitative assessments of the world. It is these qualitative assessments that are of primary interest in this book.

Part of these qualitative assessments includes evaluative judgements. Just as individuals' self-image can gauged roughly from the balance between positive and negative self-appraisals, so also individuals' general 'world-image' can be gauged by evaluating the balance of their positive and negative evaluative judgements about the world.

Looking at the overall valence of responses to our questions (particularly the third question) provided a basic first level of understanding the varieties of young adults' worldviews.

The concepts of 'world-image' and variations of positive and negatives worldviews are not new in the social sciences. Some scholars have indicated that the worldview perceptions and ideas of people across cultures may gravitate toward the *negative*. Max Weber discussed the concept of 'discrepancy' in public theology: that is, the degree of disjuncture perceived and judged by people between the world-as-idealized and the world-as-experienced.[26] Robert Bellah took up this theme, stating that it was religion that provided culture with systematic beliefs to make sense of 'ultimate frustrations', or violated expectations *vis-à-vis* the world.[27] From a psychoanalytic perspective, Sigmund Freud's 'reality principle'[28] can be understood as a challenge individuals must face – coming to terms with the ways the world fails to live up to personally treasured ideals and wishes, and accepting the reality of negative qualities of the world. These scholars suggest that people might form early hopes and beliefs about the world as a good, positive place, and then must adjust to a more negative pattern of beliefs that incorporate their sense of discrepancy, frustration and disappointment. But for other scholars, the primary assumption is that the world is a positive place. German philosopher Gottfried Wilhelm Leibniz argued that, despite the many evils and problems in the world, this was the best of all possible worlds.[29] From James Fowler's hopeful developmental perspective, people are not inevitably consigned to negatives worldviews: Fowler assumed that individuals seek a kind of world coherence, with an ultimate possibility of attaining a personal theology that affirms the world as unitive and holistic, reincorporating anything negative under a higher positive view.[30]

There has been a tendency among some researchers to think of 'world-image' only as a dipolar construct with negative and positive as the only options.[31]

---

[26]   See Max Weber, *The Sociology of Religion*, trans. Ephraim Fischoff (Boston, MA: Beacon, 1963). See also Weber, 'Ascetism, Mysticism, and Salvation Religion', in Louis Schneider (ed.), *Religion, Culture and Society* (New York: John Wiley & Sons, 1964), pp. 192–202.

[27]   Robert Bellah, *Tokugawa Religion: The Cultural Roots of Modern Japan* (New York: The Free Press, 1985), p. 6; and Bellah, *Beyond Belief: Essays on Religion in a Post-Traditional World* (Berkeley and Los Angeles, CA: University of California, 1996), pp. 266–7.

[28]   Sigmund Freud, *Beyond the Pleasure Principle* (New York: Norton, 1920) 1961 edn.

[29]   Gottfried Leibniz, 'Theodicy: Essays on the Goodness of God, the Freedom of Man and the Origin of Evil', trans. E.M. Hubbard, from C.J. Gerhardt, *Edition of the Collected Philosophical Works, 1875-90* (Peru, IL: Open Court, Project Gutenberg EBook #17147 <http://www.gutenberg.org/files/17147/17147-h/17147-h.htm>.

[30]   James Fowler, *Stages of Faith: The Psychology of Human Development and the Quest for Meaning* (San Francisco, CA: HarperSanFrancisco, 1981).

[31]   Examples include Fritz Oser's dipolar worldviews of 'hope versus absurdity', William McCready and Andrew Greeley's contrasting 'pessimistic' and 'optimistic' perspectives people might have about theodicy, and the General Social Survey's questions about the world and humanity that since the 1950s have asked respondents to locate

Florence Kluckhohn moved beyond simple dipolar perspectives and proposed three possible solutions people might choose in response to her question of worldview related specifically to human nature: positive, neutral or mixed good-and-bad, and negative. She also discussed an important sub-theme: how changeable or unchangeable people considered human nature to be.[32]

Furthermore, a simple focus on the overall valence of people's 'world-image' provides only the thinnest understanding of worldview. As Kluckhohn's work suggests, valence in worldview provides only a partial picture of individuals' conceptions of the world. Individuals' *reasons* for their evaluations of the world reveal the deep content of cultural and personal beliefs, as expressed in differing appraisals of safety, predictability, care, equity, justice, or beauty in the world.[33] These reasons and textured thoughts behind young adults' evaluations of the world are explored extensively in the chapter on worldview.

Theodicy

We asked two separate questions to elicit young adults' theodicies. The questions were asked in different parts of the interview.

1. Say something bad – terrible, tragic, unexpected – happens in your life, or to someone you know. Think about that kind of event for a minute. How do you understand or make sense of life when things are going really badly?
2. Some people believe that everything happens for a reason while others believe that things happen randomly and without purpose. Others fall somewhere in between. What do you believe along that line?

Rabbi Kushner, over 30 years ago, wrestled with the questions of theodicy in his well-known book, *When Bad Things Happen to Good People.*[34] But the questions have haunted published literature since the time of Sumer and the Akkadian

---

themselves on a Likert scale from negative to positive: Fritz Oser, 'The Development of Religious Judgment' in B. Puka (ed.), *Fundamental Research in Moral Development*, vol. 2 (New York: Garland, 1994), pp. 375–96, and William McCready and Andrew Greeley, *The Ultimate Values of the American Population* (Beverly Hills, CA and London: Sage Publications, 1976).

[32] Kluckhohn, 'Dominant and Variant Value Orientations'.

[33] 'Archaic' myths and stories emphasized different perspectives about the world. The ancient Babylonian religious myth of Tiamat and Marduk painted a picture of the negative forces of chaos being overcome forcefully by the wilful triumph of the positive forces of order and generativity. This mythic view emphasized chaos rather than injustice or inequality as the ultimate negative quality of the world: Mircea Eliade, *The Myth of the Eternal Return* (Princeton, NJ: Princeton University Press, 1954).

[34] Rabbi Harold Kushner, *When Bad Things Happen to Good People* (New York: Random House, 1978, original edn).

empire. The Hebrew Job and the Akkadian Shubshi-meshre-Shakkan gave literary voice to the questions of cosmic justice and moral law in light of the sufferings and afflictions of virtuous people,[35] and these questions have persisted through literature across cultures and historical periods.

The word *theodicy* was first used by Leibniz in the same essay that presented his positive worldview, his chief aim being to argue that the goodness of God was not diminished by the evils of the world.[36] An entire body of texts emerged in western philosophy and theology that wrestled with the 'evils' of the world, that is, the unexpected and undeserved traumas and tragedies that beset people and the seeming lack of reward or retribution for the good or bad deeds done by human beings, and the injustice of wicked and oppressing rulers and owners whose cruelty can continue unchecked. Although the word 'theodicy' literally means 'judgement about God', the core question is not primarily about God. The underlying question is about ultimate causation and ultimate purpose in causes and effects. What, if anything, causes life's tragedies and traumas to happen? And what principles, if any, guide such causes?

The most frequently recognized theodical belief, across cultures and continents, is a *deterministic* view of life events – that events happen as they do for a reason, either fated and predetermined by an ultimate plan or following a strict cosmically ordered cause-and-effect formula that transcends direct time and space (such as in classic Tibetan Buddhist theodicy[37]). Both anthropologists and religious missionaries have observed that deterministic theodicies can vary significantly, both within and across cultures and religions.[38]

---

[35]   In the book of Job of the Hebrew scriptures, Job laments, 'Though I am innocent, I cannot answer him; I must appeal for mercy to my accuser ... The earth is given into the hand of the wicked; he [God] covers the eyes of its judges – if it is not he, who then is it?': Job 9:15, 24 (NRSV). In the Akkadian *Ludlul bel nemeqi* (*I will praise the Lord of wisdom,* alternatively called *The poem of the righteous sufferer*), Shubshi-meshre-Shakkan states, 'A man who has been righteous throughout may yet be dealt with by the powers who govern existence as though he were the blackest offender ... Righteousness, the good life, is no guarantee of health and happiness. Often, indeed, the unrighteous life seems a better way to success', quoted in Haim Schwartzbaum, 'The Jewish and Moslem Versions of Some Theodicy Legends,' in *Fabula* 3 (1960): 119.

[36]   See, for instance, Leibniz, 'Theodicy', p. 61.

[37]   See the Dalai Lama on *karma* and rebirth: ' ... the consequences of various unvirtuous acts determine the circumstances of one's life [that is, rebirth] in different ways. Killing in a previous lifetime dictates a short life span and much illness. It also leads to the tendency to kill, ensuring more suffering in future lives ... Sexual misconduct, such as adultery, results in future lives in which the company you keep will be untrustworthy and which you will suffer infidelity and betrayal': The Dalai Lama, *An Open Heart: Practicing Compassion in Everyday Life* (New York: Little, Brown, and Company, 2001), pp. 67–68.

[38]   Theodical differences across cultures and religions can be easier to spot. Ethnologist Sir Raymond Firth documented notable contrasts between more 'benevolent' deterministic theodicies of major monotheistic religions and more 'malevolent' deterministic theodicies

Richard Shweder and his associates, in their thorough study of theodicies across cultures, outlined seven alternative theodical positions, most of which were deterministic or *humanistic* (that is, linked to human cause-and-effect) formulas focused on interpersonal, biological/medical and moral explanations of cause.[39] An example of a cultural theodicy that locates cause in human beings is the 'evil eye', a form of envy understood in Hindu and Santal cultures to exert a spiritual force to cause negative events in the lives of persons being envied.[40] This form of theodicy locates cause within humanity – but rather than the victim, it is another person with malicious or ill-willed intent who is the cause, and the mode of cause is magical or spiritual in a way less familiar to Western ears.

Shweder and his colleagues also mentioned a more radical and rare position: suffering is neither good nor evil, and does not necessarily yield meaningful outcomes – it just *is*. A contemporary and increasingly popular western variant, expressed crassly in the popular culture catch-phrase 'shit happens', is that suffering is devoid of moral meaning or cause, and emerges from impersonal natural forces acting on humanity. According to Shweder and his associates, it is also a favoured position within the sciences, medicine and much of contemporary western philosophy – but not found frequently in other parts of the world.

Theodicies that focus on human responsibility and scientific explanations of impersonal natural forces may be more common in modern western cultures. This leaves western investigations of theodicy with a bias favouring these more 'evolved' perspectives on ultimate causation. Both developmental and socio-historical theorists have tended to view theodical beliefs in a developmentally hierarchical manner, with supposedly more evolved or actualized people and cultures emphasizing more rational and individual-focused theodicies. Paul

---

in polytheistic or pagan religions of various pre-industrial and historic cultures such as the Tikopian religion in the Solomon Islands. This stark contrast between theodical – and accompanying cosmological – perspectives was given vivid illustration in the account of missionary Don Richardson in Papua-New Guinea. But such stark cross-cultural contrasts are often overly simplistic: within-culture and within-religion differences can also be quite pronounced. For instance, theological anthropologist Wendy O'Flaherty Doniger documented several Hindu theodical perspectives in India, many ultimately deterministic but with clear differences: Raymond Firth, *Rank and Religion in Tikopia: A Study in Paganism and Conversion to Christianity* (Boston, MA: Beacon, 1970) and Firth, *The Fate of the Soul: An Interpretation of Some Primitive Concepts* (London, UK: University of London, 1956); Don Richardson, *Peace Child* (Ventura, CA: Regal, 1976), and Wendy O'Flaherty Doniger, 'The Origins of Evil in Hindu Mythology', *Hermeneutics: Studies in the History of Religions*, vol. 6 (Berkeley: University of California Press, 1976).

[39]   R.A. Shweder, N.C. Much, M. Mahapatra and L. Park, 'The "Big Three" of Morality (Autonomy, Community, Divinity) and the "Big Three" Explanations of Suffering', in A. Brandt and P. Rozin (eds), *Morality & Health* (Stanford, CA: Stanford University Press, 1997), pp. 119–69.

[40]   Marine Carrin-Bouez, *Inner Frontiers: Santal Responses to Acculturation* (Bergen, Norway: Chr. Michelson Institute, Dept. of Social Science and Development, 1991).

Ricoeur, Brian Hebblethwaite and Mircea Eliade presented theodicy as a progressive development in the historical evolution of religious thought[41] – theodical positions have historically 'developed' from deterministic views that emphasized the actions of malevolent deities, to a determinism focused on impersonal fate, to dualistic explanations that juxtapose good and evil as cosmic competing forces, to a determinism emphasizing benevolent deities, to explanations that focus on human responsibility and impersonal natural forces.

However, deterministic theodicies appear to be not only normative but typical for most people in western cultures, regardless of the assumptions made by scholars. Melvin Lerner demonstrated through repeated social psychological studies that people seek to preserve a fundamental 'belief in a just world'[42] – attributing events to fate, God, or some other purposive force or moral formula. This is expressed in how people treat perceived victims of misfortune differently, attributing blame and responsibility to victims for their misfortune. Lerner proposed in his work that more deterministic theodicies (and theodicies that emphasized direct human responsibility) are basic and nearly ubiquitous as a fundamental human belief – despite some people's effort to move away from this position toward a more naturalistic or materialistic understanding.

Theodicy likely includes a more complex set of variations, within and between individuals as well as cultures. In addition, theodicy as an explanatory belief serves a coping function. Different theodical beliefs are likely to serve different functions in people's methods of coping with negative life events. Young adults' responses to the questions we asked will provide further insight into the range and function of people's theodical beliefs.

Life Purpose

Following the set of questions about worldview, we asked participants two questions together about purpose in life:

> What do you see as your place in the world?
> How do you 'fit' into the world?

Questions of life purpose are at once both personal and general, bringing into focus each person's ideas and beliefs about his own location, purpose and function in society and in the world as well as ideas and beliefs about what human beings in general can and should do in relation to the world of being. Beliefs about life purpose orient intention or motivation *vis-à-vis* the world. Thus, questions

---

[41]   Paul Ricoeur, *The Symbolism of Evil*, trans. E. Buchanan (Boston, MA: Beacon, 1967); Brian Hebblethwaite, *Evil, Suffering and Religion* (Wiltshire: Cromwell, 2000), and Eliade, *Eternal Return*.

[42]   Melvin Lerner, *The Belief in a Just World: A Fundamental Delusion* (New York: Plenum, 1980).

of purpose are not abstract considerations but are intrinsically linked with what Sharon Parks has called vocation: 'awareness of living one's life aligned with a larger frame of purpose and significance'.[43] From psychiatrist Clemens Benda's perspective, life purpose is a sense of devotion or dedication based on beliefs about humanity and ultimate ends, which in turn shape ultimate values.[44] Thus, solutions to the questions of human purpose are both personal and universal, providing a framework for how individuals and humanity relate to and influence the greater surrounding contexts of human culture, nature and the supernatural.

Expressions of life purpose vary widely, related in part to what people believe about the *telos* or ultimate meaning and end of human life. For example, the sage in the biblical book, Ecclesiastes, commends the reader to finding purpose in the moments of daily life in one's immediate context, detached from concern about the vanities of the world: 'Go, eat your bread with enjoyment, and drink your wine with a merry heart ... Enjoy life with the wife whom you love ... Whatever your hand finds to do, do with your might ... .'[45] A quote commonly attributed by Erik Erikson to Sigmund Freud echoes this sentiment in his synopsis of healthy life purpose as *lieben und arbeiten*, to love and to work. Max Weber only considered one religious alternative to this more 'ascetical' religious mindset (as expressed in Ecclesiastes), in which the good person begrudgingly and humbly engages the world through limited localized roles: a 'mystical' or contemplative religious mindset which fosters an active withdrawal from the world and thus protection from entanglement and wrong.[46] For Weber, religion rarely supported a sense of life purpose focused on active and transformative engagement in the world.

But other scriptural and theological perspectives on life purpose find expression in Christianity as well as in other religions. In his classic *Christ and Culture*, Richard Niebuhr outlined five different historic Christian theological orientations with Christ as a symbolic figure of human *telos* or destiny, the exemplar of and redemptive gateway to highest human purpose intended by God, in relation to human culture.[47] In his five types, the exemplar is understood as setting a path and ideal pattern for followers of intentional withdrawal from, resistance to, full participation in and acquiescence to, fulfilment and transcendence of, or struggle for the transformation of, human culture. Niebuhr's theological orientations offer a religiously based depiction of distinct ways that humans seek to express and understand their place or 'fit' within humanity and their reason or *telos* for existence. In *Religion and Community*, Keith Ward took a similar approach in discussing how people in the world's major religions have come to perceive themselves and

---

43   Sharon Parks, *Big Questions, Worthy Dreams: Mentoring Young Adults in Their Search for Meaning, Purpose, and Faith* (San Francisco, CA: Jossey-Bass, 2000), p. 26.

44   Benda, 'Existential Approach'.

45   Excerpts from Ecclesiastes 9:7–10 (NRSV).

46   Weber, 'Ascetism, Mysticism, and Salvation Religion', pp. 192–202.

47   H. Richard Niebuhr, *Christ and Culture* (New York: HarperCollins, 1951).

their religious communities' common purposes *vis-à-vis* the surrounding culture or perceived 'world.'[48]

As psychiatrist Erich Fromm has indicated, human purpose is not only built on goals, but on a set of beliefs that provide a map for movement in the world. Expressions of purpose in life begin with teleological questions such as 'Why am I/are we here?' and 'How do I/we belong in this world?', yielding an explanatory set of beliefs that can orient one's goals and motivations toward an ultimate end.

Fromm outlined the following telic themes that people must face: rootedness (focused on connections with others), unity (focused on a sense of congruity in oneself) and effectiveness (focused on accomplishment). People then vary in their choices to withdraw from, partially engage with, or fully embrace each of these three telic challenges.[49] For instance, in relation to a *telos* of rootedness, individuals may abandon relational ties in favour of narcissism, cling to old connections, identify with new people through role-adoption and group identity, or actively pursue new mutual connections. In terms of unity, individuals may opt for self-forgetfulness, adopt a set of roles and actively ignore inner questions of congruence, or pursue an understanding and acceptance of their own complexity through education and active care.

Fromm's discussion of life purpose suggests a continuum of engagement, ranging from active and passive withdrawal from the world, through role-based engagement within specified contexts, to more open-ended engagement. People's beliefs and choices along this continuum are likely to be shaped in part by religious and cultural differences in concepts of the ideal human *telos*.[50] But individuals may also depart dramatically from their surrounding culture in how they view human purpose and act in accord with their views. For instance, in ethicist Kristen Monroe's (1996) now classic study of highly altruistic people, she found that altruists had different orienting beliefs and intentions than those surrounding them.

The pattern of relationship between religious person and surrounding world in Niebuhr's and Ward's taxonomies is similar to what Florence Kluckhohn described as three alternative beliefs about humanity's role *vis-à-vis* nature: overcoming (and active in), in harmony with, or subjugated by (and passive to) nature.[51] Those with a 'mastery over nature' orientation might adopt a sense of human purpose marked by either acquisition or altruism, whereas those with a 'subjugation to nature' orientation may adopt a sense of defensive withdrawal from the world, marked more by anxiety and self-preservation than by any recognized potential for personal influence.

---

[48]   Keith Ward, *Religion and Community* (New York: Oxford University, 2000).

[49]   Fromm, *Destructiveness*, Chapter 10.

[50]   Robert Bellah (in *Tokugawa Religion*) and Dorrine Kondo have both pointed to role-fulfilment as a salient feature of life purpose in Japanese culture, from the Tokugawa era to the present: Dorrine Kondo, *Crafting Selves: Power, Gender, and Discourses of Identity in a Japanese Workplace* (Chicago, IL: University of Chicago Press, 1990).

[51]   Kluckhohn, 'Dominant and Variant Value Orientations'.

In Chapter 6, I will examine more closely the varied ways in which young adults articulate their thoughts about life purpose.

Ultimate Values (and Vices)

We took a multifaceted approach to tapping young adults' ultimate values, drawing on open-ended questions in our face-to-face interviews, survey questionnaires, and Likert-scale rating questions in our initial interviews. The open-ended questions were asked in three sets, as follows:

Think for a minute about what it means to be a person in society and the world.

1. What do you feel are the best and the worst human attributes?
2. What types of people do you admire most, and what types of people disgust you or turn you off the most? Why?
3. What is the most important ideal or belief in your life?
4. Is there a principle by which you try to live your life?
5. Are there principles or ideals that make no sense to you, or that seem really unimportant?

Values have been the most widely studied and explored facet of personal theology, across academic disciplines. Beginning with the earliest scriptural and philosophical texts, scholars and researchers have concerned themselves with questions about how to live and how to orient one's motivations. Alasdair MacIntyre's historical-philosophical work in *After Virtue* and Robert Emmons' psychological study of *Ultimate Concerns* are both markers of increasing scholarly interest in values, virtues and vices.[52] The emerging field of 'positive psychology' has particularly highlighted this interest through studies of character, as found in *Character Strengths and Virtues: A Handbook and Classification*.[53] Many of contemporary researchers' ideas about character, virtue and values are rooted in discussion of the ethical, moral and teleological ideas of ancient scholars such as Aristotle and Thomas Aquinas, Confucius, or the Buddha.

From the 'terminal values' or 'ultimate concerns' of Milton Rokeach and Robert Emmons to 'instrumental' means-to-end values, from personal aspirations to socio-political opinions, values carry directional heft. They are not static ideas: they all direct choices in attention, thought and behaviour. In an oft-cited definition, Florence Kluckhohn's husband, Clyde, also an anthropologist of values, stated, 'A value is a conception, explicit or implicit, distinctive of an individual or characteristic of a group, of the desirable which influences the selection from

---

[52]   Published citations for MacIntyre's *After Virtue* and Emmons's *Ultimate Concerns* currently exceed 15,000.

[53]   Christopher Peterson and Martin Seligman, *Character Strengths and Virtues: A Handbook and Classification* (Washington, DC: American Psychological Association, 2004).

available modes, means, and ends of action.'[54] MacIntyre further noted that values influence us by how they 'instruct us how to move from potentiality to act, how to realize our true nature and to reach our true end'.[55]

Core orienting values then help to shape the relative emphases and energy given to other values and goals. Hierarchically at the peak (or at the deepest core) reside the values that aim toward ultimate, unifying ends. Aristotle (and later, Aquinas) named the primary ultimate end as happiness. For the Buddha, the ultimate aim of freedom from suffering was the core orienting value. The ancient Jewish value of *shalom*, evocative of communal peace and harmony, carries resonances similar to core values in Confucianism.

These core values have been called ultimate ends, terminal values, or ultimate concerns, which theologian Paul Tillich described as giving 'depth, direction and unity to all other concerns and, with them, to the whole personality'.[56] Core values, and those values closely related to the core, are what I am calling *ultimate values* – those ideals of human qualities of being and intentions for the good to which individuals aspire as ultimate ends. Conversely, core anti-values or vices may be understood as those intentions and qualities of being and acting that gravitate toward an ultimately undesirable end.

Researchers select and classify values differently according to the questions they asked, the cultures in which they asked them, and the implicit or explicit assumptions and interests guiding their choices. In his review of values research and theories, Richard Kilby outlined 28 different broad classifications, each encompassing a variety of specific values.[57] This presents a confusing array of studies. Ultimate values must be understood as distinct from values specific to relationships and work, and from day-to-day means-to-end values. Without this distinction, any multivariate or qualitative attempt at categorizing values into value-sets will be fraught with confusion.

A focus on the ultimacy or centrality of values only somewhat limits the range of values that might be studied. Milton Rokeach outlined what he considered 18 independent 'terminal values', distinct from 18 independent 'instrumental values'. His label 'terminal values' indicated a set of 'end-states to strive for',[58] reflective of Paul Tillich's 'ultimate concern'. Terminal values included mature love, a life of excitement, world peace, accomplishment and salvation. Instrumental values, in contrast, were behavioural means of attaining those desired end-states (for instance,

---

[54]   Clyde Kluckhohn, 'Values and Value-Orientations in the Theory of Action', in Talcott Parsons and Edward Shils (eds), *Towards a General Theory of Action* (Cambridge, MA: Harvard University Press, 1951), p. 395.

[55]   MacIntyre, *After Virtue*, p. 50.

[56]   Paul Tillich, *Dynamics of Faith* (New York: Harper & Row, 1957), p. 105.

[57]   Richard Kilby, *The Study of Human Values* (Lanham, MD: University Press of America, 1993).

[58]   Milton Rokeach, *The Nature of Human Values* (New York: The Free Press, 1973), p. 11.

being honest, polite and friendly). More recently, Robert Emmons also worked with Tillich's construct of 'ultimate concern' to develop twelve categories of what he called 'personal strivings' (for instance, achievement, affiliation and power).[59] Drawing on the work of Rokeach and Kluckhohn, Shalom Schwartz outlined a theory of ten broad types of values, including power, hedonism, universalism, benevolence and security, and demonstrated their general 'pan-cultural' hierarchy of their importance in people's lives.[60] Philosopher William Gerber, musing on 27 human values, settled on a hierarchical solution similar to Thomas Aquinas' and Abraham Maslow's by dividing ten basic physical needs (for example, food and shelter, rest, freedom from physical pain or deprivation, recreation, stimulation) from ten psychological needs (for example, understanding, belonging, freedom from guilt and shame, freedom from undue stress, self-respect, achievement and spiritual connection) and seven higher-level 'wants' which might be regarded as ultimate aims (for example, self-expression, equality, inner harmony, happiness, honesty and freedom from frequent and intense sorrowful events).[61] Abraham Maslow outlined a similar hierarchically ordered set of four ultimate values, with belongingness (that is, affiliation) necessarily satisfied prior to seeking achievement and competence, and finally freedom of self-expression – a list that is limited by its more individualistic and atomistic focus, surprisingly devoid of either hedonistic or altruistic values.[62]

The multiplicity and inconsistency in the literature – and the differences in what is regarded as 'ultimate' – has led researchers to search for broader underlying categories of values. Here is a sample of different researchers' categories derived from surveys and interviews: autonomy, personal growth, pleasure, social altruism and affiliation (Dorfman); achievement/power, hedonism, self-direction/stimulation, universalism, benevolence and security/conformity (Bilsky

---

[59]   Robert Emmons, 'Personal Strivings: An Approach to Personality and Subjective Well-Being', *Journal of Personality and Social Psychology* 51(5) (November 1986): 1058–68.

[60]   Shalom Schwartz, 'Value Priorities and Behavior: Applying a Theory of Integrated Value Systems', in C. Seligman, J.M. Olson, and M.P. Zanna (eds), *The Psychology of Values: The Ontario Symposium*, vol. 8 (Mahwah, NJ: Lawrence Erlbaum Associates, 1996), pp. 1–24, and Shalom Schwartz and Anat Bardi, 'Moral Dialogue across Cultures: An Empirical Perspective', in Edward Lehman (ed.), *Autonomy and Order: A Communitarian Anthology* (Lanham, MD: Rowman & Littlefield, 2001), pp. 155–83.

[61]   William Gerber, *Anatomy of What We Value Most*, vol. 52 of *Value Inquiry Book Series* (Atlanta, GA: Ropodi, 1997), pp. 6–8.

[62]   Abraham Maslow,. 'A Theory of Human Motivation', *Psychological Review* 50(4) (1943): 370–96. Ultimate values found by Rokeach (1973) to be highly important to young adults (and older adults) in the late 1960s – specifically, equality, freedom and world peace, indicative of concern for others and for the continuity and structure of society – are absent from Maslow's system. However, Maslow's system contributes to discussion of values by distinguishing between values focused on materialism, affiliation and eudaimonic self-image, a pattern we will find playing out among American young adults in this study.

and Schwartz); ideal-orientation, loyalty, integrity, care and trust, fairness and confidence (Walker and Pitts).[63]

More than a few scholars have assumed or commended further reductive categorization of values into dialectically polarized global values-sets – individualism vs collectivism,[64] hedonism vs idealism,[65] or self-indulgence vs self-development[66] – but in the end, simple dipolar distinctions in value systems, between passion and reason (as found in the works of Hume, Kant and Kierkegaard), personal pleasure and social good, or collectivism and individualism, may be overly simplistic. Cultural and subcultural variations reveal subtler differences in people's ultimate values rooted in their telic ideals of the good.[67]

The complexity in mapping values led me to employ multiple methods in asking young adults about their ultimate and means-end values. The questions at the beginning of this section are the open-ended questions about ultimate values we asked emerging adults in interviews. The questions invited their freeform ideas and reflections about what they considered as the good (and the bad). The first question oriented young adults toward desirable and undesirable human attributes, and further tapped the motivational aspect of values by eliciting images of types of people that evoke admiration or disgust. The second and third questions gave young adults a chance to name their most central or ultimate value or principle of how to live, and to name a principle or value foreign to them but recognizable as perhaps a core principle to other people.

We also gave young adults a Q-sort adaptation I developed for Rokeach's Life Values Survey[68] as part of a questionnaire. The adaptation allowed young

---

[63]   Rachel Dorfman, *Aging into the 21st Century: The Exploration of Aspirations and Values* (New York: Brunner/Mazel, 1994); Wolfgana Bilsky and Shalom Schwartz, 'Values and Personality', *European Journal of Personality* 8 (February 1994): 163–81, and Lawrence Walker and Russell Pitts, 'Naturalistic Conceptions of Moral Maturity', *Developmental Psychology* 34(3) (May 1998): 403–19.

[64]   See, for instance, Hazel Markus and Shinobu Kitayama, 'The cultural psychology of personality', *Journal of Cross-Cultural Psychology* 29(1) (January 1998): 63–87, and Harry Triandis, *Individualism and Collectivism* (Boulder, CO: Westview, 1995).

[65]   MacIntyre (in *After Virtue*) frames his philosophic historical review in conversation with this argument, and Radhakamal Mukerjee takes this perspective as a southern Asian scholar: Radhakamal Mukerjee,'Homeostasis, Society, and Values', *Philosophy & Phenomenological Research*, 27(1) (1966): 74–9.

[66]   Jack Bauer, Dan McAdams and Jennifer Pals, 'Narrative Identity and Eudaimonic Well-Being', *Journal of Happiness Studies* 9 (2008): 81–104. Recent discussions of eudaimonic vs hedonic values and motivations have re-engaged ancient philosophic distinctions in values that might broadly be seen as self-interests.

[67]   Alisdair MacIntyre in *After Virtue* and David Fisher in *Albion's Seed* provide rich historical studies of different cultural values-orientations: David Fisher, *Albion's Seed: Four British Folkways in America* (New York: Oxford University Press, 1994).

[68]   Milton Rokeach's *Life Values Survey* has been widely used in research and applied consultative work: Milton Rokeach, *Life Values Survey* (Palo Alto, CA: Consulting

adults to sort Rokeach's 18 'terminal' values into clusters of relative centrality or ultimacy. Responses to this exercise helped guide our understanding of the range of responses to interview questions regarding ultimate values. Additional questions related to means-end values allowed for an additional perspective on how ultimate values translated into the motivations and immediate concerns and actions of these young adults' daily lives.

These four categories of beliefs and values – worldview, theodicy, life purpose and ultimate values – are at the core of what I am presenting in this book as an initial mapping of personal theologies. As indicated above, preceding research and theory is either scant or of mixed benefit in framing the research we undertook. Global cultural categorizations or historical simplifications, developmental type-casting and positivist reductions of the beliefs and values constituting personal theologies has not always led to clarification, and has frequently obliterated or diminished attention to nuance. A grounded-theory approach was in order, to allow the themes embedded in people's speech to direct our analysis of content and to identify patterns in the beliefs and values of young adults.

Background to the Study

Throughout my training and work in psychological services, social science research and religious ministry during my first 25 years of adulthood, no small part of my focus has been related to young adults. I entered early adulthood with questions that followed me through the entire course of my graduate education, research, direct service and ministry, and teaching. Why do so many of us as young adults struggle in the process of finding our place in society? Why are there so few people my age involved in any way with religion? How are we all making sense of this world into which we find ourselves 'thrown', to borrow a term from existentialists? How are we managing to find our way, make even somewhat informed choices, and establish a sense of how to be in the world?

I found that I was not asking these questions alone. I was simply giving voice to the questions my peers in work and graduate school were asking. From my atheistic Jewish friend painting grandiose murals to explore his own ideals and purposes in light of the writers and philosophers who had stirred his imagination, to my Finnish colleague who wandered the hallways muttering as he wrestled with Wittgenstein about meaning and purpose, to my research colleague uncertain about graduate school or her boyfriend or her continuing back problems resulting from her adolescent experiments with LSD, to the daughter of a missionary in the long process of coming out as lesbian and facing the challenge of reconstructing her world and her religious faith, to a young congregation member holding his family together and coming to terms with his military experience in Operation

Psychologists Press, 1967).

Desert Storm and his work in the financial world where his boss was indicted for financial malfeasance and embezzlement – we were all asking questions, seeking meaning, constructing and reconstructing worlds. Whether motivated by discrepancy, uncertainty, cognitive dissonance, or curiosity, I found my peers and myself on a search that took us beyond our varied heritages of beliefs and values into a new, intentionally constructive space.

My research on young adulthood unfolded around these larger questions. Some of my earlier research explored young adult psychological development and identity formation. But my questions expanded beyond questions of selfhood and self-concept to religious engagement and matters of personal theology or world-concept. Two research initiatives coalesced around the communal practices and individualized content and processes of meaning-making among young adults.

The people with whom I first explored the core questions of personal theology – worldview, theodicy, life purpose and ultimate values – were young adults. My initial exploratory interviews, begun in 1995, were with young adults who were involved in unique religious rejuvenation movements within organized religion (such as found in emerging church groups), who were attempting to keep the fires of their religious faith lit in the midst of denominations on the decline and typically underpopulated by young adults.[69] This study, the subject of a documentary and another forthcoming book, provided evidence from ten different young adult faith communities not only of religious creativity and passionate spiritual interest among some American young adults, but also of the challenges young adults face in engaging their spiritual quests in religious denominations whose organizational structures and systems were at best marginally responsive and at worst oppositional to their interests and unique religious expressions.

An integral part of my ethnographic work in these young adult faith communities was the direct interviews I conducted with the young adults involved in these religious rejuvenation movements. There were two distinct types of questions I asked. With one set of questions, I inquired about their experience of the faith community in which they participated, the meaning of their experience, and how they understood the purpose and value of what the faith community offered in comparison to traditional religious congregations. With the second set of questions, I asked about their personal theologies and other matters related to their own perceptions and meaning-making perspectives related to their life experiences. It was in this work, during the 55 interviews I conducted, that I first formed and used the questions about worldview, theodicy and life purpose.

While in the midst of that first (and longer) research project,[70] I became interested in exploring these same questions with a broader sample of young adults, representative of the wider range of religious experience and interest in

---

[69]   Jacqueline Schmitt and David Gortner, 'The Challenges of Evangelism with Students and Young Adults', in Sheryl Kujawa (ed.), *Disorganized Religion: The Evangelization of Youth and Young Adults in the Episcopal Church* (Boston, MA: Cowley, 1997).

[70]   The Young Adult Ministry Research Project extended from 1995 to 2005.

American culture. I was invited to join the research team working on a study called *Making the Transition*, based at the University of Chicago, under the direction of sociologist Barbara Schneider. The three-year study, begun in 1997, tracked the unfolding lives of a sub-sample of the 1,215 emerging adults (aged 18–25) who had participated as teenagers in the preceding longitudinal study of adolescence, the *Sloan Study of Youth and Social Development*.

The *Making the Transition* Study

The initial aim of *Making the Transition* was to study the differences in life experiences, early vocational trajectories, psychological well-being and work-related values related to young adults' post-secondary transition directly into full-time work, full-time bachelor-level college education, or part-time college and work in associates- and bachelor-level schools. The study included three years of base telephone interviews conducted in the tradition of the National Opinion Research Center; more in-depth interviews primarily conducted face-to-face in the communities where young adults lived and worked; brief ethnographic site visits to the places where young adults were employed; a questionnaire with established and constructed psychological inventories, and a week-long randomized time diary called the 'Experience Sampling Method'.

Schneider graciously welcomed me to expand the focus of the project to include an exploratory study of meaning-making among young adults. Together, we created the interview protocol for the in-depth face-to-face interviews, incorporating as one segment of the hour-long interviews the core questions about personal theology that I had formed and used in my previous study as well as more basic questions about religious beliefs and practices and new questions I formed about ultimate values. In constructing the questionnaire used in the second and third years of the study, I added a modified version of the Rokeach Values Survey, to inquire more deeply about ultimate values. And, to allow for comparisons with young adults from previous cohorts in the General Social Survey (GSS), we added GSS questions about worldview and life purpose to the base telephone interview in the third year of the study.

After three years of study, the *Making the Transition* team had conducted telephone interviews with 548 emerging adults who were from the original group of 1,215 teenagers that, between eighth and twelfth grades, had participated in at least two of three phases of the Sloan longitudinal study. During the years of my involvement in the study (and my focus on personal theologies), we completed 314 of these base telephone interviews. Of these, 82 emerging adults also completed the in-depth interview, and an overlapping set of 115 completed the questionnaire. For the in-depth interviews, we travelled as often as possible to the towns and cities where our emerging adults lived and worked – in the Midwest, North-east and South. For those living in the West, we used the telephone to conduct the in-depth interviews.

The *Making the Transition* and *Youth and Social Development* studies are both examples of 'concurrent nested design' studies – studies that embed one research effort within or in direct relation to a larger research project. A qualitative phase of research may be embedded within a larger quantitative phase. Or a longitudinal study with a smaller group may begin within a larger cross-sectional population study. Or, within a longitudinal study, a subgroup may be asked to complete more intensive research tasks like in-depth interviews or time diary experience-sampling. The original *Youth and Social Development* (YSD) study was nested within a much larger nationwide study, the *National Education Longitudinal Study* (NELS) of 1988–92: YSD participants in high school during 1990 and 1992, from twelve different schools systems across the US, completed many overlapping questions from the core NELS survey. NELS, which began with 24,599 eighth-graders in 1988, tracked both high school students and dropouts through 1992 when they were old enough to graduate from high school, and again around age 20 (in 1994) and 26 (in 2000).[71] NELS itself was designed to allow for direct comparisons with two previous large-scale longitudinal studies (the *National Longitudinal Study for the High School Class of 1972*, and the *High School & Beyond* study), and so included repeat questions and new questions. NELS questionnaires were translated into Spanish and several Asian languages, allowing students with a primary language other than English to participate. Thus, careful sampling procedures and 'cohort freshening' procedures (for example, replacing unavailable participants with similar students) ensured that the large sample remained representative of the overall US student population (see Figure 2.1).

While a concurrent nested design does not ensure a representative sample at every nested level (as we shall see), it does allow researchers to situate their findings within a larger embedded sample, allowing for a greater confidence that findings have some generalizable applicability beyond the small group of people who participated in a specific nested component of the overall study.

Participants in the Study

As in the original YSD study, the subsamples studied from the second and third years of *Making the Transition* were all US citizens from diverse communities across the country. But they were no longer as clearly representative of the US population as a whole. As with many longitudinal studies, difficulties in tracking and differential attrition led to significant changes from the original demographic distribution of the YSD sample. Table 2.1 provides a demographic summary of the 314 participants in Year 2 and Year 3 of *Making the Transition* and the 82 of

---

[71]　NELS and the prior studies, conducted as partnerships involving multiple institutions, have guided federal and state-level educational evaluation and policy development: 'National Education Longitudinal Study of 1988 (NELS:88) Base Year through Second Follow-Up: Final Methodology Report', Working Paper 98-06, May 1998 <http://nces.ed.gov/pubs98/9806.pdf>.

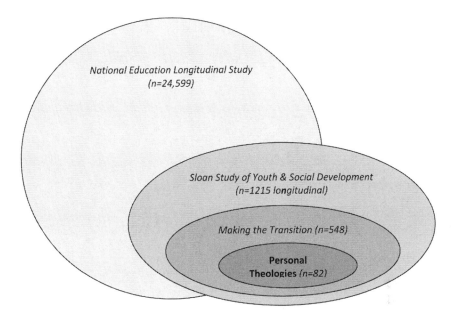

Figure 2.1   Visual representation of the concurrent nested design of *Varieties of Personal Theologies*

these whose in-depth interviews are the primary focus of this book, compared to the full sample of 548 emerging adults in the study, the 1,215 in the original YSD study, and the 24,599 eighth-graders in the larger NELS 1988 study within which the YSD study was based.

As evident in Table 2.1, we experienced a degree of differential attrition in *Making the Transition* – and more as the study progressed. Over time, we retained a higher proportion of female than male, white than non-white, and collegiate than non-collegiate participants. We had more difficulty tracking families and young adults from poor and working-class communities, and they less frequently agreed to continued participation in the study. Emerging adults participating in Years 2 and 3, especially those in the intensive studies, were more likely to be white, from more affluent communities (particularly upper-middle through upper class), from college- or graduate-educated parents with intact marriages, and had somewhat higher grade point averages in high school.[72] Only 14 per cent of these emerging adults had children, and only 9 per cent were married (almost all of them women). Most participants were involved in more than one dating relationship over a two-year span, usually sexual in nature. These patterns indicate a disproportionate

---

[72]   Comparisons were made using one-sample t-tests, using mean percentages or scores from the full *Making the Transition* group as a baseline for comparison. The differences are magnified when comparing overall Year 2 and Year 3 demographics to those of the original Sloan sample and NELS sample.

Table 2.1   Demographic summary of participants in different layers of studies

Demographics	NELS♦	YSD base year	*Making the Transition*	*Making the Transition Years 2 and 3*	*Making the Transition Personal theologies*
	n=24,599 (18,221 first follow-up)	*n*=1,215	*n*=548	*n*=314	*n*=82
Female %	50	53	59	58	63
Race (% non-white) ♠	27% (grade 12)	42	34	26***	19
Type of community %					
Poor/Working class	~39	32	22	18†	19
Middle class	~40	38	36	32	24
Upper-middle/ Upper class	~21	31	42	50***	57
Parent education %					
Less than high school ⎱ High school ⎰	10 21	33	25	19	20
Some college	41	19	21	20	17
Four-year college degree	14	20	20	22	24
Graduate school degree	12	28	33	39	39
Intact original family %	~65	63	68	74†	79
High school grade average (0–4)	2.82	3.18	3.21	3.28	3.44
Post-high school %					
College	76 (started) 29 (finished)	—	77	80	82
Most competitive colleges	—	—	24	29	39
Employed	86	—	72	81*	69
Married	39	—	10	9	8
Total serious relationships in 2 years (unmarried)	—	—	—	1.5	1.6
Have children	41	—	14	15	14
Living at home	—	—	46	46	47
Living with peers	—	—	54	54	53

Notes to Table 2.1

† *p* < .1; *p* < .05; ** *p* < .01; *** *p* < .005

♦ NELS summary data was drawn from several Statistical Analysis Reports from the National Center for Education Statistics, including Steven Ingels, 'Coming of Age in the 1990s: The Eighth Grade Class of 1988 Twelve Years Later', June 2002, NCSE 2002-321 <http://www.gpoaccess.gov/eric/200304/ed468715.pdf>, and Laura Horn and Jerry West, 'A Profile of Parents of Eighth Graders', July 1992, NCES 92-488 <http://nces.ed.gov/pubs92/92488.pdf>, US Department of Education.

♠ Among the combined Year 2 and Year 3 participants, 5 per cent were Asian, 8 per cent were Hispanic, 12 per cent were black, and 1 per cent were Native American. Fewer black and Hispanic participants completed the intensive studies. The US adult population in 2000, by comparison, was 72 per cent white, 11 per cent Hispanic, 12 per cent black, 4 per cent Asian, and less than 1 per cent Native American.

---

sample of well-educated, career-motivated group of young adults from middle- to upper-class communities that were unlikely to marry at a young age.

But in many ways, there were marked consistencies between the different study samples, and notable similarities with the overall US population of adults. Racial diversity in the Year 2 and 3 *Transition* sample was similar to the original NELS sample and roughly representative of the year 2000 US adult population. Over 70 per cent of *Transition*'s emerging adults were from intact families with their original birth parents, while the remaining 30 per cent were from blended, single-parent, or non-traditional families (roughly similar to patterns in the year 2000 US population). The majority of young adults in this study were employed either full-time or part-time, regardless of their post-secondary school enrolment status, and most held two or more jobs over a period of two years. Between 40 and 50 per cent of the young adults lived at home with their parents, and the rest lived with peers or roommates. None were living alone. These and other results were generally consistent with young adult demographic trends of delayed marriage, job instability and increased post-secondary education.[73]

The emerging adults we interviewed in *Making the Transition* thus provide an imperfect but useful baseline for glimpsing the range of personal theologies among American emerging adults. The group is over-representative of college-educated emerging adults from more economically privileged backgrounds and is under-representative of emerging adults who went straight into work after high school (or after dropping out of school) and who were from more economically challenged backgrounds. In this study of personal theologies, I discuss the overall distributions of personal theologies among these emerging adults in light of this imperfect representation, I highlight the verbal expressions of personal theologies

---

[73] See Frances Goldscheider and Calvin Goldscheider, *Leaving Home before Marriage: Ethnicity, Familism, and Generational Relationships* (Madison, WI: University of Wisconsin, 1993), and Paul Amato and Alan Booth, *A Generation at Risk: Growing Up in an Era of Family Upheaval* (Cambridge, MA: Harvard University Press, 1997).

among individuals that are more representative of the wider population, and when possible I use statistical corrections in longitudinal analyses that are based on patterns in the more representative sample from the original YSD study.

Young Adult Lives and Personal Theologies

Young adults move through a series of extended transitions in roles, rights, responsibilities and social realities. They face a fundamental shift in their lives: shaped significantly by multiple factors from their childhood and teenage years, they take on more responsibility for choosing the experiences that will continue to mould them – and they are invited by society to shape their own destinies and choose how to participate in their society and culture. As young adults begin to move beyond early concerns with personal identity, they also continue the process of leaving the home-lives of their childhood, shift roles from adolescent semi-dependence and counter-dependence to adult autonomy and responsibility, develop increasingly intricate ways of thinking about abstract issues, and embark on the pursuit of meaningful work and enduring relationships. Nuanced neurocognitive and emotional development, as well as ongoing adjustments in personality, continue well past adolescence until age 30.

Young adults' personal theologies, themselves shaped by previous contexts and experiences, can help or hinder young adults in their decisions, commitments and investments as adults. Experiences in childhood, adolescence and the transition to early adulthood give rise to the personal theologies of young adults. In turn, these personal theologies enter a dialogical and mutually influential relationship with ongoing choices and experiences in young adults' lives. As roles, purposes, responsibilities and opportunities expand and change during these years, young adults also begin to pay closer attention to the external environment in all its diversity and complexity. According to Erik Erikson and other psychosocial theorists,[74] this increased attention to and interaction with broader external environment leads to young adults' construction of a *Weltanschauung*. Lawrence Kohlberg, James Fowler and other moral and faith development theorists[75] have pointed to early adulthood as the primary period during which people step back

---

[74]   Erik Erikson, 'Identity and the Life Cycle', *Psychological Issues* 1(1) (1959): 1–171. See also Ruth Wittenberg, *Postadolescence: Theoretical and Clinical Aspects of Psychoanalytic Therapy* (New York: Grune & Stratton, 1968).

[75]   Lawrence Kohlberg and Richard Hersch, 'Moral Development: A Review of the Theory', *Theory Into Practice* 16(2) (April 1977): 53–9; Fowler, *Stages of Faith*; James Fowler, *Becoming Adult, Becoming Christian: Adult Development and Christian Faith* (San Francisco, CA: Jossey-Bass, 2000); Oser, 'Religious Judgment', 1991; Laurent Daloz, Cheryl Keen, James Keen and Sharon Parks, *Common Fire: Lives of Commitment in a Complex World* (Boston, MA: Beacon, 1996), and John Gibbs, *Moral Development and Reality: Beyond the Theories of Kohlberg and Hoffman* (Boston, MA: Allyn & Bacon, 2009).

from their previously assumed beliefs and values, assess them, and begin to construct more individuated moral and faith constructs.

Early adulthood thus affords an ideal opportunity to examine the ways in which personal theology is influenced by childhood and adolescent experiences, but then in turn influences emerging adult lives. Of particular interest is the period identified by Jeffrey Arnett and others as 'emerging adulthood'[76] – the period from age 18 to 25. As roles, expectations, opportunities and life patterns have changed in American society, so have the experiences of people during what Sharon Parks called the 'critical years' and what Arnett has called 'emerging adulthood'.

Our travels and calls to conduct in-depth interviews with emerging adults took us to college towns, major cities, suburbs and smaller working-class cities and towns across the United States. We met with them in coffee-houses, bars, their apartments, their parents' homes, their colleges and their places of work. Stories from portions of a few of these interviews will help us grasp the intensely personal nature of young adults' development and the ways they engage in meaning-making in light of their new challenges and insights. It is their widely varied contexts, experiences, attitudes and ways of thinking that give rise to the varieties of personal theologies that we will explore in later chapters.

'Recentering': Ly-Hanh, Stefani and Jacob

Ly-Hanh was a young college student headed into orthodonture as a profession, working during the summer at a high-end department store and her father's Vietnamese restaurant. Her parents, as first-generation immigrants, had raised her and her two sisters in an upper-middle-class suburb in the North-east. Through high school and college, she had worked at least halftime while getting Bs and some As in her courses. She was seriously dating, in a sexual relationship with her non-Asian boyfriend, but still living with her family. When asked about religious beliefs, she talked more about what she did *not* believe. Growing up in a very traditional middle-class Vietnamese household with regular Buddhist prayer rituals and traditional gender roles and authority, Ly-Hanh found herself as a young adult rejecting many of the beliefs and values of her upbringing:

> My mom is very traditional, where she, like, she follows my father basically. And I just don't see how she can do that in this day and age. It's like, none of my aunts do it. But, my father handles all money problems, all business affairs, everything around the whole household by himself. And, like, he doesn't even have to consult with my mother before he makes a decision. But if she has to do

---

[76]   Jeffrey Arnett, 'Emerging Adulthood: Understanding the New Way of Coming of Age', in Jeffrey Arnett and Jennifer Tanner (eds), *Emerging Adults in America: Coming of Age in the 21st Century* (Washington, DC: American Psychological Association, 2006), pp. 3–20.

anything, she has to ask him. It's like, what is wrong with my mother? Why is she doing this? Like, she could, she's a free woman. It's not like she's a slave. Why is she not thinking for herself? And, like, it just makes our job even harder. 'Cause my sisters and I, we don't want to ... be traditional. We don't want a man controlling our lives. But, because of her we can't speak up to our father. Just because he thinks he, like, owns the place. And then my father – I can't believe that he still thinks that, like, men rule over everything ... And, it's just a lot of my aunts and uncles still believe that interracial relationships or marriages still aren't right. And, I can't believe that our family is, like, it's so traditional. But the newer generation that grows up with them, it's really hard for us. And, people don't even realize it – 'cause they think that we're like really good sons and daughters and learn to just abide by all the rules. But it, we all try to break out of this, but we can't just because so many of us are still dependent on them. It's just wrong.

Later, we will see how Ly-Hanh talked about rejecting her family's Buddhist notions of theodicy. But her struggle with familial assumptions about gender roles gives voice to the perspective of many young men and women that challenge the beliefs and values of their parents, religions and subcultures.

Stefani, a 20-year-old Native American woman, had grown up in a single-parent household with her mother in a middle-class community in the South. Seriously dating but without children and living with peers, Stefani was working on her college degree at a state university while working full-time at night in print media. She paid her full college tuition herself from her earnings:

I work in the printing department, so basically I work microfiche or laser printers all day. I load paper in one end and take it out of the other end and distribute it and pigeonhole it all over the property ... It's basically a foot in the door. It looks good on the resume. Once I graduate with my MIS degree, it will be good to have some work experience within the field. But, it's extremely boring on a day-to-day basis. I just ... I don't find it challenging at all. There's not anything there for me.

Stefani grew up in the Lutheran Church, but 'after I was confirmed we, we had difficulties with the church, and so around ninth or tenth grade a large group of people left the church. And ever since then I've been kind of fumbling around trying to find my own ... what I personally believe as opposed to what people tell me to believe.' Stefani indicated strong disengagement with organized religion: 'I don't go to church anymore. For right now. When we get married, we're not having a church wedding.' Claiming no current religious affiliation for herself, she found herself navigating between religiously and anti-religiously dogmatic friends, and she was gently critical of their unexamined 'extreme' positions: 'I have a wide variety of friends that are extreme ... extreme in both ways, that there is no God and that there's one God – and it's "the way they've been taught their whole life" type of thing.'

Stefani may have left behind the explicit religious practices she inherited from her Lutheran background, but she talked about her regular practice of deep thought, pointing toward her intentional work on matters of personal theology:

> When I'm driving, I have a 45-minute drive to work everyday, so I tend to clear my thoughts and I think about myself and my situation and what's going on around me. I don't know that I think about God in general or any particular beliefs, but I will tend to ... um ... what's the word I'm looking for ... think on society and why everything is the way it is and how my life fits into that.

Both Ly-Hanh and Stefani were articulate about the frustration of working at a job that was neither meaningful nor fulfilling while they completed the education necessary to move to a new phase in their career trajectories – a common early employment experience of American young adults. They were also quite articulate about distancing themselves from the religious beliefs and practices of their families of origin. Stefani was particularly articulate about her spiritual practices and the reasons behind her leaving the Lutheran religious heritage of her childhood, a decision emerging from a painful church conflict that tore apart the religious community she had enjoyed. Religious disaffiliation in early adulthood is not simply due to attachment to some floating American myths about freedom. Conflict, even bitter conflict, is not at all uncommon in religious communities. Sometimes, religious communities and their leaders wound people – and then, trust is not easily regained. Finally, Stefani's and Ly-Hanh's beliefs and values, as we shall continue to discover, were not vacuous or shallow. Nor, in Stefani's case, was her current spiritual practice of deep reflection on life. Both were engaged in meaning-making. Both were striving to make sense of the world into which they had been thrust. Both were engaging in what psychologist Jennifer Tanner has called the 'recentering' work of emerging adulthood.[77] And they were drawing upon multiple resources to do this work, expanding upon as well as partially rejecting what she had previously inherited from their families and religious communities.

The concept of 'recentering' may be a key to understanding how many emerging adults are actively engaged in the formation and re-formation of personal theologies. To dig deeper, let us consider a bit of Jacob's story.

A young Jewish man on the cusp of graduation from college, Jacob had over ten consecutive summers moved through a kind of apprenticeship in stagecraft to become a supervisor of backstage, guiding staff members and directing backstage traffic at a major East Coast summer arts training centre:

---

[77]   Jennifer Tanner, 'Recentering during Emerging Adulthood: A Critical Turning Point in Life Span Human Development', in Jeffrey Arnett and Jennifer Tanner (eds), *Emerging Adults in America: Coming of Age in the 21st Century* (Washington, DC: American Psychological Association, 2006), pp. 21–55.

To be honest, things never got that busy until the weekends. So ordinarily I would just come in and, and fill out a few account forms, and just make sure that everything's running smoothly … And, I was put in a position where I had to mediate arguments or just patch over little glitches that occurred between my staff and other departments.

Jacob had moved through adolescence and emerging adulthood immersed in the world of the performing arts, and had been prepared to move into a permanent career in orchestral management: 'I mean, the orchestra will hire me full time. There are some open positions right now.' But Jacob also expressed skepticism about the career trajectory that was opening up before him:

As much as I love the music industry there are some things about it which I could do without. I see a lot of the ugly side of the music industry that really doesn't interest me at all. Little celebrity gripes that just have nothing to do with what goes on onstage and too many inflated egos … Unfortunately the only thing that's really familiar to me is the orchestral world. But after this summer I'm not, I'm not a hundred per cent certain if it's what I want to do with the rest of my life. But, I don't think I'll ever stray too far from the arts world.

Like Ly-Hanh and Stefani, Jacob was renegotiating his religious identity. An automobile accident had brought him face to face with his beliefs about worldview, theodicy and life purpose. But, while still regarding himself as 'monotheistic' and respectful of his religious heritage of Judaism, he admitted to being 'somewhat frivolous' and 'pretty open to new ways of thinking and beliefs'. He had studied Buddhism and had a girlfriend who was 'able to feel the presence of spirits'. He believed in a God, 'but God's not necessarily confined to the constraints of Judaism.' He remained inquisitive about more spiritually expressive parts of his religious tradition: 'Six hundred years ago, Jews were actually very, very spiritual people themselves. And, you know, if I have some free time – well, I do have a lot of free time! – I would like to investigate the spiritual side of Kabbalah a little further.'

Jacob seems to be located somewhere between Christian Smith's more pessimistic and Sharon Parks's more optimistic conceptions of emerging adults and their engagement with religion and meaning-making. On one hand, Jacob admits a certain flippancy about his religion and about his own lack of use of his free time, echoing Smith's perspective that emerging adults have passively embraced an American addiction to youthful freedom (and Jeffrey Arnett's perspective that emerging adults are dedicated to openness)[78]—perhaps exacerbated by the opportunities afforded by a wealthy society. There is not as much at stake, it

---

[78] Christian Smith, *Souls in Transition: The Religious and Spiritual Lives of Emerging Adults* (New York: Oxford University Press, 2009, and Jeffrey Arnett, 'Emerging Adulthood: A Theory of Development from the Late Teens through the Twenties' *American Psychologist* 55(5): 469–80.

seems, in what Jacob chose to believe. He had a clear and direct career path that had been provided by multiple sources. And he still inhabited the exploratory and temporary world of university life.

On the other hand, he knew and used his religious heritage as a primary reference point. He was not simply free-floating, nor was his college or summer arts training centre an amorphous nether-world of fantasy. Jacob's flippancy – evident as an interactive style throughout his interview – masked a more deeply thoughtful reality that revealed itself in discussions of theodicy and other beliefs and values. Like Stefani, Jacob was 'recentering'. Jennifer Tanner described the recentering work of emerging adulthood as a process of individuation from family, of being thrust into and progressively taking on responsibility for oneself and one's own life, of establishing and testing one's own agency, of navigating the spaces of separation and connection.[79] Recentering need not simply be considered as something emerging adults do *vis-à-vis* their families. They also recenter *vis-à-vis* their religious heritages and social positions. Like Ly-Hanh and Stefani, Jacob no longer accepted the 'standard' beliefs of his religious heritage at face value: God may be more than what Judaism teaches, and Buddhism and other religious or spiritual traditions offer expansive perspectives – perspectives that may come into conversation with earlier Jewish traditions of deep spirituality, like Kabbalah. Jacob was actively navigating his own sense of individuation from and continuing connection to his own religious heritage, drawing from the expansive encounters in his education, work and relationships.

Jacob's blending of religious traditions is an example of several contemporary trends in American religion. Besides the rapid rise in non-affiliation with organized religion, there is an increase in blending, borrowing, mixing and matching theological ideas and spiritual practices from multiple religious and non-religious sources. This may occur within a religion, as has been happening in Christianity among 'emerging church' communities of young adults, who blend pieces of tradition and practice from Eastern Orthodoxy, mediaeval Catholic mysticism, Quakerism, Evangelicalism and contemporary conservative and progressive theological perspectives. It also is occurring across religions, with Mormons attending other Christian and Jewish congregations, or Jews and Catholics engaging in Buddhist meditation. This effort does not usually reflect haziness or laziness in beliefs and values: it reflects an invested search for and exploration of what feeds the hungry heart, what fulfills or completes the empty spaces experienced in a single tradition, what reveals a deeper reality behind the surface that has been learned or accepted to this point.

---

[79]   Tanner, 'Recentering During Emerging Adulthood'.

Renegotiating Commitments: Shanille and Rachel

A young black-Hispanic single mother from a middle-class community and a single-parent household, Shanille was 20 at the time of her on-site interview. As a teenager, she had anticipated completing college. At the time of her interview, she was not in college but was working successfully for a major international bank in telecommunications in customer relations, and had just been promoted. She was living with her mother after a difficult time with a roommate who did significant damage to her apartment and left her with fines to pay the landlord for damages:

> I got a roommate that was helping me out by watching my kids at night. But, whenever I was gone, he was throwing big parties and did twelve hundred dollars worth of damage to my apartment. So. He ran me pretty well into the hole there. And that's why I moved back home, so that I can: 1) clear up my finances, get that all paid for and in my past, and then 2) it's really more convenient to be in this area.

Shanille expressed overall satisfaction with her job, not as a chosen vocation but as a career she could live with and enjoy:

> I work from 3:00 p.m. until midnight. I go in at three, we call it getting into your 'Citi-brain', get set up, get in the mode to work. I, I tend, I'm a supervisor now, so every time that somebody wants to talk to somebody's 'supervisor', that's me. And … anytime that our unit managers are out of the bank, we'll watch their teams. So this is a real good position to be in to move up … I really wasn't necessarily looking for a career. But, after being there for almost two years, I'm realizing that this is definitely the kind of place where you could make a career out of it … I'm noticing that I'm better at it than what I planned on doing. Or, at least, I enjoy it more.

Raised as a Roman Catholic, Shanille found herself butting up against some of the exclusive claims of Catholicism:

> There were always just little things about the Roman Catholic Church that I didn't necessarily believe. I didn't think that that made me any less Roman Catholic, but in finding out that … some of the things that I've always believed are quite opposite of anything that a Roman Catholic is supposed to believe. Like, I believe that my God is the same God that everybody else out there is worshipping. No matter what religion it is, I believe it's the same person – you know, 'person', or, you know, their higher power, whatever that may be. But, part of one of the prayers that we have to say is, 'I believe in one holy Catholic and Apostolic Church.' And I didn't realize that, in saying that what I was, you know, what I was saying was exactly opposite of what I believed. And that's one of the things that we say in the church every week, it's one of the things that we

stand upon. And I was just like, 'You know, I really just don't believe that. You know, I believe that everybody's church is OK.' And I just always believed that didn't make me any less Roman Catholic. But in realizing some of the things that other Catholics believed, I was realizing that I really don't quite fit in here. But I'm sure that there's a, a religion out there that fits me. And so in the last few years I've kind of been researching other religions. And, you know, just kind of figuring out where I fit in.

She found herself attracted to the growing Wiccan religious tradition:

What I have found to fit me, and it's gonna probably sound strange to you, 'cause it sounds strange to most people – and, you know, I've had a lot of people in my life that have been of this religion, that have been in *my* religion – but, I'm a 'witch'. Or, it's a, a pagan religion. Yeah. A Wiccan religion … 'Cause I've been studying lots of religions and finding that they're the ones that, they, they believe in all of the other religions that are out there. They're not saying, 'This is the right way to worship', and 'Your way is not right.' And I love that. I love that open-mindedness.

A loose association of peers turned out to become her significant religious community: 'And a lot of the *Rocky Horror Picture Show* people that I hang out with are of a similar faith. And I find that, you know, a lot of the people that I didn't know previously were of, of a, a Wiccan faith or of a pagan faith are.' Her primary religious rituals included Tarot readings and incantations circles.

Psychologists often make note of early adulthood as a period of emotional and intrapsychic volatility, with potential for both enormous creativity and extreme dysfunction. American adolescents tend to enter early adulthood with high hopes for personal achievement – and this became even more markedly clear in the affluent years of the 1990s. But early adulthood also is a period of more concentrated onset of mood, anxiety and major mental disorders and to the beginnings of substance addiction. Delinquent, criminal and antisocial behaviours are most concentrated among young adults, with 18–29-year-old men and women comprising 56 per cent of all prison inmates.[80] These contrasting psychological qualities of early adulthood support Levinson's characterization of early adulthood as a tinder-box of high potential and equally high vulnerability.[81]

As emerging adults embrace their autonomy, they also face consequences of their choices. Young women may shoulder the burden of childrearing alone and single. There are significant challenges for single parents especially, but for any young parent couples as well, in finding adequate childcare for the hours of work

---

[80]   Patrick Langan and David Levin, *Assessing the Accuracy of State Prisoner Statistics*, Technical Report, NCJ 173413: US Department of Justice, Office of Justice Programs, February 1999 <http://www.ojp.usdoj.gov/bjs/pub/pdf/aasps.pdf>.

[81]   Daniel Levinson, *Seasons of a Man's Life* (New York: Alfred A. Knopf, 1978).

necessary to earn income for a household. Attempted solutions for challenges such as childcare (or, more simply, sharing rental costs) can result in unexpected difficulties. These challenges are only heightened by the vulnerabilities of young adults' recent and incomplete maturation. High contrasts seem to mark not only the social and economic landscapes but also the mental and emotional landscapes of early adulthood, making for what can be a quite difficult period of life.

Shanille faced many difficulties – and yet was clearly dedicated and committed to her child and her work. With her, we have another example of a young adult making sophisticated decisions about religion based on the knowledge she has available, recognizing an inconsistency she is not willing to accept, actively searching for an alternative, and finding a new path – even in the midst of her life's challenges. Her agency, clarity of thought and commitment to explore possibilities places Shanille beyond the more passive and cognitively lazy religious ideas and choices of Smith's youth and young adults that hold a vague notion of what he called 'moralistic therapeutic deism'. In many ways, she epitomizes the development of what Parks describes as a 'life of commitment', a path of life entered with curiosity and dedicated eagerness to find meaning. And the importance of peers in helping her find a path for her beliefs and values reflects what John Westerhoff has called 'affiliative faith' – a pattern of belief and value that is discovered and strengthened through one's friendships and close relationships.[82]

This kind of open and creative blending or shifting between religions may appear to some theologically or sociologically as hedging one's bets, or a form of religious promiscuity, or not fully exploring the rich terrain within one's original religious heritage. And many young adults stay clearly within their religious heritage, while a few make clear breaks and convert to a new religion (or non-religion). But, even for a 'faithful' remnant, there are often challenging decisions to navigate. What do I really believe of all that is taught in this tradition? What practices and prohibitions really matter? Rachel offers a good example of a young adult committed to core religious beliefs but renegotiating practical commitments.

Rachel, a white 23-year-old lapsed Baptist, was an occasional community college student working as a research assistant at a private research company. She grew up as a single child in a religiously divided household, with a mother devoted to her Baptist church and an abusive father who 'only stepped in a church was if there's a wedding'. Her parents, who had some college education, had raised her in a middle-class community in the South. They eventually divorced, much to Rachel's relief, because of her father's physical and emotional abuse of her mother and herself.

Rachel described her religious beliefs mostly in terms of soteriology (that is, beliefs about human deliverance):

---

[82]   John Westerhoff III outlined four stages, or styles, of faith: experienced, affiliative, searching and owned: John Westerhoff III, *Will Our Children Have Faith?* (New York: Seabury Press, 1976).

I'm a Baptist. And so I believe that if you're, if you're born again and you ask Jesus in your heart, then you go to heaven. And he'll forgive you for all your sins, besides murder or suicide. And that if, if you aren't washed in his blood, then whenever, you know, when the world comes to the end ... he'll give those people the second chance to accept him. But then once you don't, who still don't want to, then they live an eternity in hell.

But her choices did not exactly match up with expectations of behaviour for faithful Baptists – she slept and lived with her boyfriend, Dan:

Ever since I met Dan, I haven't been to church. I, I used to go to church with my mom every Sunday ... I haven't been to church in over two years. 'Cause my mom lives all, lives thirty, forty-five minutes away from me. I just never got up to go, you know. I just woke up, you know, asked, 'What are we doing today, Dan?' It's like I lost interest in it. I didn't lose interest in God. I just lost interest in going to church.

Rachel had close relationships with her friends, and this brought her face-to-face with some intense life challenges. One of her friends had developed an addiction to heroin, and was on a slow downward titration off the methadone substitute prescribed by an addictions clinic:

I really hate the government right now. Because now instead of her being to addicted to heroin, she's addicted to methadone. And the government is just sitting there taking her money and allowing her to still do it ... She actually came over to my house Monday morning and was like, 'Rachel, I, I want help.' Da, da, da, da, da. I'm like, 'OK, you can stay here.' I got her a job at my company, and she wasn't there. And I haven't heard from her since ... It's sad. It's so sad.

Ironically, while early adulthood is an important period for exploration and consolidation of a personal theologies, multiple surveys indicate that early adulthood also represents the nadir of most people's involvement in organized religion – at least among more 'traditional' religious organizations.[83] But in contrast to this, both late adolescence and early adulthood also tend to be peak periods of religious conversion[84] and deeper internalization of religious beliefs into

---

[83]   See Andrew Greeley, *Religious Change in America* (Cambridge, MA: Harvard University, 1989); Max Regele, *Death of the Church* (Grand Rapids, MI: Zondervan. 1995); Robert Gribbon, *Developing Faith in Young Adults: Effective Ministry with 18–35 Year Olds* (New York: Alban Institute, 1990), and Schmitt and Gortner, 'Challenges of Evangelism'.

[84]   See Wilfrid Jones, *The Psychological Study of Religious Conversion* (London: Epworth, 1937); Sante de Sanctis, *Religious Conversion: A Bio-Psychological Study*, trans. H. Augur (New York: Harcourt, Brace, & Company, 1927); Jon Alexander, *American Personal Religious Accounts, 1600–1980: Toward an Inner History of America's Faiths*

everyday motivations and goals.[85] The harsh realities that young adults themselves face or that they witness in the lives of their peers bring the deeper foundational theological assumptions of their religious heritages into stark relief. They must contend with their own assumptions about the nature of the world, justice and the good in light of what they see and experience firsthand.

Recent books like *UnChristian* and *They Love Jesus but They Don't Love Church* document survey evidence of young adults' deep suspicion and skepticism regarding organized religion, even among Evangelical Christians – even while they might hold dearly to some of the most central themes, ideas and stories.[86] Evangelical young adults do not always adhere to prohibitions of sex before marriage. As young adults begin to navigate the realities of the world in which they must forge a life, they encounter challenging choices between competing interests – and they adapt, often making adaptations in their beliefs and values. They marry or cohabit with lovers who may or may not share their theological perspectives, and their patterns of religious life and belief change somewhat as a result of these relationships. Again, blended marriages and families are not new – but they are increasing. And adaptations go both directions. An ardently atheist young woman married a devoted Catholic man, and because of her husband had come to appreciate what religion could do for people.

The Place of Religion in the Lives of Twenty Young Adults

The experiences, issues and concerns of young adults in the *Making the Transition* study were manifold, including negotiation of financial challenges and family care, coupling and mating and child-rearing, career exploration and consolidation, and self-differentiation from families of origin and religious upbringings. But, despite a wide range of backgrounds and experiences, the consistency of their responses around religion was striking. These young men and women were actively reconfiguring their relationships with organized religion, as a result of their active work thinking through their beliefs and values in relation to their expanded life experiences and insights as emerging adults.

---

vol. 8 of *Studies in American Religion* (Lewiston, NY: Edwin Mellen, 1983), and Bob Altemeyer and Bruce Hunsberger, *Amazing Conversions: Why Some Turn to Faith and Others Abandon Religion* (Amherst, NY: Prometheus, 1997).

[85]   See Helena Helve, 'The Development of Religious Belief Systems from Childhood to Adulthood: A Longitudinal Study of Young Finns in the Context of the Lutheran Church', in Jozef Corveleyn and Dirk Hutsebaut (eds), *Belief and Unbelief: Psychological Perspectives* (Amsterdam: Ropodi, 1994).

[86]   See David Kinnaman and Gabe Lyons, *unChristian: What a New Generation Really Thinks about Christianity ... and Why It Matters* (Grand Rapids, MI: Baker, 2007), and Dan Kimball, *They Like Jesus but Not the Church: Insights from Emerging Generations* (Grand Rapids, MI: Zondervan, 2007).

If we take seriously young adults' statements about religion, religious affiliation and religious belief in the interview excerpts presented here, we will recognize that religion is not a straightforward predictor of beliefs, values and behaviour. Our sample is full of young adults who were abandoning, reshaping, adjusting and creatively blending religious ideas. Baptists were 'shacked up' with boyfriends or girlfriends who did not attend church, and began to drop their own attendance. Roman Catholics were not attending mass with any regularity. Atheists were married to Christians and developing some appreciation of how religion could function positively in people's lives. Jews were combining Kabbalah with meditative practices of Buddhism. Buddhists were abandoning simple notions of karma, dharma and reincarnation as explanations for tragedies or traumas. The pattern of religious attendance among young adults in this study echoed a national pattern among college students in the annual Freshman Survey conducted at UCLA – religious non-affiliation has increased dramatically over 35 years, and religious involvement has steadily declined.[87] Once young adults leave home, religious attendance drops far below an already low attendance rate during adolescence. Yes, there were some strictly faithful Jehovah's Witnesses, Evangelical Christians and atheists who expressed clear adherence to the religious or anti-religious systems in which they had been raised or to which they had converted – but they were a minority. Their personal theologies were no more or less articulate or coherent than those of young adults less religiously engaged or creatively blending traditions.

To get a sense of the variations and depths of emerging adults' personal theologies, and to consider some of the pathways of social and developmental influence on their personal theologies, I have selected excerpts from interviews of 26 of the 82 emerging adults with whom we conducted in-depth interviews. Throughout the coming chapters, I will refer to them and quote them generously, letting them speak for themselves of what they believe and value (all names, of course, are fictionalized). It is important to hear from this number of individuals in order to get a full sense of the range of beliefs and values comprising personal theologies. I have already introduced Jason, Ly-Hanh, Stefani, Jacob, Shanille and Rachel. Now it is time for a brief introduction to the remaining 20 young women and men who will speak about their personal theologies through the core chapters of this book.

It is not a simple thing to group these young adults even by way of introduction. These eleven women and nine men varied widely in religious background and

---

[87]   As documented by Bryant, Choi and Yasuno, follow-up to the annual freshman survey in 2000 revealed that freshman religious involvement declines significantly over a single year of college, with frequent attendance at religious services dropping from 46 per cent to 27 per cent, and with total non-attendance increasing from 16 per cent to 43 per cent one year later: Alyssa Bryant, Jeung Yun Choi and Maiko Yasuno, 'Understanding the Religious and Spiritual Dimensions of Students' Lives in the First Year of College', *Journal of College Student Development* 44(6)(November/December 2003): 723–45.

current religious involvement, career pathways, financial responsibility, and living arrangements. They varied in their degree of change in religious (or non-religious) commitments. Only a few were married, most were in serious (and, in most cases, sexual) long-term dating relationships. Social class was varied, but most representative of higher social class and upward mobility. For simplicity's sake, I will introduce them according to the religious or non-religious traditions in which they were raised. Within each group, there are young adults whose religious or non-religious commitments were intensifying, weakening, changing, or staying the same.

Let us begin with our Roman Catholics. Joining Shanille are three men and one woman raised in Catholic families: Michael (19) who was raised by Jewish and Roman Catholic parents, and Joel (22), Javier (25) and Beth (24), who were raised in singularly Catholic homes. In all four cases, their parents were still married at the time of their interviews. Michael, Joel and Beth were from the Midwest; Javier was from the North-east. Michael and Javier grew up in upper-middle class suburbs of large metropolitan cities; Joel and Beth grew up in working-class neighbourhoods of smaller cities. Javier's parents had attended some college; Michael's and Beth's parents had college degrees, while Joel's parents had both completed graduate school. All four young adults themselves had attended at least some college. Javier had enrolled in law school and was spending his upcoming summer in Guatemala 'doing human rights work' and 'research on military justice reform'. Michael had begun college with interest in medicine, but was considering switching to architecture, and was working for the summer as a store manager. Joel, an average student in high school, was completing college in agriculture but was uncertain and uncommitted about his career path, and was still living at home with his parents and doing temporary farm jobs like detassling corn. Beth, who had attended some community college, had abandoned her desire to complete college and was working three-quarters time in a dry cleaning and laundry store. She was the only one married, with two young children, and lived in a poor neighbourhood of a small city. Javier had a steady girlfriend with whom he was sexually involved. Michael had a new girlfriend, having broken up about three months previously with a girlfriend who had cheated on him. Joel was not dating.

The religious trajectories of these four young adults varied widely. Joel remained committed to spiritual activities such as prayer and monthly-to-biweekly church attendance. Michael, an example of a young adult raised in a dual-religious household, ended up gravitating toward and increasing his involvement in Catholic faith and practice. Attending one or two services each month, Michael said, 'It's become more personal for me. It was just a part of my life I missed, I think. I wasn't necessarily looking for God, as strange as that may be. I was just kind of looking for the way I felt when I went to church—it made me feel good. I'm Roman Catholic.' But regarding the Jewish part of his heritage, Michael said, 'I'll go to a Jewish holiday ... but when I go to a Passover dinner it's just like something that happens, but it doesn't have a religious impact on me.'

The remaining two, Javier and Beth, were converting or had already converted to other religious traditions. Javier was shifting away from Catholicism and becoming an Evangelical:

> I went to [Catholic] church and pretty much I went getting very little out of it. And I met some people who weren't Catholic and they were more spiritual. And I learned from them more of a personal relationship with God instead of something you do on Sunday. So that's what started changing me.

Similarly, Beth converted to Jehovah's Witness after meeting someone who demonstrated a faith and certainty that she desired.

> I was brought up Catholic and it never satisfied me. So I constantly searched for something else. In college, you know, you take your philosophy classes and mythology classes and you try out different religions and … none of it clicked. And so finely after doing that forever I was like, 'Forget it, I'm just going to pick up the Bible, I'm going to read it myself and see what it says for myself.' And when I decided to do that and take a whole-hearted, personal study of it, I met this person, Margaret.

In the case of these conversions – and Shanille's movement toward Wiccan communities and practices – there is a clear role of peer exemplars who ignite sparks of interest and resonate with personal passions for meaning-making.

Now let us consider young adults like Stefani and Rachel who were raised in Mainline Protestant families: Rebecca (21) and Karla (24), like Stefani, grew up Lutheran; Jeannie (23) grew up Methodist, but with parents who only occasionally attended services, and MeiLi (22) was raised Presbyterian. Rebecca and Jeannie had grown up in the same working-class community, a small Midwestern city. Karla and MeiLi came from upper-middle-class suburbs of major cities – Karla from the Midwest, MeiLi from the North-east. Like Rachel, Rebecca had divorced parents. Her parents were high school educated. MeiLi was part of an immigrant family from Hong Kong, and her parents had never completed high school. Karla's and Jeannie's parents had graduate degrees. Rebecca was the only one married, with a young son. She had given up ideas of college and worked flexible three-quarter time hours as an optometrist's assistant. Jeannie was completing a six-year pharmacy degree programme, lived with her parents but regularly stayed with her boyfriend, and worked part-time at a pharmacy filling orders. She had a non-committal 'meh' attitude toward her job and toward life in general – to her, the job was 'just experience, it may help me with school or help me later on, I don't know how much it's gonna help, but … .' Karla and MeiLi showed stronger career-related motivation. Karla had graduated from college as a physics major, lived with peers and was dating seriously, and worked full-time overseeing production of a major biotechnology company's annual catalogue. MeiLi continued to live with her family while completing college in biology in preparation for medical school, had dated intermittently, and worked a part-time as a research assistant.

Typical among mainline Christians, religious attendance for most of these women was more occasional. Jeannie continued the pattern of her parents with semi-annual (Christmas and Easter) attendance and a 'meh' non-committal attitude toward her own beliefs and values. Rebecca, while still committed to her Christian beliefs, was now in a dual-religion marriage with a husband who followed the nature-religion beliefs of his Native American heritage; she had significantly decreased her attendance to going only on the major Christian holidays. As with Rachel, religious life and dedication for Rebecca decreased. Karla, who grew up going to church and Sunday school, said she 'never really enjoyed it. But I did enjoy going to bible camp and the youth group aspect of it … you get the more subtle influence of, of belief and having a faith.' But, like Stefani, Karla was distancing herself from her Lutheran heritage. She saw her rigorously religious father as 'very devoted', but 'I just don't see him as being complete, I haven't seen him as being happy.' Nonetheless, she retained a modestly strong religious commitment, attending services monthly at a Presbyterian church. In contrast, MeiLi's religious commitment intensified, beginning in high school: 'I used to think differently before ninth grade and thereafter started – like, that's when I accepted Christ. And it's been constantly … well, I guess, it's been the same system of beliefs since then, but I'm learning more about it. There are changes every day as I'm learning more.' MeiLi attended religious services two times every week.

As was the case with Stefani's and Rachel's stories, these women's stories illustrate the impact of familial heritage and experiences in religion during childhood and adolescence—and significant love relationships in early adulthood.

Our Jewish young adults show similar trends in their religious affiliations, beliefs and practices. Like Jacob, Dean (23) grew up in a Jewish household, with graduate-educated parents, in an upper-middle-class community. Dating actively and living on his own, he had been employed as an entry-level financial analyst, but felt bored and 'under-utilized and constrained', and had just left for a new position at a small investment bank. More than Jacob, he claimed his Jewish heritage and his belief in God as guiding his whole approach to life, even though he only attended services on high holy days:

> It wasn't the fact that my parents told me something that made it work for me; it was the fact that I went out, and that I found that looking at the world and that sort of trying to frame it all in that sense did work for me. And eventually I just came to realize that … this was a useful and constructive way to look at the world.

Dean thought about his work in relation to higher purpose and believed that finance and commerce was the most significant arena (more than politics or social service) to contribute to the social good.

A contrast to Jacob and Dean is Adriana, who grew up in a culturally Jewish but religiously agnostic family. Also from a North-eastern upper-middle-class community, she had moved from college as a political science major into a bureaucratic position in the Council on Foreign Relations. Regarding her upbringing, she said, 'I wasn't raised with any sense of God. I was raised with a cultural sense of religion, since my mother's Jewish but not enough to really stick. You know, we put up the tree for Christmas, we put up the menorah for Chanukah, but that about the extent of it.'

Adriana had just moved in with her boyfriend Evan. She reported no religious affiliation and attended no services, but admitted to some spiritual yearnings:

> I don't know. I really sense spirituality in love and in the connections between people. I have had my moments of prayer – it's funny, 'cause I've never told anybody else that. And at the time I don't really question if there's anything that I'm actually talking to. But, on a day-to-day basis I'd say no, I don't think there's really a God, or at least a God in the way that everybody says that there is. I think, really, prayer – or, whatever I'm doing in those moments – is a way for me to use a third person to come to my own conclusions.

Many religions, like Judaism and Buddhism as well as some forms of Christianity, are deeply embedded in and shaped by the cultures in which they emerged. The American experience can contribute to a division between religious heritage and contemporary American culture. In the past, neighbourhoods provided cultural and religious refuges in American society. Increasingly, with mobility and education driven by career aspirations, young adults from non-dominant cultures in America can tend toward becoming mainstreamed, leading in many cases (like Ly-Hanh) to further distancing from their religious heritage.

Agnosticism can exist in religious and non-religious forms. Jennifer (18) grew up in a Unitarian-Universalist family (a common ground for her graduate-educated parents) and was clearly shaped by this humanistic religious tradition. From a Midwestern upper-middle -class suburb, she was studying international affairs and peace studies at an East Coast university with the aim of becoming a diplomat. She was single. Her father had just died of a heart attack that autumn – a sad tragedy that she talked about as part of her discussion of her personal theology. Other young adults like Christopher and Philip, also from upper-middle-class communities with college-educated parents, were agnostic and non-religious. Christopher, a senior lighting engineer for a summer theatre company but about to move to another city to pursue a career in civil or technical engineering, described himself and his parents as 'agnostic explorers' not committed to any specific tradition; he attended religious services, but no more than twice a year. Philip grew up with no religious tradition, even exploratory. None the less, as we shall see, as a military cadet with long-term interest in political leadership, he expressed a consistent sense of active and enthusiastic engagement in his life, whether in military training, friendships, or academics. Like Jennifer, and like Jewish agnostic Adriana, Christopher and Philip revealed deep reflection on their beliefs and values, and articulated clear thoughts about their personal theologies. Agnosticism should not be confused with lack of interest in or consideration of theological matters. In many cases, these young adults were more articulate than some of our more marginally involved as well as more intensely committed religious young adults.

So, let us end our consideration of religious heritage by meeting our last young adults: those from more conservative religious traditions, and those who claim atheism. In addition to Rachel, three young adults came from more conservative religious traditions: AnMing (23), from an Evangelical Christian Vietnamese family, Liz (23), from an Evangelical home, and Cory (22), raised in a Mormon household. All had college-educated parents. AnMing grew up in an upper-middle-class North-eastern suburb. Liz came from a middle-class community in a small Midwestern city. Cory grew up in a smaller middle-class city in the South-east. Both AnMing and Cory had been in recent serious but not sexual dating relationships, while Liz had recently been in a serious and sexual relationship with a man recently divorced. AnMing ('Amy' by her English name) lived alone, and had just begun law school, with plans to continue even further for an MBA and an advanced degree in psychology. Liz lived with two roommates as she completed her graduate schooling in food science and human nutrition. Cory lived with his parents, attended a two-year community college part-time, and worked in several part-time jobs as a receptionist in an admissions office, a security guard at a parking facility, and a ditch digger ('I quit my job waiting tables 'cause I hated it').

Cory remained devoted to his Mormon religious tradition, attending an average of two services a month as well as intensive 'Seminary' Mormon classes for teenagers and young adults. This commitment gave unmistakable shape to his clearly articulated and thoughtful personal theology. AnMing was also deeply shaped by her religious heritage: she recalled her father closing family prayers with requests to God that she would become a lawyer and her sister become a doctor. But AnMing had begun to question and explore her religious heritage, visiting churches of other Christian traditions, and attending less regularly (about ten times a year):

> I used to just read the Bible and just kind of take it for what it said, and listen to sermons and just believe what they said. But now I'm a little more critical. And I just apply things to my life based on how, what I feel is right for me. Like, I don't believe in that group faith anymore, not having to follow what everybody else says to come to do. I just take faith into my own heart and my own mind, and just apply it to myself ... I think moving away to college was probably a turning-point. I had the freedom to go to whatever church I wanted, to worship any way I wanted. And to be myself. I quit church for a while. And then I would go to an Asian church. And then I went church-hopping. And then I just wanted to see what was out there. But I still believe in God, and I still pray occasionally.

Liz echoed AnMing in her own withdrawal from what had been very active involvement in church and camp during her teenage years. "We went to church every Sunday, and so probably out of just tradition and almost fear, you know, that

I was Christian. And then we had a strong youth group in high school." Between youth group and summer camp ("probably the most moving experience I've been to"), her faith grew stronger for a time. "Then I went through, as everybody does, that time of doubt and stuff. I went through that and then slowly came around from that. And now I don't go to services as much as I probably would like to, but I think I blame that on moving around and stuff like work, and excuses." Liz wanted to return to more regular religious involvement when she started a family, to "expose my kids to all of it and let them decide what they believe."

Religious conservatism is not a guarantee of secured beliefs and values. Recentering and renegotiation occur for young adults of all religious backgrounds. AnMing, Liz and Cory, like Rachel, expressed clear personal theologies. It might appear that they differed in their degree of individuation – a benchmark signal for some theorists of individuals' moral and spiritual development. Such a theoretical perspective can sell short the depth and clarity of the beliefs and values of young adults like Cory and Rachel. But Cory and Rachel did show other signs of holding on to adolescence in a way that AnMing and Liz did not.

The same range of openness versus assuredness, or flexibility versus precision, expressed by AnMing and Cory regarding their religious perspectives, can be found among atheists. Our four atheists, Alexandra (22), Steve (23), Kasey (23) and Lillian (24) provide a good example of this range. Alexandra and Steve were both from an upper-class community in the North-east; Kasey was from a small middle-class Southern town, and Lillian was from a Midwestern working-class small city. All parents except Kasey's were college educated, and Alexandra's parents had graduate degrees. Alexandra was about to graduate as a history major; Steve was finishing a two-year culinary school degree, and Kasey had graduated in business and was contracting independently as a website developer while also working for a temporary employment agency and attempting a web-based entrepreneurial venture. Lillian was in her second year of dental graduate school. Lillian was married to a devout Roman Catholic. Alexandra, Steve and Kasey were all in serious and sexual dating relationships, and Steve lived with his girlfriend. None of them had children.

There was a clear range of openness versus assuredness among these young atheists. Alexandra described herself as a 'non-militant atheist'. Her college experience was exposing her to more 'superstitious' as well as 'traditionally religious' people than she had previously met in high school. Similarly, though a professed atheist, Lillian attended Catholic Mass with her husband about once a month, and found herself opening up recognizing the value of religion for others: 'I used to really be anti-religious. And I never really understood why somebody was religious. But then, after meeting my husband and talking about things like that, because he's Catholic … it helps me to understand lot more about why religion is important to certain people.' Steve, who described himself as 'an atheist with communist ideals' (beliefs and values that he took most from his father) was going through his own recentring process, developing a critical view of his father's idealistic communism:

I'm a dyed-in-the-wool atheist. It's had a full generation in my parents of atheism and there is no religious sentimentality left. My dad was born in South Africa. And living in South Africa, being a communist is a lot different than it typically has been in America ... He always thought that Che Guevara was terribly romantic. And that's actually one image he has of himself is, you know, a gun-toting revolutionary. But, I mean, it in no way represented an actual possibility in his life. But I grew up very much with that sense, you know? So he told me at a young age well, if I was really true to my beliefs I would be toting a gun in Latin America somewhere. Which is a horrible and ridiculous thing to grow up with.

Steve found himself increasingly drawn to Taoist philosophy and practiced meditation as a matter of self-care.

In contrast to the varying degrees of openness among Alexandra, Lillian and Steve was Kasey, who had an edgy, sarcastic attitude about many things, including her mom who had raised her, who 'hates men', and her old high school friends who moved to the same big state university with her but 'were all jackasses and dropped out'. This tone was part of how she talked about her life throughout the interview, including about her beliefs and values. As we shall see in the upcoming chapters, Kasey had little patience for religion in any form, and expressed an almost aggressive assuredness and lack of flexibility in her atheistic beliefs.

In this introduction, we have only begun to scratch the surface of variations that emerge from a closer look at religious affiliation, involvement and beliefs. Signs of uncertainty or certainty, hesitancy or confidence, exploration or security, volatility or stability emerged with regard to religious and non-religious identity – but also in all other contexts of these young adults' lives as they faced expected and unexpected challenges in a much larger and daunting world, wrestled with their own sense of purpose and place in the world, and began to define the ultimate good worth pursuing.

It should now be clear, even from this cursory introduction to 26 young adults, that espoused religious affiliation cannot be taken anymore as an emblematic stand-in or methodological shortcut for personal theology. Nor, as we shall see, can prior religious heritage or current religious activity level accurately predict young adults' personal theologies. Indeed, at a time of life when personal religious commitments tend to be at their lowest and in an American culture when religious affiliation was continuing to wane, religion did not always play a significant role in shaping these young adults' personal theologies. Other developmental ecologies besides religion may exert greater influence on personal theologies. As we shall see, education, work experience, family life, socio-economic realities and peer interactions – as well as internal dispositions long in play – may all contribute significantly to the personal theologies of young adults as reflected in worldview, theodicy, life purpose and ultimate values.

Chapter 3
Methods for Uncovering Personal Theologies

A brief word about analytical methodology is warranted. We have our questions to explore personal theologies – open-ended questions that invite free response and presume as little as possible while still assuming that we are talking about matters of foundational theology. We have a set of emerging adults who will engage the questions – a somewhat diverse sample nested within larger and more diverse samples of emerging adults in America. But what are the merits methodologically of such direct yet open-ended inquiry about fundamental beliefs and values that comprise personal theologies? What is gained from open-ended responses that might not be gained from a simple questionnaire? What methods are used in the analysis of responses? And how are these qualitative responses then to be converted into categorical data and used in statistical analysis? These questions take us to the core of assumptions about grounded theory, thematic analysis and mixed methods that move from qualitative to quantitative analysis.

Why a 'Grounded-Theory' Approach?

The use of grounded theory is not new. But examining facets of personal theology using a grounded-theory approach is still somewhat unique in the study of core beliefs and values, among both theologians and social scientists. Scholars from both arenas have tended to prefer other methods and strategies. Both theologians and social scientists have used a variety of either deductive or rapid-inductive approaches as they have sought to describe or account for the beliefs and values of a culture, society, subculture, or group. A deductive method is a top-down approach that begins with an overarching theory or an accepted set of rules, principles, categories, or patterns, and proceeds to use that generalized perspective as a framework for observation and putting a theory to the test in a particular situation. In contrast, an inductive method is a bottom-up approach that begins with observations, seeks discernible patterns and categories, and moves toward the proposal of more general, overarching theory or principles from what is observed. What I am calling 'rapid-inductive' is simply a way of naming a tendency, among theologians and social scientists alike, to rush from a few observations to general theory without spending more time and effort in more careful, longer-term, wider-ranging observation.

My colleagues in both fields tend to favour deductive and rapid-inductive approaches. For theologians, not to begin from a deductive stance can lean perilously toward abandoning the truth claims of one's religious tradition. Thus, the deductive (or, at best, rapid-inductive) stance of theologians is also typically a prescriptive stance – a commitment to a set of deeply held convictions and commitments that colour interpretation of what is observed in light of what 'ought to be', and can even shape one's choices of what to observe. The social sciences are not by any means free of such normative commitments (nor, for that matter, am I): theories and traditions of research are grounded in prescriptive stances.

If I were to take a deductive approach, I would begin by using preconceived categories of responses to particular questions. For the study of beliefs and values, I would derive these categories either from primary sacred and philosophical texts of a religion or society, or from dominant observed practices in both organized and 'civil' religion,[1] and in society in general. If I suspected that there have been significant shifts or divisions between people of different times and places, I might also look for the big cultural or historical events that contribute to such shifts in beliefs and values.[2] I might even take a rapid-inductive approach and draw quick inferences from some bits of observed behaviour, speech, printed material, or popular cultural media, bringing those observations under the lens of my overall frame of reference.

And there are certain advantages to such an approach. I can construct a study quickly by moulding questions from the ready-made metrics supplied by religious, philosophical and social scientific traditions.[3] I can draw conclusions more rapidly by drawing upon a priori categories from these traditions. I can access support for my a priori commitments by accessing source documents and archival material that tends to capture dominant strands of beliefs and values from a selected perspective. And I can to a certain degree count on a measure of verification of

---

[1]	Classic examples are Max Weber's discussion of different understandings of salvation, and H. Richard Niebuhr's typological analysis of Christian religion's engagement with culture,

[2]	Examples of this approach are as varied as Tom Beaudoin's popular culture analysis of religion and spirituality among American young adults who were part of 'Generation X' (in which he used popular music, celebrities and fads like tattooing and body-piercing as evidence for the beliefs and values of a generation), and Alisdair MacIntyre's analysis of historical cultural differences in ultimate values (in which he used primary philosophical texts of figures that he regarded as archetypal of a particular cultural theological and philosophical system): Tom Beaudoin, *Virtual Faith: The Irreverent Spiritual Quest of Generation X* (San Francisco, CA: Jossey-Bass, 1998).

[3]	Examples include Stark's and Glock's classic typological questionnaire that neatly distinguished between Christian denominations and Kothari's study of religiously based differences in beliefs and values: Rodney Stark and Charles Glock, *American Piety: The Nature of Religious Commitment* (Berkeley: University of California, 1968), and Saroj Kothari, 'Impact of Religion upon Development of Moral Concepts', *Psycho-Lingua*, 24 (1994): 65–72.

my overarching perspective, because I have designed my questions in line with assumptions I was seeking to verify.

A common practice among social scientists is to construct survey instruments and vignettes with forced-choice solutions to evaluate religious beliefs, political views, moral development and general life philosophy, as well as worldview, life purpose, theodicy and values. These instruments are often designed and vetted by fellow academicians and representative 'experts' – prior to direct interviews and conversations with the people among whom the instrument is supposed to measure and account for their beliefs and values. Such instruments, once published, are then taken up by other eager researchers and applied across multiple settings, as much a matter of convenience as a continuation of an intellectual conversation begun.

But significant limitations and problems arise from this approach. First, such instruments, despite their proliferation and wide use, are methodologically limited due to the predetermination and imposition of a set range of possible responses. Many such instruments are theologically biased or religiously and culturally limited, having been designed through the emic lenses of their authors and contributing 'experts'. Take, for example, three items from the 'Religious Problem-solving Scale' of Kenneth Pargament and colleagues:

> When I have a problem, I talk to God about it and together we decide what it means.
> When a situation makes me anxious, I wait for God to take those feelings away.
> When deciding on a solution, I make a choice independent of God's input.[4]

These questions, intended in three separate subscales to flag collaborative, self-directive and deferential religious approaches to problem solving, are shaped and informed by American strains of Protestantism influenced by Calvinistic evangelicalism and Lutheran pietism. The instrument was normed with data from Midwestern Presbyterian and Lutheran churches – and, not surprisingly, the scales were found statistically to be both reliable and valid. But they are not constructed in a manner that allows for their use with people from other religious traditions, or with Christians whose theological assumptions differ from the presuppositions driving the construction of these scales. This is a frequent problem with instruments designed with a priori categories: they are not easily transportable across cultural and religious lines, they narrow the possible range of responses, and they obliterate nuance in differences. In this way, the deductive approach can be limited by the not-so-universal perspective of one's overarching theory.

Secondly, these Likert-scale questions, dipolar questions and vignettes with forced-choice responses (such as those conducted by the National Opinion

---

[4]   Kenneth Pargement, Joseph Kennell, William Hathaway, Nancy Grevengoed, John Newman and Wendy Jones, 'Religion and the Problem-solving Process: Three Styles of Coping', *Journal for the Scientific Study of Religion*, 27(1) (March 1988): 90–104.

Research Center), themselves based upon the theological assumptions and limited perspectival range of the 'experts' designing them, can be fraught with potential effects of social demand and social desirability. Respondents will read such questions as those above not only in an effort to understand the question and answer honestly, but also with some interest in what the researcher might *really* want to know and then attempt to enhance one's appearance to the researcher. The most sophisticated assessment instruments include validity scales to help correct for self-enhancement and social desirability effects. But most instruments designed to measure responses about specific beliefs, values, or behaviours do not include such corrective measures. In this way, the verification of theory in the deductive approach is fraught with the undesired but very real effects of people's motivations for their responses.

These are not new problems in social scientific research, nor are they unique to the study of theological beliefs and values. They were recognized as part of a growing problem arising from a nearly exclusive focus on deductive research in the 1960s. Into this space stepped the pair of sociologists, Barney Glaser and Anselm Strauss, drawing heavily from best practices in anthropology to propose and promote the practice of 'grounded theory' as a core practice in exploratory and discovery-oriented sociological research.[5] Their aim was to address what had become a problem in sociology: a turn away from theory creation toward theory verification. Testing and verifying existent grand theories is an important part of any good academic enterprise – until scholars slip off course and begin imposing assumptions from grand theories in settings and situations in which they were not meant to be applied, or attempting to use previously constructed concepts from one time, place and circumstance to 'measure' something that does not fit within those concepts. While they later parted company on matters of process and coding procedures, Glaser and Strauss at the time offered to sociology a defined methodology for exploratory qualitative research and for generating theories from the ground up – through careful analysis of people's responses to focused but open-ended questions.

When dealing with interviews, grounded-theory method as a bottom-up inductive approach begins with people's responses. Analysis begins with the identification and categorization of themes in people's responses, while ignoring, as much as possible, literature that might colour or skew one's work, 'in order to assure that the emergence of categories will not be contaminated by concepts more suited to different areas'.[6] While contemporary grounded-theory users like Kathy Charmaz have recognized the impossibility of absolutely 'pure' freedom from influence of prior knowledge on thematic coding, one core commitment keeps researchers relatively close to the ground: as much as possible, grounded theorists

---

[5] Barney Glaser and Anselm Strauss, *The Discovery of Grounded Theory: Strategies for Qualitative Research* (Chicago, IL: Aldine, 1967).

[6] Ibid., p. 37.

are to permit the categories to emerge from people's own words.[7] This means that analysis is iterative – that is, new categories and codes may emerge along the way as new responses are encountered, or different nuances and patterns of meaning are found. As structures and ideas begin to emerge, a theory begins to take shape, and the task turns to reducing the number of categories, through prioritization or hierarchical generalization. These refined categories become the basis for presentation of a new theory and provide a basic roadmap for other researchers to follow, adapt, or even verify or refute.

The premises and methods of grounded theory are increasingly common in both the social sciences and theological studies – particularly in the wake of postmodernist critiques of modernist and positivist assumptions about research. In the social sciences, various psychologists and sociologists have attempted to uncover 'folk' understandings of morality,[8] perceptual and mental processes, and the nature of selfhood[9] and personal identity.[10] Rick Shweder and his colleagues embarked on their international study of theodicy beginning first with direct conversation with people. Looking for deep thematic structure of beliefs and values in Indian culture and subcultures, they drew upon interviews and then surveys developed in part from themes found in interviews, employing discourse analysis, thematic cluster analysis and discriminant analysis.[11] These scholars' efforts represent attempts to move away from a tendency to take preconceived theoretical constructs and impose them as forced categories on people's responses. For theologians, they represent efforts to emphasize 'the intelligibility and publicness of theological thinking *for anybody* inside and outside the Jewish and Christian tradition'.[12]

Rather than relying on analysis and received wisdom from primary texts and observed historical events, it is the task of the grounded theorist – like the

---

[7]   Kathy Charmaz, 'Grounded Theory Methodology: Objectivist and Constructivist Qualitative Methods', in N.K. Denzin and Y. Lincoln (eds), *Handbook of Qualitative Research*, 2nd edn (Thousand Oaks, CA: Sage, 2000), pp. 509–35.

[8]   Lawrence Walker and Russell Pitts, 'Naturalistic Conceptions of Moral Maturity', *Developmental Psychology* 34(3) (May 1998): 403–19.

[9]   Nicole Chiasson, Lise Dube and Jean-Pierre Blondin, 'A Look into the Folk Psychology of Four Cultural Groups', *Journal of Cross-Cultural Psychology*, 27(6) (November 1996): 673–91.

[10]   Dan McAdams, *The Stories We Live by* (New York: Guilford, 1993).

[11]   Richard A. Shweder, N.C. Much, M. Mahapatra and L. Park, 'The "Big Three" of Morality (Autonomy, Community, Divinity) and the "Big Three" Explanations of Suffering', in A. Brandt and P. Rozin (eds), *Morality & Health*, (Stanford, CA: Stanford University Press, 1997), pp. 119–69.

[12]   Paul Tillich, James Loder, George Lindbeck and Ellen Clark-King are theologians who hold this standard in high esteem: Quote from Werner Jeanrond, 'Theological Method', in D.W. Musser and J.L. Price (eds), *A New Handbook of Christian Theology* (Nashville, TN: Abingdon), p. 484 (italics added).

anthropologist and the pastoral and practical theologian – to hear, record and interpret the 'living texts' of individual statements of beliefs and values. And, in order to understand the nature of individuals' personal theologies and cosmologies, and the impact of these personalized belief systems on people's lives, one must persist in asking direct, open-ended questions.

There is something a bit ironic in the manner that many researchers have asked people about their ultimate beliefs and values. Rather than trusting that people might have constructed or collected systems of meaning for themselves which they might articulate, most researchers instead turned to elaborate means of getting at people's personal theologies through preconstructed questionnaires, vignettes with a few limited response categories, or indirect observations of 'more accessible' attitudes shown through behaviours. This belies an assumption that people are untrustworthy, incapable, or simply too uncomfortable in articulating their own most fundamental beliefs and values about the world, humanity and existence, and that they need the help of specialists to unearth what is 'really' there under the surface. To a certain extent, this assumption may have some merit. Social psychologist Roy Baumeister noted that people tend to get nervous or dismissive when confronted with questions regarding the meaning of life. He concluded that 'people were more willing to discuss intimate sexual matters than issues of life's meaning and happiness.'[13]

Nonetheless, a 'lay' or 'folk' perspective helps move research and theory away from constructivist models in which individuals are retro-fitted into presupposed philosophical hierarchies or categories. In a grounded-theory and data-driven perspective, individuals' beliefs, values and ideologies are taken at face value and used as a principal means of generating theories and models. Using such an approach, researchers engage people directly in open-ended questions, take people's responses at face value as basic data which reveal meaningful themes, and look for patterns within and across people's responses. The researcher moves away from what might be regarded as a 'hermeneutic of suspicion of human stupidity', and the consequent tendency to create artful means of looking for hidden elements in people's speech and meanings. Any discomforts or difficulties people experience in articulating their responses are regarded by grounded-theory methodologists as positive signals of people's thoughtful and honest engagement with questions. Just as a therapist will not too quickly intrude on a client's silence, so a grounded-theory researcher will not too quickly offer alternative responses to someone who is struggling for an answer.

Taking an inductive grounded-theory approach to the study of personal theologies does not require me to abandon classic theological and philosophical perspectives. I simply engage them in a different way. In a grounded-theory approach, the on-the-ground perspectives of individuals set the direction for analysis. I suspend use of classic theological and philosophical ideas until I have a clear sense of these on-the-ground perspectives. Then, I can bring them into

---

[13]   Roy Baumeister, *Meanings of Life* (New York: Guilford, 1991), p. 4.

conversation with the valued perspectives of individuals, not from a position of superiority, but from a position of parallel interaction.

The Projective Nature of Personal Theology Questions

A related form of research that values open-ended responses is projective testing. Projective tests (or, as they are now being called, 'open response measures') grew out of both Gestalt and psychodynamic schools of psychology. In clinical and personality research, projective tests invite respondents to offer free responses to some kind of basic stimuli – pictures, words, or phrases – or simply to produce free visual or verbal depictions of requested stimuli. Projective tests are used in tandem with more 'objective' questionnaires and assessments to provide a richer and fuller picture of each person's perceptions, thoughts, emotions, motivations and attachments. The projective stimulus – the picture, word, or phrase – is intended to be ambiguous or relatively value-free, allowing the person who interprets the stimulus to bring meaning to it from their own internal associations. Over time, elaborate scoring systems have been constructed and (to varying degrees) empirically tested, which help create a better picture of relative strengths and challenges in individuals' ways of being in the world, and disclose patterns of thought and mood that can more easily be masked by a person in questionnaire responses. But the fundamental assumption behind projective tests is that individuals will reveal important things about themselves when invited to speak, write, or draw freely in response to an image, phrase, or word offered.[14]

In the same way, direct but open-ended questions about the world, purpose in life, reasons for traumatic events, and ultimate human values can provide a fuller and more complex picture of each person's beliefs, disclosing beliefs and values that may differ from responses to preconstructed questions for which people might to resort to what they perceive are more socially desirable responses. The questions we asked young adults about their personal theologies, as outlined in Chapter 2, were designed with projective tests in mind. Nobody has a complete or 'accurate' evaluative picture of the world. Nobody has a clear and precise picture of the good person or the good society. Nobody has a complete handle on cause and effect or on the idea of justice. The questions presented something like a blank screen to our young adults, and thereby invited their internal associations and, as psychodynamic theorists would put it, projections.

---

[14]   Of course, no stimulus is engaged completely freely. The influence of the researcher or examiner can still be strong – even if that influence is in part also a projection of the person taking the projective test.

Basic Thematic Analysis

An inductive approach and the use of qualitative data do not give licence for sloppy or haphazard analytic methods. As interviewers, we all took careful notes on people's responses to questions. I placed high value on actual verbatim responses to questions, since the study was focused on analysis of content in people's responses. I asked all interviewers to write down verbatim sentences and phrases that captured people's responses to open-ended questions. We also tape-recorded all in-depth interviews and listened to these tapes when we needed more complete notes. We transcribed 33 of the taped interviews as verbatim texts. I then analysed these 33 interviews in depth. I also used these interviews and interview coding to verify the content and coding of interviewers' notes, and to test note-coding reliability.

Drawing on my memory of the themes I had already heard in my previous study of religious young adults and in the initial interviews I conducted in this study, I developed an initial taxonomy and set of categories of the beliefs and values within each facet of personal theology. Interviewers' notes then were used as the first and most basic interview data. Three of us coded these interview notes according to themes I had previously identified, as well as themes we found arising across interviews. We soon developed coding dictionaries for themes that were recurring, and used these while adding to the categories as necessary. This followed classic grounded-theory process: grounded theorists code, read and digest data as it is collected; the process leads to preliminary definitions and categories for open-ended interview responses; the emergent definitions and categories then help focus the attention and intention of research, leading to further refinement in future data collection and field study.

Close content analysis of narrative responses to open-ended questions is the primary basis for this exploration of different facets of personal theology. Each facet of personal theology was examined separately, in the responses to questions targeting that specific facet. Coding and classification methods varied slightly for each facet of personal theology, but always began with clausal analysis. These specific methods are outlined later in this chapter and described in detail in Chapters 4 through 7. A general summary of each classification scheme is outlined below.

Worldview

We coded interview notes by classifying statements as evaluations of the world (as negative, positive, or mixed), citations of specific qualities about the world (for example, political, economic, religious, intellectual, moral), statements of uncertainty such as 'I don't know', and ways of making sense of the world (for example, reason, conversation with others, ignoring). Clause-by-clause examination of responses in 33 transcripts served to clarify and confirm the reliability of broader coding methods, and to give further opportunity for coding breadth or narrowness of perspective about the world. These procedures, as well as more in-depth discussion of qualitative content of responses, are presented in Chapter 4.

Simply for the purpose of comparing *Making the Transition* young adults with cohorts of other adults across generations from the General Social Survey (GSS: 1972–2000)[15] on matters of worldview, two scaled items derived from the GSS and added to the Year 3 phone interview. These two dipolar questions, rated on a 7-point scale, inquired about beliefs about the ordered vs. chaotic nature of the world, and about the generally positive vs. negative quality of human nature.

Theodicy

Two questions were asked about theodicy. From responses to the first, more open-ended question, we developed categories not only for types of theodical beliefs, but for how young adults deal with theodical events – for instance, through reference to beliefs (that is, cognitive reframing), or through coping behaviours. We coded responses to the second question primarily according to what young adults expressed as their beliefs about and explanations for negative events. As a classic demonstration of the value of grounded-theory methods, we found quickly that two a priori higher-order categories of theodical thinking (deterministic and randomistic) were insufficient to account for the diversity of responses. As a result of close content analysis of responses, we added a third major category of theodicy. The three categories of theodical belief are as follows:

1. Deterministic: divine or other fatalistic and predeterminative forces are guiding events, for example, 'God is in control', 'We are meant to learn from things that happen to us';
2. Humanistic: human and particularly intrinsic forces are guiding events, for example, 'We make our own fate', and
3. Randomistic: events happen without any clear cause, for example, 'things just happen.'

We also coded responses for how young adults cope with unexpected negative events. A full discussion of responses and coding procedures is presented in Chapter 5.

---

[15]　James A. Davis, Tom W. Smith and Peter V. Marsden, *General Social Surveys 1972–2006* [Cumulative File]. ICPSR04697-v4 (Storrs, CT: Roper Center for Public Opinion Research, University of Connecticut/Ann Arbor, MI: Inter-university Consortium for Political and Social Research [distributors], 2009-12-04.doi:10.3886/ICPSR04697.v4 <http://dx.doi.org/10.3886/ICPSR04697.v4>.

Life Purpose

Upon seeing and hearing responses that focused specifically on the self-described action-level of each participant *vis-à-vis* the world, we categorized responses according to *degree* of engagement or withdrawal, ranging from ignorance and disregard to active engagement. We also coded for the *type* of engagement young adults sought or envisioned for themselves. Five broad categories emerged from participants' responses, which were further reduced to three general categories: 1) retreat and avoidance; 2) engagement defined and delimited through roles of family or job, and 3) broader engagement as an intentional agent of change in society. A thorough presentation of responses and coding procedures follows in Chapter 6.

Again, simply for the purpose of comparison with cohorts of previous generations of adults, we asked Year 3 participants a single dipolar 7-point scaled item from the GSS (1972–2000), inquiring about avoidance vs. engagement as the proper response of the good person to the world.

Ultimate Values

For the coding of values, we stepped aside a bit from classic grounded-theory practice. Young adults mentioned a wide variety of values, virtues and vices, and it was challenging without some additional reference points to create clusters of these values. I ended up using another source of values-related data from our study participants: I used young adults' rankings of the Rokeach 'terminal values' (as well as ratings of more basic motivational or instrumental values that had been part of the *Making the Transition* study from the beginning) as the basis for classification of values expressed verbally in the interviews.[16] Beginning with the Rokeach 'terminal values', I used a statistical method called 'cluster analysis' to identify values that were ranked similarly and seemed to be 'clustered' more closely in young adults' rankings. Once I identified the thematic coherence of these clusters, we used those themes to categorize open-ended interview responses. Any values that did not fit these larger categories were coded under a new category.

We also used our young adults' Rokeach 'terminal values' ranking scores for cohort comparison with previous generations of young adults in the original Rokeach studies held in the National Opinion Research Center (1967–71). This mixed-method procedure is discussed more completely in Chapter 7.

---

[16]   Prioritizing or rank-ordering of values yields better predictors of behaviour than mere categorization or rating on a scale: Shalom Schwartz, 'Value Priorities and Behavior: Applying a Theory of Integrated Value Systems', in C. Seligman, J.M. Olson, and M.P. Zanna (eds), *The Psychology of Values: The Ontario Symposium*, vol. 8 (Mahwah, NJ: Lawrence Erlbaum Associates, 1996), pp. 1–24. This was also Kluckhohn's and Rokeach's methodological position.

Following this focused process of categorizing responses, I return to an examination of whole responses, exploring for each facet of personal theology the similarities and distinctions between different sets of young adults featured in this book. Their whole responses, in conversation with each other, open more nuanced insights into personal theologies, revealing patterns in young adults' narratives of meaning-making, and illustrating the surprising ways that young adults from very different religious and cultural backgrounds can express similar beliefs or values. I offer commentary and interpretation on young adults' responses, in relation to their lives, and conclude these exploratory discussions by bringing into conversation with their responses some similar classic theological and philosophical perspectives.

A Closer Look: Clausal Analysis of Transcripts

A challenge presents itself to researchers working with interview, meeting, or event transcripts: how should I code this verbatim document of a person's (or group's) verbal statements? Do I code line-by-line, by looking for key words and synonyms, at a more global level, or somewhere in between?

Line-by-line coding can be problematic, due to syntactical variances in line breaks that can either break up or cause double coding of a meaningful theme. Extreme versions of content analysis find a solution in coding at the word-unit level – a solution that often results in higher coding reliability, but with a trade-off loss of context and narrative meaning. Coding broad units of text, such as paragraphs or whole passages, usually cannot be done effectively without a priori hypotheses and constructivist categories brought to bear on the data – often at the expense of subtle or not-so-subtle nuances that clearly differentiate between individuals.

Mid-level solutions between the word and the paragraph have been proposed by Holsti and by Trabasso and Stein.[17] These researchers propose coding individual thematic or *clausal* units – units that include a stated (or previously or contextually implied) subject and verb/predicate. Coding at such a refined level, while laborious, allows for more nuanced categorization of clausal units based on their syntactical, semiotic, or thematic content. For instance, the following interview response regarding theodicy – presented in clausal units – includes coding categories developed from the clausal units themselves.

---

[17] See Ole R. Holsti, *A System of Automated Content Analysis of Documents* (Standford, CA: Stanford University Press, 1963), and Nancy Stein, Susan Folkman, Tom Trabasso and T. Anne Richards, 'Appraisal and Goal Processes as Predictors of Psychological Well-Being in Bereaved Caregivers', *Journal of Personality & Social Psychology* 72(4) (April 1997): 872–84.

Well, usually, well number one I believe that there's reasons for everything that happens.	→	*Belief –* a reason for events exists
Ah, God doesn't put anything in front of you that you can't handle	→	*Belief –* deity in control *Coping concern*
and um, that maybe you may not see the reason	→	*Current mental state* and *Belief –* a reason exists
for something happening now,	→	*Current situation*
the positive [for something happening now – implied antecedent],	→	*Belief –* a positive reason exists
but you'll see it in the future.	→	*Belief –* a reason will emerge

The young adult in this passage focused primarily on a belief-system, rather than on goals or coping behaviours, as a means of making sense of unexpected negative life events. The dominant beliefs are 1) events in life happen for a reason, 2) a deity is in control of events, and 3) the final reason for negative events will eventually be understood as positive. From this simple example, we might readily recall – and be tempted immediately to impose – Aristotelian categories of causal thinking or Fowler's constructivist model of 'maturity' in faith development.[18] However, in most analyses, I initially attempt to stay closer to the data by relying on the content of responses to guide the creation of categories.

In this study, I adopted clausal coding strategies as a means of offering a more exhaustive exploratory analysis of young adults' beliefs and values. This method also provided a means of checking the reliability of broader impressionistic coding we employed when we examined interviewers' notes and listened to audiotapes of interviews.

More often than not, responses about beliefs and values contain multiple themes and perspectives. The theodical response above was easily categorized as a predestinational or deterministic theodicy, with a theistic basis. But such global categorization of an individual's response can become problematic in more complex or seemingly contradictory responses, where two or more distinct types of beliefs are cited. In these cases, the dominant pattern can often (but not always) be ascertained by examining the frequency of clausal units in each category of belief. By coding responses so closely, categorizing clausal units or phrases from interviewers' notes, we could look at relative frequencies of various themes within and across respondents. In other words, we could count the total number of clauses in a response and compare the proportions of different thematic types of clauses in a single individual and across all the young adult participants. When there was a clearly more dominant type of clausal theme, we judged that theme to be primary.

In cases too close to call, or when individuals used a lot of modifiers in their speech, syntactical and semantic cues provided further clarification. For instance, a respondent might state an overarching theodical belief as a topic

---

[18]   James Fowler, *Stages of Faith: The Psychology of Human Development and the Quest for Meaning* (San Francisco, CA: HarperSanFrancisco, 1981).

sentence (*'Generally*, I belief things happen randomly'), offer a brief discussion of a secondary theodical belief ('I mean, of course *sometimes* people do things that result in tragedy for themselves or others. And we are *often* the cause of our own destruction'), but conclude with a return to the first belief ('But *overall*, shit happens. There's no guiding reason behind it'). In this situation, a belief in a random world of causation subsumes a theodical belief related to human efficacy. The semantic clues of 'generally' and 'overall' set the statements of belief in a random world in a superordinate relationship to statements of belief related to human efficacy.

This final complexity in clausal coding and categorizing led to an adapted coding strategy for *life purpose*. As will be discussed in Chapter 6, many young adults seemed to feel some social demand to acknowledge, at the very least, a life purpose of helping others in society – but this engagement-oriented sense of life purpose was not necessarily their primary response. For these passages, clausal length and syntactical and semantic cues were examined, as in the previous paragraph, to generate final categorizations for individuals.

Because of such high value given to the direct speech of individuals, this study might be regarded as overly idiographic. But the study's assumptions are grounded in a hermeneutic of trust in people's capacity to express thoughts and perceptions with clarity when given the opportunity – a Socratic perspective, some might say romantic (in the sense of Rousseau), but really more of a trust in human capacity when people are given the opportunities to express themselves clearly. The analytical 'tricks' and methods are employed to hear more clearly what young adults have to say. They are also used to uncover patterns of association and meaning-making across interview responses. Semantic clustering is one of the implicit strategies in thematic analysis, to answer a simple question: what themes or ideas belong together? Martha Feldman outlined some semiotic strategies such as semiotic clustering or semiotic chains,[19] as ways to make explicit some of the connections and contrasts in a text. I make some judicious use of these strategies, for instance, in examining what types of assertions are made about the world when a worldview is negative. However, any method can become a bit too fancy and encumbered by its own jargon and sophistication for its own utility. Analytical methods for qualitative research were considered only if they maintained a fundamental respect for face-value integrity of young adults' statements.

Once categorized, people's responses are 'reduced', allowing for analysis of statistical comparisons and patterns. But, since we are attending to the nuances in so many verbatim responses of individual young adults, we can then set aside this complexity and examine some broad patterns. First will be the relationships between different facets of personal theology. How does worldview relate to theodicy, and life purpose to ultimate values? Is there any coherence that emerges across groups of individuals? This is the first question.

---

[19]   Martha Feldman, *Strategies for Interpreting Qualitative Data*, vol. 33, Qualitative Research Methods Series (Thousand Oaks, CA: Sage Publications, 1995).

Next is the developmental question. What influences each facet of personal theology? What social and developmental factors contribute to a particular worldview, theodicy, sense of life purpose, or ordering of ultimate values? Here we find one of the greatest advantages of a mixed methodology that uses grounded theory within the context of a longitudinal study. The categories for each facet of personal theology become dependent variables (that is, predicted outcomes) of a variety of factors that preceded young adults' articulation of these core beliefs and values. Qualitative analysis has generated categorical classifications that can be used in longitudinal correlational analysis.

Given the exploratory and theory-building nature of this book, traditional hypothesis testing is not in order. I am generating theory and seeking patterns, not verifying a priori hypotheses. However, we can anticipate certain patterns to emerge. These include expectations that certain themes will emerge as culturally dominant types of beliefs or values within each aspect of personal theology, that there have been some socio-historical changes over the past 40 years in young adults' core beliefs and values, and that there will be some variations in beliefs and values due to socio-economic and demographic factors. Given the riches of the longitudinal data, I also have the opportunity to explore possible influences of family, education, work, peers, leisure, religion and personal dispositions on beliefs and values. The specific relationships – and strength of relationships – of various cultural, familial, educational, vocational, religious and personal factors with personal theology will be one of the contributions of this exploratory study.

Additional Measures Used in Correlational Analyses

Beyond the classifications of personal theology, there are four broad sets of specific measures used in this exploratory study: demographic data, adolescent and early young adult predictors of personal theology, concurrent young adult life experiences and attitudes, and psychosocial maturational outcomes. These sets of specific measures are described below.

Demographic Measures

Demographic variables were examined to evaluate any gross differences in aspects of personal theology. These variables included gender, age, race, socio-economic status, family 'type', (that is, original parents still married, parents divorced, single-parent, or blended), family size, English as a primary language, and summative life stressors experienced during adolescence[20] – all drawn from the Teenage Life

---

[20]   Adolescent life stressors included school violence or theft, neighbourhood violence, parental divorce, death, or job change, family delinquency, violence, dropout, illness and teenage pregnancy.

Questionnaire[21] completed in the initial *Youth and Social Development* study. Two measures were used for socio-economic status: a) social class of the community (SCC: poor and working class, middle class, or upper-middle and upper class),[22] and b) level of parent education.[23]

Adolescent Predictors of Personal Theology

To examine predictors of each aspect of young adults' personal theologies, more extensive data from the Sloan Study and *Making the Transition* were used. These measures focused on some objective qualities and subjective evaluations of several areas of adolescents' and young adults' lives: family, school, work, extracurricular activity and religion. Measures, as follow, are drawn from the Teenage Life Questionnaire, the Experience Sampling Method, or the Career Orientation Survey:

- Family – perceived family support and family challenge, parental knowledge and limits on free time, parental school investment, time spent with family members, household capital goods (for example, books, televisions, dishwasher, magazines, computer), family distress and eustress (negative and positive stress), and parental financial support for college.
- School – high school grades, level of math and science courses, time spent in school, hours spent on homework, scholastic and civic service awards, perceived school support, teacher support, school distress and personal school problems.
- Work – teenage employment status, work hours, percentage of time in work, job type and wages.
- Leisure – teenage extracurricular involvement, time in active and passive leisure, time with peers and peers' values.
- Religion – teenage religious affiliation, attendance (per month) and perceived religiosity.

---

[21]   This questionnaire was designed using questions and measures from the National Education Longitudinal Study (NELS).

[22]   See Barbara Schneider and David Stevenson, *The Ambitious Generation: America's Teenagers, Motivated but Directionless* (New Haven, CT: Yale University Press, 1999), and Mihaly Csikszentmihalyi and Barbara Schneider, *Becoming Adult: How Teenagers Prepare for the World of Work* (New York: Basic, 2000), Ch. 2. Each of the twelve communities was given a broad categorical code based on the 1990 Census data for that community.

[23]   Parent education level was found to correlate highly with the 1994 revised Duncan occupational prestige index for parents' occupations in a subsample of original Sloan participants. Parent education level was used because of greater data completeness: K. Nakao and J. Treas, 'Updating Occupational Prestige and Socioeconomic Scores: How the new measures measure up', *Sociological Methodology*, 24: 1–72.

- Psychological traits and dispositions – teenage self-esteem, self-efficacy, chance locus of control,[24] educational aspirations, optimism and future outlook; motivational values related to expected career, and average day-to-day ratings of cognitive and affective states, including positive mood, motivation, personal control, and challenge and perceived importance of activities.
- Emerging adulthood life status – post-secondary marital status, number of children, post-secondary education status,[25] employment status and habitation.

I explore relationships between these various measures from participants' adolescent years and the subsequent statements of personal theologies. From the strongest relationships, I generate linear regression analyses to see how strongly various adolescent social and developmental factors predict later worldviews, theodicies, life purposes and ultimate values. Results of this process are presented in Chapter 8.

Young Adult Correlates of Personal Theology

The final question is about the relationship of personal theology to the everyday current life experiences and longer-term plans of young adults. The following *Making the Transition* measures (from the phone survey, in-depth interview, questionnaire and experience sampling method) were gathered during the time that we asked young adults about personal theologies:

- Relationships – social relationships, premarital dating and sexual relationships in the previous two years, relationship ethic, investment in relationships.
- College – grades, school problems, school satisfaction.
- Work – job type, hours, earnings, advancement opportunity, responsibility; job relevance to education and life purpose, job satisfaction, duration, permanence, dedication; investment in career, work-life balance.
- Leisure – hours, investment in individual interests.
- Religion – involvement in religious organizations, monthly religious attendance, religious beliefs.
- Psychological traits and dispositions – current life satisfaction, self-efficacy, optimism, internal and external locus of control; context-specific

---

[24]   Locus of control items for the TLQ were drawn from the original Rotter scales: John Rotter, 'Generalized expectancies of internal versus external control of reinforcements', *Psychological Monographs* 80(609).

[25]   Post-secondary school status was classified according to four categories: no post-secondary schooling, attendance at a 2-year college, attendance at a 4-year less competitive college, and attendance at a 4-year more competitive college (see Csikszentmihalyi and Schneider, *Becoming Adult*, Chapter 2). The competitive level of colleges was classified by truncating the academic prestige codes in *Peterson's Guide to Colleges and Universities*.

challenge, concentration, motivation, personal control, self-esteem, mood, motivation, interpersonal trust, self-differentiation.

In the interlude following Chapter 8, I provide a summary of a limited investigation of relationships between these various experiences of emerging adulthood and facets of concurrent personal theology. From identification of the strongest relationships, I suggest directions for further research.

An Exploratory Study

This is an exploratory study. As such, I committed myself not to testing hypotheses but to exploring possibilities and generating hypotheses. Furthermore, the study at best provides only a limited snapshot of the beliefs and values of American emerging adults from twelve different communities, in the years at the turn of the century, just prior to 11 September 2001. Even with the advantages of a nested design which situates our study participants and their responses and life patterns in a larger context, the picture is incomplete. But a nested design provides some additional advantages that allow for some more accurate estimation of the patterns that might exist among the general population of emerging adults in America.

Since this study is focused on theory building, rather than theory testing – and, given the restricted statistical power due to small sample size – I was more generous than is customary in looking for statistical patterns, accepting a higher tolerance for what statisticians call 'Type I' error (that is, a 'significant' difference that occurred simply because of the 'luck of the draw' in random variations). Researchers focused on hypothesis testing and theory verification are typically more concerned with committing Type I error (pointing to the presence of something that isn't really there) than they are with committing Type II error (dismissing the presence of something that really is there). To reduce spurious positive claims, they set the bar high for finding a real difference, pattern, or effect. Concern for spurious negative claims ('there's nothing discernible there') is not as strongly emphasized:[26]

> *Type I error*: Claiming a significant pattern or contrast that was not really present in the population, but was only due to chance distributions of data in the given sample.

---

[26]　In medical research, Type II error is taken a bit more seriously. If a drug or other medical intervention has a small or inconsistent positive effect on patients' health, it would be somewhat more grievous to dismiss its usefulness simply because it didn't make the stringent statistical probability cut-off of most other research. Rather than disregard research because results do not reach the tolerance level of 5 per cent chance of an erroneous positive claim, medical researchers are often willing to tolerate a bit more chance (up to 10 per cent) of spurious positive claim because missing a real difference might keep them from finding and using some effective treatments.

Type II error: Dismissing the presence of a significant pattern or contrast that was really present in the population, because it was masked by chance distributions of data in the given sample that yielded non-significant results.

In his frequently referenced statistical textbook, Geoffrey Keppel suggested that significance levels in psychology have become reified and remained at an unexamined standard of a 5 per cent tolerance level for possible Type I error (the well-known p-value, or probability value, of .05 or less). He warned that 'an overconcern for Type I error in any particular experiment may actually impede progress in that area of research.'[27] Keppel further advocated exploratory analysis, submitting several criteria exploratory researchers might use in adjusting tolerance levels in order to strike a more appropriate balance between Type I and Type II (that is, 'non-significant' statistical results that, due to multiple factors, mask a legitimate and present pattern). These criteria include the following: (1) adjust tolerance (probability cut-off values) to more lenient levels, (2) conduct all primary and follow-up (post hoc) tests without adjusting tolerances to more restrictive levels, and (3) with small samples, conduct power analyses to discern minimum sample size for which questionable effects would meet traditional criteria for 'significance'. By doing so, researchers engage in productive 'exploratory data analysis, the unearthing of interesting and unexpected findings, [which] often generates the planned comparisons studied and examined in subsequent experiments'.[28]

I have adopted many of Keppel's recommendations – particularly the first two: a less restrictive tolerance level ($p \leq .1$), and all primary and follow-up tests treated independently with the same tolerance level. This strategy (in addition to occasional references to non-significant but suggestive patterns) assures the broadest acceptable tolerance of Type I error and prevention of Type II error – essential in theory building. However, I also employ a 'convergent evidence' strategy of interpreting results, as a means of evaluating the logical coherence of effects. For example, if young adults with different types of theodical beliefs came from families of different socio-economic status, then other factors related to family life and social/financial capital should also differentiate between these groups of young adults. Evaluation of 'convergent evidence' affords an emergent strategy for testing the validity of findings. Finally, I only use those variables with statistically significant or suggestive relationships with personal theology in any multivariate regression analyses.

---

[27]   Geoffrey Keppel, *Design and Analysis: A Researcher's Handbook* (Englewood Cliffs, NJ: Prentice Hall, 1991), p. 178.

[28]   Ibid., pp. 183–4.

Interlude

An Interview with Rebecca

Before launching into a close analysis of different facets of young adults' personal theologies, it will be helpful to get a sense of a typical interview. We tried as much as possible to meet with young adults in their homes, and always in the towns or cities in which they currently resided, for these more intimate interviews. In all our interviews, we attempted to create a natural flow of conversation from topic to topic, giving each person space and structure in which to describe more about their experiences in college, work, relationships and leisure. We moved from these topics easily into conversations about worldview, life purpose, theodicy and ultimate values, touching along the way on their ideals about relationships, work and the good life. Our interviews took us into neighbourhoods across America – from working-class and poor communities to middle-class to upper-class neighbourhoods in small and large cities, villages and rural communities, from New England to the Southeast, across the Midwest and into the West.

The following is an example of where and how we met each young adult who agreed to participate in an onsite interview. It shows the typical flow of conversation as we worked through our interview questions, and it reveals how interviewers were able to elicit greater depth of responses even from young adults who had never been asked questions directly about different facets of their personal theologies. This interview with Rebecca in particular also offers a glimpse into an American way of life that is becoming less common in early young adulthood.

I met Rebecca at her home, a small house on the outskirts of a small city in the rural Midwest. Rebecca was a married white young mother who worked as an optometrist's assistant. Her life is representative of a pattern of many – but a decreasing percentage – of young adults in America. She married and had children at an age that was once more normative in this country, but is now several years earlier than the national average. Like most married young parents, both she and her husband worked, and faced the challenges of juggling work schedules with family life. Her investment in work was primarily utilitarian, as she described it:

> Oh, let's see. Patients come in, I pre-screen them, ask them if they can see colours, if they can see words, if they can see all kinds of things, if they can see 3-D. Hand them off to the optometrist, and then do it again. That's all I do all day. And talk about glasses. The only farther I could go would be an optometrist and obviously I can't do that without schooling. So ... it's a job. It's close to home.

She described her prior work setting as chaotic and unkind compared to a more predictable and friendly new work environment:

Well, we used to get in yelling matches at my old job. On Saturdays and Sundays, especially. I'd want to get out of there early on Sunday, cuz that was our report day, and they decided that they wanted to have an appointment at seven o' clock at night, and I'd be stuck. And oh yeah, many yelling, yelling matches. And here, now, I have a set schedule. If it's nine o'clock, I leave at nine. It's an easygoing environment. There's lots of people around. Everyone there is nice. I mean, I don't have anyone who I'm intimidated to talk to. There's, and they'll talk about anything with you. Just bring it up, and they'll talk forever about it. So, I mean, it's just one of those jobs where you just feel really comfortable.

Rebecca was deeply grateful for her friendships. Her closest friends, like her family, lived in the same region. She spoke warmly of her closest friend, an optician who was 'dating my cousin, which is kind of weird. They're now just moving in together this weekend, so, I don't know.' The world in which Rebecca lived evoked images of an American middle-class family and community that was once more common – but with values that have shifted in how people live their lives. What follows are some of the questions we discussed about what she values most in her relationships:

David: What do you value most about your friendships? What do you look for in your friends?

Rebecca: Being there. And being truthful, honest. No back-stabbers. And she was there for me when, the night I got the phone call that my grandfather died, she was there. She sat there all night with me. So … Someone else to talk to. Just, someone to be there, I guess. Just to … I need those shoulders to lean on.

David: What about dating? What did you look for in the guys you dated? What did you value in dating relationships?

Rebecca: Just fun. Having a great time. Being relaxed with each other. Not having to impress each other. Just, I guess just being comfortable, I guess. But definitely having fun. I don't like those guys that just sit there and do nothing. 'What do you want to do this Friday night?' 'I want to sit home and watch a movie.' No.

David: So, then, what about marriage? You're married. (Laughter) So, what was important to you about the man you married? What do you value most in him?

Rebecca: He's always there. If I need something, he's there. And, I mean, we're just … it's … I guess it's just that we were, I don't know, I think we were meant for each other. We dated when he was 18 and I was 14, and he went away to the Navy. And just by some incident, we just met up again and been together ever since that day. So I don't know. It's just … There's got to be the reason we met again. And we've gone through a lot and we're still together, so. I figure if we could work through the tough times, I think we'll be okay. There's one tough time upstairs [motioning toward a room where her son was playing loudly], so.

David: Now, a tougher question. What reasons would cause you to consider divorce as a serious choice?

Rebecca: Him cheating. That would be one. And that would pretty much be the only one. Because we've pretty much worked through everything. We're able to work through everything.

David: Like what?

Rebecca: We weren't honest with each other before. I should have said I wasn't honest with him before, and now we are. And we haven't, we haven't had any problems since.

David: That sounds like a big step.

Rebecca: Yeah. I had to grow up. A lot. I went from living at home to jumping into this, and it, I didn't have anything in between. So, I needed to learn a lot. But I have now, and now it's much better.

A few more questions followed about relationships, drawn from a Gallup study of beliefs about marriage. Then the conversation shifted to the questions tapping into personal theology:

David: Think for a minute about the world as you know it. How do you make sense of the world? What do you do to make sense of the world? What kind of a place is the world, to you, in general?

Rebecca: Well, I don't know. I don't know how, I've never actually asked myself that question. It depends on what part of the world you're talking about. I mean, there are some horrible, horrible parts. But there are some cool parts, like Australia, and I want to go to Ireland. I think Ireland would be kind of, you know, on the, you know the peaceful parts, which are scattered.

David: Well, yeah! What are the horrible parts and what are the good parts?

Rebecca: The horrible parts are where people are massacring, doing things where it is totally inhumane to do. The good parts are just, I don't know, you hear a lot of vacation, like the vacation areas and stuff. I think that would be fine. But …

David: If that's all that were there?

Rebecca: If that's all that was there, that would be just fine. Like the Kosovo thing, you know. Who would want to be there? You know. That's a horrible, horrible, horrible thing that's going on.

David: Overall, what do you, what's the balance do you think?

Rebecca: I think there is right now in this world more bad than anything good. You got the school shootings, you got everything going on that I think is, bad things are taking over I think. Too many, too many people dying.

David: You think it's getting worse?

Rebecca: Oh yes. Much worse. My son, we don't even allow guns in our house and my son knows how to shoot a gun. He runs around 'pshoo pshoo-ing' everybody, you know. And it's like, he's two! I mean ... .

David: I don't know what it is about little boys, somehow they, they learn ...

Rebecca: They learn how to shoot a gun! And it's, we don't even have guns in the house! You know? And it's, we don't even have toy, you know, no toys or anything that are guns. And he just knows how to do it.

David: How do you feel about that?

Rebecca: I hate it. I hate it. He will pick up a golf club and hold it like a rifle. I mean, that's scary. And I mean, it's ... and he doesn't know that he's doing anything bad. Which he could get his hands on a real gun and be playing and shoot somebody, and he doesn't even know he did anything bad. He learned what he watched on television.

David: Shifting a bit now, what do you see as your place in the world? How do you 'fit' into the world?

Rebecca: Oh ... these are difficult questions. I've never actually thought about any of this. I don't know how to answer that ... I'm a mom. How else can you fit in? You're one of the most influential people when you're the, when you're a mom.

David: How? What ... ?

Rebecca: See him walk up the steps – he cries, I mean, that's, you know, it's just, you have more impact. The parents have more impact on a child than anyone else. And it's what you do at two, when they're two or three that they imitate. And that's they, that's how I think they learn. So I think my place is pretty much being a role model right now. I mean.

David: OK. Now. Say something bad – terrible, tragic, unexpected – happens in your life, or to someone you know. Think about that kind of event for a minute ... How do you understand or make sense of life when things are going really badly?

Rebecca: I don't know. I just, something happens for a reason. So.

David: Mmm-hmm.

Rebecca: Like, my grandfather dying. He died because he was in pain. I mean, that's, he died for a reason. Obviously someone greater than him didn't want him to suffer any longer. I mean, it's, everything happens for a reason.

David: So, for, for him, his dying was because he wasn't supposed to be in pain any more.

Rebecca: Right. I think that's, I mean, yeah, I think they should have let him, when he was alive – what happened was he had like seventy-some tumours in his brain and one hundred and some lining his entire body. He had cancer really bad. And he fought it for a good year and a half. And it just got really bad. And I kept saying you know what, let's let him go. But then once he went, then I got mad. I didn't want him to be gone when he went, but he wasn't hurting any longer. So. That's, I think that's why.

David: What do you feel are the best and the worst human attributes? Or, another way to think about this – What types of people do you admire most, and what types of people disgust you or turn you off the most? [Rebecca laughed and shook her head.] *Kind of strong way to ask something?*

Rebecca: I know it is! Just people who don't care what anybody, you know, people who ... You really shouldn't care all that much what people think, but you shouldn't, I mean, walk around and do horrible things or say horrible, horrible things. People who don't respect others are horrible people. I mean, it's ... [noise in background] It's just, and people I admire the most are people who are trying to help others, I guess. I mean, when you're out there trying to improve society, I guess that's ...

David: Like what?

Rebecca: Oh, I mean, from anything. It could be from a vet working on an animal, trying to save the animal to a doctor to parents, to teachers. I mean, it could be any number of people who are not, you know, making society worse.

At this point, the interview questions turned toward a focus on religious background and ways of learning a system of belief:

David: So, how did you come to believe as you do?

Rebecca: My grandma plays the organ for our church, my parents used to be the janitors, and I live ten feet out my parents' back door's our church. So, I mean, it was, it's there.

David: Have you had to face any situations that made you rethink your outlook on life?

Rebecca [her son has appeared at her side]: I don't know. It just, you know, it just it makes you feel as if God put you here for something. [Child: 'What?'] Now, my position in this world is to take care of him [motioning to her child]. It's not my, me anymore. It's him. I guess that's what it kind of is.

David: That's really, that's great.

Rebecca: My position here is just to nurture him now. [Child: 'I have to go.'] Make sure he chooses the right path. It's just difficult now because he has, my husband's got different beliefs than I do.

David: Sure.

Rebecca: My husband believes in Indian beliefs, and I don't. I believe in God and everything. So, I mean, it is different. We have our little conflicts over that, but, we don't persuade each other to change, so. It's good.

David: OK, thanks. Let's move on. Some people believe that everything happens for a reason, while others believe that things happen randomly and without purpose. Others fall somewhere in between. How about you? What do you believe along that line? Try to be specific.

Rebecca: Just like before. I think everything happened for a reason … Not that everyone's got a plan, but that everything happened for a reason. I don't, I think everybody else chooses, I think everybody chooses their own fate. But when things happen, I think they're for a reason.

David: Can you give an example of what you mean?

Rebecca: Yeah, well when, like, one prom at school, you know, kids go out and drink and everything. Well, right before prom, there was a car accident, some kids died. They put the crashed car in front of there, and I don't think one … and I think it set an example. I mean, it just saved some more lives. I mean, I think that it happened for that reason. Cuz on prom, everybody's …

David: So their death teaches other people.

Rebecca: I think sometimes it does. I mean, it's not good to die, but I mean, sometimes ... [Child: 'Mommy!'] Shhhhhh sweetheart.

David: [Pause] Thanks for so much time, Rebecca. We are close to the end here. One more question? What is the most important ideal or belief in your life? Is there a principle by which you try to live your life?

Rebecca: Just to be a good person.

David: And what's a good person?

Rebecca: Someone who is, oh, I don't know how you describe a good person. Someone who isn't, who isn't hateful. Who isn't, you know, angry, I don't know. Just, just a good person in general. I mean, I want others to respect me as I respect others. I want to set good examples. I want to just be a good person, you know? I don't know how you would explain being a good person. It's .. not doing anything bad.

Rebecca and I continued talking for just a few minutes. I thanked her and brought the interview to a quick conclusion, to allow her to get her son ready for bed.

In many ways, the interview with Rebecca was typical of the interviews we conducted over the course of this phase of the *Making the Transition* study. While few of the young adults in the study had young children, many were living busy lives in school and work and found it challenging to make time for these interviews. However, once into the interviews, time passed quickly as they engaged the questions we asked.

Chapter 4

Worldview:
The Troubles and Wonders of the World

My people are foolish, they do not know me; they are stupid children, they have no understanding. They are skilled in doing evil, but do not know how to do good … I looked, and lo, the fruitful land was a desert, and all its cities were laid in ruins.

Jeremiah 4:22, 28a

The mind is burning, thoughts are burning, consciousness of thought is burning … Burning with what? Burning with the fire of lust, with the fire of hate, with the fire of delusion; I say it is burning with birth, aging and death, with sorrows, with lamentations, with pains, with griefs, with despairs.

Samyutta Nikaya xxxv.w 8: 'The Fire Sermon'

When men get together to pit their strength in games of skill, they start off in a light and friendly mood, but usually end up in a dark and angry one, and if they go on too long they start resorting to various underhanded tricks. When men meet at some ceremony to drink, they start off in an orderly manner, but usually end up in disorder, and if they go on too long, they start indulging in various irregular amusements. It is the same with all things. What starts out being sincere usually ends up being deceitful. What was simple in the beginning acquires monstrous proportions in the end.

Chuang Tzu 4

The world itself is the will to power – and nothing else! And you yourself are the will to power – and nothing else!

Friedrich Nietzche, 'The Will to Power'

These quotations from varied religious and atheist traditions offer examples of worldviews, opening a window into how these writers saw the world in which they lived and the human beings among whom they lived. The writers' views are negative, rather pessimistic, and filled with images of chaos, desolation, corruption and injustice. They emerged in a variety of settings – the destruction of a city and its civilization, the ongoing poverty and inequities of a caste-based society, the life of leisure in an empire's citadels.

Personal theologies do not emerge in a vacuum or begin with abstract, disembodied notions of the good. They are rooted in and begin with perceptions and impressions of the world in which people find themselves living. It is this sense of the world (worldview, cosmology, or *Weltanschauung*) that is fundamental in the formation of other beliefs and values that comprise personal theologies. As they embark on their transition from adolescence to adulthood, what do emerging adults say about the world in which they find themselves? What kind of a world do young adults think is the larger ground of their existence? And what perceptions and impressions form the basis of their worldviews?

Worldview (first known use 1858): The overall perspective from which one sees and interprets the world.

Weltanschauung (first known use 1868): A comprehensive conception or apprehension of the world especially from a specific standpoint
Merriam-Webster Online Dictionary, 2011

American young adults participating in the *Making the Transition* study were asked to articulate their beliefs about the world by responding in individual interviews to the following question: 'Think for a minute about the world as you know it. 1) How do you make sense of the world? 2) What do you do to make sense of the world? 3) What kind of a place is the world, in general, as you see it?'

It is the third question that elicited most clearly young adults' worldviews. Participants gave a variety of responses, in terms of valence of worldview (that is, the negative, positive, or ambivalent quality of statements about the world), clarity of content, and breadth and specificity of evidence and examples cited.

Negative, Positive, or Ambivalent?

> Lillian: I think, the world is a basically, although there's a lot of bad things happening in the world, the world that I live in – this small little world that is, you know, where I exist – it's a pretty good place. I mean, nothing terrible has really happened. But the world as a whole, I think, sometimes bad things happen, but as a whole I don't think that's a commonplace thing to happen. For the most part, I think people act in their own best interest, and that can lead to problems.

When presented with our questions about the world, Lillian, our atheist dental graduate student married to a devout Roman Catholic, responded from two vantage points: the larger world with a 'lot of bad things happening' and a human compulsion toward self-interest, and her smaller known world of school and family, where 'nothing terrible has really happened'. Her view of the world at large was negative, distinct from the small world in which she lived her life.

Lillian's negative view of the world at large was typical. Among the 82 American young adults we interviewed, these questions about 'the world' most frequently evoked negative feelings, impressions and evaluations.[1] Overall, the world was not a good place. Over 57 per cent of young adults we interviewed expressed a negative worldview. Only one-fourth of young adults expressed a generally positive view of the world. The remaining young adults were clearly ambivalent about the world, seeing both negative and positive qualities and expressing deep uncertainty. Thus, the dominant pattern that emerged among these young adults was a general pessimism about the world: over twice as many expressed negative worldviews as expressed positive worldviews. This pattern for the full sample was nearly identical to the pattern found when examining a subset of interview transcripts in close detail, and when examining the ratio of negative-to-positive clausal statements within each interview[2] (Figure 4.1).

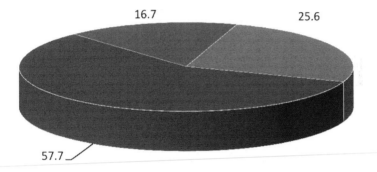

16.7   25.6

57.7

■ Negative   ■ Mixed/Ambivalent   ■ Positive

Figure 4.1   Valence of worldview among *Making the Transition* young adults

The dominance of a negative worldview was clear and dramatic. When presented with an open-ended question about the world, American young adults gravitated toward the negative – either in the form of pessimistic appraisals of

---

[1]   As a research team, we recorded the interviews and took careful notes during the interviews for all 82 young adults. Using interviewers' written notes, two raters worked on coding each interview response, consulting audiotapes when written notes were either unclear or incomplete. We coded overall responses for worldview first based on overall valence (positive, ambivalent or mixed, and negative), and second according to the central examples cited by young adults as evidence for their worldviews.

[2]   Three of the 82 interviews provided no indication of individuals' assessments of the world. This was due to a mixture of interviewers failing to ask the appropriate question and respondents refusing to state an assessment of the world. These three respondents were excluded from analyses of worldview but included in analyses in the next chapters.

individual and social behaviour and intention, or as diffuse anxieties and fears about the overwhelming nature of the world.[3]

Two major organizing themes arose as American young adults described the world in negative terms: chaos and injustice. The ways they talked about the world echo images of the world expressed in sacred texts of many religions. Positive images, ideas and impressions of the world were often cast in terms of potential, new development, or general beauty. Ambivalent young adults tended to be less clear in the examples or reasons they offered for either their positive or negative perceptions.

The dominance of negative worldviews from our interviews reveals a different pattern than what one finds from dipolar Likert-scale questions found in traditional sociological surveys – and a distinctly different pattern than what we found when we used such items in our own final phone interviews with a larger group of young adults (*n*=192) participating in the *Making the Transition* study. We included two questions that picked up on the common themes of chaos and injustice – questions that have been used for over 50 years in the General Social Survey. These questions were as follows:

People have different images of human nature. Where would you place yourself on these scales?

a) Human nature is basically good.   Human nature is fundamentally perverse
                                                              and corrupt.

| 1 | 2 | 3 | 4 | 5 | 6 | 7 |

b) The world is a place of strife   Harmony and cooperation prevail in
   and disorder.   the world.

| 1 | 2 | 3 | 4 | 5 | 6 | 7 |

Participants placed themselves on a scale between 1 and 7, depending on what they judged their view to be. Not surprisingly, young adults responding to these Likert-scale questions presented more optimistic views of human nature and more moderate views of chaos versus order in the world. There is an effect on people's responses to such questions, called the 'social demand effect':[4] people respond with overly positive evaluations on scales as a way of managing self-presentation and managing other people's impressions of them. Given the potential for 'social

---

[3]   The pattern found in interview responses in the *Making the Transition* study is replicated in a parallel study of 60 young adults involved in recreating religious communities, who responded to the same questions.

[4]   'Social demand' is a methodological effect that persists in survey data. An example of this is shown in Myers' (2000) summary of sociological database response patterns to questions about people's happiness, and also in Chartrand's (2002) review of a frequently used job skills inventory: in both cases, data were clearly skewed, with people rating themselves most frequently as very or extremely happy and as highly skilled at a majority of job tasks.

demand' effects in these forced-choice questions, no conclusions were drawn regarding the overall positive vs. negative valence of worldviews. But these questions are useful for another purpose. They allow *relative* comparison of worldview valence of the young adults in the *Making the Transition* survey with that of young adults and general adult populations from different periods of the *General Social Survey* (GSS).

For these questions, we compared *Transition* young adults' responses with responses from three birth cohorts of GSS young adults (ages 18–25): 1946–60, 1961–75 and 1975–82 (closest in age to *Transition* young adults). *Transition* young adults did not differ significantly in their responses from these three different generations of GSS young adults. Also, on the question of order versus chaos in the world, all three generations of GSS young adults answered similarly. But, comparing the three generations of GSS young adults, there was a slight trend toward a more pessimistic view of human nature since the 1970s – with the GSS young adults closest in age to our *Transition* young adults significantly more negative about human nature than all other groups (Figure 4.2).[5]

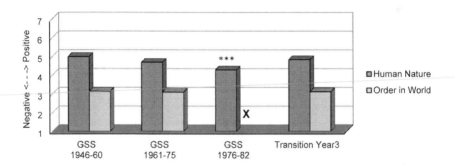

Figure 4.2   Average ratings on human nature (reverse coded) and world order questions by GSS and *Transition* young adult cohorts

This increase in pessimism about human nature was not unique to young adults: over time, adults of all ages selected progressively more negative views of human nature.[6] But in any decade of GSS surveys, emerging adults were typically the most negative of any adult age-group about human nature.[7] It should be noted that these variations in views of human nature are not large: there was just over one-half of a rating-scale point's difference between the highest and lowest group means, on a seven-point scale. And, interestingly, neither generational nor age-based comparisons yielded any differences in views of world order versus chaos.

---

[5] ANOVA, Human nature, omnibus $\underline{F}(3,1901) = 4.34$, $\underline{p} = .005$, post hoc <u>Least Squared Difference</u>, p< .005.

[6] ANOVA, Human nature, $\underline{F}(5, 11966) = 14.64$, $\underline{p} < .005$.

[7] ANOVA, Human nature, $\underline{F}(5, 11937) = 9.96$, $\underline{p} < .005$.

This suggests that overall, there appears to be noteworthy stability in worldview across age-groups, birth cohorts and generational cohorts of young adults, but with a trend toward more negative views of human nature. Age-group differences in worldview, particularly focused on human nature, may be related to historical events or to progressive socio-economic increases in household wealth and social opportunity over the course of the twentieth century in the United States – although it is interesting to note that the most negative views expressed by young adults were during a period of remarkable economic prosperity (and increased disparity between the richest and the poorest).

A Closer Look

What does a more refined and precise qualitative analysis of young adults' responses reveal? I closely studied 33 of the transcripts and coded responses to worldview questions using a form of clausal narrative analysis.[8] In each young adults' worldview response, I classified each clause as one of the following: negative worldview, positive worldview,[9] coping or sense-making, confusion, and acknowledged ignorance of the world.

This close reading of interview transcripts was revealing. Across the interviews, there was a preponderance of negative statements about the world. Even young adults who overall had positive worldviews usually made some clearly negative appraisals of the world. Negative clauses accounted for an average of 39 per cent of clauses in each young adult's narrative worldview response and were nearly twice as frequent as positive worldview statements, which accounted for only 23 per cent of clauses, on average, in each worldview response. The remaining clauses were indications of confusion (for example, 'I'm not sure,' 'I don't know'), ignorance of the world (for example, 'I've never given it thought'), or coping and making sense (for example, 'try to put your own perspective on it'). Coping or sense-making clauses accounted for 23 per cent of narrative worldview response clauses.[10]

---

[8]   The method used for clausal analysis for this study is similar to that used by Nancy Stein, Susan Folkman, Tom Trabasso and T. Anne Richards, 'Appraisal and Goal Processes as Predictors of Psychological Well-Being in Bereaved Caregivers', *Journal of Personality & Social Psychology* 72(4) (April 1997): 872–84. This method gave insight into how young adults constructed their responses, and provided a means to evaluate the accuracy of raters' more general coding from interviewers' notes. See Chapter 3 for more discussion of this method.

[9]   Ambiguous or mixed worldview was not coded, because at a clausal level of analysis, statements are typically unidirectional in valence.

[10]   A research colleague coded clauses for three interviews, allowing us to check coding consistency. Our coding consistency was relatively high (Cronbach $\alpha = .92$). We then classified these 33 young adult worldviews based on clausal response patterns. Those with a higher proportion of negative clauses were classified as negative. Those with a higher proportion

Table 4.1 provides examples of clausal excerpts from young adults' responses that reveal the ways they described the world in positive and negative terms. Naturally, some statements are stronger than others. For instance, 'I think it's a very positive place' is more unambiguously positive than 'I wouldn't say that it was unsafe'. These variations may indicate differences in degree of affirmation: a worldview could be extremely positive or marginally positive. Additionally, some statements are more vivid than others, either as examples of specific events ('you got the school shootings'), or as general summaries of specific human behaviours ('horrible parts where people are massacring'), compared with vague statements that indicate a visceral reaction but provide no specific reasons for the reaction (for example, 'It's scary' or 'It's pretty').

Going Deeper ...

There is greater complexity and richness of pattern lurking beneath a simpler, more straightforward empirical analysis of worldview as negative, positive, or ambivalent/mixed. Here, we turn to the transcripts to see directly how some of our young adults talked about the world. The following pages peer more deeply inside the responses of ten young adults to reveal four distinctive patterns of positive and negative worldviews: the chaotic negative worldview of Jeannie and Joel, the clear and nuanced positive 'world of potential' of Dean and Shanille, the religiously rooted negative 'world of corruption' of Beth, Cory and Mei Li that includes a pathway of escape, and the partially negative 'corrupt but mixed world' of atheists and agnostics like Steve, Stefani and Kasey. These are by no means the only possible worldviews. Their responses demonstrate only some of the varieties of worldview found in young adult personal theologies, in terms of valence, clarity, breadth and content. Commentary and interpretation follow each excerpt, providing a window into the varied ways young adults think about and express their thoughts about the world, as well as their mental and emotional reactions to the world and their ways of dealing with the world they perceive.

A Chaotic World: 'There be monsters out there'

Jeannie and Joel, both 22-year-old white college students from working-class communities but whose parents held advanced degrees, differed from each other in the clarity of their job aspirations and their general motivation. Jeannie was a

---

of positive clauses were classified as positive. And those with equivalent negative and positive clauses, as well as those offering no clearly valenced clauses, remained classified as 'mixed' or 'ambivalent'. In the end, our more global coding from interviewers' notes was generally consistent with classifications from my overall clausal analysis of transcripts (Cronbach α = .80), with only a few differences. In the cases of disagreement on classification of worldview, clausal analysis results were used to adjust, following the criteria described above.

Table 4.1   Examples of clausal coding of young adults' views of the world, and summary coding statistics

Negative worldview	Positive worldview
It's scary.	It's not real bad.
When you just think about it, it's so depressing.	It's pretty.
An unjust world …	You'll always find a way.
Horrible parts where people are massacring.	There are some cool parts, like Australia.
There is right now more bad than anything good.	People are inherently good.
Never underestimate the stupidity of humankind.	Most people are normal.
There are still places where people don't have freedom.	In the US, you have a lot of freedom.
It's hard to think why people have this thing called 'ethnic cleansing'.	This little world where I exist, it's a pretty good place.
People's priorities are kinda mixed up.	A lot of people are out for the betterment of society.
People are looking out for themselves.	I wouldn't say that it was unsafe.
Quite often very lonely.	It's a very positive place.
Human society is quite awful, in many respects.	[It is] evolving, changing.
[There are] intolerable amounts of unhappiness and despair in many parts.	Never in any point in history has there been more potential for good.
There's always people that try and stop you.	I have faith in people.
It's driven by money.	People can make a difference.
Church – it's everywhere and you can't get it out of your life.	A lot of people are working to make it better.
[There are] too many, too many people dying.	[There is] the possibility of being just.
It's steadily getting worse.	It's a rational world.
You got the school shootings [Columbine].	I find myself to be in a very lucky place in the world right now.
It's a dog-eat-dog world.	You're generally rewarded for the work you do.
It's difficult to make people hear each other.	
People are doing things that are totally inhumane.	
Average negative clauses per interview: 4.1	*Average positive clauses per interview: 2.1*
Proportion of negative/all clauses: .39	*Proportion of positive/all clauses: .23*
Per cent of respondents with negative worldview: 57.6	*Per cent of respondents with positive worldview: 27.2*

bright student in high school with a 4.0 GPA, and had committed (if somewhat half-heartedly) to a vocational identity as a pharmacist. Joel had drifted through high school with a 2.5 GPA, was not working while in college, and had not yet decided what he wanted to do after college ('I don't know. Maybe I'll be a teacher, or a manager'). Jeannie was raised with minimal connections to the Methodist tradition, while Joel was a devout Roman Catholic.

Both Jeannie and Joel expressed negative views of the world, with vague images of chaos and disorder. Here are their responses:

> Jeannie: It's scary, 'cause you never know what to expect, and there's just so many people too – it's like, sometimes when you just think about it, it's so depressing, 'cause you're like just one person, just like everybody else. But, but you have to have your own private area too, like your home or whatever, where you can be with family, and then it's not so depressing, 'cause you don't just feel like everybody else. I don't know how I would make sense of the world. I really don't. I just try to deal with it the way it is I guess … I would say just having my own place to go, probably like my boyfriend's house or my parent's house, just get away from everything else.

> Joel: It's a lot of clutter, there's a lot of people. And sometimes people don't always get along but I think sometimes you'll always find a way even though there's conflicts between all the people. And once you get older, I think you learn to get along a little better. When you're in high school it seems like there's more conflict than any other time. But now that I'm in college and I'm getting out of college, people settle down and get a little more mature and it's not quite as bad … That's one way of looking at it.

Both Joel's and Jeannie's speech became more disorganized at this point in their interviews, as they grappled with the question about the world. Jeannie's speech became more punctuated by phrases of adolescent and young adult uncertainty such as 'like' and 'you know'. Joel's descriptions of the world on the largest scale became muddled with juxtapositions of absolutes like 'always' and disclaimers like 'sometimes'. This disorganization in speech further amplifies the sense of chaos and confusion they conveyed as their perceptions of the world – and it suggests an underlying response of anxiety.

Jeannie painted a picture of the world as overwhelming, frightening and unpredictable. Joel's first thoughts were of the somewhat chaotic, crowded, uncertain nature of the world, and his focus on the broader world, like Jeannie's, was negative and diffuse. Consideration of the world in general seemed to evoke in each of them a sense of dislocation, insignificance and deep uncertainty about how to navigate any direction. Jeannie cited no specific examples, and her descriptors of the world were vague and diffuse. Her sense of anonymity in an uncertain world left her with feelings of fear, sadness and hopelessness. Joel also described the world as a whole in rather fuzzy terms, but became a bit more focused when he named conflict as one of the negative features of the world.

Their way of dealing with this diffuse, chaotic, unpredictable reality of the world as they perceived it was to withdraw from the world in general and to focus more narrowly on their immediate friends, families and people they knew. This is an important feature of Jeannie's and Joel's worldviews, and will replay itself on a larger scale in the shape of young adults' most important ultimate values. Jeannie's way of dealing with the overwhelming nature of the world was to leave the world alone and to seek a safe and defined place. For Jeannie, her diffuse but clearly negative worldview corresponded with a retreat and avoidance of the larger social order by seeking the shelter of her family or lover where she did not feel anonymous and could feel safe. Joel demonstrated this coping strategy in the very way in which he responded to the question. As he continued to speak, he withdrew his attention from his rather fuzzy and disorderly picture of the world to a more controlled focus on his experiences of interpersonal conflicts in high school and college. His attentional shift from the vagaries of world as a whole to his experiential world of high school and post-secondary life in a working-class community allowed him to adopt a somewhat more positive but not clearly optimistic view of the world ('it's not, not quite as bad '). This narrowing of the world down to his own frame of reference—a narrating strategy we saw earlier in Lillian's response—appeared to be Joel's chosen strategy of dealing with the world. When asked how he makes sense of the world, he stated two strategies: layering a personal perspective on events in the world, and focusing on his own life:

> Joel: All's you can do is kind of try to put your own perspective on it, you know? Let other people know what you think and if they don't agree with you, I mean, that's their choice too, you know? So, basically you just gotta live your own life. Sometimes you gotta learn to work with other people. Usually you do.

Early psychodynamic and Gestalt-based investigations charted similar echoes of anxiety and withdrawal in studies of human perception of and response to ambiguous stimuli.[11] Anxiety is a natural response to stimuli that are beyond the capacity of an individual to organize or classify them into categories that one typically uses to make sense of things. A consequent behavioural response can frequently be withdrawal or avoidance. The self-protective function of this response is, basically, 'If I do not see it, it will not exist to trouble me.' An alternative form of withdrawal is intentional narrowing of the field, so that prior

---

[11]   Hermann Rorschach's famous Inkblots (1921) and Henry Murray's and Christiana Morgan's Thematic Apperception Test (1935) are examples of ambiguous stimuli used to provoke anxiety and uncertainty, and to see how individuals responded. Gestalt psychology is focused on the interplay of ambiguous stimuli, arousal (excitation or anxiety), and perceptual choice.

ways of organizing things still work: 'If I return to my established categories and patterns, I can keep it at bay.'

Wendy Doniger hinted at a similar pattern of withdrawal in her essay, 'Inside and Outside the Mouth of God'.[12] To illustrate her point, Doniger uses two different Hindu myths from the *Bhagacata Purana*, in which Krishna comes in the guise of a human to individuals – in one myth to the young mother Yashodha, and in another myth to Markandeya, a Brahman sage. At a certain point in interaction with each character, Krishna opens his mouth, and the person falls into or out of 'the mouth of God'. In this experience, each person falls through 'the mouth of God' (a metaphorical portal or gateway) into a much more expansive vision of being. In the case of Yashodha, she experiences a vision of all of the vastness of nature, the universe, the aeons, and the life of the gods passing before her eyes and swirling around her. She is overcome by the experience and cannot bear the overwhelming magnitude of this expanded perspective. Krishna has mercy on her, allows her to forget and withdraw from this experience of a much larger reality, and transfers the power of her emotions into deep and vigorous attachment to himself who was the young son in her lap. In the case of Markandeya, a sage who has lived in the religious world of the 'belly of the god', he experiences an altering vision of the world destroyed in fire and flood by Vishnu who now sleeps. At his first experience, he withdraws in fear back into the 'belly of the god'. But later, when he experiences a similar vision, he is able to hold more of the experience and not withdraw in terror but stay in the midst of the vision that alters his view of the world and of himself. Vishnu, appearing to him as a child, blesses him with expansive insight.

These myths point out differences in phenomenological responses to what Rudolf Otto called the '*mysterium tremendum et fascinans*' – the experience of the numinous, or the undefined vastness of the realm of being in which all of us exist. Jeannie's and Joel's responses to questions about the world signal an impulse to withdraw, like the reaction of Yashodha, from the vastness and the perceived chaos of the world at large – and from the consequent self-perception as insignificant or impotent. The smaller, contained world of known existence and predictable patterns becomes an important source of solace, comfort and support for a belief in their significance and a measure of control in life.

The chaotic and overwhelmingly unpredictable world of Jeannie and Joel is quite different from the world of other young adults we interviewed. Let us turn next to the more positive view of the world offered by Dean, Shanille and Karla.

A World of Vast Potential: 'We can make this world better'

Dean and Shanille came from very different backgrounds. Dean, a white 22-year-old college graduate, grew up in an upper-middle-class community with parents

---

12   Wendy Doniger O'Flaherty, 'Inside and Outside the Mouth of God: The Boundary between Myth and Reality', *Daedalus* Spring 1980: 95–6.

who had graduate degrees. He lived alone, worked part-time at a bank after having left an entry-level position in financial planning, and expected to go to graduate school and work in commerce. Shanille was a 20-year-old Latina woman who grew up in a middle-class community in a single-parent household, with a mother who had attended high school. Although she had intended to go to college, at the time of her interview she was working full-time at a bank in customer relations. Shanille had grown up in the Roman Catholic Church, but was active with a Wiccan coven and a network of devotees to the *Rocky Horror Picture Show* subculture. She lived with her mother.

Coming from very different places, they both spoke in more positive terms about the world, and, while acknowledging worldwide problems, focused on the potential of human beings to change course and to make things better than they were. Both were also far more invested in exploring the question with their interviewers, as can be seen in the excerpts below.

> Dean: I think the world right now is moving in the right direction. I think there is still untolerable amounts of unhappiness and despair in various parts of it.

> *Laura: Why is there despair and unhappiness? I mean in what realms? Economically, politically, individual people?*

> Dean: I think economically some parts are very distressed. And I think based on my training in academia, I would say that the economic depression leads to social and cultural problems. Not to say that if someone is economically depressed, their culture is at fault at all. But just that economic stresses cause other stresses, for example, you take a place like Sudan. You know, tremendously economically depressed and then you have the civil war going on and everyone stuck in the middle is starving and dying and miserable. At least I assume they're miserable, I can't imagine living like that … And that's as much a part of cultural and ethnic strife as it is just the fact that no one has any money. When no one has any money, it doesn't take too much to say, let's pick up guns and shoot the guys next door, because what do we have to lose. And all it takes is one demagogue, one firebrand to start that up.

> *Laura: Okay, then, given the despair and the misery, how do you make sense of the world? What do you do to make sense of the world?*

> Dean: To make sense of it I'd say that I feel that things are moving in positive directions. I think that there are good things happening in the world.

> *Laura: Ah, like what?*

> Dean: I think that technology and advances in technology which are in many cases spurred on by economic growth are helping people in less fortunate areas live better. And I think more people are getting brought into the growth area

as opposed to the decline area ... I also think the globalization of capitalism is not universally a good thing, there are probably plenty of awful things that it's caused. But still, more people are doing better than they have before. Which is not to say that there aren't people doing horribly because there are people in very desperate situations. But I feel like in general things are moving forward. All I can affect is my life and the various people I can touch and influence, so if I can do good things and help the people around me then maybe they'll do that too and it will work out. But I feel like trying, I mean I don't think any one person, I mean save for a few leaders at the very top, can really change things vastly. But if everyone does a little bit, if you just try to make everyone else a little bit happier, the net effect can be pretty powerful.

* * *

Shanille: Kind of a hard question, since the world that I live in is so much different from the rest of world. Being a United States citizen, you have a lot of freedom that the rest of the world doesn't have. Even in the year 2000 where it seems like the whole world should be free of everything. I mean, the world's come a long way but there are still the places out there where people don't have the freedom to do just what we pass off as our day-to-day freedom. The world as I see it right now is a little unbalanced. And has a lot of growing and changing to do yet ... And I think that there are a lot of people out there saying the United States needs to worry about its own problems and quit worrying so much about everybody else's. But I also see where we have so much more than everybody else and we probably should be out there helping other people at least get to where we are. Before we worry so much about the little problems that we have.

Charles: Yeah. When you see events in your world as you experience it or the world in general, what do you do to make sense of the world?

Shanille: Wow. I find a lot of time that the world doesn't make sense to me ... I used to believe the idea that people were inherently good and that people were all out there doing what was right and that there were just situations that cause people to do things that weren't necessarily good but, you know, I see all the negative things going on out there and I just don't know that I can believe that people are inherently good and doing things that way ... I know that I do things that are good just because they're good and I don't imagine ever doing anything negative. And the only time that I could imagine doing something bad is when I really needed something. I don't know ... I try and make sense by saying that people were only doing those negative things because ... there's something causing them to do it. But now sometimes I have a hard time making sense of what's going on in the world.

The contrast between these two responses and those of Jeannie and Joel are striking. Both Dean and Shanille offered more richly developed, nuanced views of the world, in both positive and negative terms. Their negative statements were not vague or diffuse; they offered clearer perspectives on specific issues such as economic disparities and political unrest, they had clear opinions about issues like globalization, and they offered some clear pictures of causal chains of worldwide problems. They also had much more to say about the world that was positive in valence – mostly having to do with growth, change and potential. These positive statements were not stated with as much clarity as their negative statements; they were in the language of hope, faith and trust ('I've always believed that people are inherently good').

Dean's view of the world was more positive, with a sense of potential for improvement in the world, but with a notably negative baseline. Dean was, with a simple prompt from his interviewer, quite articulate and specific about situations related to both negative and positive qualities about the world. He was aware of difficult situations in the world and was able to talk about them in both general and specific terms. His positive worldview was based in an optimistic belief in dynamic development and upward movement, linked to technological and economic development, regardless of the negative baseline from which development emerged. Dean talked in similarly hopeful terms about coping with or making sense of the world: while he did not expect to have a momentous impact, he remained optimistic that his positive focus on himself, his family and friends, and his local connection, combined with other people's efforts, might help foster and perpetuate upward movement in the world.

Like Dean, Shanille was articulate, astute and reflective in her response to the question about worldview. She began with an unambiguously positive view of life in the United States and concluded with a dubious assertion of the general good intentions of most human behaviour. But in the middle of her statement, she recognized an 'unbalanced' quality of the world, a need for ongoing change, and a specific political objection to the United States' inadequate treatment of national and local problems. She further admitted that her usual belief in the inherent goodness of human intentions was difficult for her to sustain. Shanille focused on political aspects of the world, clearly stated her ideas and thoughts, and indicated an active mental engagement with political and social issues. Her initial positive response, which she acknowledged was based on her experience of being a United States citizen, was overtaken by negative assessments of world situations, national and international practices, and people's motives. None the less, she was actively interested in issues of the world and had clear opinions, even if she had become more uncertain about how to make sense of world events. Shanille admitted that her usual coping strategy of assuming the best of people's motives was not always helping her make sense of world events. But she did not respond by withdrawing, and she never indicated perceptions or feelings of being overwhelmed by the magnitude, chaos, or inequality of the world.

Karla likewise held a more positive view of the world rooted in a faith in progress and human potential. Like Dean and Shanille, Karla recognized the presence of negative events in the world, but she was particularly focused in turning attention deliberately away from the negative to the positive, even disavowing the negative as part of that hope and faith in human progress:

> Karla: That's sort of a big question. Well, it amazes me how – I guess I have a kind of a scientific view of it – how every organism can be broken down into smaller things and smaller components. Or the opposite way around, smaller components make up larger organisms. Just like, companies, friendships, things like that. And I guess to make sense of it, just seeing how different things influence each other. Even if you're just looking at problems either at work or with friends, trying to help them through problems. You just kind of see how the smaller things can affect the bigger picture.

> *David: And so, what kind of a place is the world to you, in general?*

> Karla: Evolving, changing. I like to look at the world in a positive way. And I don't black out the pictures that aren't like that. But I have faith in people. So I don't try to see the negative when people are being melodramatic about, not melodramatic but really concerned with all the hatred and things like that in life. I think that people can make a difference and a lot of people are working to make it better.

Karla, who had grown up in a very religious Lutheran family but had found other perspectives through her education and peers, stated an intriguing balance in ways of perceiving the world. She did not ignore or refuse to see events in the world that are more negative, but she did make a conscious choice in how much attention she pays to the negative, and refused to make the negative her predominant focus. An analytical sensibility, fostered in her scientific training and work in a biotechnology firm, supported these mental habits of perceiving and making sense of the world. Karla's response demonstrates the choices made by people holding this more positive, progress-oriented view of the world: they directly acknowledge the difficulties in the world, but rather than withdrawing from the world, they make a choice to focus on the positives of human potential, an underlying order in the structure of the world, and the evidence of things getting better.

One finds streams of this positive worldview in a variety of theological traditions, both religious and secular. Perhaps most salient from the twentieth century are the theological visions of Pierre Teilhard de Chardin, who painted a cosmology of progressive evolution of being into the unity of the cosmic Christ,[13] and of Jürgen Moltmann, who used a mixture of negative and positive descriptions of the world, but leaned heavily toward a positive vision of creation as God's habitation and of the Holy Spirit as God present everywhere in creation and

---

[13]   See J.A. Lyons, *The Cosmic Christ in Origen and Teilhard de Chardin* (Oxford: Oxford University Press, 1982).

in the best of human nature.[14] One finds similar streams in process theologies and philosophies that trace their lineage to Alfred North Whitehead, who wove together scientific notions of progressive evolution and theological concepts of God to offer a hopeful and positive cosmology.[15]

These, and earlier, expressions of positive worldviews – from Benjamin Franklin's optimistic pragmatism to the harmonious universe of the Jewish philosopher Wilhelm Leibniz, and from Julian of Norwich's gentler view of humanity to Muslim scholar Ibn Rushd's view of a world of order and beauty – can function as a benefit to societies who are emphasizing movement, development, renewal and progress. However, they can also serve to minimize 'the troubles of the world', as the old spiritual puts it, where one intentionally turns all negatives into positives and strives to make everything good and happy, sweet and light. Interestingly, there were hardly any young adults in our study that showed such a tendency toward denial. For Dean, Shanille, Karla and others, positive worldviews were consistently qualified with acknowledgment of tragic and chronic problems in the world, but then undergirded with a choice to see fundamental goodness in nature and the world, and to believe in and point to progress and potential.

Positive worldviews were far less frequent than negative worldviews, which focused most frequently not on chaos and unpredictability but on corruption and injustice—and as we see in the interviews with Beth, Cory and Mei Li, this perspective was taken by theist and atheist alike.

A World of Corruption, a Path of Escape

Beth, Cory and Mei Li also came from and inhabited different parts of American society. Beth, 24 at the time of her interview, grew up in a Midwestern working-class community in a home with college-educated Roman Catholic parents. With a 4.0 GPA in high school, she had expected to go to college, but her life took a different turn. At the time of her interview, she and her husband were raising their two children in a rundown duplex apartment in a poorer working-class neighbourhood. She had attended a two-year community college, was working 30 hours a week in a laundry and dry-cleaning business, and had converted to become a Jehovah's Witness. Cory grew up in the South as part of a white Mormon family, and remained devoted to this religious tradition, attending a young adults' seminary as well as worship services on a regular basis. From a family of college-educated parents, Cory was more of an average high school student, and was at the time of his interview attending a two-year community college and working in several part-time jobs as a receptionist, security guard and manual labourer. He lived with his parents, paid his own way to college, and had no specific career goals. Mei Li arrived in the United States on the cusp of adolescence, with her

---

[14] See Jürgen Moltmann, *The Spirit of Life: A Universal Affirmation,* trans. Margaret Kohl (Minneapolis, MN: Fortress, 1992).

[15] See Alfred North Whitehead, *Process and Reality* (New York: The Free Press, 1978).

Chinese parents, from Hong Kong. At the age of 18, at the time of her interview, she was still adjusting to life in college. She relied heavily on her close friendships with other Christians.

With different voices and different experiences, Beth, Cory and Mei Li spoke of a world of corruption and desolation, but with a path of hope offered in their religions:

> Beth: I make sense of the world through the Bible. And what kind of a place is the world in general? The best word that I can say is decaying.

> *David: Can you explain?*

> Beth: I think the world is horrible. I mean there are some bright spots, but ... for the most part it is getting steadily worse and ... But there's also reasons for that.

> *David: Like what?*

> Beth: I don't want to get too much into everything, but it's not an accident or a tragedy. It's supposed to be that way. It has to happen that way. So I accept the world the way it is, but I don't like it.

* * *

> Cory: I think there's a lot wrong with the world. There are a lot of horrible things that happen in the world. A lot of pain and suffering. But I also feel at the same time that never in any point in history has there been more potential for good, you know? We've got so many advantages that people before us have never had. And how we use those advantages is really what it's all about. I think there's more good in the world than a lot of people realize. It's so often overlooked and the bad is sensationalized. And, but yeah, that's kind of my view of the world.

> *Joe: And how do you make sense of the world?*

> Cory: How do I make sense of it? Well I believe firmly that everything that happens in this life is a part of a divine plan. How exactly it all fits in, I don't know, but I know that there's a deeper meaning and a deeper reason why things happen the way they do ... I believe that this life is a learning process. And if you didn't have challenges, if you didn't have hardships, you probably wouldn't ever learn anything if you always had everything handed to you on a plate. You wouldn't appreciate anything.

* * *

Mei Li: I understand the world from the point of the Christians.

Joe: Can you be a little bit more specific?

Mei Li: Well, God created the world and we, as his servants, need to find his will in our lives and carry that out.

Joe: And then, what kind of a place would you say the world is, in general?

Mei Li: Ah, I would say hectic, confused.

Joe: Okay. What is it that you do to make sense of the world?

Mei Li: Pray. And, I believe that God is in charge and that there is a reason behind that happening. And that I can't explain it, but I just have to rely on my faith.

These young adults thought of the world on a large scale. For them, there was a positive world – but it was a small world within the world whose boundaries were defined by a common faith and by a path of escape from the world, provided by God. Overall, the world at large was at best a mixed and uncertain place and at worst corrupt and literally hell-bent on destruction. Mei Li described the world, briefly, as 'hectic and confused', later pointing to misplaced priorities. Beth's response pointed directly to evil and corruption – a negative worldview filtered through an explicit religious perceptual system and expressed in unambiguous moral terms. She was not very specific in her descriptions; but she had definite ideas about reasons for the state of the world. Cory's worldview was more mixed: on the whole, it was moderately negative, and the negative qualities of the world were tragic and horrific, ones that he chose not to elaborate in detail. In contrast, the positive qualities had to do with 'potential' – what he perceived as opportunities and benefits resulting from historical progress.

All three cited reasons for why the world was the way it was, drawing from theological assertions in their chosen religious traditions. Beth's way of coping with and making sense of the world was primarily through a theodical explanation – that the world was a negative place by design or cosmic reason. So, Beth accepted the negative status of the world, but with a kind of distasteful endurance, rather than withdrawal into family or self-absorption. She later revealed that facets of her personal theology – and particularly her worldview and theodicy – were influenced significantly by her Jehovah's Witness training. For her, the increasingly negative quality of the world was a necessary process in the cosmological battle between forces of evil and forces of good, with a concluding future destruction of all corrupt and negative things. In this cosmology, a deity functions quite differently from the more benevolent deity described by Cory – and the negative events in the world are not infused with purpose or deeper meaning, but seen as something to endure prior to eternal reward. For Cory, negative images of pain and suffering had to be understood within a context of several positive compensatory beliefs: 1) that historical human progress was possible, and human capacity for good was higher than in previous periods; 2) that the horrific events of the world tend to be magnified out of proportion by journalists, and 3) that events in the world are part of a meaningful learning process framed by a divine being. Mei Li similarly focused trust in a divine plan, and it was the quest to discover and follow this divine plan that undergirded her most important Christian relationships that offered a path through the world.

These young adults perceived the world through moral lenses. Psychologically, their positioning of the world in moral terms of wickedness and distortion disposes them to approach the world as a place to suspect, fear and resist. Their religious traditions provide them with moral and cosmological language for perceiving this basic human corruption, and they interpret these perceptions through a particular set of organizing religious narratives that locates them among a group of people who have been given greater clarity to see the world as it truly is and to follow a different path.

Richard Niebuhr described a particular stream of Christian theology that similarly positioned the Christian community of faith as a bastion against the corrupting forces of the world. He called this theological tradition the 'Christ against culture' position.[16] From this theological position, the world is seen as thoroughly corrupt and tainted by the fallout of sin, and Christ is seen as the antithesis of the world and the provider of a path of escape to a select community of people who are given eyes to see the world as it truly is. There are similar strands of this type of worldview present in other religions. In some Jewish circles, the 'chosen' identity of the children of Israel stands in contrast to the confusion, corruption and lesser good of the *goyim*. Among Wahabbi Muslims, the evils of the world call for radical separation from the patterns of life so easily embraced by the West. Buddhism's wheel of suffering is understood as inevitable in life in the world, and can only be transcended or escaped through a fundamental change in awareness that is attained through a process of detachment.

These worldviews, embedded in variants of different religions, begin with a picture of the world as a mess—and not simply a mess of undefined chaos, but a mess of distortion and corruption. Beth's theological perspective goes so far as to see Satan, the Prince of Darkness, holding sway over all of humanity and creation, and to locate God's ultimate sovereignty and victory in a distant (or not so distant) future following a cosmic overthrow and a final destruction of all that is corrupt. In all three cases, a path of deliverance, a different reality, and a different way of being can only be given – otherwise, it is outside and beyond humanity's potential.

---

[16]   See H. Richard Niebuhr, *Christ and Culture* (New York: Harper & Row, 1951), pp. 45–82.

A Corrupt World from the Atheist's and Agnostic's Perspective

With Steve, Stefani and Kasey, we have a similar negative perspective of a world fraught with human fallibility and corruption, but without the possibility of a *deus ex machina* escape. Humans must simply face the difficult truth of life in a world that is far from ideal.

Steve, a 22-year-old culinary student, grew up in a two-parent household in a middle-class community and regarded himself as a 'dyed-in-the-wool' atheist. Stefani, a 20-year-old Native American college student working full-time at night in a printing company, grew up in a middle-class community, in a single-parent household due to divorce, and in a Lutheran church whose disharmonies left her with a bad taste for organized religion. Kasey, from a Southern non-religious household, at age 24 worked on a contract basis as a web designer and was deeply skeptical about there being any value to religion. These three young adults articulated a 'raw reality' perspective on the disorderly, selfish and coercive quality of human behaviour:

Steve: It's a little difficult at the current moment. But more or less I just try and see what's going on, you know? There's a lot of unbelievable things. And a lot of awful things. But when you sort of lose yourself in looking at other things and looking at other people in particular, you try and figure out what the right thing to do is.

Benita: OK. What kind of place do you think the world is in general?

Steve: Kind of place? It's a very big place. But, I don't know. Quite often very lonely. But also strange and wonderful and brutal and ... The world is neutral. But human society is quite awful in many respects.

* * *

Stefani: The world? I wouldn't say it was safe, but I wouldn't say that it was unsafe, if that makes any sense at all. And, people are not universally well-intentioned toward others. A lot of people are out for the betterment of society, but those people are fewer in number than the people that are out more for themselves.

Charles: And then, how do you make sense of the world?

Stefani: I try not to let what other people tell me influence my thinking or my thought process. My grandfather is extremely political and every time I go over to his house, he tries to talk me into, you know, political conversations. And I try not to let that affect the way I think. I try to find source data and learn from the true meaning or the true aspect.

* * *

Kasey: Ohhh. It's pretty corrupt, basically. It's all I can think of. Power struggle all over the world. It's pretty much how I look at it. It's driven by money … I mean, I don't know what else to say.

David: Do you have any other thoughts about the world as it is?

Kasey: No. I don't, I don't know … I can't think of anything else to say. 'Cause I don't really know. I would just say if I had to say, it's just driven by money, church. Religion's a huge thing, too. Religious stuff everywhere.

David: How do you mean?

Kasey: Oh, just everybody's thing about church. How it's everywhere and you can't get it out of your life. Everybody wants to comment on it everywhere. Everybody, everywhere in the world there's different religions, though. So that doesn't really make sense.

David: Great. Thanks. And how do you make sense of the world?

Kasey: I don't really try to make sense of it. I mean, I didn't create all this stuff so it's not my position to try to figure it out. I mean, I'm like, younger than most people living here, so I, I'll leave that to older people whose made these rules and made it the way it is. That's their problem.

These are worldviews of three young individualists. Their ambivalent and negative perspectives were not mitigated by more positive experiences in their local 'tribes' of friends and family, or within a larger community or orienting philosophy of a religion. They were on their own in a world that is recognized as strange, wonderful, brutal and driven by self-interests – a world that 'is what it is'.

These young adults, coming from an atheistic or agnostic perspective, indicated an implicit resistance to being influenced too much by others in their views of the world. They were committed to finding their own paths and making their own decisions. For Kasey, religion was one of the problems of the world rather than a solution. Stefani similarly resisted the overt efforts of her grandfather to impose his own political perspectives on her thought, instead asserting her own responsibility to seek sources of information and make her own decisions about the world. Steve addressed his concern about the potential of 'losing' himself in the larger environment of the world by attempting to understand 'what's going on' and to 'figure out what the right thing to do is', rather than simply seeking refuge with family and friends. These three young adults accepted as a given that the journey through the world and life was an individual journey and that they were responsible for making sense of the world.

Psychologically, their worldviews seem rooted in a resigned realism and self-reliance that Sigmund Freud would have regarded as signs of health (or, at least, freedom from delusion and neurosis). The world for Steve, Stefani and Kasey was difficult. But they did not depend on religion, family, or local tribe as a crutch. They knew, admitted and embraced their singularity and their individual responsibility for making sense of a world that was risky and uncertain.

The 'raw realism' of this kind of worldview can give way to a focus not on underlying virtues or purposes but on evidence of power, strength and influence. Strength to stand up to the world and find one's own path becomes a primary virtue. And the inherent suspicion of religious and political scripts presses toward self-reliance and individual thought as a virtue. These are the virtues of Nietzsche's individualistic *Übermensch*, standing alone against the suppressive forces of modern society.[17] They point toward the ascendancy of self-interest and self-affirmed consciousness, as espoused by Ayn Rand.[18] The worldviews that shape this way of living might be summed up in a quote by the Dread Pirate Roberts in the movie *The Princess Bride*: 'Life is pain, Highness. Anyone who says differently is selling something.'[19]

Prevailing Themes about the World

American young adults at the turn of the twenty-first century varied widely in their worldviews – beyond the four types presented above, and despite a dominant tendency toward negative perspectives about the world and human nature. American young adults also varied widely in the examples and images they offered to further articulate their worldviews. What follows is a summary analysis of how frequently different types of themes were mentioned by young adults when they discussed their worldviews.

Nearly half of young adults with negative worldviews were *exclusively* negative in their clausal statements – but no young adults with positive worldviews were *exclusively* positive. Diffuse or generic descriptions were frequent – but only a

---

[17]   Nietzsche decries the forces of conformity in society that suppress individual strength: 'High and independent spirituality, the will to stand alone, even a powerful reason are experienced as dangers; everything that elevates an individual above the herd and intimidates the neighbor is henceforth called evil; and the fair, modest, submissive, conforming mentality, the mediocrity of desires attains moral designations and honors': Friedrich Nietzsche, *Beyond Good and Evil*, trans. Walter Kaufman (New York: Random House, 1966), pp. 113, 114.

[18]   Rand used fiction to frame a personal theology (atheistic) focused on the necessary ascendancy of the individual for the sake of true human freedom and dignity: 'When you listen to a mystic's harangue on the impotence of the human mind and begin to doubt your consciousness, not his, when you permit your precariously semi-rational state to be shaken by any assertion and decide it is safer to trust his superior certainty and knowledge, the joke is on both of you: your sanction is the only source of certainty he has': Ayn Rand, *Atlas Shrugged* (New York: Signet, 1957, 1989), p. 960.

[19]   From *The Princess Bride*, directed by Rob Reiner (MGM, 1987).

few young adults, like Jeannie, referred solely in diffuse terms to the negative or positive qualities of the world. Most young adults discussed more specific reasons for both negative and positive worldviews. Reasons cited for negative worldviews were most frequently moral-interpersonal (for example, selfishness, chaotic and misplaced values, violence, untrustworthiness, lack of human affection), or political (for example, corruption of power, ethnic cleansing, competition between countries, religious zealotry), with some economic examples as well, such as poverty, or inequity of distribution. Only two young adults mentioned religion as a contributor to negative elements in the world, particularly citing religious zealotry and intolerance; nobody mentioned religion as part of a positive view of the world. Reasons cited by young adults' for their less frequent positive worldviews were most often relational (for example, people well-disposed to care, friendships, the promise of maturity, the haven of one's family and community), but also occasionally included political (for example, freedom, altruistic action and intention, potential for justice) and economic examples (for example, technological and economic opportunities, enjoyments of leisure). Political images and examples were four times more frequent among young adults with negative worldviews than among those with ambivalent or positive worldviews (Table 4.2).

Table 4.2   Percentage of young adults who stated one or more examples or images in their worldview responses

Worldview focus	Overall %	Negative worldview, %	Mixed worldview, %	Positive worldview, %
Interpersonal/Moral	44.3	47.7	23.1	55.0
Economic	10.1	13.6	7.7	5.0
Political	27.8	43.2**	7.7**	10.0*
Religious	1.3	2.3	0.0	0.0
Familial	1.3	0.0	0.0	5.0
General/Diffuse	53.2	40.9*	84.6*	65.0

Note: * $\chi^2 = 8.92$, p < .05; ** $\chi^2 = 10.76$, p < .01

Confusion, uncertainty and vagueness were expressed by over half of the young adults interviewed. such These included statements as 'I don't know' or 'It's hard to say', as well as other diffuse claims or vague generalizations without any associated details or supporting evidence. These were most frequent among young adults who expressed ambivalent worldviews, and also quite frequent among those expressing positive worldviews. They were significantly less frequent among those expressing negative worldviews. Young adults with ambivalent worldviews also offered fewer specific examples and images of interpersonal/moral, economic and political reasons for the state of the world, adding to the lack of clarity inherent in such a position.

American young adults in this study were disposed to negative views of the world at the 'macro' level, with a more frequent focus on national and international problems in morality and politics at the turn of the century. Examples such as ethnic cleansing in Kosovo, President Clinton's affair with an intern, the bombing of Iraq during the Kuwaiti conflict, and economic and educational policies in US domestic affairs were among their specific citations. Those who had positive worldviews based on the broader national and global contexts were also likely to acknowledge negative qualifiers of their optimism – sometimes, to the extent that their worldview valence shifted from positive to negative in the course of their responses. This was a somewhat surprising pattern, given the unprecedented era of peace and both national and international prosperity in which these young adults developed and matured. Yet, despite a world in which some of the major threats and anxieties such as the Iron Curtain had disappeared (and prior to 11 September 2001), young adults focused on forms of political corruption and interpersonal moral violation as the bases for their worldviews.[20]

Making Sense of and Responding to the World

Given their varied views of the world (with a strong tendency toward a negative view), how did these American young adults respond to the world they perceived? Responses to the world ranged from withdrawal and avoidance to toleration to active and thoughtful analysis. Thinking about the world seemed to overwhelm some individuals with feelings of anonymity, powerlessness, unpredictability and lack of control; but for others who had internalized resources of knowledge, confidence and systems of belief, thinking about the world seemed to trigger deeper cognitive and emotional engagement.

An individual's response to the world forms a bridge in personal theology between basic worldview and a sense of life purpose. As shown in the excerpts earlier in this chapter, young adults showed a range of coping and sense-making strategies in regard to the world. These strategies range from retreat or intentional blindness to detachment, to observation and analysis, to more direct engagement. Some, like Jeannie and Joel, made sense of the world by redefining the world in narrow terms of local family, friends and communities. Others, like Dean, Shanille and Karla, took a position of being optimistic and engaging locally to make a difference. Some talked about seeking perspective – either by drawing on personal resources or using religious perspectives provided for them – to find a path through the perceived corruptions and distortions of the world. One stated

---

[20] I continued to interview young adults through 2004, as part of another national study of young adults creating religious communities. These young adults showed the same pattern overall—gravitating toward negative worldviews and citing political, economic, and moral/interpersonal examples—but this time, the bombing of the World Trade Towers in New York City also figured in their examples.

a form of perspective-taking influenced by Eastern thought: 'You live for the contemplation of beautiful things and exquisite personal relationships.'

But some young adults were quite disengaged, expressing a sense of unimportance and detachment in their worldviews: 'I don't really mind, if it's not a big deal', or 'I'm not going to get too obsessed with anything, I'm just going to take life as it comes.' Disengagement came in the form of a fundamental and unquestioned habit ('I've never actually asked myself that question'), or it was expressed as a conscious choice ('I figure whatever doesn't affect my life personally, I really shouldn't worry about it,' or 'I kind of just, subconsciously, pretend it doesn't exist'). Sometimes the dismissive attitudes were stark, utilitarian and self-focused: 'I mean, I didn't create all this stuff, so it's not my position to try to figure it out.'

Summary

Results from the *Transition* study suggest that negative worldviews are dominant among American young adults, with prominent themes of chaos and corruption. These themes of chaos and corruption appeared even among many of the young adults with more positive beliefs about the world or humanity. In American culture, there seems to be a general underlying script for a negative worldview – regardless of religious affiliation. Does this ubiquitous undercurrent of seeing the world in negative terms reveal a deep cultural script deriving from the predominantly Judaeo-Christian heritage of American life? Or does it point to a common human apprehension about the world that can be found across religions and subcultures, and perhaps across cultures? And what role do factors, such as social class, family life, education and intrinsic motivation during adolescence, play in the development of young adults' negative worldviews? How are their worldviews related to the opportunities and challenges they experience day to day as young adults in their work and collegiate education? We will explore these questions later in Chapter 8.

A negative worldview is by no means universal. There are three distinctly valenced ways young adults view the world: negatively, positively, and with a mixed or ambivalent orientation. Ambivalent or mixed worldviews are least frequent, but there is a marked qualitative difference in them, making them more than simply a midpoint between positive and negative worldviews. The key difference is the level of clarity versus vagueness in how young adults perceive and make sense of data about the world. Ambivalent young adults' descriptions of the world were far less clear than negative or positive young adults' descriptions, and were peppered with far more statements of uncertainty. Mixed worldviews seem to signal a disregard of the world, expressed in a form of anxious self-protection that denies engagement even in terms of formulating an opinion, or in a local absorption in oneself and one's immediate relationships and surroundings, to the extent that the external world is shut out. Interestingly, mixed worldviews are associated with greater family instability and less psychological maturity.

Positive worldviews are more frequent, and (as will be seen in Chapter 8) clearly associated with socio-economic and educational benefits. While taking account of negative realities in the world, they are most frequently based on hope and a greater sense of trust in fundamental human benevolence, natural order and potential for growth and development. Images and examples cited to support a positive worldview tend to be a bit less clear than those used as evidence for a negative worldview.

These distinct patterns in responses suggest that worldview is not simply represented on a single continuum from negative to positive. There is another important dimension in individuals' worldviews: the degree of clarity in images and descriptions. Clarity is signalled by more decisive thought and well-defined, sharp images and ideas.

Figure 4.3 shows a spatial representation of worldviews according to valence and clarity. Each worldview is represented by a sphere which is sized proportionally to the percentage of young adults reporting a given worldview. The freeform shape surrounding the outside of the spheres outlines the plausible range of worldviews.

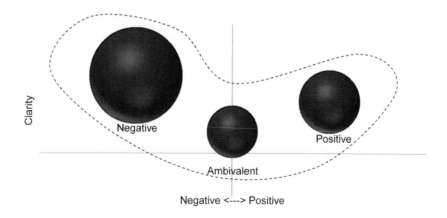

Figure 4.3   Spatial representation of worldviews

As this visual representation indicates, worldviews that are more clearly negative or positive are likely to be stated with more clarity. The more ambivalent the worldview, the less clear and decisive an individual will usually be, and the more vague and diffuse descriptions will be of the world. The more distinctly negative or positive the worldview, the clearer the perceptions and interpretations of the world. Negative worldviews will likely be stated most clearly and specifically.

Beyond basic classification by valence and clarity lay other meaningful but more nuanced variations in worldview. These include the fundamental sense behind a negative or positive view (for instance, chaos vs. corruption and actual good vs. potential good), frameworks people use when thinking about the world (for instance, political or moral/interpersonal), the level of interest expressed in the larger world beyond one's immediate surroundings and experiences, and the resources people access for making sense of the world. Worldview alone provides a rich field for further study of patterns and variations in personal theologies. And it is the fundamental ground for personal theology, which begins with the question 'What is this place into which I have been born?'

Chapter 5

Theodicy: Making Sense of Tragedies and Traumas

Whatever affliction may visit you is for what your own hands have earned.

Qur'an 42:30

Like a clear mirror, according to what comes before it, reflecting forms, each different, so is the nature of actions.

Garland Sutra, 10

The net of Heaven is cast wide. Though the mesh is not fine, yet nothing ever slips through.

Tao Te Ching, 73

The Lord has made everything for its purpose, even the wicked for the day of trouble.

Proverbs 16:4

What has been is what will be, and what has been done is what will be done; there is nothing new under the sun ... What is crooked cannot be made straight, and what is lacking cannot be counted.

Ecclesiastes 1:9, 13b, 15

Ambrosia can be extracted even from poison; elegant speech even from a child; good conduct even from an enemy, gold even from impurity.

Laws of Manu, 2:239

Why do tragedies and traumas occur? How are we as human beings to make sense of the unexpected, the events that disrupt our lives and assail our sense of order, control, dignity and justice? These are not simply abstract questions of theodicy. They are questions that become deeply personal, that arise naturally for people in the face of tragedy, or assault, or unexpected trauma. Behind the narrowly focused question 'Why did this happen to me?' (or, empathically, 'Why did this happen to her?') is the much larger question, 'What causes the tragic?' It is a haunting question for a humanity that wants and seeks order, peace, stability, predictability and happiness in the world in which they find themselves and live their lives.

The term 'theodicy', first used by Leibniz in 1710, is currently defined specifically as a theological 'defense of God's goodness and omnipotence in view of the existence of evil' (Merriam-Webster Online Dictionary). Despite its etymological roots being tied to a deity (θεος, or god), the actual philosophical function of theodicy is not to justify God. That conception of theodicy is too simplistic and reductionistic. Rather, the philosophical function of theodicy is primarily to justify attributes associated with God and with the cosmos of God's creation – purpose in design and function, benevolence, constancy, rationality and justice. The term is used by philosophers and sociologists as a shorthand term for understandings of the problem of evil – with or without reference to a deity.

The quotes at the beginning of this chapter, from diverse religious texts, illustrate varied theodical responses. Even within the same religion, there are often varied answers to the questions of theodicy, including human responsibility for what occurs, divine or cosmic purpose, meaninglessness and redemptive end that makes sense of the tragic, traumatic, or evil that is experienced.

Young adults, increasingly exposed to the realities of the world and life as they launch lives independent of their families and learn about a wider range of human experience, come to struggle in varying ways with the questions embedded in theodicy. They, like older adults, have formed and perhaps re-formed responses to these questions which help them cope both with the reality of known tragic and traumatic events and with the possibility of unexpected tragedy in their futures.

One might view the question of theodicy as a bit ironic, in the face of a predominantly negative worldview. If the world is a place of chaos and corruption, then why are tragedy and trauma questioned? And yet, there lurks behind the theodical question of ultimate cause a treasured image – perhaps never articulated but merely assumed – of a better way of life, a 'peaceable kingdom', and an ideal of cosmic justice or balance. Responses to the questions of theodicy may be the vital fabric of what Peter Berger describes as the sacred canopy that religion provides for a society – a constructed theological barrier against the unknown, the unreasonable, the unpredictable terror beyond. They allow for a reinforcement or reconstitution of beliefs in greater cosmic or divine attributes, ideals about human life, and structural order and purpose in the world that cause, direct, guide and shape events and their outcomes.

We sought to open a window onto young adults' theodical beliefs by asking two different types of questions. One question located the problem of theodicy (or ultimate causation) in relation to traumatic and tragic life events. The other question invited young adults to locate themselves in their general beliefs or scripts regarding theodicy:

1. Say something bad – terrible, tragic, unexpected – happens in your life, or to someone you know. Think about that kind of event for a minute. How do you understand or make sense of life when things are going really badly?
2. Some people believe that everything happens for a reason, while others believe that things happen randomly and without purpose. Others fall somewhere in between. How about you? What do you believe along that line? Try to be specific.

Most young adults had thought about the classic theodicy problem. Only two out of the 82 interviewees stated that they had never thought about it. Most young adults were able to think of specific negative life events that were traumatic or unexpected, ranging from deaths and diseases to accidents and assaults, either in their own families or among close friends. Some young adults reported that, since nothing bad had happened among their own families and friends, they could not mentally imagine such a specific situation. It is hard to tell whether these young adults were indeed blissfully ignorant of tragedy or trauma, defended against this level of vulnerability in the context of an interview with someone they just met, or responding out of a habitual stance of withdrawal and disengagement from the world.

Deterministic, Humanistic, or Randomistic?

To see how young adults talked about these questions, let us turn to Jacob's responses. Jacob, a young Jewish college student from the East Coast, had just completed a summer working as a stage manager at a major performing arts centre for classical music and dance. He described himself as a 'hopeless romantic', specifically referencing his experiences while living in Florence for a period of study ('next door to the Palazzo Pitti, the home of the Medici family – and they pretty much funded the Renaissance'). Jacob was quite willing to discuss the questions of theodicy. But it took him a while in his response to uncover the specific incident that registered most intensely with his personal solution to the theodicy problem. He talked his way toward significant tragedies and traumas, beginning with a distant friend whose father died of cancer, then moving to a fellow student who had committed suicide and a failed relationship, and finally focusing on a directly personal incident:

Jacob (responding to Question 1): ... I actually, I, my brother was almost killed in a car crash last summer.

David: How do you make sense of something like that?

Jacob: Well, I, I wasn't, my friend was driving. And he fell asleep on the wheel. At the wheel. And he swerved to, to miss a tree by about a millimetre. And we crashed into the guard rail on the Hudson Parkway.

David: Mmm! Oh, man.

Jacob: In New York. And when I stepped out of the car, realized what had happened, the very first thing that came to my mind was that I was missing my glasses.

David: Wow!

Jacob: And, and like, I refused to assess the situation or, or, or to try to remedy it somehow until I found my glasses. And I eventually did and was able to go from there. That event made me realize how much I treasure my existence and I understand that sometimes I owe it to divine intervention. I mean, we so easily could've been killed. And I honestly believe that somebody was looking out for us at that moment. So I try to respect it. In all aspects of life that I can. And I understand that there are going to be times when, when tragedy occurs but I also know that the human spirit is pretty strong and it has the ability to recover from these things. I don't know. That accident I had was a pretty big turning point. And I think from that moment I just appreciated more what was around me. I didn't take as many things for granted. And I also began to understand the delicacy in life.

Jacob (responding to Question 2):Oooh. I'm not sure if I'd go as far to say as there's one collective consciousness that connects all of us. But, yeah, I attribute a lot of things to destiny. To something that's already been divined. I partly believe that I can choose my own destiny, but I do believe there's some higher force guiding me along the way ... I truly believe that there was a reason that I didn't die that morning ... And it may not have even had to do with me. It could've had to do solely with my friend who saved us.

Jacob's responses reveal some of the range of thinking young adults expressed when articulating their theodical beliefs. Jacob found his way toward reflecting on a frightening event: what could have been a fatality while driving. He described how this event heightened his sense both of human strength and of a possibility of divine or cosmic benevolence. Later, in response to the second question, he returned to an affirmation of a guiding higher power, at the same time affirming the importance of human action.

Jacob expressed two of the three primary theodical positions found in young adults' interviews: the *deterministic* position, asserting that events happen for a reason or are intended and guided by forces beyond human understanding; and the *humanistic* position, asserting that events are the result of human action and are given meaning by human intention. The third *randomistic* position, that such events are random and without causal explanation linked to purpose, was not part of Jacob's response.

A Closer Look

Responses to on-site interview questions about theodicy were coded for all 82 interviewees.[1] Coding of responses for theodicy focused primarily on belief, using several general categories as derived from responses themselves:

1. *Deterministic with reference to a deity* (emphasizing supernatural forces behind events),
2. *Deterministic without reference to a deity* (emphasizing formal or final causes for events, in which the events occur due to a future purpose),
3. *Humanistic* (emphasizing human responsibility for events),
4. *Randomistic* (emphasizing chance occurrences and a lack of purpose or cause in events).

Secondary coding focused on coping responses – behaviours enacted and interpersonal milieux sought when facing a traumatic or unexpected negative event.

Responses to Questions 1 and 2 were coded and analysed separately. Responding to the first, open-ended question, most young adults answered by offering some causal explanation for negative life, with 57.3 per cent favouring a deterministic explanation that life events have a divine or fated origin and will make sense later, and only 3.7 per cent stating that negative life events are the results of random or chance probability. The remaining respondents emphasized how they would cope with the situation rather than seeking a causal explanation. Their coping responses focused on redirecting mental attention, ignoring or letting go (18.3 per cent), focusing more narrowly on daily goals (11 per cent), or relying on relational contact (7.3 per cent).

In response to the second, semi-structured question about theodicy, the vast majority of young adults (68.7 per cent) favoured a divine or fated explanation for life events. Only 13.3 per cent stated that there is a level of randomness in life events. The remaining 18 per cent introduced the thematic category of 'humanistic' theodicy, stating explicitly that life events were mostly the result of human action.

To both questions, the majority of young adults in *Making the Transition* stated a deterministic theodicy,[2] asserting in varying degrees that 'everything happens for

---

[1]   As in previous chapters, two raters worked on coding, relying primarily on interviewers' notes and consulting audiotapes when notes were either unclear or incomplete.

[2]   This overall pattern found in interview responses in the *Making the Transition* study are replicated in a parallel study I conducted of 60 young adults involved in creating new Christian religious communities, who responded to the same questions. While references to a deity were more frequent, the overall distribution of deterministic, humanistic and randomistic responses was similar among these committed Christians (D.T. Gortner, 'Young Adults and Religion: How Three Distinct Approaches Influence Personal Theologies, Self-Concepts, and Behaviors', paper presented at the American Academy of Religion Annual Meeting, Boston , MA, November 1999, and D.T. Gortner, *Feast in the Desert: Five*

a reason.' Some explicitly spoke of God, gods, or other divine beings as part of their explanations. But more often, their deterministic statements did not include reference to a deity: the organizing principles, reasons, and purposes behind the tragedies and traumas of life were simply assumed as attributes and forces in the nature of being.

We compared and combined our coding across the two theodicy questions to arrive at final theodical categorizations that best fit each young adult's overall narrative response. This heuristic coding process resulted in the following distribution: 62.6 per cent determinists, 16.9 per cent humanists, and 20.5 per cent randomists. The dominant theodical orientation among young adults was deterministic, with a frequency over thrice that of either humanistic or randomistic orientations (Figure 5.1).

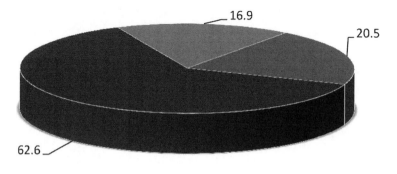

■ Deterministic　■ Humanistic　■ Randomistic

Figure 5.1　Theodicies expressed by *Making the Transition* young adults

We again used 33 transcribed interviews for closer clausal narrative analysis. First, we separated clausal belief statements from coping-response clauses and other clauses indicating uncertainty. This allowed us to check the reliability of raters' more general coding of theodicy, and to generate a more refined and precise qualitative analysis of verbatim responses.[3] We divided theistic and non-theistic

---

Young Adult Ministry Approaches, and Their Critique of Traditional Organized Religion (forthcoming).

[3]　Clausal analysis of transcripts was moderately consistent with more general coding by research assistants from interviewers' and audiotape listeners' notes ($\alpha = .82$), across categories of theodicy. Because of its greater precision, we used clausal analysis results to correct raters' original theodicy classifications for the 33 young adults whose transcripts were analysed, based on majority proportion of clauses of a particular theodical category. Distribution patterns between heuristic coding by research assistants ($n=82$) and intensive clausal analysis ($n=33$) were quite similar, indicating a good cross-section of personal

statements of determinism. A summary of the types of clausal statements of theodicy made by young adults is in Table 5.1.

Over 69 per cent of the clauses comprising young adults' responses to questions of theodicy were belief statements about causes. Most of the remaining clauses were indications of coping responses (21 per cent), divided as follows:

1. relying on others – 2.7 per cent;
2. refocusing attention or reframing the situation – 5.4 per cent;
3. attempting to change the situation – 2.0 per cent;
4. learning from the situation – 3.6 per cent, and
5. simply enduring until the situation abates – 7.3 per cent.

Other clausal statements made in response to the theodicy questions included indications of a lack of coping responses or beliefs regarding negative life events (11 per cent on average). I will explore the relationship of these coping responses to beliefs later in the chapter.

The distributions of young adults' primary theodical positions among the 33 young adults whose interviews were transcribed mostly matched the distribution found in the full collection of 82 interviewees (with 5 per cent lower percentage of determinists). Across the 33 transcripts, deterministic theodical clauses (combining both theistic and non-theistic) were nearly twice as frequent as either humanistic or randomistic clauses.

Going Deeper ...

As was the case for young adult worldviews, greater complexity lurked beneath a simpler, categorical analysis of theodicy. Religious heritage is much more clearly related to young adults' responses to questions of theodicy – but it is not an absolute relationship. Examining verbatim responses of some young adults more directly reveals distinctive patterns of causal reasoning. I have used the Aristotelian concepts of material, efficient, formal and final cause to discuss these different types of causal reasoning present in young adult responses. There are patterns in coping statements as well, that cohere with causal reasoning and provide a roadmap (at least intended, if not yet used) for dealing with tragic and traumatic events. And there are degrees of difference in how strongly young adults are drawn to positive reframing of the situations they encountered or imagined encountering.

As previously, young adults' verbatim responses with commentary provided a window into the depths and varieties of theodical beliefs about ultimate causation in the face of tragedy or trauma, as well as the clarity, breadth and basis of these beliefs. To illustrate how I coded these interview excerpts, I have marked the

---

theologies in the transcripted interviews (deterministic, 62.7 per cent vs. 57.6 per cent; humanistic, 16.9 per cent vs. 15.2 per cent; randomistic, 20.5 per cent vs. 27.2 per cent).

Table 5.1　Examples of theodical clausal statements, by category of theodicy (n=33)

Deterministic clauses – active deity	Deterministic clauses – non-theistic future purpose	Humanistic clauses	Randomistic clauses
God has a plan.	I try to think of the reason this is happening.	Some things happen because people deserve them.	People sometimes have bad luck.
God has a reason.	Everything out there is happening for a purpose.	You have opportunities to make it what you want.	I don't think that anything's like totally predetermined – you just go along with it.
I look to religion.	There may be a reason, but it is unexplainable.	Ultimately you can choose your own way.	Some things happen randomly.
It's part of an ultimate plan	I try to learn from it.	The way that you play the game is really the important part.	You're dealt the cards.
There's probably a group or a culture of higher beings that uses us for entertainment.	Sometimes, numerous things happen to you that cause you to learn one lesson.	I had some control over it and that's why it happened in a way.	I don't think you can justify everything that happens.
There's not just the material world that we see going on.	There is something out of every event that you need to learn.	Every event has its own separate causes which you can trace to a certain extent.	Nothing causing them – that implies that something else is in charge of it.
It's God and Satan and angels and all this stuff we can't see that affects everybody's lives.	If you don't have these challenges … then you wouldn't be as strong a person.	People that might have some kind of personality problem set themselves up for certain things.	When shit happens, it's shit, shit is happening – and it doesn't go beyond that.
God doesn't put anything in front of you that you can't handle.	We're on this earth to learn	I think we give things purpose.	For the most part, tragic things don't have any logic or sense to them.

Deterministic		Humanistic	Randomistic
God's showing you that it's not meant to be for you to have X.	If it hadn't happened, then something else wouldn't have happened.	People's individual lives, we were created with a choice	Some things are just like coincidence.
They happen because of the Devil.	Some things happen for a reason.	You have control over some things.	Bad things can happen at any time.
It's like *something, somewhere* rolls the dice for you.	There are certain variables that are preset	And the rest is up to you.	Look at it as sort of the law of averages.
Average clauses per interview: 1.5	*Average clauses per interview* (both categories) per: 2.7	*Average clauses per interview:* 1.9	*Average clauses per interview:* 2.3
*Average proportion of deterministic clauses (both categories) per response: .37**		*Average proportion of humanistic clauses per response: .14*	*Average proportion of randomistic clauses per response: .20*
Respondents with a primarily deterministic theodicy: 57.6%		*Respondents with a primarily humanistic theodicy: 15.2%*	*Respondents with a primarily randomistic theodicy: 27.3%*

Note: ** $p < .01$, comparing proportions of deterministic clauses to humanistic and randomistic clauses.

first excerpt (Joel's) as follows: belief clauses are underlined, coping clauses are italicized, and each belief clause is marked as deterministic (D), humanistic (H), or randomistic (R).

Randomists Without a Cause

We begin with the randomistic orientations of two young adults whose responses contain little causal reasoning and few ideas about coping. Joel, raised by college- and graduate-educated Roman Catholic parents in a rural working-class community, and Christopher, having grown up in an upper-middle-class small urban community as an agnostic whose parents who had attended college and had come from different religious worlds and socio-economic subcultures. Joel continued to live with his parents and take temporary jobs; Christopher was in the process of changing career paths and entering engineering school.

Joel directly acknowledged the likelihood of negative events happening in people's lives. But aside from noting the possibility that tragedy could strike at any time, he offered no explanation of how this unpredictability was part of the fabric of existence. Unpredictability and randomness were accepted as givens. Thus, Joel focused more on coping responses than on explanatory responses:

> Well, I mean, things go wrong in everybody's life, and even though some things might be going good <u>bad things can happen at any time</u> (R) and *you have to be ready for them* and *expect them to happen.* I mean, <u>a lot of times that's unexpected, something bad happens</u> (R). *So you just gotta deal with it.* And *try to use your friends and loved ones to support you.* That's the main thing … I don't know. *I just try to do something I enjoy. Like listen to music* or something, yet, talk with, *talk it out with somebody.*

Joel's theodicy hinted at randomistic expectations. For Joel, something unexpected might happen at any time – but without any specific reference to causal explanations. Joel's coping responses included anticipation and vigilance, seeking out social support, and self-soothing activity. None of these coping responses point toward a desire to find a reason or cause behind negative events (a form of cognitive reframing of situations). Rather, his responses were focused on emotional recovery and prevention.

In his response to the second question, Joel once again tended toward a randomistic theodicy, but with ample acknowledgement of human causes:

> Joel: I kinda fall in between. <u>You have control over some things</u> (H), and <u>some things you don't have control over</u> (R). So it kinda balances out I think.
>
> Joe: Do you think you could be more specific?

Joel: It's hard to say whether or not, you know, things happen for a reason or not. I mean, if you say that things happen for a reason, I guess you could say, 'Well, I had some control over it and that's why it happened in that way' (H), you know? Or I didn't do this, or I did do that (H). I mean … It's really hard to say.

In the end, Joel acknowledged that negative events might happen for a reason, locating such a possible reason in human efficacy, not predestined causes. In Aristotelian terms, Joel briefly considered efficient cause by humans as a theodical explanation. But this response was conditional, indicating that Joel tended not to think about causes as a response to negative events. Perhaps Joel, adrift and without clear direction in his life, was not sanguine in considering causal thinking in relation to theodicy because it led to thinking about his own responsibility for how things happened in his life.

Christopher gave responses that were more typical of the randomistic orientation. He believed that certain events were due to human causes and others weren't. But he attributed the events not within human control – particularly traumatic or tragic events – to chance or seemingly random causes:

Oh, I don't think there's a purpose behind everything. But I wouldn't say necessarily random. I mean every event has its own separate causes which you can trace to a certain extent. Though I guess some things just do happen randomly. Things, like I suppose somebody dies unexpectedly for whatever reason, um, seems to be basically random.

In response to traumatic or tragic situations, Christopher's randomistic orientation was expressed in this belief statement that hints at a belief in fate, fortune, or a law of averages: 'I just think that things will inevitably swing back up.' In a random world, negative events are unlikely to continue to happen to the same person over a prolonged period – or, stated colloquially, lightning should not strike twice in the same place twice. A randomistic orientation seemed to provide Christopher with hope that, according to a folklore-like law of probabilities, negative events are highly unlikely to persist or continue in one person's life. This belief was paired for Christopher with one primary coping response of perseverance: 'You just have to plough through the bad stuff and keep on trying until they get better.' It becomes easier to persevere and endure hardship if one believes that, according to a 'law' of probabilities, life events will soon become less negative. But this law of probabilities also must retain the possibility of further unpredictable disruption. In this theodical perspective, positive cognitive reframing is a kind of heroic test of will and survival.

The heroic, or at least survivalist, coping response was shared by AnMing, a searching Evangelical Christian from a Chinese household in a North-eastern upper-middle-class suburb, and two atheists, Alexandra and Kasey – one from the same community as AnMing, and the other from a small middle-class southern city. Again, their backgrounds were different, but their theodical orientations were quite similar.

AnMing put into words the language of fate or fortune. Her focus was entirely on coping – and she explicitly eschewed any attempts to explain or justify the negative events of life:

> I think, drawing from my own experiences, I think the bad things that have happened in my family, I really just justify it with, that you gotta take, you know, the card that you're dealt. You know? Just make the best of the card you're dealt. Just kind of make the best of what you have. I think that's the only way. I don't think bad things like that require justification. In the sense that, I don't think you can just, justify everything that happens. But if you can just deal with it as a family, I think that's really important.

> I think that things happen randomly, but the way that you deal with it has a purpose. Or what you come out with has a purpose. So, like I said, it was like, you're dealt the cards and the way that you play the game is really the important part. Not so much that you were dealt really bad cards.

AnMing's language began to express a randomistic theodicy in deterministic terms: her repeated use of the phrase 'the card you're dealt' conjures images of fate, fortune, nature, or the law of probabilities acting upon human lives. She did not explain this latent allusion to cause. 'The cards you're dealt' could refer to genetic inheritances, the unfolding of events in just such a way as to intrude upon one's path, or the will of Allah or ultimate plan in the mind of God; but she made no reference to any source of 'the cards'. Her central causal orientation was randomistic, with no easily identified cause and a sense of the unpredictability of life's unfolding. But more central for AnMing was the response to the tragic or traumatic. For her, the process of making something from one's situation was most important; she sought to reframe negative events in light of her own response of how to live, alluding to family as a source of strength and resolution. AnMing's theodical stance is not entirely unfamiliar to theists: it is found in the biblical books of Ruth, Esther and Ecclesiastes, as well as in medieval poems from Catholic and Muslim societies.[4] As the old English proverb goes (borrowing from Jesus' statement in Matthew 5:45), 'The rain falls on the just and the unjust', and it is in how one responds afterward that sense emerges from what would otherwise be senseless trauma or tragedy.

Kasey, like AnMing, decried any value in attempting to understand reasons and causes for negative life events. She denied any deterministic purposes in the events themselves – except for the purpose of recovery itself. Interestingly, she spoke of the negative life event as carrying an embedded purpose of evoking a

---

[4]   See *The Rubáiyát of Omar Khayyam* and the 13th-century anonymous European monastic poem, *O Fortuna*.

survivalist or heroic coping response. This almost sounds like the language of a 'test', a kind of trial of merit or test of mettle – a theodical explanation found in ancient polytheistic as well as monotheistic stories. For Kasey, the reframing is in the shift to a focus of 'moving on' with life, and in the implied view of the situation as a test of her capacity to survive:

> I think those kind of situations, most of them, you're not supposed to figure out why there are tragedies. Why it happened, why is it you – that's not the purpose of it. The purpose is to see after that happens if you can find something small, anything, out of it to at least go on. The whole purpose of it is just to see if you can get on from there. Basically. it's not that the actual horrible thing has anything to do with you. It's totally, it has nothing to do with you, basically.

Kasey's implicit heroic or survivalist script, perhaps expressive of a social Darwinist ideal of survival of the fittest, moved her to a mixed randomistic/ humanistic theodical orientation. This mixture came through in her response to the second question:

> I think for the most part things are random. But certain people that might have some kind of problem in their personality, they set themselves up for certain things and they wonder, you know, why am I always getting fired? Why do all my cars break down? Those situations I think, they don't realize it, but they put themselves in it. So some things kind of happen like that. But for the most part I think things are random. 'Cause I'm more of a science person anyways. But … it has to be somewhat, a little bit of your own fault. You can't always say it's random. So, I guess I'm in the middle.

Along with the ideal of survival in the face of tragedy or trauma, Kasey held a belief that, frequently, people bring negative events upon themselves due to the choices they make. In Aristotelian terms, this belief is expressed with material and efficient causal reasoning – some negative events occur because of the constitution (that is, the personality) and the continuity of choices of a person. It is a naturalistic explanation, and a natural flip side to her social Darwinist ideal of positive coping. In the end, Kasey's primary orientation was randomistic – but with a strong humanistic leaning and considering just a hint of deterministic 'purpose' embedded in negative events.

Alexandra offered a response that expands on Kasey's perspective. For Alexandra, there were only two possible responses to tragedies and traumas: recovering or not recovering. Like many others with a randomistic perspective, she focused much more on coping responses and beliefs about coping than on causal explanations:

> Alexandra: I, it's not an issue of making sense of it. I don't. But the alternative to recovering is really lousy. The alternative to recovering is not recovering.

And I have no interest in doing that. And, not that I would count myself among the people who have overcome adversity, but I've had a tragic experience. My mother died when I was young. I don't, for example, revert to a god or dismiss a god as a result of a tragic experience. If anything, it's a sort of pragmatic approach. There's nothing to be gained by not recovering. And everything to be gained by recovering. In so far as I explain tragedy, I don't – except that it's neither good nor bad. I mean, I don't attach moral significance to it.

Phaedra: So how do you cope?

Alexandra: When I'm upset? I do very particular things. I write. I read. And I run. But those are to deal with symptoms. Not to deal with the actual event. I don't expect to deal with the actual event. I don't expect to do away with it either.

Alexandra described her own approach as 'pragmatic'. She came to accept tragedy – the death of her mother – as a given, something amoral that is simply part of reality. Her focus was almost solely on coping. For her, recovery was the only alternative, and self-care through personal interests was the path. In essence, she expressed a central belief in human resilience and determination to thrive, regardless of any circumstances. Even though events happen 'randomly and without purpose', for Alexandra the resilient human response is what gave meaning to negative life events: 'It's up to the individual to create a purpose or a meaning. Not after the fact in retrospect: "The cup fell because such and such." But, by my own actions I'm going to endow [this event] with such and such a meaning.'

Perhaps the most compelling account of a randomist without a cause is that of Ly-Hanh, our Vietnamese college student who had left the Buddhist faith of her parents. For Ly-Hanh, it was not simply a matter of not recognizing or finding causes for negative life events; she was actively opposed to such theodical causal reasoning and found its hopes and promises empty. Her opposition to causal reasoning – both humanistic and deterministic – had translated for her into active disbelief rooted in disappointment. To the question 'Why do the good suffer?', she had heard nothing but silence underneath the traditional folk beliefs and practices of her parents. And the lack of deliverance from suffering for herself and for others left her with an active belief in herself as heroically coping, and in nothing else:

I liked to believe the saying that bad things shouldn't happen to good people, but of course that's never the case. I just say that. But I guess I'm jinxed, you know? And, like, if I told my parents, then they would just go and get me an amulet or something or say that I'd probably done something wrong, like, during a celebration I must have not prayed to Buddha, and that's why he's not blessing me. Some kind of crap like that. Myself? Just get out of life [what you can]. Like, your life can't be all happy and perky all the way through. You have to go through some bad things. You go through one bad thing, you have to get back up.

I guess that's the challenge that you have to go through. Can't get back up, then why bother with your life? You just stay in that little slump hole. But it takes a lot more energy and courage to actually get out of that ordeal. Especially if it's a death or even your friend's going through a lot of hard stuff, or yourself. And you just have to get back up, get past it. Get beyond it.

Similar to Alexandra, Ly-Hanh held on to a belief in her own will and fortitude to survive the traumatic and tragic moments resulting from the laws of probability. In her response to the second question, Ly-Hanh laid out her case against both deterministic and humanistic theodicies:

Well I'm like the random. 'Cause, why would everything happen for a reason, you know? Why? Unless you control it yourself. But accidents and stuff, they're accidents. You can't cause them. Well actually you could cause them. But you can't prevent them if you don't know when they're gonna happen. If you're saying that that happened for a reason, why? Is it because you were bad? A lot of bad things happen to good people. And everybody knows it. So it has to be random. I don't believe that everything happened for a reason.

Ly-Hanh later discussed how her beliefs had changed significantly. Her conversion to disillusionment is striking in its absolutism. And her interpretation of one of her experiences – a car accident – is dramatically different from Jacob's interpretation (discussed earlier in the chapter):

My parents taught me to believe in Buddha. But in these past couple years I've come to the point where I just don't believe any more. I don't believe that there's a greater being. [There was a time when] I did as my parents told me. And yet, bad things still happened, you know? Why do we believe in this greater being if they're the one that's supposed to protect us but we still have to go through all this crap? I believe that's part of life. But, when multiple [bad] things just show up at the same time it's just like, who is looking over us, you know? It's like, 'Is it good? Is it bad?' It's come to the point where I just don't believe in it anymore. I'll do whatever my mom says when it comes to ceremonies or praying or even offering incense. But I don't really believe it truly. It's just an act to please my mother. I truly don't believe in anything. All I believe is in myself. 'Cause you're the one that's gonna getting everything done, you know? And you're the one to have to walk through life. So why do you believe that there's somebody greater than yourself? It's just like, to offer you security. So I don't believe …

Right when I started college that year, one of my friends got really really sick. And she's supposedly a Buddhist too, and what not. And she was only 22, and she got diagnosed with cancer. And, even after chemotherapy she's so weak right now and, like, she's not even herself anymore. It's like, why is this happening to her, you know? She's always done as she's told. She never objected to anybody, her parents, her beliefs, anything. But when the point where she, she really needed some support and, like, just there's nobody there. No greater being. But why, you know? This shouldn't be happening to her.

And then, this past year, I've had a series of things happen to me, like I got into a car accident in my car. Another car accident out of my car while I was a pedestrian. And then I was like, near death I think. There was nobody with me. I had to, like, control the car myself. I had to jump out of that car's way, you know? Near-death things where you know there should be somebody there but there wasn't. And like, you had to control it all in your hands.

It's just, I think it's bullshit what my parents say. They're so traditional and believe exactly what their parents taught them. And they expect the same from me. But, they don't want me to think freely about religion or anything like that. I don't believe in what my parents do.

Ly-Hanh's stark refutation of her parents' theodical beliefs may seem to some wonderfully parsimonious, but to others cognitively impoverished and psychologically immature. On the one hand, Ly-Hanh presents a simple either-or question to the universe – something like 'Either there is a powerful and benevolent force that can and will intervene in people's lives, or there isn't.' This reads on the surface like an insightful and economical reduction of the question of ultimate causation – requiring the universe's adherence to Occam's Razor. But Ly-Hanh's belief was rooted in disillusionment of a similarly simple and economical solution, that the world and its unfolding events were ordered by a moral economy that would have immediate consequences and provide immediate payoffs. And her solution – 'All I believe in is myself' – brings this emphasis on the most simple, economical and predictable solution to a solipsistic conclusion. But on the other hand, the absolutism of Ly-Hanh's stance may reflect her own cognitive development as an emerging adult leaving adolescence; in Piagetian terms, formal operations have not yet bloomed into post-formal, dialectical and synthetic thought. To borrow an idea from Sharon Parks,[5] Ly-Hanh's conversion merely brought her from absolute endorsement to absolute refutation, but it left her thinking at a parallel stage of absolutism. Ly-Hanh's absolutism and disengagement from thinking about ultimate causes of negative life events, common among other randomists, may short-circuit the inquisitive mind just as much as an overly simple deterministic or humanistic set of explanations.

In 2001, Pascal Boyer in *Religion Explained* argued that the beliefs of the religious mind are simply the epiphenomenal consequences of naturally occurring psychological processes, such as the search for causal agents, distortions of

---

[5]   Sharon Parks, *Big Questions, Worthy Dreams : Mentoring Young Adults in Their Search for Meaning, Purpose, and Faith* (San Francisco, CA: Jossey-Bass, 2000).

memory and the confirmation bias.[6] Boyer's argument can be extended to examine the beliefs of the randomist as well as the determinist. Few randomists spent time citing material or efficient causes – because these are, ultimately, not satisfying explanations. Without an accompanying sense of consolation or moral good or justice, the quest for causal explanations is quickly abandoned as meaningless, and the claim of randomism, that 'shit happens,' is cited – but this then slips toward an assent to the Fates or the overarching laws of probability. Pragmatic concern with how to live and how to recover takes precedence over concern about causes, because it is more emotionally and motivationally satisfying. So, in place of causal thinking comes an emphasis on the hero's quest – the heroic narrative of the surviving and thriving Self. Such a pattern of theodical belief might be found in an atheist, a mature Buddhist, or a questioning Christian pilgrim.

Theistic Determinists: A Benevolent Deity, a Guiding Force and a Path for Growth

In contrast to randomists, deterministic young adults expressed beliefs in an ultimate purpose behind all situations and events encountered in life, including the tragic or traumatic. Many deterministic young adults based their belief in ultimate purpose in a belief in God. They described God as a benevolent deity who was a master architect, the ground and guiding force behind all individuals' lives. They stopped short of saying that God directly caused tragedies or traumas, instead saying that God directed all events toward a higher purpose for each person, either guiding or allowing situations to unfold so that new growth or development can occur. Excerpts below are from Cory and MeiLi, whom we have already met, and Michael and Liz. All of them grew up in religious households and had significant exposure to religious thought and practice – Cory as a Mormon, MeiLi and Liz as evangelical Protestants, and Michael as both Jewish and Roman Catholic. These young adults had all experienced difficult and trying situations which they discussed in their responses. Michael was a pre-med college student in biology, and had broken up with his girlfriend who cheated on him. Liz, a graduate student in food science and nutrition who served as a teaching assistant and kitchen manager for a lab kitchen professor notorious for yelling at students, discussed the death of her grandmother. MeiLi, an immigrant from Hong Kong, continued to wrestle with her sense of cultural displacement even in the face of improved opportunities. Cory, our young Mormon, talked about the death of his friend and the way he came to terms with it in the context of unexpected conversations with strangers during his work as a missionary. These circumstances, while not violent or disruptive on the scale of rape, war, or natural disaster, were high-impact stressors over which they had no control and which significantly disrupted their sense of order and security.

---

[6]   Pascal Boyer, *Religion Explained* (New York: Basic Books, 2001), pp. 297–330.

Cory's responses to questions about theodicy were drawn primarily from the doctrines and personal experiences in his religious tradition, Mormonism. His response to the second question was out of a deterministic orientation, but with a decidedly benevolent deity as the driving force behind life's events. Cory took pains to clarify his deterministic theodicy: all events for Cory had their cause in a deity whose intention was not for amusement or punishment, but for each person's growth and education. Cory's religion provided him with opportunities for experiences that could further imprint this belief. This was exemplified in Cory's response to the first question – Cory drew directly from his personal experience as a missionary, after a personal tragedy:

> How do I make sense? Probably an example would be when my friend was killed while I was in Australia. I was just, as you can imagine, I was just totally upset about it, being so far away from home and not being able to come back for the funeral … That, that was really difficult for me and I was really depressed and my mind was just totally not on the work that I was there to do. In our church we teach that Christ has made it possible for us to be with our loved ones or our family, friends, when we leave this life. That we have the possibility of being with those people again. And that really gave me hope.

> And it was the weirdest thing … I was a missionary while I was there and we were out knocking on doors, and a lady answered the door, and she was a middle-aged woman and I could tell she had been crying. And I asked her, what's the matter? Are you ok? And she said that her sister had just died. And I just started to cry. And I told her what had happened, you know, with my friend. And I told her that you can see her again, that death doesn't, isn't the end. That it's not the end of the story. You can be with them again. And being able to convey that belief to her, I mean, it comforted her, and she felt better and I felt better. Even though I had known that before, it took me talking to her and just realizing how blessed I was to know that I can be with my loved ones when I leave this life.

> I believe that everything that happens to us has a purpose. I don't believe that God, that he's the kind of person that puts things in our lives to hurt us or to cause us pain. I think he allows those things to happen to us in our life to teach us, to help us to learn, and to grow.

Cory's experience of soothing himself through the process of reciting his beliefs to another distressed person, and his sense of being in the right place at the right time for someone in need, imprinted his deterministic theodicy more deeply. He was attempting in his story to convey how, without experiencing his friend's death, he would not have been able to talk in the same way to the middle-aged woman during his missionary experience. An implicit script seemed to undergird this story that gave structure to his theodicy: 'What follows explains what precedes.'

MeiLi, a young Chinese Evangelical Christian, offered a similar perspective. She was explicit in saying 'I think everything happens for a reason.' When pressed further for an explanation, she attempted haltingly to articulate a belief in a God who draws all events toward a purposeful, redemptive future. This future desired growth explains the past and makes the past a necessary path: 'I think each event, or each thing that happens, somehow God is behind it and he's using that to shape you and to build you up and to make you a stronger person.' For MeiLi, 'God is in charge', 'there is a reason behind what happens', and 'the reason – and cause – comes from a preordained future.' And that 'I can't explain it, but I just have to rely on my faith.'

In Aristotelian terms, both MeiLi and Cory make use of final and formal causal reasoning. Things are as they are because God has made them for a purpose, and that purpose is one that unfolds toward a future ideal form. The language of becoming is embedded in their responses: for them, God is drawing them through hardships and difficulties to some fuller form of completeness, new growth, and learning – to become fuller forms of MeiLi and Cory. This focus on learning and growth is not far from randomists' heroic narrative of the self – except that the emphasis moves beyond survival or recovery to growth and learning, and beyond self alone to self under divine guidance. The trauma or tragedy is reframed not only in light of a belief in a benevolent Deity, but in light of a belief in a future ideal state of being, toward which one is moving and being moved.

Michael drew on both his Jewish and Roman Catholic heritages and on some core ideas given to him by his parents as a foundation for his theodical framework:

> Michael: I guess if things were going really badly then all I would do is try to find a way to change it. I wouldn't necessarily try to make sense of what's happening. I would just try to find whatever I could do to make it better … Both my parents have always told me to do whatever I can to change what I can and to accept whatever I can't change, so … That's pretty much how I live my life, I change what I can and I accept what I can't. I definitely think everything happens for a reason. I just feel like anything that's happened in my life I can see how if it hadn't happened then something else wouldn't have happened.

> *Laura: Can you give me an example of what you're thinking?*

> Michael: Well, if I hadn't broken up with the one girl [who cheated on me] I never would have met the other one. And it just seems like everything that happens is kind of interrelated.

Michael stated a deterministic theodicy, and rooted the determining reasons or purposes of events in future outcomes and pathways that result from such events. It can be expressed simply in the following axiomatic theodical formula: what follows explains what precedes. This axiomatic formula is an underlying belief expressed by many young adults we interviewed. Michael might express a more nuanced formulation: what precedes leads directly to what follows, and what follows was meant to happen. In Aristotelian terms, this is final-cause reasoning: the future explains the past, and is in some way determinative of the past itself. This kind of causal thinking depends upon some sense of purposeful form and design in the universe and in the unfolding of individual lives. For Michael, this was God: 'I'm a Roman Catholic, so I believe basically everything that's there. I mean, there's certainly a lot of contradictions in the Bible that you've got to get around, but in general I go with what the church says.' His response to difficult situations, rooted in his parents' teaching, was to attempt to make a difference and to accept what could not be changed.

Liz, who grew up as an evangelical Protestant and was shaped significantly in her youth by Christian camp and youth group experiences, described herself as 'not involved' religiously for several years and moving through many doubts but 'beginning to come around'. Her responses were a bit more complicated than Michael's. For Liz, religion was a way to make sense of bad events in a positive way:

> I think I usually go to religion as something. Like I just pictured a tragic car accident killing family members or something. And I think I usually just … that's pretty much the only way you can make sense of it in a positive way. It just kind of gives me hope that things can be worse and they get better. And I think with religion too, you can never really know everything so it's almost kind of reassurance that, okay, someone else is taking care of that. And I can deal with Now and know that there's Something Else working.

> I go to the same thing, like you know, God wants this to happen. Well, it could be that the reason just isn't quite visible yet. I mean, if I can go back to a break-up, it seems so terrible, but of course I broke up with him so long ago so I can find the person that I actually will love more. I think I might be in the middle, but I think I would tend to sway more towards things happen for a reason. At least the big things, some things … I don't know why I really think that. It just seems like usually the picture becomes clearer after a while. You know, something happens and at least there's a positive end to … My grandmother died and it was terrible. However, she was in so much pain that … um … things like that. I've never come across an experience like a car accident or something where someone's died. I don't know how I would explain that.

For Liz, religious affirmations and beliefs in a higher order of structure and direction in the cosmos and in individual lives helped her let go of events she could not understand and trust that, in the long run, good things would result. Liz was able to examine her own religious beliefs and thoughts with some distance. As a result, she was clear about the way such theodical beliefs in a benevolent, directing deity functioned: they allowed her to carry on with everyday life 'and know there's Something Else working' at a different level of reality – so that what was beyond her control was still under control, and with the intention of good. And yet, Liz did not seem entirely satisfied with her own response and recognized its limitations in the face of deep tragedy or trauma. She could not even quite bring herself to say aloud a theodical explanation she likely had heard in relation to her grandmother's death – a purpose of alleviation of suffering.

The reference points for these young adults differed widely, from family deaths to relationship break-ups. Their direct experience with significant loss also varied widely. As Liz implied for herself, these young adults' theodicies were not yet fully tested in the crucibles of truly significant tragedies or traumas. But their experiences of negative life events did not differ that dramatically from those of their randomist counterparts. It is little more than a game to attempt to weigh whether or not persons have experienced losses significant enough to justify their theodical beliefs.

Liz's theodicy was most closely akin to what Christian Smith in *Soul Searching* described as the normative cultural belief pattern of American youth: 'Moralistic Therapeutic Deism'.[7] This generalized belief-system can be summarized as 'God is out there, I've got to be good, and God is watching out for our best and wants us to be happy.' But it's not an exact match. There is a sense, in Liz's responses, of a deity who is an ultimate designer and architect, giving shape and meaning not only to the world but to individual lives – not merely a detached deity ready to help when needed, and not simply interested in Liz's happiness (although Liz expects that ultimately good will result from tragedy or trauma). Furthermore, the theodicies of Cory and MeiLi do not match with Smith's moralistic therapeutic deism. For Cory and MeiLi, God's benevolent direction was not for their comfort and happiness, but for their growth and development (and, by way of consequence, for their *ultimate* happiness). Divine intention for them moved beyond securing human self-esteem. The focus was on how growth might be found through tragic or traumatic experiences. Michael expressed a similar trust in the potential for growth – and for his own agency – in his family's version of the well-known Serenity Prayer, attributed to theologian Reinhold Niebuhr. His deterministic orientation allowed him a means by which to accept the things he could not change, while remaining actively engaged in changing things he could:

> God grant me the serenity to accept the things I cannot change; courage to change the things I can; and wisdom to know the difference.

> Living one day at a time; enjoying one moment at a time; accepting hardships as the pathway to peace; taking, as He did, this sinful world as it is, not as I would have it; trusting that He will make all things right if I surrender to His Will; that I may be reasonably happy in this life and supremely happy with Him forever in the next.

---

[7] Christian Smith, *Soul Searching* (New York: Oxford University Press, 2005), pp. 118–71.

The prayer summarizes better than 'moralistic therapeutic deism' the expressions of personal theology found among these young adults. A deterministic theodicy focused on a benevolent deity functions as a basis for acceptance of life as it comes, space for personal agency to change and learn, and trust and optimism that things will change for the better. At its worst, it might result in a passive stance toward life and toward any process of survival or recovery; it might keep one from looking at more material and efficient causes of negative events and addressing people with responsibility for such events. At its best, its function is not far from the function of a randomistic theodicy that calls forth the heroic self. Between randomism and theistic determinism, it is the *locus* of survival, recovery, growth and thriving that differs. And for the theistic determinist, the self is not merely passive: the self searches in an open posture for opportunities presented in the world and by God for recovery and thriving.

Vaguely Theistic Determinists: The Future Explains the Past

There are a number of deterministic theodicies other than those above. One type may be described as a 'vaguely theistic deterministic theodicy'. Young adults who expressed this kind of theodicy – such as Stefani and Shanille featured below, and Jacob featured earlier in this chapter – were often among those renegotiating their relationship with religion. For these young adults, causal reasoning reflected the idea that 'what follows explains what precedes.' References to a deity were oblique or somewhat conflicted.

Stefani described her response to negative life events as optimistic, an intentional search for the 'silver lining': 'I will probably find what was best ... what came out of it. For instance, I hate my job, but it's how I found my fiancé ... so I typically try to find the good thing out of it, out of a bad situation.' This coping response suggests a deterministic orientation, which she stated more explicitly in her response to the second question. While she claimed to believe 'somewhere in between' a deterministic and randomistic orientation, her specific statements of belief were all deterministic in nature. Having rejected her Christian (Lutheran) background, she did not believe in a benevolent deity, but entertained the possibility of a group of puckish deities whose intervention in human life is for amusement – a religious belief more akin to ancient Roman or Greek polytheism:

> 'I don't believe that there's one ... all-knowing God who ... the typical Christianity way that I was brought up. I tend to believe that there's probably a group or a culture of higher beings that basically just use us for entertainment and fuck with our lives every now and then. That's about it.'

Stefani's response to the second question seems generally pessimistic – she saw negative events as predetermined or manipulated by higher beings who had no benevolent intentions. However, her coping response of looking for good consequences of negative events belied a quest for benevolent determinism –

'what follows explains what precedes, and the end is meant to be good.' While she wrestled with how to describe this in relation to anything like theism, her optimism kept her looking for positive events that, as outcomes of other negative situations, justified and gave her a reason for those situations. It is a kind of final or reverse-efficient causal reasoning.

Shanille stated a theodical orientation that was unambiguously deterministic. For her, 'everything happens for a reason', and the reason is for the purpose of learning something. In this way, Shanille's theodical beliefs were similar to those of Philip: the purpose behind negative life events is for learning and the building of character. But she differed from Philip in one fundamental way: she believed in an external source, undefined but benevolent, guiding the occurrence of negative events. Shanille's upbringing in the Roman Catholic tradition could have shaped this belief, but her immersion in Wiccan religion could also have contributed to her sense of order and benevolent purpose in the universe, guiding events in people's lives:

> I've always believed that everything happens for a reason. And that every event, whether it be good or tragic, is gonna be something where we can learn and grow from it. And that there is something out of every event that you need to learn. And even sometimes you have numerous things happen to you that cause you to learn one lesson. Because you're not learning it. When tragic things happen, I try not to say this is the reason that it happened. But at least take it as it is and try to learn whatever it is that I need to learn from it. Or to help the people that need to learn from it, learn something.

> Yeah. I do believe that some things happen randomly. I think that I fall with it somewhere in between. The majority of things happen for a purpose. And I think that actually, everything happens for a purpose, somewhere. The purpose may not lie with me. So that particular event may have happened randomly to me, but it happened for a purpose for somebody else. So, you know, everything out there is happening for a purpose. I guess.

Shanille's acknowledgement of some events happening randomly is none the less subsumed by a more global assertion – that a seemingly random event to one person might have occurred for a purpose in another person's life. In such a strong deterministic orientation, even seemingly random events had an explanation and predestined function – if not for her, then for somebody else. In Shanille's theodical orientation, nothing was purely left to chance. From a contemporary Wiccan perspective, Shanille might have assumed animistic forces of nature at work, or, from her Catholic background, Shanille might have continued to draw on ideas of an all-knowing God. In either case, it was possible for Shanille to assume benevolence at work in the unfolding of life events, with an ultimate end of learning and development.

The Determinist and the Devil: The World as a Cosmic Battleground

Beth's theodical orientation, though deterministic like Shanille's, was not necessarily benevolent. For Beth, negative events happened for a reason, but the reason was not for the purpose of human learning. With some coaxing to overcome fear of embarrassment, Beth stated explicitly, 'I know that when bad things happen to people it's not because of God or God's not making it happen … They happen because of the Devil … That's who the bad things come from.' Beth viewed reality from a dualistic perspective: material versus spiritual, and the Devil versus God. From this perspective, negative events in people's lives might often be outcomes or reflections of a more cosmic conflict between evil and good:

> It helps me make sense of it because there's not just the material world that we see going on. There's, you know, God and Satan and angels and all this stuff that we can't see that's going on that affects everybody's lives but that they don't…see it. It's going to change the world. So for me, looking at it through that perspective instead of just the material world you can understand better why things happen.

Beth's deterministic theodicy shared similarities with that in ancient Greek polytheism, in which human life was often used as a staging by the gods to act out their conflicts. It bears kinship to Zoroastrian theology, in which the deity of malevolence and chaos is almost equal in power to the deity of benevolence and order. As such, there is little benevolent or purposeful in negative events – they are caused by the Devil, without any higher purpose but to harm people. In this theodicy, there is a type of aggrandizement of human experience, in that negative events are full of meaning beyond the simple tangible qualities of the events.

But Beth's cosmic determinism did not eliminate human responsibility in her theodicy. In her second response, Beth emphasized the importance of human choice and responsibility for consequences: 'I think there's some things that are planned and that are going to happen, but ultimately you can choose your own way.' It seems that Beth's cosmic determinism magnified not only the meaning of negative events, but also the meaning and purpose of her own behaviour in daily life – not only did the events impacting her life have some cosmic relevance and purpose, but also her behavioural choices were rich with meaning in terms of her following or rejecting a divine plan.

Navigating Between Humanistic and Randomistic Theodicies

Not all young adults expressed a theodical orientation that was purely from a single perspective. Many young adults indicated some mixture of two of the three orientations, with one clearly dominant position. Combinations most likely were deterministic/humanistic and humanistic/randomistic. Lillian, an atheist dental student married to a devout Roman Catholic, and Jennifer, a Unitarian-

Universalist college freshman, are two intriguing examples of young adults with theodicies blending humanistic and randomistic beliefs.

Lillian offered several real-life examples in the process of responding to the theodicy questions. She began by talking about her cousin's suicide, later mentioned people who cheated on tests, and ended by referring to the murderous shootings at Columbine High School in 1999. She vacillated between a randomistic perspective and a humanistic perspective – even in reference to her own cousin, which struck her more personally:

> Lillian: My cousin committed suicide a couple years ago, and so that was sort of a bad thing. But I mean, it takes a couple days for you to even realize it happened. And then you just talk about it and talk about your feelings. After a while, after it happens, I don't know, after a couple months it sort of gets a little better.

> *Charles: And, how did you make sense of that?*

> Lillian: I don't know. It's really hard to rationalize something like that. But I guess you just figure that he was unhappy and that was his way of dealing with the situation. Not necessarily the best choice, but that was … Well, I mean, you had to find some sort of way of explaining it. I guess … I don't know. You don't really ever really explain why he did it. But you try to figure out reasons why.

It was difficult for Lillian to talk about this situation, and particularly challenging to talk about how she thought about it afterwards. Lillian focused on efficient causal reasoning, but this brought her close to the psychologically uncomfortable place of assigning responsibility and blame. In the case of suicide, how comfortable is it to assign moral responsibility to the one who has died – especially if it is one's kin?

Lillian's tension between randomistic and humanistic orientations continued in her response to the second question. She struggled with articulating what she believed, but talked herself through her thoughts to draw a clear distinction between types of situations to which she assigns different beliefs:

> I think I fall somewhere in between. Like, for instance, I don't think tragedies [happen] just because somebody's bad or anything like that, you know what I mean? I think it's sometimes random. But then other things happen for a reason, like, if somebody is not studying or whatever then they don't do well on a test because they didn't study. I mean, some things have reasons, sometimes they don't … Pretty much I think that it's when you can control things that things happen for a reason. But I don't know. I mean, like, the Columbine thing … they couldn't control that. That was just sort of a random thing. I mean, the people that actually committed the act could've controlled. But the people who actually had it happen to them, that was just a random thing.

For Lillian, the distinction came down to the question of agency. If something happened to someone because of actions that person took, she assigned this kind of situation to a humanistic theodicy – human actions beget human consequences. But, if something happened to someone simply because of being in the wrong place at the wrong time, she assigned this kind of situation to a randomistic theodicy.

Most intriguing about this distinction is the rift in causal reasoning and assignment of agency that it reveals. The Columbine High School case, in Lillian's causal reasoning, yielded two theodical explanations: (1) for the shooter, a clear assignment of cause and responsibility; (2) for the victims, a random universe acting on them. Lillian correctly assigned not causal agency to the victims – but she described the event as random from their vantage points. And yet, the event was not random. It was unanticipated, and news media and investigators expended significant efforts looking for missed signs that, if read and understood correctly, could have led to prevention of the shootings. Who was wounded or killed was not planned – but that people would be wounded or killed was planned. In this case, who became victims might be described as a matter of chance or randomness. But the cause of suffering and death was a person.

The rift in Lillian's causal reasoning may be related to how she talked about her cousin's suicide. Talking about humans as causal agents of negative life events quickly approaches the assignment of responsibility and blame, and may in some people's minds be synonymous mental actions. Additionally, assigning randomness to cruel tragedies such as the shootings at Columbine High School may in an odd way afford the victims a dignity that could not be expressed in the same way as simply sticking with the cold, diffuse murderous intent of a fellow student.

Jennifer talked about her father's sudden death, just six months prior to her interview. When we as social scientists or practical theologians come to such moments in our research, we must pause and be prepared to listen with care and presence:

Jennifer: My father died in September. So I have, I can use that.

David: I'm sorry ...

Jennifer: Yeah ... Thanks ... So, he had a heart attack suddenly. Apparently he had some warning signs but he didn't tell us about them. So we had no idea. So it was completely sudden. Just basically died instantly. I kind of explain the fact that it was instant as that would be what he wanted, because he's not a person who could sit still ... He didn't even like to sleep 'cause you weren't getting anything done. It was counter-productive. So I kind of looked at the fact that it was sudden as a good thing ... Because he would've been a horrible hospital patient or anything. I kind of always thought that if something horrible happened that I would use religion. I don't really, I'm not religious now ... But I've kind of always been well, if it's ever necessary, then I'll do that. I'll take that route. But I still haven't felt that it's necessary. I don't know ... I mean, people just come and go and you can't, can't really control it. So.

David: So in terms of making sense of all of that, how have you done that?

Jennifer: I just move on. I mean, I think it kind of helped actually that I was at school, because I had already been at school for a month. So I did have friends at school already. So obviously I came home, I was home for a week, and then I went back to school because that's what he would've wanted and that's what I had to do. There isn't really choice. A month into the semester, you know. Have to continue with your grades and everything. So.

Jennifer was still in a process of coming to terms with her own loss and grief. She had not taken or been given much time to grieve. For people her age (18) and younger, delayed grief responses are not uncommon. Her coping response of 'moving on' and her citation of deterministic beliefs that attempt to explain her father's sudden death in light of a possible alternate future that would have been undesirable are among the standard fare of responses heard by clergy and counsellors who work with people in bereavement.

Perhaps in the face of death, even the most ardent humanist or randomist might leak deterministic claims. But Jennifer later returned quite clearly to a humanistic orientation to theodicy, with an underlay of randomism. In response to the second question, she located herself as 'probably in between':

I think everything between life and death happens with the purpose of somebody on earth. I don't really believe in fate. I think there are a lot of coincidences in life. And I don't believe that things are completely random and happen for no reason at all. So, I believe that most things are driven by people. There are, you know, human reasons. And then everything else I just kind of go, I don't know where that came from. But I don't really try to explain everything. Just, there are some things that are not explainable. As far as I'm concerned.

Jennifer's stance was in keeping with her religious tradition: Unitarian Universalists often describe their religion as a humanists' religion. Her focus on human agency even found its way into her discussion about her father. His death was in keeping with how he lived his life – in other words, the form of his death was consistent with the form of his life. Formal and efficient causal reasoning served Jennifer well – and when she encountered circumstances that taxed such reasoning, she was comfortable dismissing them as unexplainable and thus 'random'.

Courageous Humanists: Acknowledging Real Causes, Coping Through Strength of Will

Philip, in the midst of discussing theodicy, revealed his history of serious and potentially life-threatening medical emergencies. His way of making sense of his

situation at the time was not to look for a reason behind his health problems, but to shift his priorities and motivations for how he wanted to live his life:

> I remember my freshman year was probably the worst. The doctor told me oh, I probably wouldn't make it to graduation. I thought that was pretty cruel thing for him to say. It was a misdiagnosis, but for a few weeks I didn't think that I would have very many more years left to live. So. It was weird because I thought about, well, finally, if you only have a year left to live, what are you gonna do? Go to Disney World? Do all the other stuff? Travel the world? And then I realized that I really didn't want to do all that stuff anyhow. I want to do what I'm doing right now. And I want to live exactly the life that I have going on right now.

Philip's no-regrets, no-nonsense approach to his own negative life events framed for him his theodical orientation. An agnostic who had been raised Roman Catholic, Philip believed that negative events served as character-building experiences in people's lives:

> I look at people that were, something bad has never happened to that person. And I say, you know, what have they experienced in this world? How do you know when the really good times are unless you've had a really bad time? And you become a better person with every bad experience. There's a saying that we use at West Point that that which does not kill us makes us stronger. And I kind of believe it. Every bad experience I've ever had just makes me have a better perspective on life.

This orientation is not strictly deterministic in the sense I have presented so far. Philip's statements above strongly imply a mixture of two theodical beliefs: 1) negative events serve a function in people's lives, and 2) it is up to the individual to learn what he or she can from the experience. This combination of beliefs left Philip with a generally optimistic outlook on negative life events: not the optimism of 'things can only get better', but the optimism of 'this will make me a better person.' Philip's focus was not on causal explanations, but on outcomes.

In Philip's response to the second question, he refuted the validity of any predestination of negative life events. He vacillated in his response between a randomistic and humanistic orientation, in the end gravitating more toward a humanistic perspective – but drawing a clear distinction against determinism by arguing that events have prior causes but are not caused or planned by something in the future:

> In my life I don't think I have a lot of things that just happen. Occasionally you get ... a wrench thrown in the conks ... I think things do just happen, but I think they're built upon the past, things that happened. Rather than built backwards in time from ... this purpose thing ... Nothing causing them. Because that implies that something else is in charge of it. So there's a reason for them happening.

But I guess the reason would be that things that have come before. I don't know
if anything's pushing all the events to happen.

Philip's sense of meaning in negative events was derived primarily from prior
causes and outcomes – both localized in human action. For Philip, there was a
logical causal chain leading to many events (although many things 'just happen');
but the primary meaning derived from negative events was found in learning and
character development – both human outcomes. In Aristotelian terms, Philip relied
on both efficient and final causal reasoning. Philip's theodical orientation did not
subscribe to the statement 'what follows explains what precedes.' Rather, Philip's
underlying belief might best be summed up in two statements: 'What happened
before explains what follows, but what follows gives value to what precedes.' The
focus on growth holds out a final form of a future ideal Philip, as yet unrealized,
that will impart meaning to events through the growth that is pursued.

Steve, our atheist chef, presented another compelling example of how a
humanistic theodicy functions when a person encounters unexpected negative
events. In Steve's response to the second question, he clearly placed himself in
a theodical orientation that was neither deterministic (in the sense of divine or
fatalistic predestination) nor randomistic. Steve attributed causes of events to
factors and qualities endemic to the situation or actors: 'They [negative events]
happen for reasons, but it's not a reason that exists outside of them. I mean,
everything has its own internal logics and processes have their tendencies and
their paths of their development, but they don't have an extrinsic determination.'

Steve's response points to a humanistic theodicy, in which one looks for
the causes of events within the individuals and groups involved. His response
carries reference to both efficient and formal causes – people and situations affect
each other directly, but also unfold according to their 'tendencies' and 'paths of
development', which are in some way intrinsic to their nature.

With such an undergirding belief, Steve did not look for hidden causes in the
face of negative events. Rather, he focused on his emotional responses as important
resources for coping and change – as stated in his response to the first question:

> There isn't any way to make sense of it. I mean, you could figure out the causes,
> but that doesn't, in some sense, explain why it could happen to a good person.
> I mean, it doesn't explain why it happened to you. But, essentially I think the
> emotion that's designed to make sense of it is anger. You know? You, you feel
> angry about what's happened and the course that things have taken. Or, if it's
> completely unavoidable then, I mean, to the degree of which it's unavoidable
> you just have to accept it, you know? And the degree which it's changeable
> and needn't have happened, well that's when I think that anger steps in. Anger
> is what helps you make sure that it doesn't happen to other people, you know?
> A tool that connects you to the rest of world and re-establishes a connection
> where ... if you feel rejected because you didn't get the help, the world let this

happen to you in some sense. I mean, I think that's the primary feeling of anger,
is, 'How could this happen to anybody?'

Steve outlined his own struggle with theodicy from a humanistic perspective.
While there may be objective causes to negative events, those explanations did
not provide Steve with an adequate explanation for why the events happened
to a specific person. As for a randomistic theodicy, the causal explanations in
a humanistic theodicy do not imbue the negative event with personal meaning,
and one is left with the struggle for 'making sense' of it. Steve highlighted the
particular challenge of sense-making in situations of injustice or in situations that
still might be altered. Without the satisfaction of causal explanations, Steve was
left with emotion as a starting-point for constructing meaning. For Steve, anger
was a primary emotion activated in negative situations in which the outcome might
be changed for himself or for others in the future. He indicated that anger was an
emotional signal of a deep sense of injustice or unfairness, which in turn motivated
him to act for change. In other words, anger was a signal that things were not as
they should be – that an ideal had been violated. And it was the motivation to
act for change that created personal meaning in the event – meaning that helped
him reconnect with the world by looking for ways to prevent similar things from
happening to others.

The closer look at these narratives reveals both complexities and consistencies
in young adults' theodical beliefs. Overall, there is a consistent quest for the
heroic narrative of the self that survives tragedy and trauma, grows and develops
as a consequence, and arrives at a place of thriving. It is a common thread that
echoes the tone of the redemptive narratives among American middle-aged adults
as documented by Dan McAdams in *The Redemptive Self*.[8] There is a consistent
disinterest in relying upon material and efficient causal explanations for tragic
and traumatic events for purposes of sense-making. There is some consistency
to an underlying assumption (rooted perhaps in an array of mental images,
formulas and ideas about idealized existence) that tragedies, traumas and other
such negative events should not occur. But there are also complex differences
in how various deterministic and humanistic theodicies are expressed. There are
limits, inconsistencies and disengagements in the logic of each of the theodicies
expressed. They are not elegant. But they are at least somewhat functional, with
differing degrees of cognitive maturity and sophistication.

Patterns at Play

In 1980, Melvin Lerner published *Belief in a Just World*. In this book, Lerner
presented social psychological evidence that 'belief in a just world,' a folk theory

---

[8]   Dan McAdams, *The Redemptive Self* (New York: Oxford University Press, 2006).

of naturally occurring retributive or instructive justice, is quite common and nearly pervasive, transcending cultural and historical boundaries, and operating at subtle levels of social interaction and social judgement.[9] 'Belief in a just world' holds that events occur because people deserve them or need them in order to become better people. Divine, fated, or human causes are used by people to explain how people 'get what they deserve'.

On the surface, the overall pattern of theodical orientations among our emerging adults lines up with Lerner's documentation in prior generations of people seeking some causal explanation for suffering. A divine or fated source of life events – that is, that all life events have a purpose or 'reason' directed toward an intended or instructive future – which is the most typical belief associated with a 'belief in a just world', was the most common orientation among *Transition* young adults. Add to this the humanistic theodical orientation, which relies on efficient and formal causal reasoning to arrive at conclusions that humans are the source of their own and each others' misery, and nearly all of our young adults expressed some form of Lerner's 'belief in a just world'.

But Lerner's model does not adequately account for the depth of variations in theodicy. Lerner does not differentiate between humanistic and deterministic theodicies, nor does he differentiate these from a randomistic orientation. Lerner's linear continuum ranges from ardent affirmation in cosmic justice to disavowal of cause. But the preceding qualitative analyses in this chapter does not support such a linear relationship.

The difference between determinists, humanists and randomists can be further clarified through cross-tabulation of responses to our two interview questions about theodicy. I used the categorizations of young adults' causal explanations for Question 2 to look for similarities and differences in their belief and coping responses to Question 1. Figure 5.2 shows differences and similarities in the percentage of young adults expressing coping and belief responses to Question 1, among the three theodical orientations categorized from responses to Question 2.

There was not only a clear consistency of belief types across Questions 1 and 2, but also a clear relationship between coping responses to Question 1 and belief types from Question 2. Determinists were least likely to state coping responses, but most likely to state divine or fate-related explanations. Both humanists and randomists were more likely to state coping responses, and unlikely to state divine or fate-related explanations. Overall relationships between responses to the first and second questions were statistically significant and robust.[10] Determinists are different from humanists and randomists in how they express behavioural intentions related to coping with negative life events.

Closer analysis of actual coping responses reveals a further qualitative distinction between humanists and randomists. We thematically coded the coping

---

[9]   Melvin Lerner, *The Belief in a Just World: A Fundamental Delusion* (New York: Plenum, 1980).

[10] $\chi^2 (2,3) = 25.18$, $\underline{p} < .005$

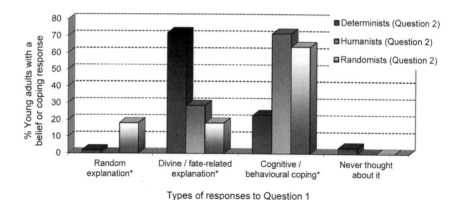

Figure 5.2   Cross-tabulations of belief and coping responses in Theodicy
              Question 1 by categories from Theodicy Question 2

responses for indications of personal striving, reliance on other people, and passive
endurance or acceptance of a situation. Both groups of young adults were similarly
likely to mention indications of personal striving. But humanists were more likely
to express reliance on other people (30 per cent), while randomists were far more
likely to attempt to endure, ignore, or let go of the negative situation (86 per cent),
stating that 'there is nothing you can do about it.'

Further clarification comes from a study of the correlations between explanatory
clausal statements and coping clausal statements in the 33 transcripts analysed
in depth. As seen in Table 5.2, there are distinct patterns of coping statements
associated with each type of theodical explanation. Randomistic explanations
were positively correlated with coping statements having to do with learning from
or simply enduring negative events. In contrast, humanistic explanations were
positively correlated with coping statements having to do with reliance on others

Table 5.2   Correlations between frequencies of different types of clausal
             statements (*n*=33)

	Deterministic explanation	Humanistic explanation	Randomistic explanation
Coping – rely on others	-.26	.37*	.29
Coping – refocus	-.22	-.08	-.06
Coping – learn from it	.14	.16	.39*
Coping – change it	-.18	.01	-.03
Coping – endure	-.38*	.22	.48**
No coping or explanation	-.22	.03	.10

Note: * p < .05; ** p < .01

in times of crisis. Deterministic explanations, however, were negatively correlated with all coping responses except learning, and significantly negatively correlated with simple endurance of negative events.

Thus, what young adults stated as their theodical beliefs was directly related to how they expected to cope or deal with negative life events. Determinists anticipated learning from negative events, but also seemed able to derive sufficient coping from their deterministic beliefs alone, and did not express an expectation of reliance on others, attempts to change the situation, or attempts to refocus attention or cognitively reframe the event. Much of this coping work tended to be implied in their reliance on deterministic beliefs. Humanists, on the other hand, stated that they would cope primarily through reliance on others, but also through simple endurance or attempting to learn from the situation. Randomists, finally, were most likely to state coping responses of simple endurance, attempts to learn from the situation (that is, construct their own meaning for negative events), or reliance on others – or acknowledge that they did not know how they would cope.

Lerner's linear-continuum model of theodical explanation might be inadequate. Humanists and randomists appear to respond quite differently than determinists to tragic or unexpected negative life events. When cued to think about such events, and given an open-ended, projective-styled question, determinists seem to reach first for their divine or fatalistic causal explanations, primarily as a source of comfort for themselves or others. In contrast, humanists and randomists tend to reach first for coping responses as a means of dealing with such events and situations by redirecting mental attention – either reaching out to other people, focusing on daily goals, or ignoring or dismissing the situation. These coping responses may indeed become more pronounced as necessities in the absence of a deterministic belief system. But the types of coping selected most by randomists and humanists further distinguish between these two sets of beliefs. Randomists might see less value in any overt or extra reliance on people as a means of 'making sense' of negative events or as a contributing factor to recovery from them.

Relationships between Theodical Orientations

A primary difficulty with any linear model of theodicy results from how one arranges the 'continuum' of theodical beliefs. Two competing linear models are graphically presented below. In the first model (the one most similar to Lerner's), the continuum is arranged according to the degree of overall perceived influence of causes in the world, ranging from total external influence (determined through omniscient forces) to localized influence as imposed by humans (that is, humans creating their own order through choices), to complete lack of any influences (that is, a random universe). In the second model, the continuum is arranged according to the locality of responsibility assumed, ranging from no responsibility whatsoever (that is, randomist) to responsibility recognized but localized generally in external and omniscient forces (that is, determinist) to responsibility localized more specifically in human action (that is, humanist). In each model, the theodical categories are represented spherically, with sizes based on sample proportions for each type of theodical belief.

The first linear model of theodical orientation, most akin to Lerner, would be arranged according to extent of causal forces as shown in Figure 5.3.

Figure 5.3   First linear model of theodicies

The second linear model of theodical orientation, arranged according to locus of responsibility, would be arranged as shown in Figure 5.4.

Figure 5.4   Second linear model of theodicies

Neither model adequately explains the similarity of humanistic and randomistic responses, and their distinction from deterministic responses in terms of coping responses and explanatory beliefs. A more comprehensive model of theodical orientation would represent theodicy along two axes, according to two distinct Aristotelian types of causal explanation: 'final' causes (predetermined causality, where future outcomes or 'ultimate realities' are used to explain a current event), and 'efficient' causes (sequential causality, where prior events or patterns are used to explain a current event).[11] Imposing this perspective, the three theodical categories would be represented as portrayed in Figure 5.5.

This two-dimensional model helps clarify the non-linear relationship between the three theodical positions. A primary reliance on final causal explanations of tragedy or unexpected negative events (deterministic theodicy) is likely to coincide with less reliance on efficient causal explanations of the same (humanistic theodicy). A randomistic theodical orientation signals an absence of reliance on either final or efficient causal explanations. As will be seen in Chapter 8, these three distinct theodical orientations were shaped by unique social and developmental factors.

---

[11]   Aristotelian 'formal' causes may be cited by both humanists and determinists, and are not distinguishing features of either theodical position.

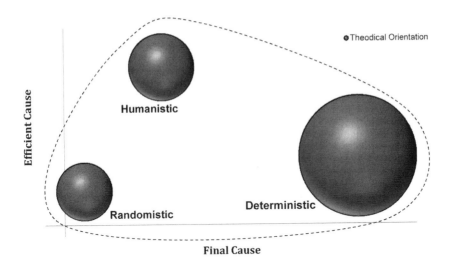

Figure 5.5   Spatial model of theodicies

Is Theodicy Related to Worldview?

Following more constructivist or deductive approaches to theory development, one might be tempted to propose 'logical' connections between theodicy and worldview. For instance, one might assume an inherently 'logical' connection between negative worldviews and randomistic theodicies: a world that is unsafe, chaotic and unpleasant certainly could not be planned or guided in terms of the negative events that occur in it. But there are multiple problems with such an approach to the study of personal theologies. First, there is the untested assumption that people's beliefs are 'systematic' and 'logical' as determined a priori by external standards and systems. Secondly, it is possible to draw 'logical' connections in different ways, depending on one's starting-point. For instance, a competing 'logical' connection could be drawn between negative worldviews and deterministic theodicies, linking them both to underlying religious beliefs: if one is religious in a traditional sense, then one is more likely to view the world as a negative place, and to view negative events as necessary events through which one learns, is tested, increases in faith and is prepared for a final destiny.

This study allows for a unique opportunity to examine relationships between different facets of personal theology – in this chapter, the relationship between theodicy and worldview. Neither case-by-case analysis nor non-parametric statistical analysis suggests any clear connection between categorizations of theodical orientation and worldview.[12] Determinism remained the dominant

---

[12] $\chi^2 (2,2) = 1.27, p > .1.$

theodical orientation in each worldview category, and negative worldview remained dominant in each theodical orientation.

There was the slightest hint of patterns worth mentioning, although there was no statistically significant difference marking them: (1) humanists were less negative and more positive in their worldviews; (2) randomists were more likely to have mixed or ambivalent worldviews, and (3) determinists were more frequently negative in their worldviews – but no less frequently positive than were randomists. But these relationships were very weak and did not provide any clear indication of results one might expect from a larger sample.

The more striking result is the persistent dominance of determinism and of negative worldview, independent of variation in the other facet of personal theology. Worldview and theodicy appear to vary independently and are likely shaped by different life experiences and situations, as we will discover in Chapter 8.

Chapter 6
Life Purpose: Belonging, Place and Impact in the World

Happiness, then, is something final and self-sufficient, and is the end of action.

Aristotle, *Nichomachean Ethics*, book 1:7

This is what I have seen to be good: it is fitting to eat and drink and find enjoyment in all the toil with which one toils under the sun the few days of the life God gives us; for this is our lot.

Ecclesiastes 5:18

The pebbles are the strength of the wall.

Buji proverb, Nigeria

Supporting one's father and mother, cherishing wife and children and a peaceful occupation; this is the greatest blessing.

Sutta Nipata 262

Achievement of your happiness is the only moral purpose of your life, and that happiness, not pain or mindless self-indulgence, is the proof of your moral integrity.

Ayn Rand

O Messenger of God, a man who is oppressed I am ready to help, but how does one help an oppressor? 'By hindering him doing wrong,' he said.

Hadith of Bukhari 3:624

Wash yourselves; make yourselves clean; remove the evil of your doings from before my eyes; cease to do evil, learn to do good; seek justice, rescue the oppressed, defend the orphan, plead for the widow.

Isaiah 1:16–17

Inherit the kingdom prepared for you from the foundation of the world; for I was hungry and you gave me food, I was thirsty and you gave me something to drink, I was a stranger and you welcomed me, I was naked and you gave me clothing, I was sick and you took care of me, I was in prison and you visited me.

Matthew 25:34–36

What is the chief end of man? Man's chief end is to glorify God and to enjoy him for ever.

Westminster Shorter Catechism, 1647, question 1

For all those ailing in the world,
Until their every sickness has been healed,
May I myself become for them
The doctor, nurse, the medicine itself.

Bodhisattvacharya Avataraby Shantideva (700 CE)[1]

Questions of purpose in life are deeply personal as well as cosmological. They are not merely self-referential. Questions of life purpose are about the self *vis-à-vis* the world, the place in which one exists and moves. Life purpose is grounded in location, or place. But it also involves identity. It emerges from the internal conversation between one's sense of identity ('Who am I?') and one's sense of location ('What is this place in which I find myself?'). The conversation yields questions of a person's fit and place in the world as perceived: 'Who am I in this place? What does this place call forth in me? In what ways do I connect or not connect?' From responses to these questions emerge questions of function, purpose and ultimate end.

The questions are not simply personal. We consider the questions not simply in light of our personal identities and personal senses of local place. We engage the questions in light of our greater sense of identity as part of humanity and any larger group identity found therein, and our sense of the whole of the world. Likewise, the questions of purpose and place are not fully engaged only by imagining the static present; the questions are future-oriented, evoking thoughts, plans, imaginations and beliefs about the time ahead of us and an ultimate end that helps to set the trajectory.

The questions we asked young adults about purpose and place in the world are personalized analogues for more broadly conceived philosophical and religious questions of purpose, such as 'Why am I here on this earth?' or 'What is the purpose of humanity?' or, as stated in the Westminster Catechism, 'What is the chief end of man?'[2] Most generally stated, the undergirding question of human meaning is 'What are we here for?' – a question that some philosophers, such as William Gerber, regard as a post-philosophical question better answered by religion.[3] But others, such as anthropologist Florence Kluckhohn, have understood that questions of human meaning and purpose are important parts of cultural systems of values

---

[1]   From Shantideva's *Guide to the Bodhisattva Way of Life*, trans. V. and T. Wallace (Ithaca, NY: Snow Lion Publications, 1997).

[2]   Westminster Small Catechism (1648),in *The School of Faith; The Catechisms of the Reformed Church*, trans. and ed. T.F. Torrance (New York: Harper Press, 1959).

[3]   William Gerber, *Anatomy of What We Value Most*, vol. 52 of *Value Inquiry Book Series* (Atlanta, GA: Ropodi, 1997).

and beliefs – for her, captured partially in how cultures addressed the question of humanity's relationship to nature.[4]

Questions of human purpose have haunted humanity for millennia. They appear in the texts of major religions from Confucianism and Buddhism to Judaism and Islam, from Santeria to atheism, from Christianity to Aboriginal and Native religions. They have guided the quests of religions' founders and authors of those religions, and are discussed in the texts of philosophers from many cultures. These philosophical and religious texts reveal a range of possible human responses to the question of existential purpose and place, each emerging from a particular perspective shaped by experience. Human place and purpose may be conceived in terms of survival, social or environmental impact, attainment, creation and achievement, and ways of belonging. People's worldviews interact with and may contribute to their sense of life purpose – but not necessarily in a simple linear manner.

Why Am I Here?

As emerging adults begin to explore and be exposed to different options, responsibilities, consequences and realities in the broader world, they wrestle in new and expanded ways with their sense of identity. The question of identity now has expanded to location: 'Who am I in relation to this enormous reality of life in the world? How will I pursue living in this world?' For some, this expansive and telic question of purposeful identity may be pursued through a vocational passion: 'I am here to make a difference in the world.' For others, it may be pursued through vigorous enjoyment: 'I am here to take in all that the world has to offer.' For others, purposeful identity may be understood as a matter of survival: 'I am here to make it through and to take care of my own, regardless of the world around me.'

Emerging adults in *Making the Transition* were asked this question about their life purpose: 'What do you see as your place in the world? Or, how do you fit in the world?' We put these questions of human meaning baldly before young adults, with no suggestion of how they might answer. Furthermore, I crafted the question so that it was intentionally framed not broadly about the meaning and purpose in human existence, but specifically about meaning and purpose of one's own life. This was not a departure from previous or subsequent questions: for worldview, we asked young adults about their perceptions of the world *as they knew it*, and for theodicy, we asked how they *personally* understood negative life events. A more generic rating-scale question about the meaning of human life (drawn from the GSS bank of questions) was asked during phone interviews in the third year of the study, allowing once again for generational or historical cohort comparisons.

---

[4]   Florence Kluckhohn, 'Dominant and Variant Value Orientations', in Clyde Kluckhohn and Henry Murray (eds), *Personality in Nature, Society, and Culture*, pp. 342–57 (New York: Alfred A. Knopf, 1956).

The choice of wording of the core interview question was critical. Asking about purpose can too easily evoke social demand effects in a person's response; that is, internally, one may think, 'Oh, I am supposed to have a purpose. How shall I respond so that it seems like I have a purpose?' While any term can potentially evoke social demand and self-enhancement effects, the word 'purpose' suggests a trajectory, whereas the words 'place' and 'fit' are a bit more ambiguous. This ambiguity invited young adults to engage the question projectively, sparking their imaginations, impressions and internal images and ideas about the world and themselves in the world.

Not all emerging adults had thought about the question of their place and purpose in the world, at least not in such direct terms. As we shall see, the question evoked a wide range of responses, evenly distributed between isolation and withdrawal from the world, role-defined understandings of one's place and contribution (for instance, within one's family or specific work), and larger visions of contribution to and engagement with the world. To begin, let us start with the example of Joel.

It was in his response to the questions about life purpose that Joel first discussed his interest in being a teacher – a markedly different career than the vocations in agriculture or small-business management to which he originally aspired. Joel's deliberation about becoming a teacher came out of his recognition that he was socially motivated and had a particular concern for high school students:

> I'm a people person. Especially once I get to know people better. And I think I can make a difference with students in high school if I get a chance to, you know, to be that. Especially since I'm pretty young and all, so maybe it's kinda, well, easier to earn the respect of high school kids if you're more on their level ... And I'm kinda on their level now, so I'd like to get an early start in that.

At this point in his response, Joel's sense of life purpose seemed somewhat restricted to a specific career-based role. However, Joel went on to indicate that he saw teaching as a springboard for mentoring and helping teenagers, and for preventing delinquency:

> A teacher's important 'cause you kinda mentor some kids, be a role model. And a lot of times the teachers get involved coaching, and I think I'd like to do that, keep kids out of trouble or give them some guidelines of what they should do with their life, what they want to do with their life. Just give them some good insight.

Here, Joel became more focused in describing the type of impact he wanted to have on high school students – to change and shape the direction of their lives, through example, prevention and wisdom. This level of individual and group engagement requires a more intense personal investment and commitment than a simpler, function-oriented idea of what it meant to be a teacher. Joel's purpose in being a teacher transcended a more role-constrained desire to pass on specific knowledge about a specific field of study to certain students. Joel made clear that he was searching for a place through which he could contribute to society in the way he felt compelled and interested. His sense of purpose was not defined by his career choice. Rather, his new vocational considerations came out of his emerging sense of purpose as someone with something significant to contribute to others.[5] As such, his response communicated what may be summarized as the following: 'I want to be here for others, and teaching is one avenue for achieving that goal.'

Joel's response provides an example of how emerging adults wrestle with questions of place and purpose in life. Emerging adults bring perceptions of the settings they encountered or imagined, their own capacities, and the particularities of their own identities into conversation with broader perceptions and beliefs about the world and humanity, which needs to be addressed in the world in light of ideals about the good, and the relationship of the human person to the world.

A Closer Look

In our grounded-theory approach to content analysis of interview texts and interviewer notes, we classified young adults' responses by categories of withdrawal from or engagement in the world and human life that emerged from the interviews themselves. To cover the variety of responses, we created five categories:

1. *Ignore the world* – indicated by responses suggesting a lack of consideration or awareness of the world, at times including intentional disregard.
2. *Retreat from the world* – indicated by responses suggesting intentional alienation, passivity, or self-preoccupation.
3. *Define purpose through immediate relationships* – indicated in responses focusing one's sense of purpose primarily within the relationships of family and close friends.
4. *Define purpose through career* – indicated in responses focusing one's sense of purpose primarily within the roles and duties performed in one's job or career, or within one's passive social roles (for example, a taxpayer), without a specific sense of broader contribution beyond the scope of one's work.
5. *Engage directly in the world* – indicated in responses directly stating a sense of purpose and impact on society as a whole, ranging from local to international focus, but beyond the scope of relational or career-defined roles. Engagement was signalled by responses focused on 'making a difference', or 'having an impact.'

---

[5] Joel returned at several points later in his interview to the consideration of teaching as a vocation, confirming that his response to the life purpose question was not a cursory response.

As with other facets of personal theology, we used interviewer notes, audiotapes of interviews, and transcripts to code young adults' responses, using the most frequent and/or salient type of engagement mentioned by each young adult, which became that young adults' category.

As an example, Lillian's response to the question of life place and purpose helped us clearly identify the theme of purpose defined in the context of family and close relationships and in the context of her work. Lillian, our relaxed atheist dental student married to a devout Roman Catholic, not only clearly articulated role-defined purpose through family and work, she also somewhat vaguely talked about wanting to make a contribution to the community – but she eschewed a grander or more expansive perspective that moved beyond the more circumspect roles she conceived: 'I mean, it's, it's not like a really big leadership role. I'm not running for president or anything. But, I mean ... I want to be a good wife and a good mother someday. And a good dentist. I want to be able to serve my community and be able to give something back to my community.'

As with worldview and theodicy, our closer analysis of 33 verbatim responses about life purpose allowed for more refined examination of clauses and of overall response intent. Examples of clauses in each category are found in Table 6.1. It should be noted that total responses were somewhat more complex in quality than they were for worldview or theodicy – when discussing different possible approaches to life purpose, young adults made more frequent use of semantic modifiers and amplifiers to make distinctions and mark differences in the *degree* of their withdrawal or engagement. Because of this, I based final coding not only on a tally of clauses but also by the narrative 'weight' or emphasis given by young adults to certain clauses.

The five categories are thematically and semantically distinct in these statements of life purpose. The language of ignoring indicated a disavowal of involvement, an acquiescence to the non-efficacy of a single person, and a sense of autonomy from the world. Withdrawal- or retreat-focused language was marked by themes of survival (for example, 'I'm just here to get through it') and self-focused objectives, as well as some of the ignoring language of disavowal and non-efficacy. Role-defined responses were either in terms of career or in terms of familial and otherwise close relationships. These role-defined responses ranged from passive to active: some young adults saw themselves 'fitting' in a network of immediate relationships or in subservient work roles, but did not describe themselves as agents making significant contributions to others. Other role-defined responses were more active and purposeful in quality; in these statements, young adults saw themselves contributing to others only within a narrow career-defined or relationship-defined domain of influence. Finally, statements pointing toward a broader sense of engagement in the world typically included any combination of the following: simple statements of a desire to make a difference in people's lives – beyond the narrow scope of immediate familial or job-specific activities, direct references to future efforts or having an impact in the larger local or global community, and naming of personal capacities and attributes by which one might make a broader contribution.[6]

These five categories suggested a continuum of life purpose, with each new category demanding increasing movement out beyond oneself and involving increased expansion of the boundaries of 'world'. Young adults whom we might call *ignorers* came close to disavowing the existence of the world as a concern. In contrast, *retreaters* acknowledged the existence and impact of the world, but adopted avoidance as a coping strategy. The *family-defined*, those who restricted their purpose to family roles and relational roles, moved further into engagement, but set boundaries on their willingness to engage the world outside their immediate relationships – and some respondents specifically referred to their familial relationships as havens and safe barriers against the world. The *job-defined*, who confined their purpose to career- or job-related roles, moved outward from themselves as well, and acknowledged engagement of others outside their immediate family – but their engagement was safely contained within the boundaries of well-defined work behaviours and job performances that performed a helpful function for others. Finally, *engagers* expressed a sense of purpose broader than familiar relationships and defined work behaviours, with a more enduring impact on others in terms of addressing deep physical, psychological, developmental, or moral needs. This progression echoes Erikson's description of the continuum between self-absorption and generativity.[7]

We collapsed these five categories into three. Figure 6.1 below shows the distribution of young adult responses in the three categories – *avoidant, role-defined* and *engaged* (in the outer ring) – as well as the original five categories (in the inner ring). When asked about their sense of purpose in life or 'fit' in the world, 35 per cent stated an avoidant response – that they did not think about any broader purpose in life, preferring to ignore the world (16 per cent), or desiring to retreat from prolonged contact with the larger world (19 per cent). In contrast, 26 per cent of young adults indicated an engaged sense of life purpose – that they wanted to have a broader influence on society beyond their roles and behaviours in their work and immediate relationships. The remaining 39 per cent of young adults described a role-defined sense of purpose or 'fit' – that they saw their place and purpose within a narrowly defined set of contexts and clear roles, either in their jobs (15 per cent) or in their relationships with family and friends (24 per cent).[8]

---

[6]   More intensive close coding of text was generally comparable to impressionistic coding by research assistants and interviewers – using semantic and semiotic coding classifications as a benchmark for impressionistic coding, reliability was found to be moderate ($\alpha = .78$). Seven cases were reclassified to conform with the more intensive semiotic coding.

[7]   Erik Erikson, 'Identity and the Life Cycle', *Psychological Issues* 1(1) (1959): 1–171.

[8]   This distribution across our heuristic coding from interview notes and audiotapes closely matched the distribution derived through intensive semiotic coding of the 33 interview transcripts (35.3 per cent avoidant, 35.3 per cent role-defined, 29.4 engaged).

Table 6.1   Examples of young adults' statements of life purpose or 'fit' in the world

Ignore the world	Retreat from the world	Define purpose through close relationships	Define purpose through career, job, or societal role	Engage Directly in the world
I just live my life.	I definitely consider my main part of my life to be worrying about myself.	I'm going to try and be a friend ... And hopefully it won't be too much of an effort, just kind of mutual.	I'm just another citizen of the United States.	I hope to make a difference in that way.
I don't feel I have any great duty to do ... anything.	I'm not in that war personally, why should I be paying out money for them	The parents have more impact on a child than anyone else ... So I think my place is pretty much being a role model right now.	I want to have a job that I like and that I can succeed at.	My goal is world peace, which is of course something lot of people say ... But I definitely want to be somebody that tries to facilitate that.
There's nothing you can do, do about it.	I play the passive role. That's why people think I fit in.	I want to be a good wife, a good mother and a good dentist	I want to be a good wife, a good mother and a good dentist	I try and become involved in charities and stuff.
It's just there.	I think we are to a large degree alienated. I mean, it's an actual.	I fit ... in a network of personal relationships that exist in this moment of family and friends.	A lot of times teachers get involved in coaching, and I'd like to do that.	I expect to have an effect on this world that's greater than the effect of my own body.
What happens, happens	I don't think that every person has to have some kind of purpose.	But maybe dedicating my life half to myself, half myself, my family, my goods.	I suppose as an engineer, I would like to improve, maybe, make things run more smoothly	... as one of God's children and designed to help other people.

One person doesn't matter.	… and to just do generally, generally what is, what is best for me.	I try to, like, in relationships I try to help people see the positive side of things.	I'm just a slave to the government.	I want to be able to serve my community and be able to give something back to my community.
This may not sound right, but honestly I'm the centre of my own world.	I honestly aim to be a hermit – to escape society.	As a parent, I'm shaping the future – at least for my own children.	I need to find a job that I enjoy and that accomplishes something.	I think I can be a good example and role model for teens.
… nobody special, no hero, no big important person, I'm just here to get through it.		I don't know that I want to sacrifice myself for humanity if it means taking myself away from love.	I enjoy working with music and with computers.	I think I'm a good leader, and I'm put here to lead other people

These results suggest that, unlike for worldview valence and theodicy, there was no clear culturally dominant category of belief about human life purpose. The closest type of belief to a dominant pattern was the set of role-defined beliefs, in which young adults stated their life purpose as specific familial or vocational roles (for example, father, wife, pharmacist, engineer), locating themselves within society as participants with clear and delimited expectations but with little attention to or interest in their impact on society or the world. A sense of life purpose devoted to broader societal engagement was least frequent among emerging adults, but still with over one-fourth expressing this as their belief. These three life-purpose beliefs are telic in nature, thus potentially linking to goals and ultimate values.

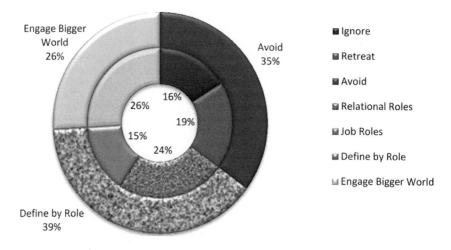

Figure 6.1   Life-purpose orientations of *Making the Transition* young adults

Historical Consistency and Age-related Change in Life Purpose

In the third year of the *Making the Transition* project, we asked emerging adults to respond to a dipolar Likert-scale question about human life purpose from the GSS. The question was as follows:

People have different images of human nature. Where would you place yourself on this scale?						
The good person must be deeply involved in the problems and activities of the world.				The good person must avoid contamination by the corruption of the world.		
1	2	3	4	5	6	7

As was the case with questions regarding worldview, there was higher potential for 'social demand' effects in this forced-choice question, and young adults tended to respond more on the engagement-oriented end of the scale – the opposite gravitation in responses of that emerging from the interviews. Thus, no conclusions were drawn from the results of the survey question regarding any overall young adult patterns of engagement or avoidance of the world. These data were more useful for relative comparisons with other birth cohorts of young adults and age groups of adults across generations. To look for generational shifts, I compared responses of emerging adults in *Making the Transition* with responses emerging adult GSS respondents from two prior birth cohorts: 1946–60 and 1961–75.[9] To look at possible developmental differences over adulthood, I also compared different adult age groups in the GSS dataset, combining cohort years of survey response.

Transition participants' responses did not differ significantly from previous cohorts of GSS young adults.[10] Figure 6.2 below illustrates the pattern of responses across years. The overall response pattern is quite stable, with no significant shift in life purpose across generations of young adults. Even young adults in the baby-boomer generation (born 1946–60) did not respond differently, as might be expected. Their ratings about human engagement in versus avoidance of the world did not differ significantly from subsequent generations.

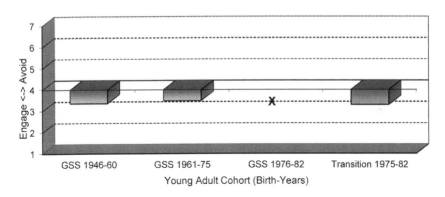

Figure 6.2   Average life-purpose ratings by GSS and *Making the Transition* young adults

While there do not seem to be generational differences among American young adults, there were subtle but noteworthy differences between different

---

    9   The GSS did not include the question about life purpose during the years that emerging adults born in the years 1976–82 – the concurrent birth years of *Making the Transition* emerging adults – would have answered.

    [10] $F_{(2,417)} = 0.54$, $p > .1$.

age groups of American adults, regardless of generational cohort.[11] As shown in Figure 6.3, adults in early middle age (36–50) were much more prone to favour an engagement-oriented life purpose than were emerging adults (17–26), older young adults (27–35), or older adults (76 and older). These variations are not particularly strong, with one-half of a rating-scale point's difference between the highest and lowest group means, on a seven-point scale. Overall, there appears to be general stability in life purpose across age-groups, but with a modest but noticeable tendency toward greater engagement among younger middle-aged adults. Adults in this age-group (36–50) are more often in the midst of significant parenting responsibilities with children and adolescents (as well as beginning to address concerns with ageing parents), and are reaching peak creative output in their careers.[12] These two factors alone likely contribute to greater outward focus and social engagement: parents gain increased concern about matters of safety, education and financial security for children and for parents; and adults growing in their careers are more likely to have more responsibility in the form of meaningful projects and management of others.

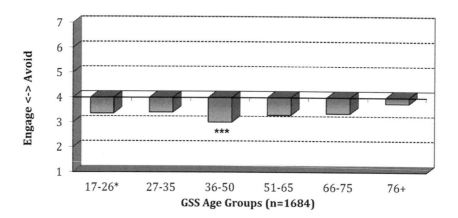

Figure 6.3   Average life-purpose ratings by GSS age groups

The above results point to historical consistency over forty years in emerging adults' life-purpose beliefs. They also suggest a modest shift, as life unfolds, toward greater social engagement in early middle adulthood. Broader social engagement or contribution can be understood as a belief undergirding Erikson's concept of generativity. It is interesting to note that such 'generativity' or social engagement does not remain as strong in later adulthood.

---

[11] $F(5,1683) = 3.39$, $p = .005$.

[12]   See Wayne Dennis's classic study, 'Creative Productivity Between the Ages of 20 and 80 Years', *Journal of Gerontology* 21 (1966): 1–8.

Going Deeper

Once again, verbatim responses with commentary offer a deeper glimpse into the depths and varieties of emerging adults' beliefs about human place and purpose in the world.

Young adults almost always framed their responses as an individual *vis-à-vis* the world and human society. They tended to draw clear distinctions between the three different types of life purpose. For some, broader social engagement was for 'superstars' and beyond their ideas about themselves in the world. Others saw potential for broader social impact emerging from their moral action or interpersonal involvement in local concerns – but there was still a distinction between larger-scale social contribution and a more limited focus on family or career-related contribution. These two categories were, in turn, distinct in young adults' responses from protective withdrawal, dismissive disregard, or clearly stated exclusive self-interest in relation to the world. While it is possible to view these types of life purpose along a continuum from full withdrawal to full engagement – and I will later make use of this perspective – it is also important to recognize the clear demarcations in young adults' beliefs that make these types of life purpose qualitatively different.

Through their responses to the question of life purpose, young adults also communicated beliefs about personal identity and agency in relation to society, ranging from the diminutive to the grand. Some young adults saw themselves as small players in a large production – but contributors none the less. In contrast, some young adults viewed themselves as passive agents, cogs simply to be plugged into an impersonal social or vocational machine.

Responses also revealed a range of vagueness and clarity, linked to a grasp of the social systems in which young adults conceived of fit and purpose. Knowledge of and exposure to social systems from an insider's perspective can create opportunities for greater clarity of life purpose, and a more precise connection between imagined or desired life purpose and vocational venues in which to pursue that purpose.

The following are examples of different expressions of life purpose among emerging adults, in their own words, interpreted with commentary. They are grouped in sets of responses expressing similar themes.

Isolated Existence

Let us begin with emerging adults' statements of withdrawal from the world. We initially coded two types of withdrawal-related statements: ignoring or dismissing the world, and intentionally retreating from the world. But a closer look at young adults' responses reveals a bit more complexity. If we look at Steve's response, he described a sense of being at a loss for how to navigate the world in order to find any sense of fit or purpose – as it were, 'Lost in the forest without a clue', alienated, without a trail of breadcrumbs, yielding a basic stance of complete uncertainty. Rachel and Ly-Hanh indicated a similar stance of passivity, but rooted in a sense of their own diminutive and inconsequential presence in an overwhelmingly large world set in its patterns of cause and effect; for them, a roadmap exists, and it primarily points toward passive acceptance of the world as it is. Kasey and Beth – atheist and Jehovah's Witness respectively– were similar in their stance of somewhat aggressive disregard of the world, recognizing that the world's problems were neither their creation nor ultimately their responsibility. The language of withdrawal from the world can come in the form of confused alienation, passive co-existing acquiescence, and aggressive disregard.

Steve, our Taoism-influenced atheist chef, expressed no clear ideas about life purpose, in vocational, moral, or interpersonal terms. But he recognized that answering the question of purpose was one of his tasks as a young adult – rooted not in some sense of a normative developmental task, but related to recognition of his own intentions and capacities, and consideration of their telic purpose. This suggests that Steve at least considered a broader sense of life purpose possible. However, he also believed that experiences of individual alienation were normative in contemporary society, suggesting that he himself often felt alienated from the world: 'I don't know exactly how I fit in yet, I guess. But I have my own will and I have my own powers and I have to figure out exactly what those are for. It's not a question of simply feeling it. I think we are to a large degree alienated. I mean, it's an actual.'

In his sense of alienation, Steve did not deliberately seek retreat or separation from the world; neither did he seek or imagine engagement or social contribution. Steve expressed some desire to find fit and purpose, but, accepting alienation as a given, was at a loss for how to construct or accept a roadmap.

Rachel, a creationist Baptist living with her non-religious boyfriend and who had 'lost interest' in going to church but not in her faith, stressed personal salvation but expressed feeling lost in the vastness of the cosmos. This in some ways framed her sense of life purpose. But so did her history of growing up with a physically and mentally abusive father, which left her with a deep imprint of feeling trapped and insignificant:

> If there's physical abuse, there's always going to be mental abuse. I went through it. My mom went through it. I mostly went through the physical. Like, my mom just was mentally abused. And it's because they have your self-esteem so low that you think that that's what you deserve. And you keep hoping and thinking that the man you fell in love with will come back.

The backdrop for Rachel's sense of life purpose was a frightening world and universe, unrelenting in their patterns of cause and effect:

> The world's very scary. I mean, I hate to see what the world's going to be like when I have kids … I just live my life and what happens happens. And you can't change the future. You can't change the past. You can't change the way people

are. So you just live day by day. What happens, happens. You gotta have fun at what you're doing.

One might be tempted simply to consider Rachel's framing of the world as completely negative and her life purpose akin to that of the grasshopper in the old Aesop's fable and as a form of reactive recovery from her past. But there is more lurking behind the surface that suggests an even greater passivity and, dare one say, submissiveness to a universe in which her own agency is so miniscule and irrelevant:

> There is something bigger. I mean, we're just one little galaxy. There's tons of them out there. What amazes me is sometimes I sit there and I think, there could be other people in a totally different galaxy, 'cause, you know, space is huge – someone sitting there thinking the same thing that you're thinking … We're like ants to something else. Floating in space.

This cosmic vision of the vastness of all time and space was the backdrop Rachel offered before finally answering the question of life purpose: 'How do I fit? I just fit. I'm just there. I don't know really how to explain it.' Rachel did not see herself as alienated from the world. But she did not express any sense of agency or potential for impact in it.

Ly-Hanh, our ex-Buddhist Vietnamese orthodonture student, used language and images similar to Rachel's to describe her sense of life purpose. But there were some important differences in her speech. She expressed intention for impact and fit, and expressed greater discomfort at feeling dislocated:

> How do I fit in the world? Just a small little ant. In, like, a big crowd. I know I'm going to make my mark. I'm going to do something. But right now I don't really feel like I fit in – which is because I play the passive role. That's why people think I fit in. I'm a typical young adult. But, deep inside me I know that I don't fit. I can't explain why. But I know I don't.

Ly-Hanh was uncertain of place and purpose in the world, and used the image of 'ant' to indicate her sense of insignificance. But she also envisioned the possibility of purpose related to impact and agency. Her disquiet about her own passivity indicates some conception of difference that she had not yet expressed.

Both Rachel and Ly-Hanh experienced fathers whose influence was one of control and diminishment – in Rachel's case, cast within a context of abuse; in Ly-Hanh's case, within a culture of male dominance and female submission. For both, a broader cultural or subcultural inheritance of acquiescence (particularly for women) may have left them with fewer resources for construction of an alternative personal theology. Ly-Hanh wrestled internally with competing passive and active constructs for life purpose; but Rachel had chosen to 'ride the wave' of existence without any explicit consideration of other purpose.

Beth offered a brief response about place and purpose that was clearly linked to her negative worldview and her deterministic theodicy. She viewed herself as 'kind of like a seat-filler' – a passive stance seemingly similar to that of Rachel and Ly-Hanh. She stated no aims of contributing significantly in any domain – even her job or relationships: 'I mean, [I'm] nobody special, no hero, no big important person; I'm just here to get through it.' Her last clause, 'I'm just here to get through it,' indicated a goal of survival in a negative atmosphere, pointing back to her religious beliefs as a Jehovah's Witness. For Beth, the world was a 'decaying' and corrupt place, and negative life events were caused by a cosmic evil force (the Devil) as part of an ongoing battle between good and evil. In such a cosmology, one's best hope might be to survive uncorrupted in this life, awaiting something better after death.

Beth's survivalist expression of life purpose carried no reference to vocation or relationships, even to her own husband and children. She spoke about her job in the same dismissive way she spoke about her place in the world: 'I'm just a clerk … It's just the same every day.' And she spoke even more clearly in distancing terms about her working-class neighbours and neighbourhood:

> This isn't really the best neighbourhood, so it's not a neighbourhood that you want to talk to your neighbours in. I don't want to sound like a snob, but I see this … um … I just don't want to associate with them. I don't really know why, they could be nice people. I just don't know. We're pretty much too involved with our own little lives, work lives and stuff. We don't have time to go next door and associate anyways.

Beth's overall life purpose was echoed in how she thought about her surroundings. Hers was a posture of resistance and withdrawal from what she perceived as an adversarial environment.

Though an ardent atheist, and though responding in an oppositional manner to the question itself, Kasey framed life purpose in adversarial terms similar to Beth's. Hers is a language of self-against-the-world. But while Beth framed her withdrawal-oriented sense of life purpose in terms of allying herself with a deity and with a people who sought to be different (in Niebuhr's language, a classic 'Christ against culture' stance), Kasey framed her explicit disinterest in the world in terms of self-interest:

> Hmm. I don't know. I'm just here to do whatever. That's a really weird question! Hopefully I'll help someone somehow, something. I don't know what, though … But I don't think that every person necessarily has to have some kind of purpose. If you're religious I think that's what you would think. But I'm not religious, so I wouldn't. I don't look at things like people that are Christian or whatever … I don't really try to make sense of it. I mean, I didn't create all this stuff so it's not my position to try to figure it out. I'm like, younger than most people living

here, so I'll leave that to the older people who made these rules and made it the way it is. That's their problem.

Kasey spoke from a perspective of owing nobody anything: 'I am not responsible for the messes other people have made.' But she did not even express the kind of purposive will toward achievement or attainment that atheist philosophers like Rand or Nietzsche espoused. She eschewed a sense of purpose, associating the concept with religious thought. The alternative she left herself was to move toward a vacuous, non-defined existence, on the border of nihilism and solipsism, where 'I'm here to do whatever.'

In the end, this is not very different from Beth's stated life purpose to 'just get through it'. In both cases, the world was something to survive, and the responsibility for any of its problems resided elsewhere. In both Kasey's and Beth's formulations of life purpose, the matter of agency and self-efficacy was not as important as sense of autonomy and distinction from the surrounding world – and their sense of a negative world to which they owed no responsibility.

Positive Engagement and Broader Impact

At the other end of the spectrum of life purpose is the belief that people have a telic purpose of positive engagement with the world, whether in the form of contribution to the common good of humanity, or in the form of general moral goodness, that offers something positive to the society in which one lives. Interview segments from six young adults – Cory, Javier, AnMing, Dean, Jennifer and Adriana – give us glimpses into the thinking of young adults about engagement-oriented life purpose. For them, there are no questions about personal agency, potential for impact, and responsibility for others. They offer occasional grandiose visions of impact. And the primary difference between them is not around the question of agency; rather it is around the question of deployment of their agency. How, and in what venues, and through what means, can they best find a path of engagement and impact?

A Life of Integrity

Cory, our young Mormon living at home and holding three part-time jobs, expressed a life purpose dedicated to broader social impact in his life. Cory placed his sense of purpose in a moral frame. He indicated that he wanted to have an impact on other people – not limited to his family or work environment – through his modelling of a moral life:

> Oh, I think I have a responsibility to be a good example to others. Try and do the right thing. You know, because if we want to change, each of us needs to start with ourselves … So being an example. Just trying to be kind and considerate of other people. And respectful of other people's beliefs.

Cory desired to make a contribution, but did not link this ideal to a specific vocation from which he might do that. When prompted for a more focused response, Cory reiterated his general moral response, and then offered some tongue-in-cheek grandiose ideas of contributions in areas outside his field of study, such as finding a cure for cancer:

> How do I fit? Sometimes I really wonder. Just basically the same, you know, being an example. Hopefully I have something useful to contribute. You know, later on in the future, come up with a cure for cancer. You know, something really awesome like that. Hopefully I can contribute something good.

This response further suggested that Cory saw his life purpose as one of broader social contribution, but in dispersed moral and individual terms – somewhat akin to the themes in the classic American movie *It's a Wonderful Life*, in which social impact is made through the accumulation of daily moral decisions and interactions. In this way, Cory's sense of life purpose contrasts dramatically with Beth's and Kasey's. Although Cory also had a negative worldview, he saw the potential for individual human efficacy through the witness of a life oriented to the good. Cory's life purpose was intentionally ubiquitous – not dependent upon a particular relationship or vocation, but applied across all contexts as a patterned principle of purposive engagement through a committed way of living.

For Cory, this sense of life purpose was thoroughly grounded in his religion. It is a telic perspective, akin to Niebuhr's 'Christ transforming culture,' and also similar to a core Jewish understanding of the way in which a surrounding culture is changed by the pattern and witness of a people dedicated to a way of life. Later, Cory went on to state that he did not fit with dishonest people – another framing of life purpose in moral terms. He concluded with an affirmation of the religious basis of his sense of purpose, which nurtured his sense of grandiosity and potential, but did not specifically focus his sense of purpose:

> In the church that I belong to, you know, I've always been taught that each one of us is a child of God. And because each of us is a child of God, we're something special. We have the potential to become something great because, just like the saying, 'God don't make no junk.' You know, I really believe that. I believe each of us has the potential to be something wonderful. And that's where I feel like I fit in.

Throughout his response, Cory clearly communicated a sense of life purpose, summarized as 'I am here for others, but I don't yet know how in more specific terms other than being a good person.'

Paying it Forward

Javier, our young Latino law student about to leave for Guatemala to do human rights work, was clear throughout his interview about his commitment to the common good and his belief that people at their best offered themselves for the betterment of others. His beliefs and commitments around life purpose, thoroughly grounded in some of (but not all) the theological traditions of Roman Catholicism and evangelical Protestantism, provided him not only with a roadmap for living but with a sense of place connected directly to his contributions and efforts on behalf of the world. Javier found his sense of place where he was living out his sense of purpose. And his beliefs about life purpose were, in fact, a deeply internalized reflection of his ultimate values:

> I think people come together in times of tragedy and help each other. And act as real neighbours. Unfortunately it is in times of tragedy, and not a daily thing. The worst thing is the competitive nature of our society. The fact that money is the driving motivation a lot of the time [is unfortunate]... I admire people that are willing to, to sacrifice for others.

Javier's response to the question of life purpose was directly reflective of this belief in self-giving – a belief and commitment found in his responses to other questions about work ethics and relational ethics. Simply stated, Javier believed in a 'pay it forward' kind of theology of life purpose. He believed that whatever gifts and benefits he had received were for contributing to other people's lives:

> Javier: I think, with my life, whatever I do, I try to help those who lack opportunities – because I've had many, and a lot of it's been because of chance. A lot of it is because I've had the right people around me. So I hope that I, I can do that for other people, to provide those kinds of opportunities.
>
> *Benita: Okay. You said that you think the world is generally dog-eat-dog. So are you sort of, is it your role to sort of change that?*
>
> Javier: Right. I think in the small [ways wherever I am]. I think my job is to do that.

Even though Javier had a more negative worldview, his telic perspective was one of vigorous engagement in the world for the purpose of transformation. His vision of impact was wide-ranging like Cory's, but more focused. And the means of impact was not so much through the example of morally upright living as through the direct addressing of human needs.

AnMing also saw her life purpose in terms of 'paying it forward', a belief in the good of offering to others the things that have benefited you. Like Javier, AnMing was a law student, and spoke specifically of a desire to help second-generation Chinese Americans based on the challenges of her own experiences and her parents' experiences when new to America. AnMing also mentioned more grandiose hopes for social reform achievements related to life purpose:

> I guess I want to be the one to change things like, really big problems, like education. And going to psychology, I want to help people who are having problems assimilating from Asian culture to your 'American-Western' culture. So I want to be the one, I guess, to help the second generation or whatever number [of generations] we're up to.

Again like Javier, AnMing linked her sense of purpose integrally to her choice of career, and both of these to her religious heritage: 'I think my religion is really so far ingrained in me that anything I'm going to do is reflecting of my religion.' AnMing recalled how her household was immersed in Christian practices, including regular prayer – and how her thinking about the world and her place and purpose formed within that nexus: 'When I was younger I wished that there were a lot of people out there mentoring the younger kids. I wished that a lot of my friends made it ... or would better themselves.' Within this religious universe, her father played an integral role in helping her think about a career path that matched her interests in helping others: 'I think that he really pegged it, you know. He looked at what we were good at and then said that you could be paid to be a good lawyer, or you might like it. And I do like the material that we're learning.'

Both AnMing and Javier believed in a life purpose of dedication to the betterment of the world and the addressing of social ills. They did not view a career as a narrow path of limited engagement with the world. Rather, they viewed their law studies as an avenue to assist them in doing expansive work. AnMing even planned to continue beyond law school to get an MBA and a psychology graduate degree, to further strengthen her capacities to serve: 'Nothing that is gonna pay well'.

Selecting a Sphere of Impact

The belief in human agency, responsibility and altruistic impact does not always lead to non-profit career paths and human service vocations. Dean provides a good example of a young adult making a thoughtful selection of a sphere of impact. As a young professional entering a career in corporate finance, Dean had given serious consideration to questions of life purpose. He reported that he and his college peers had discussed issues related to life purpose and the choices they were making in careers. The following excerpt offers an example of the lucidity of Dean's career-related decision-making process, filtered through his overarching sense of life purpose:

> Dean: There was sort of a big conflict with this when I left college, because all of the international relations people were sort of debating, you know, 'Do I sell

out to a big company, do I go to consulting or banking ... or should I go to the, you know, do something in an NGO or work in the public sector or something like that, or at least a non-private sector?'

Laura: Right. Do you view your choice as selling out?

Dean: Um, no, I actually gave it a lot of thought then, and I've been thinking about it since then. Ideally I'd like to make the world a better place for my children and other people's children. And I thought about how can I as one person get that done. I felt like, if I'd signed on to some sort of grassroots project, if I'd gone to some sort of NGO as an untrained and fairly naïve undergrad, I'd be bringing very marginal value and my personal contribution would be worth pretty little ... Whereas I figured if I went into the private sector which is probably the cause of many of the problems that the public sector is fighting against as much as anything else, then I could at least understand how that works and meet and know influential people or other people who are in positions to make decisions that affect other folks ... I think if you're inside Exxon or you know people in that company, it would be easier to affect how they conduct business than if you're Greenpeace and you're tying your boats to their oil rigs and things like that.

Dean described a conscious and calculated decision about the career-base from which he would try to have an impact on the world. A Jew with occasional religious commitments, Dean did not consider social contribution too grandiose to pursue, nor did he consider it fulfilled solely through being a good person. His response communicated what may be summarized as 'I am here for others, and I have made career decisions based on the degree of potential for impact on others.' Dean's sense of purpose gave him motivational clarity and provided him with a set of organizing principles for important decisions in his own career development. He further explained that his desire to work from within the system was not revolutionary, but cooperative in nature:

Yeah, and it's not like I want to overthrow the system or anything like that. I mean I don't have any of that kind of a notion. Certainly the system is what allowed me to go to college and live comfortably, so it would be completely hypocritical of me to cast it down. And I think it's done the same thing for a lot of people, but there are still problems that need to be addressed.

This recognition on Dean's part may be important to understanding how young adults' sense of life purpose may be influenced and shaped by their experiences of social systems. Dean, who grew up in an upper-middle-class community with highly educated parents, understood at many levels of personal experience the benefits and opportunities derived from the 'private sector'. Dean had been exposed by his parents to discussions and behaviours that gave him an insider's understanding of corporate culture, so Dean was able to imagine more specifically the ways in which he might make a social contribution within the system of the private sector. But Dean also recognized that his own education and job opportunities were benefits of being raised by parents who were within this system. Dean's social position as an adolescent and young adult had given him insight and knowledge of a system that remained foreign, intimidating and impenetrable to others his age who were from less advantaged communities and families.

Jennifer, just at the outset of her emerging adult journey through college, framed her sense of life purpose completely in terms of broader social engagement and contribution to the common good. Like Javier and AnMing, she identified a clear direction for pursuing greater social impact. And, like Javier and AnMing, her perspective on life purpose was in keeping with her religious (Unitarian Universalist) heritage. But, like Dean, she also considered benefits to her own life as part of the equation of life purpose dedicated to the common good. She expressed a sense of being made or prepared for mediation work; but she also considered personal interest and enjoyment (that is, interesting work, travel) as important side benefits:

> Jennifer: I guess I want to contribute to the world. Obvious, my goal is world peace, which is of course something that a lot of people have. But I definitely want to be somebody that tries to facilitate that, personally. Like, doing peace mediation or something like that. Non-political but more, more getting people to communicate. I did peer mediation in high school. I didn't know about it before then, but I mean, it's difficult to make people hear each other. But so many people just block out other people's philosophies and just, you know, say their own without listening. But I think I can help that. And I think we need to kind of help people listen to each other ... And I think that working with people can never be boring. It's never boring. There's always something interesting that's going to happen. Could be awful, could be wonderful, who knows? But it's never boring. So. Do something with people, but I'm more interested on an international level.

> *David: And what, why do you suppose on an international level?*

> Jennifer: I'll be able to travel a lot ... My father had a travel bug, as we call it. And I do, too. And I've travelled a lot internationally with my family. And twice without. And I just, I love to travel. And I love to see new places. I just can't stay in one place for that long.

The benefits enjoyed in upper-middle- and upper-class communities and families may contribute in multivalent ways to life purpose. On the one hand, the enjoyment of a type of lifestyle can shape choices and interests – and also a sense of the scale of work necessary to support such a lifestyle. On the other hand, the benefits of travel and exposure to places beyond one's immediate community and family can alter one's personal theology – as one comes face-to-face with human needs not as familiar, in places with less social and financial capital. The early conversion narrative of Siddhartha Gautama, later the Buddha, begins with his journey out from his contained Brahman household and his encounter with human suffering and death. For young adults from more financially secure families and communities, beliefs about life purpose may form through a mixture of perspectives on the world, personal agency and responsibility, and a balance of benefits for others and for oneself.

A Divided Sense of Purpose

Philip, our agnostic military officer candidate, provides a good example of the internal dialogue and debate between concern for broader social impact, self-interest and investment in family and home. Just about to graduate and be commissioned as an officer, and with an interest in entering politics in the future, Philip did not express a clear idea of the venue in which he hoped to have an impact on the world, and he tended to focus more on caring for himself and his family. But he remained strongly disposed toward broader engagement in society:

> I'm an individual just like everyone else. And if I want to have a big impact, I can go about and do that by working hard and dedicating myself to others. And I think that the best impact that you can possibly have on the world is by helping everyone else. Not coddling everyone else, but just giving ever, pushing forward society ... And not taking from it something just for myself. But maybe dedicating my life half to myself, my family, my goods, and the other half to making it a better place.

This excerpt indicates that Philip saw a division of purpose between self-interests (that is, self, family and possessions) and broader social engagement. He also insinuated that he intended to observe this division of purpose, devoting himself partially to self-interests and partially to social contribution. Unlike Cory, Philip exhibited no grandiosity in his response. But, like Cory, he simply stated a desire to have an impact as an individual. While he did not offer any specific ideas about where and how to make such social contributions, Philip showed some internal clarity regarding what he meant as appropriate social engagement: not coddling people, but helping people by pushing them forward.

The Allure of a Role-defined Life

The dream of making a significant impact on the world – and the belief that human beings have a purpose toward a larger good – can be deeply motivating, but also frustrating in its seemingly unattainable aim. Contrasting with this, the allure of a more narrowly defined life – and the belief that human beings have a purpose toward contentment – can be quite strong. Adriana, an administrator for the Council on Foreign Relations who lived with her boyfriend Evan, spoke of this allure of the local focus and a life purpose defined by local roles and relationships. She was clearly drawn to the world and its challenges and wanted to make a difference, but was navigating the space between self-sacrifice and enjoyment of a life discovered with another person:

> I really don't know. I think, if you were to ask me five years ago – not five, seven, before I got into a relationship – I would have said that I would have been one of those people who would sacrifice their lives for the good of humanity. But then I discovered that, well, there's humanity, but, you know, Eric's really cool. And that I don't know if I want to sacrifice myself for humanity when it means taking myself away from love. So I'm not sure yet. I know that I want to try to make the world a better place. But I don't know how, you know? I don't know if that means being a good person in any way possible ... a good mother, good wife, good sister, good daughter, whatever. Good citizen. Or if it means doing that sacrificial ... like, being a martyr for a cause. I also think less globally too. And try to think of my place in my family. And what role I want to play in my family as well. I've found that as I got older that's become a lot more important to me. I considered briefly thinking well I could move anywhere I wanted ... But being near my nephew and being a part of his life and stuff like that is important to me now. So ... I think I have been cultivating a value for an extended family that I never had before. So I think that's also where I'm trying to find my place.

Adriana expressed poignantly the tension emerging adults face between the vision of 'lives of commitment', as Daloz and Parks put it,[13] and the vision of home, hearth and local connections. She held a belief in the possibility of impact and broader social engagement, but she also found new meaning and purpose in her localized affections for her boyfriend and her nephew. Her background as an agnostic Jew likely had little impact on this internal dialogue. The choices were not about whether or not she had agency or responsibility. Her choices were about the expanse of her engagement in the world. It is as if she was asking, 'Yes, we are here to make a difference – but how global does that need to be?'

The Role-defined Life: Local Purpose, in the Family and on the Job

Along the middle of the spectrum of beliefs about life purpose, between withdrawal from the world and purposive engagement with the larger world's challenges, were expressions of life purpose defined by and limited to role. A closer look at emerging adults' responses reveals that role-defined life purpose can vary from more self-oriented to more socially oriented perspectives. Michael, Stefani, Shanille, Rebecca, Christopher and Jeannie all expressed a role-defined sense of

---

[13]   See Laurent Daloz, Cheryl Keen, James Keen and Sharon Parks, *Common Fire: Leading Lives of Commitment in a Complex World* (Boston, MA: Beacon, 1999).

life purpose, focused either on the immediate relationships of friends and family, or on the defined activities of a specific career. The common thread is found in how they viewed deployment of their own agency in a narrowly focused way – but they differed in the degree of inward versus outward focus of their care and responsibility. Is human purpose primarily a matter of self-interest? Is it a tribal matter? Or is broader social impact the inevitable result of localized care for a few other people?

Self and Family

Some emerging adults expressed a sense of life purpose defined and delimited within the roles and relationships of family and friendship. This more tribal focus of agency, responsibility and impact were articulated by both men and women (although more frequently by women). Some responses were more akin to a withdrawal-oriented life purpose, but extended beyond the self to encompass family and friends as a stronghold against the world. Other responses revealed a sense of interconnection between localized focus on family and friends and more global patterns and influence – that is, influence in the family was a gateway to and participation in influence on the world.

Michael, a young upper-middle-class college student beginning to embrace his Roman Catholic heritage, was unapologetically self-focused in his sense of life purpose. The locus of his response was first on himself, then on his family and peers. While granting an unlikely possibility that he might contribute to society as a whole, his concern for others was limited to the extent of his immediate relationships of connection and care: 'Mainly just to take care of myself and the people I care about. And I *suppose* if I can find some way to have an influence on the world in general I would do that. But I definitely consider my main part of my life to be worrying about myself and people that are close to me.'

Michael's sense of purpose, similar to that of other young adults, can be summarized simply by the statement 'I am here for myself.' His interest in broader influence or purpose was minimal and subsumed by his concern with self-care and concern for those in immediate relationship to him. Because of his interest in and care for others most immediately connected to him, his response qualifies as a role-defined life purpose rather than a withdrawal-oriented life purpose – but he is on the border of withdrawal. Michael's life purpose is an extension of his worldview ('I think the majority of the world is looking out for themselves first. I'm not even necessarily saying that's wrong'). It is also in keeping with some of his core values: Michael admired people who made something of themselves and was disgusted by 'people that expect hand outs'. In this somewhat solipsistic universe, Michael even described relational values in terms related to self-interest: 'I feel more self-worth, I guess, when I'm giving to someone else. I don't know. That sounds odd, I'm not really sure how to phrase it.' In developmental terms, Michael may have been at the beginning of a movement from a focus on identity to a focus on generativity. But self remained first, family and friends second, and world a distant third.

Stefani, our ex-Lutheran Native American student in information sciences, provided another example of how broader societal engagement was seen by many young adults as qualitatively distinct from a more limited form of engagement within the narrow contexts of immediate family or career. Stefani's sense of life purpose was focused specifically on family, and she drew two distinctions: one between purpose devoted to family and purpose devoted to career, and one between family and society at large:

> I don't ever see myself as being any superstar or [anything] politically, but I do see myself being an important person in that I will have my husband and I will have a life, maybe children. Maybe. And try and live that way through making a relationship standing and not so much a career that's important to the world. Just making my contribution as a small contribution.

Stefani stated a sense of life purpose that was relational, not vocational, and directed within a narrow band of relationships – those that comprised (or would in the future comprise) her innermost circle of relationships (for example, husband, children). Stefani seemed to view broader societal engagement as something for 'superstars' or political giants, people who had a larger-than-life sense of purpose. Later, when discussing core values, Stefani returned to the idea of 'extremes' in life purpose, and here she stated clearly her beliefs about human *telos*:

> I have a hard time believing in the radical … either way, the extremes of … um … priests or … that you know, the vow of poverty or the … I have a hard time believing that that's the only way and that's the right way. I tend to believe, if there is a God, he's … he's there to … 'God helps those who help themselves'- type thing where it's not just, you know, 'I'm going to give my life to work.' Well, he gave us this life for our own purpose.

Neither Michael nor Stefani raised questions about their own agency. They did not view themselves as ants. Nor did they question some basic sense of responsibility. Their beliefs pointed toward a more narrowly defined scope of responsibility and more focused deployment of their capacities. For Stefani, part of the *telos* of human purpose was about self-determination.

Shanille expressed a bit more interest in broader social engagement than did Michael and Stefani. Her sense of life purpose was more narrowly and specifically focused on her family as the primary context of her human impact:

> I kind of see my place in the world as just a small piece of the big pie. And that I just need to do what is best, best for me and my family and to just do generally what is best for me and what is best for my family. And anything that I can, anytime that I can help on a grander scale, to do that also. Be it, like, I used to

tutor. It's not a huge thing. But it's helping out *some* people that need *some* help. And that aren't within my immediate family or immediate surroundings. But I'm helping on a grander scale.

Shanille's view of herself in terms of life purpose was as a 'small' unit that would not have a 'huge' impact. Helping on a 'grander scale' included any small efforts beyond her immediate family or surroundings – but care of herself and her family were primary life concerns. While she remained open to *some* broader altruistic sense of engagement, her adjectival modifiers ('*some* people that need *some* help') signalled her lack of interest in any major or continuous effort. A synopsis of her response would be 'I am primarily here for myself and my family, but I will engage in broader contexts as opportunities arise.' The basic premise for Michael, Stefani and Shanille is that the larger world does not matter in comparison to the local concerns of one's own family, friends and tribe. One finds expression of this kind of personal theology not in the *bodhisattva*'s vow of Buddhism but in Herman Hesse's *Siddhartha*; not in Jesus' parable known as 'the Good Samaritan', but in the biblical wisdom text of Ecclesiastes.

Dedicated to One's Work

Other young adults identified a role-defined sense of life purpose that was focused on their work. Their descriptions of contributions to the world through work were not because of a deep sense of vocation or calling, nor from a perspective that their chosen work was for the betterment of the world. Rather, they described their impact more narrowly in terms of a few people helped or a few improvements made as a result of their chosen role.

Jeannie, the young pharmacist-in-training, saw any life purpose beyond her immediate family only within the confines of her chosen career. She hoped that dispensing proper medication would help some people have healthier and happier lives – but she did not imagine or desire any broader social impact:

> Like for pharmacy and stuff, I hope to make a difference in that way, because so many people could live so much better lives if, like, their medicine, if they were on the right one, or you know that it worked or if they knew how to use, stuff like that. I think that it'd make a few people happier. I don't think it's going to have any like worldwide implications or anything like that, but hopefully a few people.

Jeannie's life-purpose script could be summarized as follows: 'My work makes my contribution to the world – in a specific, limited way and within a system which I did not create and do not seek to change.' In other words, 'I am for others only through the roles and activities of my work.' Interestingly, her sense of life purpose in work was much more active (albeit role-constrained) than her sense of purpose in family and relationships. Recalling Jeannie's worldview response, she saw family connection as a personal refuge and safety, not as a place of significant contribution or purpose.

Christopher was also most invested in his own career development – particularly at a point when he was shifting from theatre crew supervision to engineering. He considered the possibility that his work might contribute in some small way to the greater social good:

> I don't feel I have any great duty to do … anything. I think that I need to find a job that I enjoy and that accomplishes something. I suppose as an engineer, I would like to improve, maybe, make things run more smoothly. And that may be on a very small scale, in a single company, or something.

It should be noted that Christopher cast his career-based life purpose in terms of enjoyment first, and social contribution or accomplishment second. Any contribution beyond his own job enjoyment was envisioned as small and limited within the scope of his career-related activities.

Like the family-focused responses, these job-focused responses offer a picture of life purpose defined by a role or set of roles and confined to the people encountered in a clearly understood setting. The common feature in the life purpose of these five young adults is the carefully defined parameters of engagement in a world beyond oneself.

Impact Through Being the Imprint

A role-defined life purpose is not always synonymous with a conception of limited impact or agency. Some young adults articulated a clear sense of deep impact with a small number of people in a limited sphere of influence. In these cases, beliefs about life purpose were infused with an acceptance of limitations ('I'm not going to change the whole world'), as well as an embrace of responsibilities and opportunities for deeper influence with a few people.

Rebecca, our young mother working and living in the small city where she grew up, initially puzzled over the question of life purpose, but came to articulate her role-defined life purpose as a place of great influence. Her role as a mother was to her a gateway for her child's future. Her impact was through the imprint she left on her child during what she saw as the critical years of his toddlerhood – and she understood that impact as enduring and as having ripple effects through his future:

> Rebecca: I'm a mom. How else can you fit in? You're one of the most influential people when you're the, when you're a mom.
>
> *David: How?*
>
> Rebecca: See him walk up the steps, he cries, I mean, that's, you know, it's just, you have more impact. The parents have more impact on a child than anyone

else. And it's what you do at two, when they're two or three, that they imitate. And that's they, that's how I think they learn. So I think my place is pretty much being a role model right now.

Emerging Patterns

We can hear in these narratives the ways that these American young adults at the turn of the twenty-first century were searching for and finding answers to the telic question of human life purpose. The question was deeply personal for them, more than other questions of personal theology. Perhaps it is because the question of life purpose taps directly into the developmental quests of young adulthood for belonging and for meaningful vocation. In this sense, the questions 'How do you fit in the world?' and 'What is your place in the world?' strike at a core issue of emerging adult identity – they are the questions that most bring personal identity into relationship with personal theology.

Young adults' responses to our open-ended questions brought to light themes of agency and responsibility *vis-à-vis* the world, potential for impact beyond oneself, power of the world on one's life and choices, domains of deployment of human effort, choice between competing goods and motivations, and depth and breadth of impact. Telic understandings of human place and purpose ranged across differing perspectives on human happiness and thriving, from the hedonic (focused on securing extrinsic pleasure and comfort) to the eudaimonic (focused on fostering personal development) and the altruistic (focused on securing well-being for others). They ranged across different loci of attention, from the individual to the tribal to the global. These themes will become even more central in the discussion of ultimate values. Young adults' beliefs about the purpose of human life spread across the entire landscape, expressing ends of comfort and pleasure, magnanimity, moral excellence, and social or ecological improvement; indicating passivity, resistance, proactive intention, and participation in the stream of being – with differing degrees of intensity. Their responses reveal how life purpose as a facet of personal theology is informed but not determined by worldviews and ultimate values, as well as by personal identity and life experience.

In her study of South-western American subcultures, Florence Kluckhohn addressed the question of human place, purpose and power by asking people a forced-choice question about humanity's relationship with nature.[14] Her question presupposed three types of response: (a) humans can direct and master nature and forces of being; (b) humans can live in balance with forces of nature and being but exert some control, and (c) humans are passive recipients of the forces of nature and being. In our study of American young adults, similar themes have surfaced. But the question of telic human purpose in the world cannot be reduced simply

---

[14]   See Florence Kluckhohn and Fred Strodtbeck, *Variations in Value Orientations* (Evanston, IL: Row, Peterson and Company, 1961).

to a matter of agency. Beliefs about human agency *vis-à-vis* the world form one starting-point – but so do beliefs about individual and collective responsibility for the state of the world (nature, humanity and being).And what follows may be a kind of decision-tree of beliefs about life purpose. If humans have agency and responsibility, then how much of each do humans have (and by extension, do I have)? And what are the best venues for the deployment of human powers for maximal, ubiquitous, or enduring impact?

Non-responsibility is the first belief behind an avoidant or withdrawal-oriented life purpose – one may believe in human passivity and non-responsibility before the forces of nature and being, and so opt for a personal theology of acquiescence; or one may believe in human agency and potential for impact but also believe in a refusal of responsibility (as did Beth and Kasey), and so opt for a personal theology of resistance and self-interest. But as belief in human responsibility for the state of the world increases, belief in human passivity becomes an untenable theological position; people do not choose to hold a personal theology that 'I am responsible for the state of the world but have no power in the world.' Belief in responsibility assumes belief in agency.

Once a person responds affirmatively to the question, 'Am I my brother's keeper?', that person assumes both responsibility and agency. The next questions are 'Who, then, is my neighbour?' and 'What, then, is required of me?' From these questions, more nuanced beliefs emerge about location and deployment of agency. For some, responsibility is addressed by living with integrity regardless of a particular setting or venue. For others, responsibility is taken up in the form of a focused cause or effort for change. And for others, responsibility is understood in more bounded terms related to the settings and people most in contact with one's intentions and actions. Degree of responsibility seems partially to differentiate between role-defined versus engagement-oriented life purpose – although a degree of grandiosity may also differentiate engaged young adults' beliefs about agency and impact.

Figure 6.4 provides a visual representation of different beliefs about telic human purpose, along dimensions representing agency and responsibility. As indicated visually, the three general orientations of life purpose lie roughly along a continuum – but with some qualifiers. First, the avoidant orientation is most distant from other perspectives on life purpose. Secondly, the role-defined and engaged orientations are closer in beliefs about human agency but more distant from each other in beliefs about responsibility.

I have mentioned previously some of Richard Niebuhr's categories from *Christ and Culture,* and Keith Ward's categories in *Religion and Community.* These are analogues from Christian theology and from the study of world religions, describing different religious beliefs about human purpose and ends. The two works offer a glimpse of the varied perspectives within and across religions regarding the place of the good person and community within the world, from resistance and withdrawal to participation in a greater mystery of being, to transformation of the world through example, to transformation of the world through vigorous action.

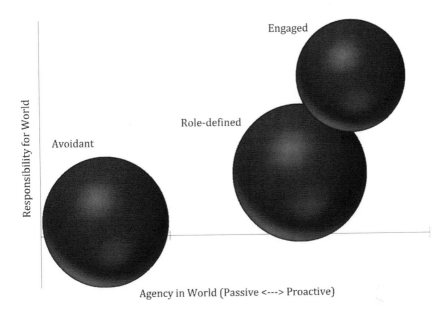

Figure 6.4   Spatial representation of life-purpose orientations

As our research from *Making the Transition* has shown, individuals from atheistic and theistic religious perspectives alike can be aligned in similar perspectives on human responsibility for the world, agency in the world, and potential for impact in different places in the world. A very basic continuum, from self-preservation to tribalism or vocational functionalism to more broad-based altruism, can map personal theologies of life purpose – and can illuminate surprising similarities in beliefs about telic human purpose, regardless of differences in religious heritage.

Is Life Purpose Related to Theodicy and Worldview?

One last word in this chapter: what, if anything, do beliefs about life purpose have to do with beliefs about the world and about ultimate causation? As shown in Chapter 5, worldview and theodicy seemed to function as independent facets of personal theology in the minds of these American young adults. But what about life purpose? How do worldviews and theodicies interact with life purpose? Are young adults with randomistic theodicies and negative worldviews most likely to express an avoidant sense of life purpose?

Relationships among beliefs of the 82 core young adults were examined, once again using non-parametric statistical analyses. Results revealed that life purpose was indeed significantly related to worldview valence, but not to theodicy.[15] But, as seen in Figure 6.5, the association between life purpose and worldview as not in any simple linear relationship. Negative worldviews were just as frequent among avoiders and engagers. Positive worldviews were most common among engagers, but least frequent among young adults with a role-defined sense of life purpose. The reverse pattern appeared among young adults with mixed or ambivalent worldviews: no engagers expressed ambivalent worldviews, and the highest percentage of young adults with mixed worldviews was among those with role-defined life purpose.

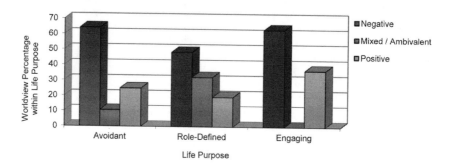

Figure 6.5   Worldviews within each life-purpose orientation

Previously, I discussed that a mixed or ambivalent worldview might suggest an indecisive position often linked with disregard or disinterest, and correlated with other experiences and attitudes that suggest a form of uncertainty and withdrawal *vis-à-vis* the world. That the majority of young adults with mixed or ambivalent worldviews espoused role-defined orientations to life purpose – and none espoused a broader engagement-oriented life purpose – suggests that their indecision and uncertainty about the world had a limiting impact on their sense of agency in and responsibility for the world. James Marcia would likely have called this an example of ideological identity diffusion, with the consequent lack of vision for seeking an impact on something beyond oneself and one's immediate family.[16] But in this case, it is not uncertainty about the self (a question of identity) that contributes to the tendency to withdraw; it is uncertainty about the world.

Theodicy did not vary systematically across types of life purpose. Determinism remained the dominant theodical orientation among avoiders (69 per cent), engagers (64 per cent), and the role-defined (56 per cent). Humanism was somewhat more frequent among role-defined young adults (22 per cent) – but the differences were

---

[15]   Worldview x life purpose: χ^2 (2,2) = 10.47, p < .05; theodicy x life purpose: χ^2 (2,2) = 1.72, p > .1.

[16]   James Marcia, 'Ego Identity Status: Relationship to Change in Self-Esteem, General Maladjustment, and Authoritarianism', *Journal of Personality* 35(1) (1967): 119–33.

not significant. About 20 per cent of young adults in each type of life purpose endorsed a randomistic theodical orientation.

There were no notable three-way interactions between worldview, theodicy and life purpose. Theodicy seemed to function as an autonomous belief system that did not interact in any predictable manner with worldview or life purpose.[17] Once again, theodicy appears to serve young adults as a deeper, fundamental belief that remains largely unaccessed, except when one encounters times of significant or unexpected distress, as an explanatory system to provide (or impose) a sense of meaning on events that otherwise violate an undergirding belief in systemic justice or logic.

The relationship between these three facets of personal theology and ultimate values remains to be seen.

---

[17]　Examination of relationships between GSS items used in Year 3 for estimates of worldview and life purpose also yielded no significant interactions. Further examination of two theodicy-like items from the GSS used in the Year 2 and Year 3 religious-beliefs scales demonstrated no clear-cut relationship between theodicy and either worldview or life purpose.

Chapter 7

Ultimate Values – To Be What Kind of Person?

Whoever saves the life of any person from Israel, is regarded by scripture as one who has saved an entire world.

Sanhedrin, chapter 4, Mishnah 5:3

O ye who believe! Come, all of you, into submission (unto Him); and follow not the footsteps of the devil.

Qur'an, Surat Al-Baqarah 2:208

They ask you, [O Muhammad], what they should spend. Say, 'Whatever you spend of good is [to be] for parents and relatives and orphans and the needy and the traveller.'

Qur'an, 2:215

Filial piety and fraternal submission! – are they not the root of all benevolent actions?

Analects of Confucius, 1.2.2

The three cardinal values of the Objectivist ethics … which, together, are the means to and the realization of one's ultimate value … are: Reason, Purpose, Self-Esteem, with their three corresponding virtues: Rationality, Productiveness, Pride … Productive work is the central purpose of a rational man's life, the central value that integrates and determines the hierarchy of all his other values.

Ayn Rand, 'The Virtue of Selfishness'

Now the works of the flesh are obvious: fornication, impurity, licentiousness, idolatry, sorcery, enmities, strife, jealousy, anger, quarrels, dissensions, factions, envy, drunkenness, carousing, and things like these. I am warning you, as I warned you before: those who do such things will not inherit the kingdom of God. By contrast, the fruit of the Spirit is love, joy, peace, patience, kindness, generosity, faithfulness, gentleness, and self-control. There is no law against such things.

Galatians 5:19–23

Having explored three types of beliefs and identified experiences that shape those beliefs, I now turn to a brief exploration of values. Values are carriers of both beliefs and intentions. Values convey one's assertions about the good worthy of pursuit and the evil worthy of avoidance. They also convey one's aspirations or intentions to pursue such good and avoid such evil.

Values are complex. Defining values is complicated by the plethora of meanings given to the word 'value'. As a noun derived from the Latin *valere* (to be strong, of great worth), its principal definition in the American lexicon (according to Merriam-Webster) is related to marketplace exchange and purchase, but also has meanings related to numeric quantities, durations of musical notes, and qualities of light and speech sounds. Value also is understood as the 'relative worth, utility, or importance' of something, or a 'principle or quality intrinsically desirable' (Merriam-Webster). As a verb, it is synonymous with 'appraise' and 'evaluate' (implying an external benchmark), as well as 'prize' and 'esteem'(implying internal orderings of what is regarded as desirable).

Valere: to be strong, to be well, to be worth'
Latin-English Dictionary

These varied definitions point to a commitment on the part of Americans to counting, rating, arranging the world according to relative quantities and qualities. But an obsessional American, western, or modern commitment to quantitative and utilitarian determinations of worth is only one form of valuation. Valuation is a fundamental human enterprise, emerging from what we experience, feel, learn and believe. In the basic human act of valuing something, people construct and draw upon images and ideas of the good – as well as images and ideas of the bad. We make evaluations of the good through use of external criteria, intrinsic feelings and relationally based judgements of outcomes.

So, when we turn to questions of values, we consequently turn to questions of the good. What is deemed to be of value? That is, what is good? The meanings of the Latin root imply an association of strength, health and worthiness with the good. But these may not be the only associations people make with the good. In the biblical book, Philippians, Paul suggested a different basis for valuation: 'Finally, beloved, whatever is true, whatever is honourable, whatever is just, whatever is pure, whatever is pleasing, whatever is commendable, if there is any excellence and if there is anything worthy of praise, think about [in Greek: take account of] these things' (Phil. 4:8). The quotes at the beginning of this chapter exemplify only some of the range of ultimate values (or most central organizing values) found in different world religions and philosophies – from Muslims' submission to the will of Allah (*islam*) to Christians' love of God and humanity (*agape*), from Jews' upholding of enduring kindness and steadfast allegiance as well as commitment to the totality of Jewish life (*hesed* and *klal yisrael*) to Confucianists' ethos of caring reciprocity, moral correctness and decorum (*ren, yi* and *li*), from Aristotelian happiness to Enlightenment modernists' focus on 'rationality, productivity and pride'. The array is striking. Certainly, there are common threads across religions and philosophies. But even these commonalities (for instance, the 'Golden Rule') may hold different nuances, applications, expressions and interpretations from religion to religion.[1] Additionally, there is marked diversity within specific religions and philosophies. The apostle Paul was particularly adept at addressing in his letters a wide array of values in different communities and cultures across the Mediterranean regions of the Roman Empire, as well as amplifying particular values that he believed needed further nurture in those communities.

People vary widely in their definitions of the good and their ordering of values that exemplify and move toward that good – and away from what is regarded as bad (distorted, erroneous). The Ethics Resource Center, committed to helping organizations develop and follow solid ethical standards, lists 130 different values terms commonly found in organizational codes of conduct.[2] Individuals likewise hold a wide array of competing or complementary values, and prioritize them in accord with their aims and goals, situational demands and beliefs. These values are not simply static beliefs about the good and the bad. These values function as standards and trajectories for ways of being – vectors that direct attention, perception, thought, emotional response and action.[3] And so, within the social sciences, within theology, and in common public discourse, the term 'values' covers a broad range of motivations, aspirations and intentions. Values are goals. Values are not simply descriptive – they are prescriptive. Values carry intentionality, and reveal how people direct their interests.

Because of their prescriptive nature, stating not merely what is but what should be, values are often expressed most basically as desirable actions: 'It is good to be fair-minded in dealing with different people', or 'I want to help people in need', or 'We like to have plenty for ourselves and our children.' In the negative, 'anti-values' (or values to eschew) are expressed similarly: 'It is not good to be lazy', or 'I do not want to be a religious fanatic', or 'We refuse to give in to greed.' These statements capture the prescriptive nature of values through the use of the infinitive form of a verb,[4] most frequently a verb of being or striving (for example,

---

[1]   See Jacob Neusner and Bruce Chilton for a helpful examination of differing understandings of the Golden Rule within and between religions, cultures, and historic and current periods: Jacob Neusner and Bruce Chilton (eds), *The Golden Rule: The Ethics of Reciprocity in World Religions* (New York: Continuum, 2008).

[2]   See the Ethics Resource Center for an alphabetical listing of 130 values 'typically found in codes' of ethics: Ethics Resource Center, 'Definitions of Values', 29 May 2009, at <http://www.ethics.org/resource/definitions-values>.

[3]   For a review, see Robert Emmons, *The Psychology of Ultimate Concerns: Motivation and Spirituality in Personality* (New York: Guilford, 1999); Susan Folkman and Richard Lazarus, 'Coping and Emotion', in Alan Monat and Richard Lazarus (eds), *Stress and Coping: An Anthology*, 3rd edn (New York: Columbia University Press, 1991), pp. 207–27, and Charles Carver and Richard Scheier, *On the Self-Regulation of Behavior* (New York: Cambridge University Press, 1998).

[4]   See Nancy Stein, Susan Folkman, Tom Trabasso and T. Anne Richards, 'Appraisal and Goal Processes as Predictors of Psychological Well-Being in Bereaved Caregivers', *Journal of Personality & Social Psychology* 72(4) (April 1997): 872–84.

trying, intending, aiming).[5] This syntactical structure mentally positions values, like goals, as directional statements or assertions of intent. Beliefs are more definitional in nature, statements of static and enduring qualities of being. Values evoke more active dedication: my assertion of a value implicitly invites my own alignment of intentions and activities in order to pursue or sustain such a value.

Thus, values are rooted in beliefs about relative good and bad. But, more than beliefs, values are a direct expression of the human will, distinct from but intersecting with human thought and emotion. Values are the *raison d'être* for goals.

Not all values are given equal weight and status. Like goals, values are organized in terms of centrality or ultimacy of importance, as well as in terms of how abstract or concrete they are, and whether or not they are long-term sizeable aims or more immediately attainable 'small steps' aims. More long-term, general, and abstract values and goals are at the root or centre of people's day-to-day aspirations and intentions, guiding choices of more immediate short-term aims and goals that help people move toward their higher, more deeply central values. So, in this sense, ultimate values may not guide thought and behaviour directly: their effect may be most profound as mediated through more immediate values and goals most relevant to direct day-to-day activities. For example, ultimate values of finding stability and control in life might find more specific expression in the long-term, abstract goal 'I want to have financial security' – which in turn may find more concrete expression in the long-term, concrete goal, 'I want to save one million dollars by retirement.' This more specific goal then directs selection of more immediate goals for month-to-month savings, investment strategies, and frugal budgeting and purchase plans. Another ultimate value such as 'I want to be a loving person' may be expressed and pursued concretely in a wide array of different relationships – a spouse, children, parents, neighbours, extended family, a religious community, the customers or clients served, or people with specific needs – or all of the above. Each of these relationships calls forth different specific shorter-term goals and aspirations that make the ultimate value of love more concrete.

How, then, do American young adults order their ultimate values? What values are most important to them? What values seem distorted or wrong to them? In other words, what do young adults consider good, and how do they order their values and goals toward what they regard as ultimately good?

Let us consider Karla, the young biotechnology product manager from an upper-class community and a conservative Lutheran religious heritage she questioned due to what she viewed as the way it contributed to her father living a joyless and restrictive life. Karla had a lot to say about ultimate values – those she admired and sought to emulate, and those she considered distorted:

> There's a lot of things I admire. People who are very giving, and not expecting what they give to return, but just doing things for the sake of it ... And, people who are true to themselves. And, I guess, people who are most comfortable with

---

[5]   See Emmons, *Ultimate Concerns*, Chapter 2.

themselves – even their flaws and their features – that are just most comfortable in their own skin, are people I admire. People who have learned how to deal with things, go along with the waves. And people who have a good sense of humour.

The people that I don't like are ones who kind of have a narrow view of the world. A lot of twenty-somethings are starting to settle down, and a lot of those people give up on their friends and create an island of themselves and their significant other. And I don't want to forget the importance of friends, and just see them as distractions when the significant other's away. As we get older and we're building a family, I see why people do that. But I think a lot of times people discount friendships.

The principle I try to live by, I think, is probably love. Anything you do, I think, love is the energy. Sometimes you can hurt each other, but if you mean well then things will work themselves out. I think everything comes back to that. In general, love is kind of like an energy.

But then I see people like friends of my roommates chasing and chasing love for the past four months. And people trying to find others and to hold other people as responsible for their happiness. I see a lot of people being disappointed in life because there's not someone here to take care of them. And I don't understand that. Because I think you're responsible for your happiness. I can be unhappy because I drive an '86 Buick and things like that, and wish I had a sugar daddy to buy me a nice new car. But really, instead, I can work harder and … Now, I know, there are certain circumstances where people might have just had bad misfortune and incidences in their life. I mean, we're kind of sheltered here in America where you can have more control over your life, so it's easy to say that. But still, I really don't understand people who don't take responsibility for their own happiness.

Karla's response to our questions about ultimate values was typically complex. She indicated admiration of core qualities such as altruistic self-sacrifice, self-respect, authenticity and a lighthearted resiliency in the face of the ups and downs of life. She held love as the most central value or principle for living. And she stated a dislike for a distortion of the value of love placed on dating and mating relationships such that those relationships overtook responsibility to other friendships and to oneself. She was clearly oriented toward self-direction, emphasizing the importance of responsibility for one's own happiness. In the process of answering our questions, Karla voiced a wide range of values and 'anti-values', or (to borrow an Augustinian way of thinking) perspectives on the good and the distorted good.

Karla's values were not uncommon among young adults. Love, happiness, integrity and altruistic care were frequently among young adults' most central stated values. But their values ranged more widely: 'Be nice.' 'Be happy, without hurting other people.' 'Live the Golden Rule.' 'Try your best.' 'Be true to yourself.' 'Try everything once.' 'Have fun.' 'Be tolerant.' 'Do the right thing.' 'Make the world better.' These are just a few of the phrases and ideas stated by young adults as their values, aspirations, admired human qualities and ideas of the good.

A Mixed-method Approach to Analysing Values

More than with other facets of personal theology, we found it necessary to use several quantitative and qualitative approaches together in the study of young adults' values. The *Making the Transition* study began with a series of rating questions about values, asking 548 young adult respondents to rate on a scale of 1 (not important) to 5 (very important) a set of preselected values such as 'having lots of money' and 'working to improve society'. Many of these were drawn from questions asked in the original Sloan and NELS studies of adolescents. But the questions were limited to a narrow range and scope of values, and I was concerned about social demand effects in young adults' responses. So, we first opted to include several open-ended questions in our in-depth interviews. In one pair of questions, we asked young adults to state the core value or principle by which they tried to live their lives, and the values that made little sense to them, had little impact in their lives, or were undesirable:

> What is the most important ideal or belief in your life? Is there a principle by which you try to live your life?

> Are there principles or ideals that make no sense to you, or that seem really unimportant?

In another pair of questions, we asked young adults to state the human attributes and types of people they admired most, and those that disgusted them or 'turned them off':

> Think for a minute about what it means to be a person in society and the world. What do you feel are the best and the worst human attributes? What types of people do you admire most, and what types of people disgust you or turn you off the most? Why?

We invited further self-reflection and revelation by asking them to think about attributes they admired most and least in themselves.

Young adults' responses to these questions revealed important contrasts in their minds between values and non-values, or virtues and vices. Some young adults were particularly adept in delineating between a value that is lived and expressed in a virtuous manner and the same value that is over-extended or distorted into what they considered undesirable and non-virtuous.

But while this qualitative approach yielded richer data, we found it challenging to take a purely grounded-theory approach to sorting the values these young adults identified in their interview responses into self-evident overarching themes, categories, or semiotic chains. In responses like Karla's, I could readily identify a range of values expressed and had some hints of consistent themes and how she implicitly organized values. But, because expressed values were so diverse, and because we did not probe further for clues about implicit ordering of values, we did not have sufficient information from the responses to discern which values young adults considered as interrelated and which they considered divergent. To honour a data-driven approach to analysis of values, I had to look beyond interview responses to other quantitative measures.

This led to my choice to follow up with *Transition* young adults in the third year of the study and give them a modified version of Milton Rokeach's 'Life Values' survey (described in Chapter 3)[6] as part of a mailed questionnaire. A total of 115 young adults completed my modified version of the 'Life Values' survey, placing each value in one of five spaces of relative importance: *most important, quite important, somewhat valuable, not that important*, and *really not important*. Cluster analysis of the 18 'terminal values' ranked on the Rokeach instrument provided ample evidence of clear and discrete clusters of values, revealing a heuristic structure for how young adults were implicitly classifying core values according to overarching, unifying themes. I then returned to the 82 interview responses with these heuristic classifications as our organizing strategy for categorizing values named in response to our open-ended questions. And I returned to the original values rated by all 315 participants from the second and third years of the study, submitting these data to the same cluster analytic method used on responses to the Rokeach instrument, to see if similar patterns and clusters emerged.

Together, these different data sources and analytic approaches provide a rich picture of how *Transition* young adults organized and prioritized ultimate values. What emerged was a picture of four distinct sets of ultimate values, in descending order of importance: affiliative (relationally oriented) values, eudaimonic (self-development oriented) values, hedonistic (pleasure oriented) values, and broader social and spiritual values.

Rank Order of Young Adults' Ultimate Values

Let us begin simply, with young adults' rank ordering of values, from most important to least important. Table 7.1 below contains three lists of values. The

---

6   Rokeach distinguished appropriately between what he called 'terminal values' (values that are ultimate ends in themselves) and what he called 'instrumental values' (values that are mediating aims leading toward more ultimate ends). I have focused on the 'terminal values' as the basis for my analyses: Milton Rokeach, *The Nature of Human Values* (New York: The Free Press, 1973); Gortner, 'Varieties of Young Adult Personal Theologies' (PhD diss., University of Chicago, 2004); see Appendix A.

first column lists young adults' composite relative rank ordering of Rokeach's 18 'terminal values'. The second column lists relative rank ordering of values by all participants in the *Making the Transition* study. The third column provides the comparable relative rankings from their prior ratings of values as teenagers in the *Youth Development Study*. The midpoint in each list of values is marked by a dotted line.[7]

Table 7.1   Relative rank order of young adults' values from two quantitative inventories, from highest to lowest

'Terminal values' from modified Rokeach 'Life Values' inventory (*n* = 115)	Values from *Making the Transition* basic phone interviews (*n* = 307)	Values from prior teenage Sloan Youth Development Study surveys (*n* = 1215)
Happiness	To grow as a person*	To keep high moral standards
Mature love	To express oneself*	To learn something new
Family security	To know one's convictions*	To help people
Self-respect	To be challenged	To express oneself
True friendship	To be part of a community*	To improve society
Freedom	To improve society	To work with others
A sense of accomplishment	To create something new	To have lots of money
Wisdom	To have lots of free time	To teach others
A comfortable life	To have lots of money	To have lots of free time
Pleasure	To be famous	To create new things
Inner harmony		To be famous
Equality		To have few responsibilities
World peace		
A sense of excitement		
A world of beauty		
Salvation		
National security		
Social recognition		

Note: * Only asked of participants in the middle year of *Making the Transition* (*n* = 122).

---

[7]   More details of these results are found in Gortner, 'Young Adult Personal Theologies'.

These American young adults clearly indicated higher value of relationships and continuing self-development. They also indicated lower value of money, free time, excitement, pleasure and fame. Topping their 'Life Values' rankings were happiness and mature love, followed by family security, self-respect and true friendship. Topping their *Transition* values (which did not include relational values) were personal growth, self-expression, clarity of convictions and the experience of being challenged. In addition, when asked to consider the relative importance of family versus career in their lives, the vast majority of young adults gravitated toward placing family in the forefront of their concerns. Relative ratings of these values did not shift dramatically from adolescence to emerging adulthood – except that a greater distance in ratings emerged over time between more intrinsic values and more extrinsic values. Young adults rated self-expression and creative production as much more important than fame or wealth: but as teenagers, they had rated wealth more highly. In short, young adults became less hedonistic than they were as teenagers (see Figure 7.1 below).

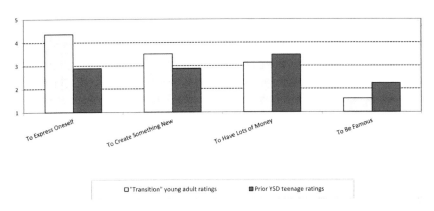

Figure 7.1   Comparison of ratings of four values, as young adults and previously as teenagers

There is one notable disparity between the 'Life Values' and general *Transition* values rankings. On the 'Life Values' inventory, young adults more frequently grouped equality, world peace, world beauty, salvation and national security as largely unimportant. But on more basic values rating questions asked in the general survey of all *Making the Transition* participants, young adults gave high ratings to values such as improving society, being part of a community and clarity of convictions. The disparity may be due once again to social demand effects, or to perceived differences in meaning, related to the wording of the more basic values questions. I will discuss this disparity later, once we have uncovered patterns in how these values relate to one another.

But one thing should be clear from this simple presentation: at least in their own self-understanding, most American young adults at the turn of the twenty-first century may not have been as hedonistic as some social scientists and theologians supposed. Their relative placement of values suggests that relationships and self-development were far more important to them than leisure, pleasure, or material goods. And, even though happiness topped the list of 'terminal values', the values immediately following in importance suggest that young adults considered happiness in conjunction with the pursuit and attainment of sound relationships and strong inner habits of mind and heart.

Uncovering Young Adults' Implicit Taxonomies of Values

Rank-ordered lists of values do not help us understand how people implicitly group values together. Other strategies are needed to find the implicit structure embedded in the proximities and distances between different values in people's rankings.

Cluster analysis, a pattern-seeking multivariate statistical method of analysis, is a tool well-suited to the exploratory, inductive nature of this kind of research. Originally developed for archaeological and biological research, it is formulated to highlight proximity of different types of items to one another. This was particularly useful for analysis of my modified version of the 'Life Values' inventory, in which individuals sorted groups of values into categories of relative importance. But I was also able to apply this method to analysis of the ten basic values rated by all *Transition* participants, once I had statistically adjusted each individual's scores according to his or her range of rating responses.[8] From the results of each cluster analysis, I created a composite score of each values cluster for each young adult by averaging the rankings (or relative ratings) of values contained within each cluster. Figures 7.2 and 7.3 highlight the results of two cluster analyses.

First Cluster Analysis

I conducted the first cluster analysis on young adults' relative rankings of the 18 'terminal values' from the modified 'Life Values' inventory. I conducted the second cluster analysis using adjustments of young adults ratings of the ten basic

---

[8]   Most published measures of values are, like Rokeach's *Nature of Human Values*, ipsative in nature—that is, they employ methods that require individuals to rank values relative to each other in order of personal importance. To bring data from the ten Likert-scale items used in the *Transition* study into conformity with this standard approach, I calculated within-subjects z-scores, which placed each person's item ratings in a narrow range of scores around a personal average rating of zero. This helped reduce the effects of social demand response and normalize each person's ratings around individually peculiar use of the Likert scale for all values, while highlighting relative proximity or distance in a person's ratings from one item to the next. This strategy was used by another Sloan study researcher, Rustin Wolfe, in his work on adolescent values that contributed to Csikszentmihalyi's and Schneider's volume, *Becoming Adult*: Mihaly Csikszentmihalyi and Barbara Schneider, *Becoming Adult: How Teenagers Prepare for the World of Work* (New York: Basic, 2000), Chapter 3.

values asked in phone interviews. These 'bubble-graphs' show how each cluster encompassed a specific set of values, where cluster fell in position of importance relative to other clusters, and how tightly the specific values in each cluster cohered with each other.

Results from the first cluster analysis revealed four distinct clusters, or implicit associated groupings, of values.[9] First, young adults in *Making the Transition* most strongly and consistently valued healthy and stable relationships. As shown in Figure 7.2, four of young adults' highest ranked values – happiness, mature love, family security and true friendship – were also most tightly grouped in what I have called the 'affiliative values' cluster. Three of these four values, regarded most frequently as 'most important' to young adults, focused on relationships – and rankings of happiness co-varied most strongly with these three relational values. I was not surprised to find young adults placing such strong emphasis on values related to intimacy, loyalty and family formation. These same concerns were noted over 70 years ago by Erik Erikson as the central psychosocial tasks of young adulthood. Young adults at the turn of the twenty-first century put positive relationships at the centre of their ultimate values – and associated their happiness most closely with strong affiliative bonds.

But these young adults also placed strong and consistent value on the types of people they hoped to be – intrinsic qualities centring around self-directedness, self-development and integrity in mind and action. The second cluster was comprised of such values. These were ranked relatively highly ('quite important' or 'most important') and somewhat tightly, although not as tightly grouped as the affiliative values cluster. This second cluster, which I have called the 'eudaimonic' values cluster, included the values of self-respect, freedom, a sense of accomplishment, and wisdom. These values bear within them images of the balanced and fulfilled person of integrity. Because of the focus of these values, I have selected the term 'eudaimonic' in keeping with social scientists' recent attention to Aristotle's ideas of *eudaimonia*, a happiness that psychologists such as Jack Bauer, Dan McAdams

---

[9]   Not all young adults completely placed all 18 values in categories of relative importance. Thus, there was missing data for some young adults, and the initial cluster solution included only a hundred respondents for whom there were no missing values. I then employed mean replacement for twelve young adults, replacing up to three of their missing values with average rankings for each of these values from the hundred respondents with complete data (three respondents with even more missing values were excluded). A second cluster solution following mean replacement yielded nearly identical results. Minkowski's (1907) metric of dissimilarity, used in tandem with Ward's (1963) agglomerative method, maximized dissimilarity between values, thus clarifying which values cohered most closely with each other: Hermann Minkowski, *Diophantische Approximationen* (Leipzig: Teubner, 1907) (see also Minkowski, 'Raum und Zeit', *Jahresberichte der Deutschen Mathematiker-Vereinigung* (1908/9): 75–88); J.H. Ward Jr., 'Hierarchical Grouping to Optimize an Objective Function', *Journal of the American Statistical Association* 48 (1963): 236–44. The restricted range of five relative rankings limited the potential for skewed results.

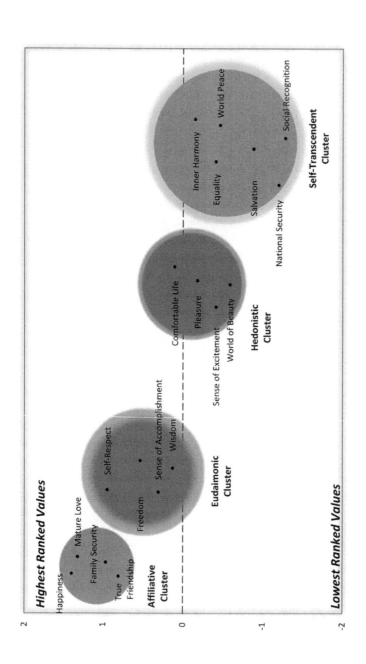

Figure 7.2   Profile of clusters of 115 young adults' 'terminal values'

and Jennifer Pals have tied to 'the highest cultivation of personal character',[10] as well as the pleasures encountered in the process of living the good life. This *eudaimonia*, focused on meaning and growth as sources of happiness, is contrasted with *hedonia*, a more raw and basic focus on pleasure and appeasement of desires.

It was in the third cluster that hedonistic values, or *hedonia*, coalesced. The 'hedonistic values' cluster included the values of pleasure, excitement, comfort and a world of beauty. Young adults typically ranked these pursuits oriented toward the pleasure principle as only 'somewhat important' or 'somewhat unimportant' – typically below affiliative and eudaimonic values.

But there was a fourth set of values that collectively fell below hedonistic values. This cluster included values related to a broader social context and to spiritual concerns: inner harmony, equality, world peace, salvation, national security and social recognition. These are 'self-transcendent' ultimate concerns. The values in this cluster were more widely dispersed in rank placement: young adults ranked some of these values in the 'somewhat important' range, but consistently placed others in the 'somewhat unimportant' or 'really not important' range. The values most tightly related in this cluster were world peace, equality, inner harmony and a world of beauty. Young adults were divided in how they ranked the importance of salvation as an ultimate value – the value most strongly associated with their religious involvement.

To summarize, young adults ranked affiliative values as their most important ultimate values, followed by eudaimonic values related to self-development and self-actualization. They regarded hedonistic values as less important in relation to affiliative and eudaimonic values – but generally more important than self-transcendent values.

These four clusters were statistically distinct and unique from each other.[11] But they were also clearly interdependent: a higher composite ranking of one set of values resulted in lower composite rankings in at least one of the other values clusters. Table 7.2 shows the strength of the contrasting relationships between the four values clusters.

Table 7.2   Correlations between values clusters

	1	2	3
Affiliative (1)	—		
Eudaimonic (2)	-.540***	—	
Hedonistic (3)	.021	-.232*	—
Self-transcendent (4)	-.228*	-.066	-.577***

Note: * p < .05; *** p < .001.

---

[10]   Jack Bauer, Dan McAdams and Jennifer Pals, 'Narrative Identity and Eudaimonic Well-Being', *Journal of Happiness Studies* 9 (2008): 82.

[11]   Within-subject differences in cluster scores were dramatic, $\underline{F}(1,114) = 824.4$, $\underline{p} < .001$. Post-hoc t-tests revealed significant differences between all pairs of values clusters.

These correlations reveal two clear pairings of competing clusters of values for young adults. In each pairing, valuing one cluster of values corresponded with devaluing the other cluster. Affiliative and eudaimonic values were pitted against each other for central focus in the minds and hearts of young adults: to emphasize relationships more results in less importance for self-image and self-actualization – and vice versa. Hedonistic and self-transcendent values were also strongly distinguished, placed by young adults in contrasting moderate to weak positions of importance.

There were also more modest contrasts between affiliative and self-transcendent values, and between eudaimonic and hedonistic values. But young adults' relative emphasis on affiliative values was not related in any clear way to their placement of hedonistic values, and the strength of their eudaimonic values had little impact on how they ranked self-transcendent values.

Second Cluster Analysis

I conducted the second cluster analysis on the transformed scores for the ten basic values that young adults rated as part of the overall *Making the Transition* study.[12] Figure 7.3 shows the pattern of four clusters emerging from this analysis: self-focused (self-expression and personal growth), self-transcendent (societal improvement, participation in community and clarity of convictions), task- or career-related (challenge and creative production), and hedonistic (money, fame and free time). Self-focused values were rated most highly. Hedonistic values received the lowest ratings, much lower than the other three clusters.

Comparison of the two sets of clusters is a bit complicated, since there were no clearly affiliative values rated on the same scale. None the less, there are clear similarities in the patterns of clusters between Figures 7.1 and 7.2, particularly between the hedonistic and self-transcendent clusters. Eudaimonic ultimate values seem to subdivide here into self-focused values (those focused more on self-improvement) and task- or career-related values (those focused on intrinsic satisfactions to be derived from vocational or avocational activity).

These four clusters branched distantly from each other, revealing clearly distinct sets of motivational values. As with the first set of values clusters of ultimate values, these clusters of basic values were interdependent. As shown in Table 7.3, correlations revealed very strong inverse relationships between hedonistic values and both the self-focused and the societal and spiritual values, and between the task-oriented values and the societal and spiritual values.

Although we did not ask *Transition* young adults directly about affiliative values in a format similar to the values above, we did ask them about the relative importance of career versus family. As shown in Figure 7.4, the majority of young adults considered family to be more important than career in their lives – but

---

[12]   I used the same agglomerative and distance methods employed in the first cluster analysis (Ward's error sum of squares formula and Minkowski's metric of dissimilarity).

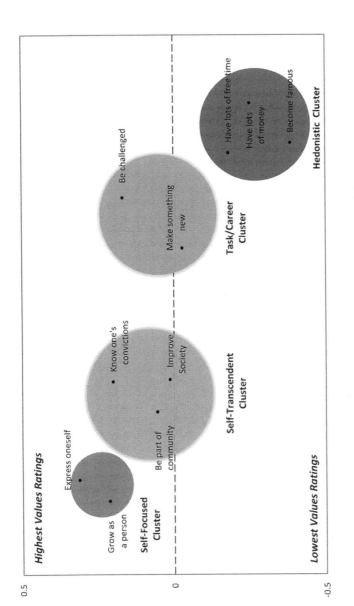

Figure 7.3   Profile of clusters of ten basic values by 315 *Transition* young adults

Table 7.3   Correlations between cluster scales of basic values

	1	2	3
Self-improvement (1)	—		
Self-transcendent (2)	.052	—	
Task-oriented (3)	-.236**	-.455***	—
Hedonistic (4)	-.504***	-.513***	-.281***

Note: ** p < .01; *** p < .005.

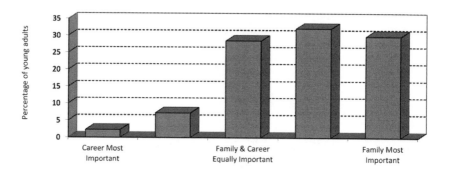

Figure 7.4   Importance of family versus career to *Transition* young adults (*n* = 305)

not to an extent of overriding career completely. Furthermore, there were strong correlations of young adults' ratings on this question with their relative rankings of affiliative values (*r* = .353, *p* < .005), and, inversely, with their rankings of self-image values (*r* = -.303, *p* < .005) – a pattern that reflects the tension between affiliative and self-image values.

Results from these two cluster analyses point consistently to clear patterns in young adults' implicit organization of values. Four distinct sets of ultimate values capture and express four distinct domains of meaningful ultimate values for young adults: affiliative, relationship-oriented values that are in marked tension with eudaimonic, self-focused values oriented toward personal improvement; and hedonistic, extrinsically oriented values that are in marked tension with broader self-transcendent values and, to a lesser degree, in some tension with eudaimonic values. A roughly similar pattern of tensions between sets of values emerged when examining young adults' relative ratings of day-to-day motivational values.

One consistent pattern worthy of note: quite different from the claims of some demographers and theologians, these American young adults at the turn of the century did not give prominence to hedonistic values. These young adults focused most on affiliative and eudaimonic values – and they were consistent in their disregard of the pursuit of hedonistic values.

Back to the Interviews: Core Values and Anti-values (Vices) in Young Adults'
Responses

Having these four categories of values in mind from the cluster analyses, we
returned to the interviews to classify young adults' verbal responses to the open-
ended questions about their values and anti-values. This close coding of interview
responses yielded a similar pattern to the cluster analyses, and provided insight
into how young adults thought about these values. Table 7.4 provides a summary
of the types of phrases and words young adults used to signal these values, as well
as anti-values that were usually distortions or extreme exaggerations of values.

Young adults' stated affiliative values were in terms of kindness, reciprocity,
love, loyalty, trust, respect, care and devotion – expressions of a self-giving
orientation to relationships. Their language for eudaimonic values included
descriptions of integrity, excellence of effort, ambition, perseverance and
tenacity, creativity, wisdom, balance and conviction – reflecting an aim toward
magnanimity of life and character. Expressions of hedonistic values were rarer
in young adults' responses; there were more frequent citations of hedonistic
'vices' or anti-values. Their few expressions of hedonism were focused on fun,
excitement, new experiences, pleasure and a 'live and let live' attitude, painting a
picture of a carefree bohemian lifestyle of the vagabond. In contrast, young adults
stated many more examples and descriptions of self-transcendent values. They
expressed values such as devotion to God, moral goodness and decency, equal and
non-judgemental treatment of others, social awareness and altruism, conviction,
and service to others.

Table 7.5 below shows how many young adults spoke directly about each
type of value or anti-value. Overall, the pattern of responses is consistent with the
profile of values-clusters from the Life Values Survey – for both core principles
and admired human attributes. Young adults were most likely to state affiliative
concerns and principles as their core values (41.6 per cent), and least likely to
mention them as anti-values (7.3 per cent). They were not as likely to state self-
transcendent concerns or principles as their core values (18.3 per cent), but most
likely to mention them as non-values (36.6 per cent). Affiliative values were
named by the most emerging adults, followed by eudaimonic values, and self-
transcendent values. Hedonistic values were named as core values by only 9.8 per
cent of young adults. Core anti-values were stated in a nearly opposite sequence
of frequency, with self-transcendent anti-values named most frequently, followed
next by a quasi-respectful refusal to answer the question because of a principle
of tolerance young adults did not want to violate – followed by hedonistic anti-
values, and eudaimonic anti-values. Affiliative concerns and principles were
named by only a few young adults as their core anti-values.

Thus, these young adults did not simply name certain values as relatively
important or unimportant: they also clearly named attributes they saw as vices or
distorted values contributing to negative outcomes when taken to extremes. Most
frequently among these distorted values or vices were broader social and spiritual

Table 7.4   Examples of young adults' key phrases indicating strongly held values and anti-values

Affiliative value phrases	Eudaimonic value phrases
Be happy without hurting people	Stand up for your individuality
Be nice	Live each day as your best
Practice the Golden Rule	Try your best
Love other people	Be true to yourself, don't imitate
Focus on family life	Keep yourself as the focus of your goals
Love your neighbour	Increase your own understanding
Understand people	Believe in yourself
Do no harm	Have goals
Show loyalty and trust	Find your own potential
Do what is best for family without harming others	Do whatever you believe in
Treat people honestly	Live with balance in life
Treat everyone with respect	Have tenacity and initiative
Have compassion	Be present in the moment
Be helpful	Be smart
Show tenderness	Have a strong will
Be caring	Pursue ambition
	Use your free will
	Persevere
	Be creative
	Use your intelligence

Hedonistic value phrases	Spiritual and social value phrases
Life goes on … live and let live	Know God
Have fun, be tolerant	Treat people equally
Make the most of life	Be a good person
Try everything once	Be tolerant
Live for today	Do the right thing
Enjoy yourself	Be a decent person
Enjoy life	Be open, don't judge
Do what one loves	Worship in more than one way
Look for fulfilment	Believe in God
	Love as *the* energy
	Self-giving
	Stand up for beliefs
	Making the world better
	Sacrifice
	Pursue women's rights
	Be ready to serve others
	Be altruistic
	Be socially aware

Table 7.5   Core value statements in 82 young adult interviews

Value type	Percentage (*n* = 82)	Non-value ('vice') type	Percentage (*n* = 82)
Core value – to live by		*Anti-value – to avoid or not live by*	
Affiliative	41.6	Affiliative	7.3
Self-image	25.6	Self-image	9.8
Hedonistic	9.8	Hedonistic	17.1
Social and spiritual	18.3	Social and spiritual	36.6
No values stated	4.9	No anti-values mentioned	29.2*
Best human attributes (first two responses)		*Worst human attributes (first two responses)*	
At least one stated attribute		*At least one stated attribute*	
Affiliative	47.6	Affiliative	51.8
Self-image	50.0	Self-image	30.5
Hedonistic	4.9	Hedonistic	26.8
Social and spiritual	36.6	Social and spiritual	31.7
No response given	0.8	No response given	1.6

* Over twenty young adults responded that there were no values held by others that they held in disdain or considered unimportant. Many of these young adults defaulted to a 'tolerance' argument, stating that they could not judge others' values as unimportant or out-of-place.

values – particularly values contributing to the dogmatism and social campaigns of political and religious movements. Strong adherence to a belief system, whether religious or political, seemed abhorrent to young adults. They tended to equate such strong adherence with vices of fanaticism, fundamentalism, intolerance and an invasive approach.

The pattern was somewhat different for responses to our questions about most admired and disdained human attributes. Only 4.9 per cent of young adults named hedonistic values as admirable attributes – even those who stated a hedonistic core value tended not to admire people who pursued similar hedonistic aims. Most young adults described eudaimonic values or affiliative values as the most admirable human qualities, particularly in examples of people who embodied the 'Golden Rule', or who were examples of the self-made man or woman. They also admired people who demonstrated strong self-transcendent values – even if only half of them stated similar qualities as their own core values by which they tried to live.

Interestingly, when naming negative human attributes worthy of their disdain or disgust, over half of the young adults named affiliative characteristics as non-values or vices. These were almost exclusively distortions or excesses of affiliative values (for instance, 'people who cling to others'). Mutated, distorted, or excessive self-transcendent qualities ('people who are religious fanatics'), eudaimonic qualities ('people who have no self-esteem', 'people who are too stuck on themselves'), and hedonistic qualities ('people who are greedy') were named as anti-values or vices by roughly similar percentages of young adults.

These patterns of responses from the interviews both confirm and provide richer understanding of young adults' clusters of values. These young adults most frequently placed their highest value on solid and healthy affiliation, both in their own lives and in the lives of people they admire. They also highly valued the attainment of self-focused qualities such as skills and abilities, positive self-image, wisdom and balance in life. They did not frequently admit to holding hedonistic pursuits as their central values, and such values focused on such extrinsic self-gratification were even less frequently among human attributes they admired. Finally, although they somewhat frequently stated spiritual and social values as central or admirable, they also frequently expressed disdain or anxiety about such values for their potential to become fanatical or absolutist ideals, which they clearly viewed as social and spiritual vices.

Going Deeper: Values in Their Own Words

To highlight the complexity in young adults' discussion of values, let us first look at Rachel's responses. Rachel, an African American who had grown up Baptist and was living with her boyfriend, revealed a somewhat bleak outlook on humanity. She began by describing what she saw as the worst of human values, or anti-values:

> I think our worst is we don't take care of what we live on. We don't own the planet. Basically, we're living on the planet and we don't take care of it. And, our good is that we are becoming more educated and technical. Computers are getting a lot better. And, you know, they're coming up with more medicines for different things and finding solutions to different human problems. But our worst, I think, is that we don't take care of the earth. Because, mostly, we don't care.

> There are *some* humane people here. There are some … very few. But our best is in those people who help each other and actually make this world a nice place to be in.

Rachel's description of most admirable and disdained human qualities reveals something not only her own ultimate values but also of her view of humanity in relation to the good. For Rachel, humanity was almost hopeless in its disregard for the earth – an ecologically informed perspective shared by many young adults. Despite advances in technology and health that were improving human conditions, ecological misuse and overuse were continuing. Rachel admired the few people she saw who were willing to step beyond their own self-interests and make the world more liveable. Interestingly, she did not mention people devoted to ecological conservation: her thoughts returned to benefits for human society when thinking about good people.

But Rachel not only admired altruistic people who cared for others. She also admired 'self-made' people – the men and women who became materially successful from meagre beginnings: 'People that I admire most are when they're not born in money and they succeed so much, do you know what I mean? Where they actually start from the bottom and make it all the way to the top instead of being born at the top.' Rachel upheld an American ideal of 'bootstrap theology': people who personally overcame adversity and became successful were most admirable and most embodied the American Dream. Rachel contrasted bootstrap successes with those who were materially secure and developed an attitude of personal entitlement and lack of concern for others: 'People that disgust me are the people who have no care in the world. They think that they own everything or think they're better than you just because they're rich.'

Rachel turned from a more individual focus to a broader social concern. She expressed disgust for the government because of policies she saw having a direct negative impact on an addicted friend in need. This was Rachel's longest exposition about values and principles. It echoes her 'bootstrap theology' and her disdain for entitlement, and voices her desire for a society that held people responsible:

Somehow, my friend got addicted to heroin. And she went to the clinic to get methadone. And it's like, wouldn't you think if she's going to the clinic to get methadone then she would have some sort of counsellor to say ok, she's been on this certain milligrams for this long, let's lower her milligrams. And lower it, and lower it. Well, she's been on methadone since '97 and she pays money to the clinic and the government still gives her methadone.

And so now instead of her being addicted to heroin, she's addicted to methadone. And the government is just sitting there taking her money and allowing her to still do it. It's so sad. The government is supporting her bad habit. That's still like getting, that's still like getting her fix, you know? I mean, she's on the lowest that you can go in milligrams. But yet the doctor's still giving it to her. And she, she's got a 4-year-old daughter that she had to give to another family – her daughter's staying with her ex-fiancé's parents. She actually came over to my house Monday morning and was like, 'Rachel, I want help. Da da da da da.' I'm like, 'OK, you can stay here.' And she's like, 'I'll be sick but it won't be that bad sick. I'll just have the chills, but I won't be really sick.' And I'm like, 'All right,' you know? And she's like, 'I want to get my daughter back, I want to get my life back. Da da da da da.' And, you know, she left. I came home from work. I got her a job at my company. And she wasn't there. And I haven't heard from her since. Because she knows that, hey I just get the money, the government 40 bucks and I can still get my fix. However many times a week I want to go. It's sad. It's so sad.

With low esteem for social and governmental structures and a dim view of human capacity for change (with a few bright exceptions), Rachel focused on a core principle of personal authenticity and integrity in the limited domain of her life and influence:

> Be the person that you are. Don't try to be somebody you're not. Be a leader and not a follower. And do what you think is right. You know? Go with your instincts and not with what everybody else says.

> In a lot of ways I try to be the person that I was taught to be. You know? I try to be the person that my mom taught me to be. I don't understand why people can't be the person that they are. You know, they try to put a front to everybody. It's like, they try to make themselves seem to be so good. I don't understand that.

For Rachel, honesty in living and responsibility for one's own choices were core values by which she judged her own life and the lives of others. She was opposed to pretence.

Rachel's response covered a wide range of values – altruistic or reciprocal care, bootstrap success and personal responsibility, ecological stewardship, personal honesty and authenticity, self-respect and respect for others. These values spanned affiliative, eudaimonic, hedonistic and self-transcendent concerns. She clearly found challenges living up to some of these values, and lamented the lack of consistent example or supportive program and standard in her surrounding culture. This drew her toward core eudaimonic values of living with personal integrity as her best path to happiness.

Not all young adults held the same values as Rachel. Not all of them faced similar challenges in their friendships and civic life. But overall, these young adults had to choose and navigate values in relation to their worlds of increasing complexity, inconsistency and challenge, as they sought to answer for themselves questions of the good and the desirable.

In their rankings of values, young adults placed happiness at the forefront of their ultimate values. They implicitly embraced a perspective offered long ago by Aristotle and the Buddha – and many theologians and social scientists since then – that happiness may indeed be the chief aim of human beings.

But happiness may be sought and realized through several paths. The clusters emerging from young adults' organization of values suggest four distinct paths: an affiliative path (in which happiness is tied to rewarding and enduring relationships), a eudaimonic path (linking happiness with magnanimity of character and fulfilment of potential), a hedonistic path (in which happiness is tied to the extrinsic experience of pleasure, excitement, comfort and beauty), and a self-transcendent path (in which happiness is linked to a spaciousness of concern for one's connection with the broader world and the afterlife).

In the following pages, I explore these four paths more intently, through deeper probing of young adults' narrative responses to our questions of values as well as other questions about relational ethics, work ethics and life dreams. Along with deeper investigation of these four paths of values, I examine the basic ethical stance of beneficence (do good) and non-maleficence (do no harm)[13] inherent in young adults' core values and principles for living.

Let us begin with the values least frequently extolled by young adults: hedonistic values.

Hedonism is Overrated

'Try everything once.' 'Live for today.' 'Enjoy yourself as fully as you can.' 'Look for fulfilment.' These are quotes from the few young adults that occasionally affirmed or asserted hedonistic values. Hedonism is understood commonly as a devotion to pursuing and indulging in pleasure. This devotion to pleasure includes the pursuit of excitement, comfort and beauty, as well as the acquisition of material goods for the purposes of maximizing these goods and for minimizing pain, discomfort, boredom, or ugliness.

Aside from the 5 per cent of young adults who most admired hedonistic qualities and the 10 per cent who claimed hedonistic ideals as their core principles for living, I did not find much esteem for hedonistic values among *Transition* young adults. Instead, I found a much higher percentage of young adults who *de*-valued hedonism in contrast to the centrality of relationships and personal development. The few young adults with hedonistic values tended to state interpersonal negligence and intentional harm as barriers or limits to the pursuit of pleasure and enjoyment – a practical ethic of non-maleficence (expressed fundamentally as 'do no harm') that acknowledged the right of others to pursue similar interests with as much freedom. For these few young adults, happiness was indeed tied more closely to pleasure, excitement and comfort. But even they were not exclusively self-focused in their hedonistic values. Beyond basic non-maleficence, a few young adults extended their hedonistic values to providing and securing comfort, pleasure, excitement and a world of beauty for their families, loved ones, or close friends and communities. Examples of 'non-maleficent hedonism' and tensions between hedonism and altruism, as well as glimmers of a more 'altruistic hedonism', came through in the responses of Jeannie, Michael, Jacob and Philip.

Jeannie (a Christmas-and-Easter Methodist pharmacy graduate student) stated no explicit core value or principle by which she tried to live. When asked about people she most admired, Jeannie replied, 'I guess I admire people who get what they want but they do it honestly, don't step on people on the way up

---

[13]   See Liam Murphy for a critical examination of the beneficence principle, and Samuel Richmond for an example of the tension between hedonism and non-maleficence: Liam Murphy, 'The Demands of Beneficence', *Philosophy and Public Affairs* 22(4) (Autumn 1993): 267–92; Samuel Richmond, 'On Replacing the Notion of Intrinsic Value', *Journal of Value Inquiry* 10(3) (1973): 205–08.

to get what you want.' She most admired human qualities involving the pursuit of self-satisfaction – within a broader context of keeping good-enough human relationships. Her practical ethic of non-maleficence set boundaries on her own pursuits of self-satisfaction so that she did not intrude on others' pursuits of the good life, but did not require additional focus on or effort on behalf of others beyond basic concerns for her own family.

Jeannie's interest was in acquisition of the desirable – but not just for herself. Her goals to attain comfort and freedom from want extended beyond herself to her future family. Her somewhat vaguely stated value system was rooted in self-interest, tipping toward hedonism, but also evoking personal eudaimonic qualities like tenacity. Her values of self-determination and dedication to provide for family came through in how she named and discussed her abhorrence for the vices of sloth and the shirking of financial responsibility: 'People that disgust me would have to be people who … *can't, like, provide for their families*, it just makes me so mad. Because, it can't be that hard. You know, if I can get a job making minimum wage – pretty much anybody can – if that's what it takes they should do it.' For Jeannie, neglect of responsibility would have a direct negative impact on one's family, and Jeannie wanted nothing to do with this kind of mindset. In fact, her concern for financial responsibility was important enough to her that she considered breaking up with her boyfriend because he bought a new truck after having a new car for only four months:

> It's a really expensive truck and I was like, 'Why do you want to buy a truck?' Then, I'm like, 'We can't get married,' and he's like, 'Yeah we can,' and I'm like, 'No, you can't afford it,' and he's like, 'Well I'm getting a raise in a couple months,' and I'm like, 'Whatever, I don't care,' and he's like, 'Well, let's get married now.'

Jeannie's argument with her boyfriend illustrates that not all hedonistic orientations are alike. There is an important distinction among hedonistically oriented young adults, related to impulse control and the timing of gratification. Unlike her boyfriend's hedonism, Jeannie's hedonism was not synonymous with instant gratification. She wanted material goods for herself and her family, but in good measure, in good time, in accord with sound financial planning. Jeannie's conflict with her boyfriend was primarily about the day-to-day disciplines required to maximize long-term pleasures and comforts. Jeannie provides an example of how it is possible to be hedonistic and not simply become a ping-pong ball bouncing from personal impulse to impulse – and how it is possible to extend hedonistic values so that they concern more than oneself but include at least one's family, beyond the present and into the future.

Michael (of Roman Catholic and Jewish background) neatly illustrated the tension between altruism and hedonism, particularly in his distinction between ethical positions of 'do no harm' (non-maleficence) and 'do good' (beneficence). On the surface, Michael seemed similar to Jeannie. He admired 'people that have made something out of themselves and been successful' and with the ability 'to provide for their family'. He stated an aversion toward the vices or anti-values of dishonesty, sloth and entitlement: 'people that expect hand outs, don't want to do anything, and just want to be successful for doing nothing.' But Michael went further than Jeannie in limiting his concern to himself and his family. When asked about other people's core values that made little sense to him, Michael named altruism as an example of a distorted ideal:

> I think people maybe carry things too far sometimes, giving to charity, whatever it may be, they just take it too far. No ideal should necessarily disrupt your own life that much. The people that dedicate so much of their life to something …
> I mean, it's the way they live their life, so obviously they're enjoying it, but I think anything that takes away from your own life is excessive.

This response pointed to self-interest as the heart of Michael's values. Unlike other young adults, Michael did not target ideological fanaticism as the excessive or distorted self-transcendent value: rather, he saw dedicated public service as potentially excessive and mis-focused, especially when it intruded on one's personal life. Such a core value might be stated as 'All things in balance, and my own life is central.' While not directly hedonistic, his response pointed consistently to underlying commitments to personal comfort and enjoyment, and a barrier to intrusion upon those commitments. He attempted to understand altruistic motivation by looking for people's personal enjoyment in such activity, further belying his underlying hedonistic orientation. Michael expressed a value system that was the closest of any *Transition* young adults to Ayn Rand's 'virtue of selfishness' – a value system that has since been echoed in the emergent values of the Tea Party movement in America. It is a position in which one may still hold a practical ethical standard of non-maleficence while standing firm against any sense of obligation toward beneficence by way of altruistic effort for others who are expected to take responsibility for their own happiness.

Despite this hint of hedonistic underpinnings and aversion to altruism, Michael turned toward personal character for his most central value, affirming honesty and trustworthiness as core eudaimonic values:

> [I aim] to be a trustworthy person. Because I think if you can't be honest with someone then you're pretty much kind of worthless. That's just a really big thing for me, it always has been. I'm not really sure why, because I've never been really crossed badly or anything. Maybe it's just because that's the way my parents are. They've always stressed honesty and trust.

Hedonistic values are not absent in religious or theological texts, nor are they only debased as distortions. Most religious traditions and texts include affirmations of life's pleasures, within bounds. Biblical texts at times assert the enjoyment of pleasures, but at other times admonish those who have allowed the pursuit of comfort and pleasure to intrude on their basic concern for other human beings and to lead them to ignore – or even add to – the plight of others in need. Hindu temple statues depict sexual scenes to indicate the delights of intimate union with the divine. The Omar Khayyam's *Rubáiyát* quatrains, written within the heart of Muslim Persia, are replete with praise of life's simple pleasures in the face of its unnerving temporality and the inevitable road of mortality. Theologians and religious leaders as diverse as mediaeval mystics like Meister Ekhart, modern feminist sexual ethicists like Christine Gudorf, and contemporary 'prosperity gospel' preachers like Joel Osteen begin with assertions of pleasure, comfort, excitement and beauty as inherently good.

But, as our American young adults have expressed, there is potential for corruption of hedonistic values through over-emphasis and placement of pleasures above other goods. This is also a common theme in the world's religions. The potential for excess, over-attachment and addiction haunt hedonic experiences. Buddhist, Confucian, Christian, Hindu, Jewish and Muslim scriptures and teachings emphasize the potential for pleasure-oriented desire to override concerns for personal integrity and honesty, relational commitments, and broader social and spiritual goods that all contribute to a sense of proportionality. Ascetic and puritanical traditions in these religions underscore this emphasis on the potential for distortion of hedonistic values to override higher, holier and more enduring concerns.

Rather than rejecting this perspective, American young adults may have taken to heart some of the deep religious perspectives still embedded in American social, political and cultural scripts. Among the *Transition* young adults interviewed, 17 per cent mentioned distortions or amplifications of hedonistic values as examples of abhorrent ways of living, and 27 per cent specifically identified excessive hedonism as a principle to avoid. Their examples of excessive hedonism were focused on overt materialistic addiction and greed, a slothful or arrogant attitude of entitlement to life's comforts, and self-absorption in meeting one's desires without concern for others. Many of these young adults set excessive hedonistic values in tension and contrast with affiliative or eudaimonic values. Fewer young adults contrasted excessive hedonism with more self-transcendent values focused on the common good or spiritual transformation.

But there were also some young adults who tempered their abhorrence of excessive hedonistic values by affirming that, within limits, people deserved to seek and enjoy life's comforts and pleasures. These limits typically referred back to relational and personal integrity – often with direct reference to the Golden Rule or its core organizing frameworks of interpersonal and social reciprocity, altruistic intention and non-violation.

Consider Jacob, a young Jewish man who expressed a tension around hedonistic values – on one hand abhorring overt materialistic greed but on the other hand valuing enjoyment and a world of beauty. Jacob was clear about abhorrent human qualities: 'People who disgust me the most are people who have a lot of avarice, or greed ... Money-makers. They just seem to make money for the sake of making it.' Jacob at first had trouble identifying admirable human qualities, and responded only with additional probing:

> Jacob: I haven't really found anyone that I admire.
>
> *David: What traits do you think are most valuable? Or what qualities?*
>
> Jacob: Well, someone who sincerely enjoys what they're doing. And has found something in life that, that they cherish in their life, in their job, in their family. It can be something literal, but that something that, that propels them to go forward, that seems to be … something on a somewhat humanitarian level.

With some gentle prompting beyond his initial noncommittal stance, Jacob was able to state what he saw as a clear admirable good: enjoyment. The enjoyment he attempted to describe was not merely a materialistic pleasure free of self-absorbed or addictive greed: its focus was completely different, linked to a cherishing of interpersonal and eudaimonic good. This became clearer in what he described (again with gentle probing) as his core organizing principle for living: 'Leonard Bernstein wrote once that a great idea never ends. I read it once and, and never have been able to find it again, but could be the underlying principles of everything that I do: "If I start with something great I'll know how to continue it."' For Jacob, enjoyment signalled a more eudaimonic focus on self-fulfilment through creativity and dedication. As an artist, Jacob linked this dedication to his passion for his evolving vocation in theatre and music, and thus to a more altruistic hedonistic value of a world of beauty. Any obliquely hedonistic interest on Jacob's part was far removed from the greed he abhorred.

Jacob was not alone. Disdain for greed was particularly common among *Transition* young adults. These young adults were appalled by what they saw as periodic signs in American society of rampant materialism and relentless commitment to acquisition. Philip, a young military cadet, spoke of greed – and contrasted the self-absorption of greed with the integrity of *eudaimonia* and the self-dedication of altruism:

> I think greed is a killer. And I don't just say greed now, but it's been greed always. People compromise their own integrity. Or they compromise what they really know is the best thing in their life. Like, they'll sell out. They'll sell out their family or anything else, because of what is right there in front of them. They'll want that apple and they'll just throw away the paradise that they had. The best thing in life that I see, is those that are willing to, I guess, not only get beyond that. That, that's almost a childish thing to say, you know? 'Take what's in front of me now. Work for just greed.' That's just such a childish thing that, if you can get beyond that, you're gonna have a whole better perspective of life. And those people that try and make the world better for every single other person in the world, those are the people that I admire.

For Philip, as for Jacob, Jeannie, and many young adults, there was nothing admirable in overt or extreme hedonism. For them, the raw pursuit of pleasure led down dead-end paths of immature self-absorption, entitlement and greedy disregard for others. For them – and for most young adults – the pursuit and enjoyment of life's material and physical pleasures were bounded by firm commitments to personal integrity, the Golden Rule and the common good, at the very least in the form of doing no harm but frequently from a more expansive perspective of providing good for others.

Eudaimonia: Valuing of Self-development

Happiness need not be tied to pleasure, and not all self-focused values are hedonistic. Many young adults stated self-focused values that were more eudaimonic, focused on self-development and self-actualization through character. Twenty-five per cent of young adults claimed such eudaimonic values as their core guiding principles, and 50 per cent mentioned these values as most admirable human attributes. These young adults named creativity, productivity, personal growth and wisdom as core values, contrasting them against sloth, materialism, ignorance and extreme ideological adherence.

Many *Transition* young adults regarded eudaimonic values as highly important. They tended to focus on becoming persons of quality, possessing and exercising admirable attributes, and expressing themselves in ways that were true to their inner character. Because young adults regarded fame and social recognition as unimportant values, we can surmise that their interests in eudaimonic values were not primarily for the sake of being admired by others. Rather, as observers of their own lives, young adults wanted to see and know themselves as people who sought to inhabit and exercise qualities of high character. They wanted to be and become the good person, and to see themselves as the good person. And their images of the good person included a wide array of admirable human qualities – courage, creativity, wisdom, personal integrity and authenticity, honesty, and balance and moderation – but they did not typically include images of moral rectitude.

Interview responses by Steve, Shanille, Kasey and Alexandra revealed the array of eudaimonic values that so many young adults claimed as most central and most admirable, irrespective of their religious or non-religious backgrounds.

Steve (a culinary student and ardent atheist with interests in Taoism) held a eudaimonic ideal focused on self-expression and personal achievement. This included his admiration of pushing beyond one's limits and bringing one's interests and passions into direct interaction with the patterns at play in the world: 'The greatest and really only basis for our interacting with the world is in finding out the extent and depth and character of what we can do, you know? What our work is of what can work in society. And that anything else is a waste of time or savage, you know?'

Steve particularly admired people's bold, unapologetic interaction with the world, stating that he marvelled at 'the way in which people are constantly *stumbling into the outside world* – and *in a thoroughly undaunted and quite striking way'*. Steve's eudaimonic values were centred on creative achievement. But they also implicitly required courage sufficient to interact with the world and to put one's creativity to the test. Steve valued an ultimate value of impact in the world – not as much through altruistic contribution to society, but more by leaving an imprint on society through personally unique contributions for which creativity and courage would be necessary.

This interest in impact through personally unique achievements becomes clearer when examining Steve's anti-values. Steve stated a strong aversion to 'people who don't want anything to change because they like things very much the way they are, thank you very much, and "only maybe if I was a little bit richer", or some other garbage, and engage in no qualitative pursuit of human enrichment'. Here he expressed aversions to sloth, greed and self-absorption. Steve later said that these vices lead to social 'morbidity' and 'savage brutes' – and he cited President Clinton as an example, alluding to the President's affair with intern Monica Lewinsky. Even though an atheist, Steve had a clear picture of vices easily linked to overt *hedonia*, and described them almost like deadly sins in terms of their consequences.

Shanille (a disgruntled Roman Catholic involved in Wiccan religion) focused on self-development and personal growth as her core eudaimonic values. Part of her self-development included learning about a sense of purpose and an intentionality in learning from life's events:

> I guess the principle I try to live my life by is that there is a purpose for me, and that I am out there trying to grow towards that – towards where I need to be. And that my life in general needs to be a growth process. And I try now to take every situation and learn something from it and grow from everything.

Shanille's interest in learning and growth was for herself primarily, and others secondarily. This was reflected in how she talked about people she admired: 'the people that are out there making a good world for themselves, and making a good world for everybody else. I admire most the people who are doing everything in their power to make things better for themselves and everybody else.' Shanille found most admirable a pattern of self-directed building of personal and shared good – starting with the personal first, but extending beyond oneself to interpersonal and societal spheres. When pairing her two statements, it seems that Shanille's value of growth and personal development (a eudaimonic concern) was linked to her value of the good life (a more hedonistic concern). Such a pairing is not new or unique to American culture: it echoes an ancient Greco-Roman image of the good citizen as both magnanimous in character and abundant in lifestyle.

While Shanille valued self-development, she counted self-absorption, selfishness and self-neglect as clear vices: 'The people that I don't like are the people that aren't trying to grow. That aren't out there for anybody else's well-being but their own.

And sometimes not even that. Those kind … that's what really turns me off about people in general. But there's a big number of those people out there.'

Shanille echoed Steve in her aversion for people whose self-focus was not oriented toward becoming and did not include any interest in others. For her, such mutated self-interest, which she viewed as commonplace in society, was not eudaimonic and was a dead-end path.

Kasey (a business professional and atheist) launched first into naming the human attributes she most abhorred: selfishness and lack of regard for others: 'Oh, yeah, that's easy. People that disgust me are basically self-serving, selfish. And, any of the things you want to add to someone that's self-serving. You know, there's "ruthless", whatever. They don't care about anybody else.' Kasey then juxtaposed ruthless self-interest with courage and conviction to stand up for others: 'The very opposite of that is people that are courageous. People that stand up for other people when they don't need to do this stuff, but they just go out of their way to do something to show other people support. That's the other side of that idea.'

For Kasey, courage was a principal virtue. This put Kasey implicitly into conversation with the rich philosophical and theological traditions of Aristotle and Thomas Aquinas. In these traditions, courage is one of the four cardinal virtues indicative of the most admirable people – and, like prudence, moderation and clear judgement, a quality to be fostered and practiced. As an atheist, Kasey would not explicitly claim such theological alliances, but her description of courage as coming to the aid of others sets her values apart from a purely Nietzschean or Randian focus on courage as strength of self-assertion in order to win. Kasey's atheism did not make space for pure, ruthless self-interest. Indeed, when asked about a core guiding principle, Kasey stated two core values: kindness (an affiliative value) and conscientiousness or dedication (a eudaimonic value): 'I guess, I try to be nice to people. There's no reason for me to want to be mean or hurt anyone else. I guess I always try to keep that in mind. And I might think about how I interact with people, like if I say something and then I see someone's face and they make a frown, I'll think about it.'

This is not the perspective of a purely Nietzschean or Randian atheist. Kasey was mindful of her impact on others. This shaped her interpersonal interactions. It also shaped her approach to work:

> As a major principle, I just naturally work hard. But I don't say that's a principle, necessarily; I'm just like that. I don't know, probably because I'm impatient. I just want to get done. I just have this mentality that I'm there, if I'm there I'm going to do it, I'm not going to be there and just fall asleep. I'm not going to waste people's time.

Kasey sought to ensure a boundary against sloth and ruthless self-interest by focusing on eudaimonic commitments to courage, conviction and conscientiousness. Kasey was almost warrior-like in her values – her happiness was tied to her exercise of personal strength in the service of her work and her care for others.

Where Kasey emphasized courage and conscientiousness, Alexandra emphasized moderation and prudence. Alexandra (an atheist dental student married to a devout Catholic) was particularly focused on finding a balance – an Aristotelian 'golden mean', if you will – between extreme polarities of zealotry and insecurity, of arrogance and pledged ignorance:

> This is sort of a study in fine lines. Because, I'm certain that zealots and fundamentalists disgust me. But people with really deep-seated insecurities I find pathetic. I don't want to associate with [them], because usually their insecurities are manifested in the ugliest ways. So people who are extremely sure of themselves, and extremely unsure of themselves, I find the most difficult to deal with … You shouldn't just have the courage of your convictions, you should have the courage to attack your convictions. And that's where I find myself in the middle of this, sort of, sureness and unsureness.

> Maybe all of the traits that I admire or that disgust me are related to this thing of moderation. I don't like people who don't privilege their own intelligence. I don't like people who privilege their intelligence above all others. If I had a choice to deal with people who were not that smart but interested in interesting things or people who were quite smart but obsessed with petty things, I'd rather deal with the not-so-smart people who are interested in interesting things. I admire people who are fully and cynically considering their situations. Who are taking as little for granted as possible, but not paralysed by it. It's all moderations, I guess.

Alexandra's stress on moderation pulled toward the focus on virtues that produce balance and wisdom – in Aristotle's and Thomas Aquinas' terms, the importance of prudence, temperance and just judgement as virtues. The Aristotelian value of a 'golden mean' of balance and wisdom implicitly included a commitment to some detachment, a resistance to being hooked by strong ideals and philosophical positions, whether other people's or one's own. But this detachment was combined with a yearning for breadth and depth of insight, an openness to understand. And she cast all of these more eudaimonic self-development values within a context of loving relationships. It is in this context of intellectual and interpersonal openness and desire to expand and connect that Alexandra named happiness as the ultimate outcome and ultimate value: 'In the broadest sense to be capable of explaining as much as possible. Which is to say making an effort to explain other people's actions, understand them. And then also to create relationships where there's love. And that's, that's towards happiness. Maybe that's the overall goal.'

Affiliative Values and the Golden Rule in Everyday Life

Transition young adults put the strongest emphasis on affiliative values, most directly linking happiness with mature love, true friendship and family security. Forty per cent of interviewed young adults named affiliative values as their core principles for living, and nearly 48 per cent named them as most admirable human attributes. Such values could not be expressed without direct or implicit reference to another person or group of persons. Young adults named mutual respect, loyalty and the anticipatory reciprocity of the Golden Rule (whether explicitly named or merely described) as core values tied to interpersonal relationships. They also frequently mentioned honesty, not only as a core value, but as an instrumental ethic for pursuing respect and the Golden Rule – and they talked about dishonesty as a hindrance to these values. When describing these interpersonal values, young adults like Dean, Christopher, MeiLi and Joel most frequently talked about family and friendship as the relationships in which these values were most clearly demonstrated – and set these values in contrast to a form of self-absorption that distracted people from deeper affiliative concerns. Dogmatism, prejudice, sloth and materialism were other competing distorted values and behaviours that undermined core relational values of mutual respect, loyalty and reciprocal care.

Dean (a Jewish financial adviser) very clearly stated the Golden Rule as his core value – and linked this more localized interpersonal value to the healthy functioning of human society:

> I think the one principle that I would say is more important than the others would just be to treat other people the way I would wish to be treated. Which is pretty basic, but I think that interpersonal relationships are the basis of society and the world as we know it. And so to talk about values and how you ought to deal with the world, I think that's the most important place to start,

Dean's first concern was to foster caring, trusting interpersonal relationships based on mutual regard and respect. His understanding of the Golden Rule as important to the good of society was further reflected in how he thought about two admirable human attributes, creativity and generosity, in the service of human care:

> I think most people are capable of being extremely generous, and those of us who are creative are capable of sort of even being more so, you know even giving things to the rest of humanity that the rest of them could never even have imagined. Making their lives better. I think the generosity thing is kind of an overarching umbrella over my view of the good things, as far as giving of yourself, and you know your time, and you know giving affection to your kids and spouse and you know your friends and whatnot.

For Dean, creativity was not simply a matter of self-expression. It was not an end in itself, but a means toward making life better for others.

Dean's dedication to the Golden Rule was set against his aversion to extreme allegiances to limited or exclusive ideals. He cited some Jewish beliefs and values he grew up with, as examples:

Within Judaism, I know there are certain kinds of exclusionary ideas. The idea that you absolutely stay within the faith because it's a small group of people, and it's bad if you marry outside or if you don't raise your kids Jewish. I think ideas like that are counterproductive. Likewise, certain groups hating other groups because of something that appeared in a book hundreds of years ago. It just doesn't make a lot of sense to me. I mean basically, when it comes down to it, life is fairly short. It just doesn't make any sense to set up superficial or external boundaries between people. Because, there are certain things that are going to naturally divide people, certain core beliefs, or what you like to do or where you live or things like that. But the notion of building up further differences just based on a certain interpretation of a certain scripture or a certain belief about how the world came to be, and then becoming dogmatic about that and at times even violent or if not violent just very opposed to any other way, it just seems very counterproductive.

Dean's opposition to dogmatism was not because of some dedication to ambiguity or sloppy theological thinking. Dean opposed dogmatism because of its divisive impact in interpersonal relationships and in society as a whole. And his concern for caring human relationships went beyond simple wishful thinking that everybody ought to get along with each other or merely tolerate each other. Dean was also repulsed by insensitivity of people to each others' needs, and the common ways in which people 'dehumanize' others by ignoring them:

I think it's amazing how insensitive people can become and how distant they can become in the same moment. You know, how you can be so generous on the one hand and on the other hand completely dehumanize someone ... And I think that's when the worst things happen, when people just aren't thinking. I think intentional acts of cruelty are probably far outnumbered by unintentional acts of, if not cruelty then just omissions of thought.

Dean specifically talked about the typical practice of passersby with homeless people and beggars: 'you just sort of walk right by and say you know don't even make eye contact and I think in that instance you really, it's kind of dehumanizing.'

Overall, Dean's ultimate value of the Golden Rule was expanded in specific ways to help Dean keep in the forefront of his mind some broader concerns for others beyond himself and his immediate family. Even Dean's choice of career in international finance was guided in part by consideration of how he could best address human needs.

Like Dean, Christopher (an 'agnostic explorer') also stated the Golden Rule directly, and named several specific ways of orienting his day-to-day ethics and motivations in order to live up to some measure of the Golden Rule:

There's a set of values people generally call Christian values: Do unto others as you would have them do unto you. That sort of general set of values – that you should be nice to people regardless, and care for other people to a certain extent, and you can never go wrong being polite to somebody.

Christopher's means by which to express his ultimate value were through niceness, politeness, and a limited amount of care for others. Christopher also echoed others in his aversion to over-amplified values. The specific anti-value he named was honour, citing both individual and ethnic acts of aggressions as examples of extreme outcomes of defending honour:

> Sometimes, honour I think is over-inflated. Occasionally you hear about somebody who kills somebody else for an insult or something along those lines. That doesn't make sense to me. Or, all of the ethnic cleansing things that are going on in Eastern Europe. I don't understand why you would hate a group of people so much – especially in some of those instances where they've been neighbours for 50 years. I suppose each person ought to be judged on their own merits.

Christopher's response to the anti-value of honour was his final sentence, which can be understood as a value that helps safeguard against hatred and prejudice: judge others according to who they are and what they do, not what they represent.

As a Christian, MeiLi expanded on the idea of the Golden Rule by focusing on love as the core virtue by which she tried to live her life. She understood this love not simply in a human sense, but as an expression of the greater love of God. 'I try to live according to the Bible. Specifically? I mean to love others as God has loved us.' MeiLi summarized a core idea of love found in the Christian scriptures and by theologians like Bernard of Clairvaux[14] – that God's love for humanity is the ideal to which humans aspire.

MeiLi contrasted love for others with selfishness and pride, and listed love for others as an admirable human quality side by side with confidence and moral commitment.

> Well, the worst, I would say, is that people are selfish. They always take their own desires first. And, the best human quality is love. People are loving when they, um, give themselves to the people that they can – not everyone, we have to choose who to be loving towards. Also, people who are not arrogant but are confident. They know themselves and they know what it is that they need to do in life. And they stick by very firm principles that they believe in. Because I think that's really noble. Even though these principles are always ones that are not selfish ones, they're ones that seem to help you more. And I think a lot of times living in this world we can get caught up in doing things for ourselves, and the fact that some people didn't yield to that is very admirable.

---

[14]   See M. Basil Pennington for a review of Bernard's 'ladder of love': M. Basil Pennington, *Bernard of Clairvaux: Lover Teaching the Way of Love* (Hyde Park, NY: New City, 1997).

For MeiLi, love as necessarily self-giving was the first and greatest ultimate value. Love combined with confidence and conviction were safeguards against falling into a life of self-absorption.

While self-giving love was central to MeiLi as a young Christian, Joel focused more on basic human kindness, even-handedness and respect as ultimate values: 'My core principle? Just treating all people the same. Try to be nice to everybody. Just try to treat everybody with respect. I think that's probably the most important thing. You do that and you get along with people a lot better.' Though an adherent Roman Catholic, Joel did not mention any religious ideals in connection with his core values – in fact, his reason for holding such values was more utilitarian. He cited as an example his admiration for good parents that care about their children and could raise their children with an even-handed, logical and understanding approach. Joel took healthy familial relationships as a template for living in public life, in all relationships.

It was the complete violation of these values that Joel named as anti-values. Joel was disgusted by crimes against humanity. He specifically cited the practice of ethnic cleansing in Yugoslavia, and returned to his core values of even-handedness and respect as reasons for his disgust:

> The people that disgust me most are people like, well, like, the problems in Yugoslavia, those kinds of things just, if, you heard about that in the news lately? Yeah. That's, that kind of stuff makes me really sick. It's killers and murderers, basically. That's the way I look at it. Just trying to keep people down for no reason, you know? They're people like anybody else, you know? Everybody deserves a chance in life. I mean, those are the worst people on earth, I think.

For Joel, holding strong affiliative values left no room for human cruelty. It was not possible to treat people so cruelly if one adhered to the values of even-handed respect and kindness.

Many young adults named eudaimonic values alongside their principal affiliative values. As indicated in their values rankings on the Rokeach Life Values survey, young adults held affiliative and eudaimonic values in tension. For many, the affiliative values of love, care, respect, and the bonds of friendship were more important. For others, eudaimonic values of self-respect, wisdom, courage, and creativity were most central. But the tension between these two sets of values never resulted in extreme diminishment or disavowal of one in favour of the other; rather, these two sets of values vied for first and second place as ultimate concerns and principles by which to live.

Self-transcendence: Values for Earthly and Heavenly Domains

In the interviews highlighted in the preceding sections, a few young adults stated core values that pointed to broader spiritual or societal concerns. Some mentioned concerns for human care, welfare, peace and equity beyond the boundaries of family and friends. Others described religious beliefs that informed and shaped their values.

But more typically, young adults' goals for contributing to social change were minimal, and typically involved a sense of the importance of 'starting one person at a time'. Very few young adults expressed great faith in institutions; rather, they expressed faith or trust in people, but indicated that they evaluated their relationships primarily in terms of trustworthiness and acceptance. As seen in previous sections, young adults frequently viewed ideology– whether religious or political – as a vice or distorted value that carried the potential for absolutism, dogmatism and extremism. Strong adherence to any ideology was repeatedly seen as a contrast to tolerance and respect, and as counterproductive to balance and wisdom in daily life. To devote oneself passionately and fully to a religious, political, or even humanitarian cause was to lose one's sense of equilibrium and to invite conflict with those who differed in their convictions. The general pattern was to view ideological '-isms' with disdain, but to uphold images of individuals who offered at least a basic level of concern for others through a practiced ethic of non-maleficence or limited beneficence.

In contrast to these stood a few young adults who explicitly placed spiritual or societal values above other values – even above affiliative and eudaimonic values. Cory, Philip and Javier all expressed a countervalent perspective that upheld dedication to societal improvement or to honouring God as an ultimate value. One young man, Cory, named both affiliative and eudaimonic values oriented toward the ultimate good of heaven and salvation. Two young men linked their ultimate values focused on the good of humanity with their vocational choices – Philip in his military service, and Javier in his work with NGOs and social reform efforts. For these young adults, commitment, passionate conviction and care for others were central values. Both sets of these young adults contrasted their core humanitarian and spiritual values against self-absorption, sloth and materialism.

Cory (a Mormon who worked multiple jobs and went to school part-time) spoke in detail about his values and their relationship to the Mormon community of faith. When first presented the question about his core values, he responded by referring to the rituals and beliefs around Mormon marriage, stating the centrality of family commitment in his life:

> Families are very important to us. I mean, you probably kind of picked up on that a little bit. We have special baptisms and marriages that are performed there in the temple. And one thing that's kind of different about a marriage in one of our temples is that, like, in most wedding ceremonies you always hear at the end the words, 'Till death do you part'. Well, in our system of beliefs we, we believe that when you're married in the temple that you're sealed to that individual for time and all eternity. And that your children, your posterity, they're also sealed to you. And after this life we're gonna be with those that we love because we're all tied together. And so that's important to me, to find somebody that I can take to the temple and, and, and have that kind of commitment. Because I mean,

forever's a long time, you know? But when I find the right person, that's where
I want it to be … I can't imagine loving somebody, to get married to them, have
a family with them, spend sixty, seventy years, however long it ends up being
with them, and then to have that just be it. I think that's kind of sad. So, that's
probably the belief that I live by the most, is the idea that we're all tied together.

Cory embraced the Mormon belief in eternal familial commitment, and stated that
this motivated his approach to dating. At first, this might seem a purely affiliative
value. But his understanding of familial commitment was grounded in broader
spiritual concerns about eternal destiny, and his core ideal that 'we're all tied
together' points to a concern for relationships extending beyond his family.

A rival core principle by which Cory attempted to live his life could be simply
stated, 'strive for perfection':

I think it's Matthew 5 where Christ says, 'Be ye therefore perfect even as your
Father which is in heaven is perfect.' And, you know, none of us is going to
be perfect. But he gave us a straight out commandment there. 'Be ye therefore
perfect even as your Father which is in heaven is perfect.' Try your best to do
everything that you can. Be the best person that you can be. I mean, we're all
gonna slip up along the way, we're all gonna make mistakes, but as long as
we're trying, we're doing honestly the very best that we can do, I think that all
that's gonna be taken into account.

Cory's concern with striving for perfection could be seen as a eudaimonic value
of personal integrity. But, like his description of family commitment, his value of
striving for perfection was expressed in relation to eternal destiny. In these ways,
Cory was explicitly oriented toward an afterlife and a final judgement.

Cory went on to explain these virtues of commitment and striving in terms
of integrity, responsibility and personal motivation. And yet, despite his strong
commitment to values of self-development and family formation, stated in
religious terms, these values did not seem to anchor his vocational and scholastic
efforts in his current life. Cory continued to work in various part-time jobs while
attending school part-time and living at home, without a clear trajectory or plan.

As an agnostic, Philip's overarching ultimate values were also self-transcendent:
'Underneath it all, I guess *it's the good of the human race.*' We previously heard
Philip's strong opposition to greed. In stark contrast to greed, he framed his own
core principles for life in both eudaimonic and self-transcendent terms: 'I think
I live a really pure life. I'm honest, I have integrity. I will look out for everyone
else. I care about every single person I think I've ever met. So most of the time
I put their needs in front of my own.' Honesty, integrity and self-sacrificial care
were Philip's guiding principles in his practical ethic of more extensive, altruistic
beneficence. Interestingly, Philip was one of the few young adults to state his
values in terms of who he was on a regular basis, and not only in terms of how he
hoped to behave. And he admired people who devoted themselves similarly to the

welfare of others: 'And those people that try and make the world better for every single other person in the world ... those are the people that I admire.'

Philip was particularly dedicated to safeguarding human life, and saw his military commitments and officer training as a means to express and meet that concern:

> People might say 'well, if you want to look out for the human race, why do you practice killing them?' Which is an interesting point. But I can counter that ... A lot of people are made for different things. And right now I think that the best thing that I was created for was to be in the military. The world needs military people, too. You can't be defenceless against – I mean, I don't really think it's a good idea to go out and fight one another all the time; I think it's a pretty bad idea, and we get to spend a lot of time thinking about that – but should there be something out there that is detrimental to the human race in the long run, then we can be a police force to cut that out.

Like many young adults, Philip initially did not want to name values held by some people as distorted, because of his own practiced underlying goal of tolerance. 'Because most of the time people who believe in something that I don't believe in ... They've spent a lot of time thinking about it. So who am I to say?' He then expressed clear aversion to racism and homophobia – but then restated that he could understand where people might arrive at such perspectives. But his abhorrence of greed (described earlier) was quite clear and unabated.

Javier's ultimate values were similar to Philip. He contrasted his core value of altruistic self-sacrifice for people beyond his family and friends against the vices and distorted values of competition, greed, racism and individualism:

> I think people come together in times of tragedy and help each other. And act as real neighbours. Unfortunately, it is in times of tragedy, and not, not a daily thing. The worst thing is the competitive nature of our society – the fact that money is the driving motivation a lot of the time, and, you know, people come second or third. I admire people that are, that are willing to, to sacrifice for others, and to put their own aims and goals second.

> And what do I, I hate? Greed. People who are racist, intolerant. And, I really don't understand blind individualism – that belief that the whole world is so much better if everyone follows my needs, my wants. I also don't understand materialism.

For Javier, self-transcendent altruistic values and a practical ethic of collective beneficence began with affiliative values expressed locally in his most immediate relationships: 'I don't know if it's a guiding principle, but I think you try to love the people you're close to, the people you know – and try to serve them as best you can.' Although this young Roman Catholic converted to evangelical Christianity, he did not explicitly restate his religious or spiritual ideals in relation to his ultimate values; his broader self-transcendent concern for humanity – deeply rooted in both Roman Catholic and Evangelical Christian religious traditions – guided his vocational choices toward activism and law, and drew him beyond his local context to work on human rights and reforms in Guatemala.

Cory, Philip and Javier had chosen ultimate values that to many other young adults made little sense. While self-interest in personal development and tribal interest in family and friendship were strongest for most young adults, only a few were oriented to self-transcendent values of equality, protection, justice and concern for the well-being of others beyond one's immediate home and community, as well as values of salvation and ultimate destiny. For this smaller group of young adults, local perspectives met global and cosmic perspectives: how one treats one's family and colleagues is how one learns to treat all human beings.

As this discussion has demonstrated, *Transition* young adults were far from vague or ambiguous about their values and anti-values. They illustrated their responses with real-life human conditions ranging from local to international. Some of their most vivid examples were offered in their discussions of anti-values: welfare dependence as an example of sloth and negligence; insider trading as an example of greed and dishonesty; ethnic cleansing as an example of ideological fanaticism; religious vows of poverty as an example of overly extreme commitment; sports icons as examples of non-heroic materialism; and political campaigns as examples of untrustworthy and dishonest behaviour. They typically referred to social institutions as settings that amplify vices and distort values, rather than as places where virtues and values could be expressed and exemplified. In contrast, it was heroic individuals who embodied core values by going to work every day, taking care of their families, getting what they wanted from life, and contributing to the social good in small ways without significant reward or notoriety. This pattern of thinking oriented young adults toward an ethic of non-maleficence or limited beneficence: do no harm, and perhaps do some good. For most young adults, minimal altruism was clearly overshadowed by their more localized relational values expressed primarily as reciprocal trust, honesty and tribal loyalty to family and friends.

Generational Change in Ultimate Values: The Shift to Affiliative Tribalism

How, then, have ultimate values of American young adults changed over thirty years? What follows are comparisons of young adults' ranking of Rokeach's 'terminal values' across generations. Table 7.6 below lists in order the average rank-placement of Rokeach's 18 'terminal values', by *Transition* young adults (1999–2000), compared with two of Rokeach's original study samples from 1968: Michigan State college students, and a national sample of American young adults in their twenties and in their thirties (conducted at the National Opinion Research Center – NORC). Values with the most dramatic change in rank placement from 1968 to 2000 (moving more than five places in rank order) are in boldface.

Table 7.6   Combined group rank orderings of values: young adults in 1968 vs young adults in 1999–2000*

1999–2000 (18–25) *Transition* (*n*=115)	1968 (18–21 Collegiate) Michigan State (*n*=298)	1968 (20s) NORC (*n*=267)	1968 (30s) NORC (*n*=298)
Happiness	Freedom	**A world at peace**	Family security
Mature love	Happiness	Family security	**A world at peace**
Family security	Wisdom	Freedom	Freedom
Self-respect	Self-respect	Happiness	Self-respect
True friendship	Mature love	Wisdom	Wisdom
Freedom	Accomplishment	**Equality**	Happiness
Accomplishment	True friendship	Self-respect	**Equality**
Wisdom	Inner harmony	Accomplishment	Accomplishment
A comfortable life	**Family security**	A comfortable life	True friendship
Pleasure	A world at peace	**Salvation**	Inner harmony
Inner harmony	Equality	**National security**	Salvation
Equality	An exciting life	**True friendship**	A comfortable life
A world at peace	A comfortable life	**Mature love**	**Mature love**
An exciting life	Salvation	Inner harmony	National security
A world of beauty	National security	A world of beauty	A world of beauty
Salvation	Social recognition	**Pleasure**	An exciting life
National security	A world of beauty	Social recognition	Social recognition
Social recognition	**Pleasure**	An exciting life	**Pleasure**

Note: * The last three columns of Table 7.6 are taken from Table 3.13 (p. 76) in Rokeach's *Nature of Human Values*.

Results suggest some dramatic changes in how young adults ordered and inherently organized their values. Not surprisingly (given the high percentage of college students and graduates in the *Transition* study), the 1968 group most comparable to *Transition* young adults were the Michigan State students: these college students ranked their values in similar order to the *Transition* sample, typically within one or less category-level difference from the *Transition* group. Michigan State students in 1968 ranked eudaimonic values higher than affiliative values – the reverse pattern from the *Transition* sample – particularly tied to a higher-rank placement of wisdom and a lower-rank placement of family security. However, in most cases, affiliative values rankings for Michigan State students were higher than other young adults in the NORC sample, closer to the importance rankings of our *Transition* young adults.

But *Transition* young adults differed more dramatically from the NORC 1968 general population samples of young adults in their twenties and thirties. The most noteworthy differences were among self-transcendent, affiliative and hedonistic values. *Transition* young adults ranked mature love and true friendship noticeably higher than did NORC young adults from 1968 – an interesting change that parallels national behavioural changes in marriage, with young adults in the 1990s and 2000s getting married later and less frequently getting divorced. But they also ranked pleasure considerably – and surprisingly – higher than their earlier hippie-generation counterparts. They also ranked world peace and national security noticeably lower than their 1968 young adult counterparts, whose survey coincided with national attention to the Vietnam Conflict and the Civil Rights Movement. And they ranked salvation markedly lower than twenty-somethings from 1968.

These patterns suggest that our young adults at the turn of the twenty-first century organized their values quite differently from the general population of young adults in the late 1960s – but not as differently from college students of that same period. The most marked differences were an increase in the importance of affiliative values, a decrease in the importance of self-transcendent values, and some increased importance in hedonistic values.

We retrieved data from Rokeach's 1968 study at NORC, and recoded the raw rank placements into my simplified five-category scheme. Statistical comparisons of rankings of 115 *Transition* young adults with 167 age-similar young adults from 1968 confirmed what is shown in the table above. The most dramatic differences were in rankings of mature love, true friendship, pleasure, world peace and national security.[15]

I then grouped the values of 1968 young adults according to the clusters that emerged from cluster analysis of *Transition* young adult values rankings, and created average cluster scores. Comparing average values cluster scores across generations reveals the more general pattern of change (see Figure 7.5 below). The most dramatic changes were in affiliative values and in spiritual and social values. Our young adults at the turn of the twenty-first century placed much greater importance on affiliative values, but much less importance on self-transcendent spiritual and social values.

Unlike the lack of generational differences in worldviews, theodicies and life purpose, generational differences in values were quite strong. It seems that American young adults in 1999–2000 constructed value-hierarchies quite differently from young adults in 1968, with self-transcendent values being viewed as minimally important, but affiliative values maximally important. There was also an increase in importance of hedonistic values, but not as strong as the increased importance in affiliative values and decreased importance in self-transcendent. The change in affiliative values most clearly differentiated between young adults from these two

---

15   The most robust differences discussed here had t-values between 6.3 and 11.6 (p < .0005). See Gortner, 'Young Adult Personal Theologies', for details of these comparisons.

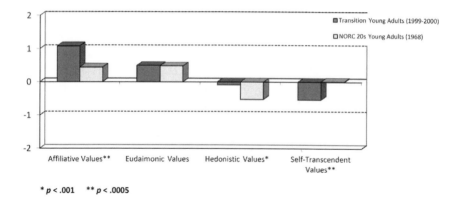

* p < .001   ** p < .0005

Figure 7.5   Average young adult cluster scores of Rokeach's terminal values,
              1999–2000, compared to 1968 (*n* = 282)

generations: in logistic regression analyses, affiliative cluster scores were most
reliable in correctly classifying 76.7 per cent of young adults into their respective
generational cohorts; classification accuracy only improved to 79.5 per cent with
the addition of scores for self-transcendent values.[16]

These results demonstrate that shifts in values from 1968 to 1999–2000 among
young adults were most strongly marked by a major increase in the importance
of affiliative values, and a major decrease in the importance of spiritual and
social values. Self-image values did not increase significantly in importance, but
were relatively more important to the 1999–2000 cohort once the importance of
affiliative values was accounted for. Hedonistic values increased somewhat in
importance, but this difference was not highly predictive.

These results stand in stark contrast to conclusions drawn by some sociologists
regarding increased hedonistic or pleasure-oriented values in American culture.
While there was some modest increase in hedonistic values from 1968 to 2000
among American young adults, the primary changes in their values from the 1968
to 2000 were not about pleasure, comfort, or consumption. Rather, generational
changes in young adults' values reflected a fundamental shift from a broader
social and spiritual concern to a narrower concern with happiness rooted in close,
intense and enduring relationships. Values of world peace and equality have been
supplanted by values of true friendship, mature love and happiness. Thus, it appears
to be affiliative tribalism, and not hedonism, that has driven the value changes

---

[16]   In a series of conditional forward logistic regression analyses, affiliative values
were the strongest predictive classifiers: *Cox & Snell R²* = .275. Prediction improved
modestly with the addition of self-transcendent values: *Cox & Snell R²* = .340. The addition
of eudaimonic and hedonistic values clusters did not improve classification accuracy.
Hedonistic values were the weakest predictive classifiers (see Gortner, 'Young Adult
Personal Theologies').

among young adults in America. Trust in political and religious institutions has eroded, contributing to diminished self-transcendent values focused on spiritual and broader societal good. In their place, young adults have focused not on hedonistic pursuits as much as they have on affiliative pursuits and the formation of localized, more nuclear bonds – even overriding their more internal eudaimonic concerns with self-image and self-development.

How Are Ultimate Values Related to Worldview, Theodicy and Life Purpose?

What, then, are the relationships between ultimate values and other facets of personal theology? How might young adults' worldviews, theodicies and senses of life purpose contribute to their choices of ultimate values? I examined these relationships for each set of values in turn, using regression analysis to predict each set of values from the personal theological beliefs of the 67 young adults who completed both in-depth interviews and 'Life Values' surveys.

Young adults' strong emphasis on affiliative values did not waver or vary by worldview, theodicy, or life purpose. Regardless of differences in other beliefs, the ultimate aims of strong, close, and enduring relationships remained central to young adults.

In contrast, young adults' eudaimonic values varied significantly with worldview and life purpose – but not theodicy. Young adults with mixed or ambivalent worldviews or with a role-defined sense of life purpose gave the lowest rankings to eudaimonic values ($R^2 = .175$).

Hedonistic values varied most significantly according to theodicy – not surprisingly, randomists gave the highest rankings to hedonistic values. Together, positive worldviews and randomistic theodicies predicted higher hedonistic rankings ($R^2 = .202$).

Young adults' low rankings of self-transcendent values did not waver or vary by worldview. But they did vary significantly by theodicy and life purpose. Higher rankings of self-transcendent values were predicted by role-defined life purpose and the *absence* of randomistic theodicies ($R^2 = .115$). As might be expected, randomists were least oriented toward spiritual and social values. But – surprisingly – role-defined young adults were significantly more oriented toward self-transcendent values than were avoiders or engagers.

There may be direct causal logic in how beliefs might shape ultimate values. For instance, a randomistic theodicy might encourage more hedonistic goals and discourage broader self-transcendent goals: in a random world with no consistent external or internal causes and with no easily predictable consequences, it might become most valuable to pursue personal gratification while one has the opportunity, while spiritual pursuits would either be meaningless or lack any meaningful influence, and social structures themselves would be seen as unstable and insecure. Similarly, a positive worldview might also contribute to more hedonistic values: the experience and mental selection of positive images and the exclusion or minimization of negative images can mitigate concerns about negative life events and their causes, inhibit the development of altruistic concern, and possibly foster a sense of entitlement and a motivational emphasis on pleasure.

But most likely, the influence between beliefs and values in personal theologies is bi-directional and cyclical. People who have become accustomed to a more hedonistic orientation of their higher-order goals may tend to avoid, ignore, or actively resist fundamental beliefs and perceptions about the world and ultimate causes that might raise unsettling questions about their motivations and pursuits.

It is noteworthy that none of the *dominant* patterns in beliefs (for instance, a negative worldview or deterministic theodicy) were predictive of values – and no beliefs predicted the *dominant* preference for affiliative values. When beliefs or values are so culturally dominant that they are nearly ubiquitous, meaningful co-variance is not easily discerned. In this situation, it becomes even more important to explore and identify the subtler, more nuanced relationships between less dominant beliefs and values in order to reveal individual differences in personal theology within an overarching cultural theology.

Chapter 8

Developmental and Social Influences on Young Adult Personal Theologies

I won the ovarian lottery. I am a US citizen; got a good education; enjoy great health; and came equipped with an 'engineer' gene that allows me to prosper in a manner disproportionate to other people who contribute as much or more to society.[1]

Kiva fellow working in Uganda

This quote comes from a blog-site for Kiva Fellows assisting with Kiva's micro-lending programme. The blogger drew the idea of the 'ovarian lottery' from a rather infamous statement by American billionaire Warren Buffett in his book, *The Snowball*. The blogger communicates a wide range of attributions for his privileged position in the world. First, he cites some kind of cosmic luck of the draw that resulted in the locations in which he found himself. Secondly, the fortune of citizenship in the United States relates to the vast resources available to American citizens in comparison to people in many other parts of the world – a matter of financial and social capital available as much as a matter of qualities of life (such as freedom) enjoyed. Third, he notes the impact of education, and links his educational attainment to his cultural and socio-economic location in the world. Fourth, his health – also linked to an 'ovarian lottery' that situated him in a family and culture and time period of strong health – affords him freedom and opportunity not easily accessible when one struggles with disability or chronic illness. And fifth, he attributes his success to something intrinsic to his nature, for which he does not take credit except inasmuch as he used what was part of his genetically inherited dispositions and aptitudes.

It is a dramatic collection of attributions for personal success. It acknowledges the impact of cultural and socio-economic forces, the power of education and of familial and cultural social capital, and the unique contributions of intrinsic capacities and qualities. There are similar accounts that tie personal success – and failure – to one's heritage and location in history. But this statement caught my eye for another reason. I began to wonder what account people might give for their own personal theologies – what they would describe as the sources and contributing social and developmental forces that shape how they believe. I also wondered how accurate these accounts would be in comparison to actual data from different points in people's lives.

---

[1]   From Kiva Fellows, 'The Ovarian Lottery', *Kiva Stories from the Field* <http://fellowsblog.kiva.org/2009/02/17/the-ovarian-lottery/>.

The last four chapters have shown the depths, patterns and varied contours of personal theologies of American young adults. While clear dominant trends appeared in almost every facet of personal theology – toward negative worldviews, deterministic theodicies and affiliative ultimate values – no clearly preferred combination of beliefs and values emerged. Young adults expressed widely varied combinations of worldview, theodicy, life purpose and ultimate values. And these diverse patterns among the 82 emerging adults whose expressions of beliefs and values form the core of this book are echoed in patterns of responses by larger groups of young adults to survey questions about beliefs and values. It might be tempting to conclude with Canadian sociologist Reginald Bibby[2] that the beliefs and values comprising personal theologies have become so atomized in a prevailing culture of individualism, pluralism and relativism, that they are now simply divergent and without predictive power. Certainly, the clustering of different young adults around particular patterns of beliefs or values did not suggest many clear similarities that drew them toward the same conclusions – nor did these clusters match from facet to facet of personal theology.

We enter this chapter with some nagging questions. What, if anything, predicts and contributes to the formation of particular personal theologies? What, if anything, is related to personal theologies in current daily life? Are personal theologies simply sets of ephemeral ponderings of individuals in the moment? Are they simply clusters of disembodied ideas, beliefs, or values that have no real connection to lived experience or to current behaviours?

This chapter provides suggestive evidence that young adults' personal theologies are indeed deeply rooted in and shaped by their life contexts and experiences as teenagers, and that meaning-making is not an isolate, solipsistic venture. More specifically, young adults' personal theologies seem most strongly influenced by their community and family social class and capital, educational experiences and some of their own personal dispositions during their adolescent years – but are less obviously or consistently influenced by the religion, family dynamics, work and peer experiences of their teenage years. In the subsequent interlude, we consider patterns of relationships between young adults' personal theologies and their experiences, assessments and choices as young adults.

At this point, we leave our qualitative focus on the individual voices of young adults, and look at quantitative relationships between patterns of beliefs or values and their social and developmental precedents. It is by far the most statistically rich chapter. I begin by exploring basic differences in the four facets of personal theology due to demographic background, adolescent social factors and adolescent psychological dispositions and attitudes. Then, through a series of regression analyses,[3] I progressively uncover the strongest related predictors

---

[2]   See Reginald Bibby, *Mosaic Madness: Pluralism without a Cause* (Toronto: Stoddart, 1990).

[3]   I utilized a method known as 'backwards stepwise regression analyses' – a systematic method of selecting variables that show indications of a possible relationship with a facet

of personal theology from each arena of adolescent life to arrive at the strongest combination of predictors of each facet of young adult personal theology.

Demographic Differences Shaping Personal Theologies

In what ways do social location and the socio-economic realities of one's context as a child shape concepts about the world, ultimate causation, purpose in life and the well-lived life? In what ways do gender, race and community and family social class affect the emergence of these beliefs and values? How do family structure and size, themselves primary training grounds for understandings of social capital, contribute to the development of personal theologies?

Gender and Race

Let us first address the question of gender. Simply stated, personal theologies did not differ between young men and young women. In terms of gender, the 'ovarian lottery' did not result in any differences among the 82 core young adults in worldviews, theodicies, senses of life purpose, or ultimate values. Similar majorities of men and women expressed negative worldviews and deterministic theodicies, and gave higher rankings to affiliative ultimate values and lower rankings to broader societal and spiritual ultimate values. Men and women were similarly dispersed across views of life purpose.[4]

Racial differences in personal theology among the core 82 young adults were a bit more complicated and challenging to gauge, given the high percentage of white Euro-Americans in the sample. With such a small sample that is not representative of the racial distribution of American young adults, it is only possible to present some suggestive patterns.

Worldviews did not differ statistically by race – although young adults who were not white Euro-American were somewhat more frequently negative in their worldviews: three-fourths of non-white young adults stated negative worldviews,

---

of personal theology, and then progressively removing those variables that fail to account for any variance. This method was used iteratively, first deriving best predictors from each arena of adolescent life, and then progressively combining these best predictors. This layering-and-removal technique – much like what one does in writing, painting and glazing – helps focus more clearly on the predictors that matter most. As the process unfolds, some variables that were originally predictive get 'bumped' by others that are more strongly accounting for variations that overlap and overlay the first.

[4]   No gender differences were found across the three global categories for life purpose; however, among young adults with a role-defined sense of life purpose, women more frequently described familial roles, while men more frequently articulated career-related roles.

compared with half of the white young adults. Life purpose and ultimate values also did not differ by race.

There was one noteworthy racial difference in personal theology: only white Euro-Americans stated a humanistic theodicy. Non-white participants never stated humanistic responses, while 15 per cent of white participants offered humanistic responses. In contrast, white participants were significantly less likely to state deterministic responses.

Hints of small gender- and race-related differences surfaced in examination of 190 *Transition* participants who responded to GSS questions about beliefs and values during Year 3 phone surveys. Women had a slightly more positive view than men of human nature, and endorsed values of societal improvement more highly than did men. Black and Latino young adults tended more toward engagement in the world than did white and Asian young adults. And black young adults endorsed far more strongly than white young adults the idea of life meaning from a divine plan, but did not differ in their views of self as the source of meaning and fate. These differences were relatively small in scope and effect.

Age

Not much variation might be expected within the narrow band of ages 18–25 – except that it is a time of significant life change. Among the 82 core *Making the Transition* young adults, age was a significant predictor of randomist theodicy, accounting for 8.6 per cent of the difference among young adults between having a randomist theodicy and having either a deterministic or humanistic theodicy. Randomists were more frequently among the older young adults (ages 23 and up) than among the younger young adults (21 and younger). The age-related increase in randomism may be related to more intensive education and questioning of deterministic assumptions, or it may be related to increased exposure, due to age and experience, to negative events and increased dissatisfaction with what might be perceived as the 'easy' answers of deterministic theodicy or the relationally uncomfortable answers of humanistic theodicy. See Figure 8.1.

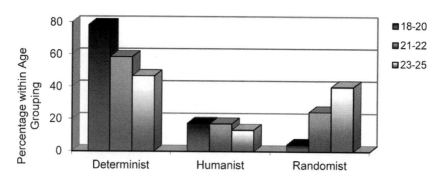

Figure 8.1   Age distribution of theodical beliefs

There were no other relationships between the age of these 82 young adults and their worldview, life purpose, or ultimate values. From the larger group of 190 *Transition* Year 3 respondents, a pattern emerged in relation to the question of life purpose – with older young adults moving toward withdrawal and away from engagement – but this was a relatively small effect.

Community Social Class

One demographic factor that affected young adults' personal theologies was the social class of the community (SCC) in which they lived as teenagers. Distributions of young adult worldviews differed noticeably by SCC during adolescence – as shown in Figure 8.2. Young adults with positive worldviews were much more frequently from higher social class communities – 75 per cent of young adults with positive worldviews were from upper-middle or upper-class communities, with higher per capita income and lower unemployment, and typically more opportunities for leisure and personal advancement, stronger educational settings and fewer conditions of significant risk. A positive worldview was only minimally present among young adults from poor and working-class communities. But a negative worldview remained dominant regardless of SCC.

Young adult life purpose was also related to adolescent SCC. Almost all young adults with engaged life purpose were from upper-middle and upper-class communities, and none were from poor and working-class communities. An avoidant life purpose was present in at least one-third of young adults from all SCC backgrounds. The higher the social class, the more possible it became to imagine and believe in a larger sense of purpose in life, with potential for greater impact than within the set spheres of local family and job contexts. Upper- and upper-middle-class communities seemed to provide adolescents with experiences and a general social milieu that fostered societal engagement.

But the social class of the community during teenage years made no difference in young adults' ultimate values – either in the core group of 82 or in the full sample of 315. Neither were young adult theodicies related in any significant way to SCC.

Parent Educational Attainment

Educational attainment is highly correlated with income and socio-economic status. Young adults with positive worldviews most often grew up in families with more highly educated parents (63.2 per cent) – and maternal education was a particularly strong predictor of positive worldviews.[5] As illustrated in Figure 8.3, the frequency of positive worldviews increased in a dramatic, linear pattern associated

---

[5]   Closer examination of worldview group differences revealed that mothers' education levels were more predictive of young adults' worldviews, $F(2,68) = 5.76$, $p = .005$, than were fathers' education levels, $F(2,62) = 1.25$, $p > .2$.

Worldview by SCC

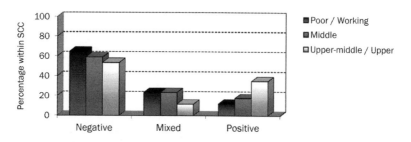

Life Purpose by SCC

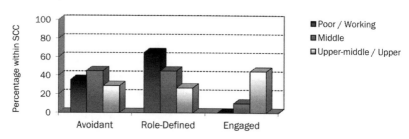

Theodicy by Teenage SCC

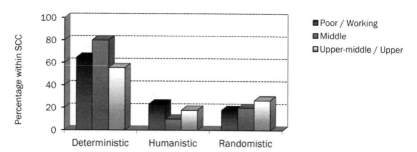

Figure 8.2 Community social class during adolescence, by later worldview, life purpose and theodicy

with parents' education. None the less, negative worldviews remained as the dominant paradigm for young adults, regardless of parent education level. Only young adults from parents with graduate degrees approached an even division between negative and positive worldviews.

In terms of life purpose, engaged young adults tended to come from homes with the most highly educated parents, particularly parents with graduate degrees.[6] Avoidant

---

[6] Planned comparisons, engaged vs non-engaged, $p < .05$.

Worldview by Parent Education

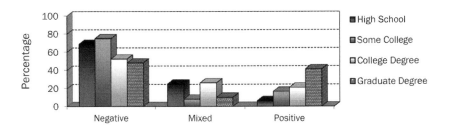

Life Purpose by Parent Education

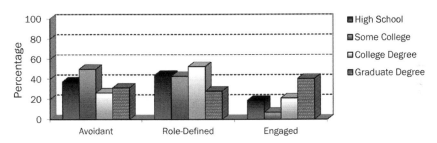

Figure 8.3   Parent educational attainment, by later worldview and life purpose

young adults had fathers with the least amount of education, while engaged young adults had both parents with the most education. Parents with graduate degrees in particular, by example and process of parenting and encouragement, may instil a stronger desire to contribute to society.

Overall parent education did not result in any significant differences in theodicy or in ultimate values among young adults.[7] The lack of relationship between theodicy or ultimate values and both community social class and parent education runs counter to some sociological and psychoanalytic suppositions, for instance, that theodical determinism might be more common in poor and working-class communities.

Life Stressors

Life-altering stresses can occur in the lives of teenagers and their families, and these stressors can have an impact on the beliefs and values that emerge in later

---

[7]   Closer examination revealed that young adults with humanistic theodicies had somewhat more highly educated mothers or fathers than young adults with deterministic theodicies, but the average amount of education between parents did not differ across theodical groups.

life. Over 70 per cent of the teenagers in the original study experienced one or more significant stressors such as major illness, death of a family member, parental divorce or remarriage, parental unemployment or major job change, relocation, or teenage sibling pregnancy or dropout. The number of stressors during adolescence was inversely correlated with parent education – the higher the parent education (and consequent access to greater social and financial capital), the fewer the significant stressors in teenagers' lives.

Young adult worldview and life purpose were weakly related to prior adolescent life stressors, in ways one might expect. Young adults with positive worldviews tended to have fewer adolescent life stressors than young adults with mixed or negative worldviews, and avoidant young adults experienced significantly more stressors as adolescents than did engagement-oriented young adults. Young adults' worldviews may be shaped in part by experiences of deprivation, risk, or stress in their adolescence. But closer inspection of the types of stressors experienced during adolescence suggests that it was family eustress (that is, positive stressors) that directly influenced worldview, rather than family distress (that is, negative stressors). Further, it was young adults with mixed or ambivalent worldviews who experienced the most family eustress and distress combined.

Neither theodicies nor ultimate values among young adults differed in relation to stressors experienced in adolescence.

A specific type of childhood and adolescent stressor often suspected as influencing later personal theologies is the experience of growing up in a 'non-traditional' household with single, divorced, or otherwise unmarried parents. There is at best weak evidence from this study that family type influenced personal theologies. Proportionally, more young adults from 'non-traditional' families had negative worldviews, deterministic theodicies, avoidant life purpose and weaker emphasis on affiliative ultimate values – and very few had humanistic theodicies – but these differences were only by a few percentage points and were not statistically significant in this small sample. In a larger study, such relatively small differences might be significant – and the pattern does suggest that experience of single-parent, divorced, or blended family life might reinforce some strong dominant cultural patterns of beliefs. See Figure 8.4.

Summary of Demographic Influences

Overall, the basic demographic realities of one's upbringing did have some impact on the personal theology emerging for these 82 young adults – but only *some* impact. Dominant patterns in beliefs and values remained dominant, across variations in demographic background. These dominant patterns of a negative worldview, deterministic theodicy and more tribal affiliative values suggest a ubiquitous cultural script for fundamental theological beliefs and values. These dominant beliefs and values may undergird the dominant pattern of beliefs about

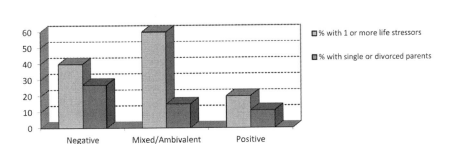

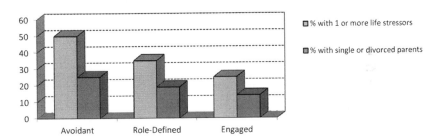

Figure 8.4   Young adults' teenage experiences of significant life stressors and of family households with single or divorced parents, by later worldview and life purpose

God that Christian Smith has called 'moralistic therapeutic deism'.[8] Culture provides the dominant templates or cultural affordances for a negative worldview, a deterministic theodicy and ultimate values stressing immediate relationships as most important. These appear to be shared and affirmed regardless of race and social class.

But this study does not support the idea of variation in theological beliefs and values due to demographic differences alone. Table 8.1 summarizes the strongest results using linear regression analyses to predict each facet of personal theology using various demographic variables. For worldview, parent educational

---

[8]   For Christian Smith, in *Soul Searching* and *Souls in Transition*, 'moralistic therapeutic deism' is the summative expression of these beliefs, which affirm the existence of a distant but personally interested deity who leaves people to their own choices but at the same time is available for protection and care in need, who expects people to be good. Reginald Bibby has described similar theistic but also non-theistic patterns in Canadian culture: Reginald Bibby, *Canada's Teens: Today, Yesterday, and Tomorrow* (Toronto, CA: Stoddart, 2001), pp. 125–8, 131–2.

Table 8.1   Best backward regression results predicting worldview from demographics

	Final model predicting worldview	Final model predicting life purpose	Final model predicting humanistic theodicy	Final model predicting randomistic theodicy
	β	β	β	β
Constant	-.88***	1.65	.238***	-1.29*
Gender (female)	—	—	—	—
Race (non-white)	—	—	-.250*	—
SCC (upper and upper-middle class)	—	.32***	—	—
Parent education	.27*	—	—	—
Family type (non-intact)	—	—	—	—
Age	—	—	—	.32***
Number of cases♦	**78**	**82**	**80**	**79**
Adjusted R²	**.059**	**.094**	**.050**	**.088**

Notes: ♦ The number of cases in the regression analyses varied due to missing data. Missing data also affected other regression analyses, as will be seen throughout the chapter.

* p ≤ .05; ** p ≤ .01; *** p ≤ .005.

attainment was the single strongest demographic predictor – accounting only for 5.9 per cent of the variance in worldviews.[9] A negative worldview remained most common among these 82 young adults, even among those coming from parents with graduate education who showed the greatest likelihood of developing a positive worldview.[10] For theodicy, race and age were the primary demographic predictors. Race accounted for only 5 per cent of the variance in humanistic versus non-humanistic theodicies. Age accounted for 8.8 per cent of the variance between randomistic and non-randomistic theodicies. For life purpose, the strongest single demographic predictor was community social class, accounting for 9.4 per cent of the variance in life purpose. Inclusion of adolescent life stressors added no predictive strength to the model. For ultimate values, there were no significant demographic predictors.

---

[9]   Family type (parental single or divorced status) was a non-significant predictor that marginally increased overall predictive power of demographic features, together with parent education accounting for 6.6 per cent of the variance in worldviews. Young adults from single-parent or divorced families more frequently indicated negative worldviews.

[10]   A cubic, or curvilinear, regression revealed that adolescent life stressors and community social class together also accounted for 5.9 per cent of the variance in worldviews, with young adults holding mixed/ambivalent worldviews differing from other young adults.

Furthermore, there is not one consistent demographic reality from adolescence that equally influenced each facet of young adults' personal theologies. Worldview and life purpose may indeed be more influenced (among these demographic factors) by parental education and consequent familial socio-economic status and relative stability; but in contrast, theodicy may be more shaped by broader racial and ethnic identities. Racial and ethnic communities may inherit, construct and foster different ways of thinking about the causes and reasons for negative life events.[11] In this study, humanists were uniformly white compared with determinists and randomists.

The social class of the community in which people grow up may have a more profound effect than familial socio-economic status on life purpose, as people become aware of the risks, limits and opportunities that shape the common life of a community and shape individuals' focus. In communities with fewer risk factors, higher tax bases and more capital investment, the range of adolescent educational and employment opportunities tends to be quite different – and the relatively higher protection from harsh experiences in families, schools and neighbourhoods can foster an engagement-oriented sense of life purpose that is less likely to emerge when one's social experience has taught a necessary emphasis on personal and familial survival and insulation. Differences in community social class may foster different ways of thinking about oneself *vis-à-vis* the world. Adolescents and young adults from wealthier communities, reflecting on the benefits of their experiences in these communities, *and* becoming more aware of social inequities and the lack of such benefits in other communities, may develop two mental scripts that lead to increased engagement orientation: 1) 'I am fortunate that I don't have to worry as much as others about my future', and 2) 'Others deserve the benefits I have received.' These two 'scripts' were mentioned explicitly by Dean and several other young adults[12] – but certainly not by all such young adults from communities of higher social class. According to Dan McAdams's research, these scripts are most common in the redemptive life narratives of highly generative adults, and are less common in the life narratives of adults who are less generative.[13]

---

[11]   For instance, Mark Musick documented trends of different constructions and uses of a deterministic theodicy among African Americans, and David Fillingim drew from country music lyrics a distinctive 'redneck' theodicy: Mark Musick, 'Theodicy and Life Satisfaction among Black and White Americans', *Sociology of Religion* 61: 267–88; David Fillingim, *Redneck Liberation: Country Music as Theology* (Macon, GA: Mercer University Press, 2003).

[12]   These 'scripts' are also outlined vividly in the conversion narrative of the young Indian member of the upper class, Siddhartha Gautama. For Gautama, who later became the Buddha, social inequity was not a problem that had a direct consequence on his own existence (a survival problem), but was a problem that he recognized as having a direct impact on his fellow human beings (an equity problem). The locus of the problem for Gautama was not personal, but transcendent of himself. It seems likely that the less one's personal survival is in question, the more such transcendent concern becomes possible.

[13]   See Dan McAdams, *The Redemptive Self: Stories Americans Live by* (New York: Oxford University Press, 2006).

The absence of gender as a predictor (including as a predictor in tandem with SCC), the predictive weakness of family type and life stressors, and the overall modest predictive power of other demographic factors like race and socio-economic status for personal theology raises questions about the conclusions and arguments that theologians might be tempted to make when attempting to speak on behalf of a particular group of people. Being female does not mean that one necessarily develops a different view of the world as a place or of the ultimate causes and reasons for traumatic and tragic events. Being African American or Asian American does not necessarily result in different worldviews, life purpose, or values. And none of these demographic 'buckets' are sufficient containers for the varieties of beliefs and values found among people in each bucket. At most, one can say that some demographic factors can either more deeply instantiate or provide opportunities to diverge from dominant cultural patterns in beliefs and values.

We turn next to a closer examination of the impact of family, school, work, extracurricular activity, peers and religion on personal theologies. Young adults' beliefs and values might be more strongly influenced by specific experiences in these different arenas of their lives during adolescence, and might illuminate the reasons for certain demographic effects.

The Influence of Family

Religious leaders, theologians and social scientists have frequently pegged parents and families as the most immediate influence on the development of beliefs and values. Among NELS adolescents, parental involvement and familial learning environment helped bolster educational and behavioural outcomes.[14] But, as we found in the *Making the Transition* study, the influence of family experience on young adults' personal theologies was neither simple nor straightforward. Nor were parents necessarily the strongest influence on personal theologies.

We have already noted the impact of parents' educational attainment on some facets of personal theology. Certainly, financial and social capital during one's teenage years may influence later beliefs and values. But there are other factors worth considering. The degree of family stability and family closeness may be powerful crucibles for the formation of later beliefs and values.[15] The emotional and motivational environment of a family, expressed through support and challenge, can open or shut down pathways to different beliefs and values. And

---

[14]   See Beth Simon, 'Family Involvement in High School: Predictors and Effects', *NASSP Bulletin*, 85(627) (October 2001): 8–19.

[15]   Concepts of family stability and closeness are drawn from David Olson's 'circumplex model' of family systems. See David Olson, Candyce Russell and Douglas Sprenkle, *Circumplex Model: Systemic Assessment and Treatment of Families* (Binghamton, NY: Haworth, 1989).

the connections between different arenas of ecological development in teenage life may be vital in shaping later personal theologies.[16]

The overall influence of parent education on the personal theologies of young adult offspring might indeed be mediated through these three different forms of family influence. First, parents with higher education might exercise parenting responsibilities differently – spending more time with their children, offering greater latitude in teenagers' free time and association with peers, and pushing stronger academic achievement. Secondly, parents with higher education might be more aware of the value of networks within their communities – and thus might communicate more actively with their children's teachers and school systems. Third, parents with higher education are more likely to own and purchase more material goods for their households and to provide significant monetary support to their children's development, including financial support for college. None of these factors of parental impact is solely the result of parent educational attainment and consequent socio-economic status. But the links of each of these factors to parent education are strong. And each of these may have its own impact on beliefs and values. I have examined the impact of each of these familial factors in turn, on each facet of personal theology.

Family Stability and Stress

We have already touched on matters related to family stability and stress. Family stability and stress encountered during adolescence was directly – but only weakly – related to the worldviews, theodicies and ultimate values of the core *Transition* young adults. Significant changes in the pattern of family life – and consequent changes in family social capital and parental involvement, either positively or negatively – may unsettle adolescents' overall perception of the world and introduce a degree of uncertainty that persists into early adulthood. Regarding theodicy, adolescent family distress was least among young adults with a humanistic theodicy. In terms of life purpose, avoiders as adolescents experienced the fewest positive family stressors along with more negative family stressors. Significant stress weakens family stability[17] and consequently can set a template for uncertainty about the world and strengthen an avoidant sense of self *vis-à-vis* the world. In contrast, a stable family environment relatively free of major

---

[16]   Urie Bronfenbrenner mapped a powerful meta-theoretical perspective on the total ecology of child and adolescent development, drawing attention to the multiple small ecologies where people are shaped and are also influential, as well as the degree of connectedness between ecologies – for instance, between parents and schools: Urie Bronfenbrenner, *The Ecology of Human Development: Experiments by Nature and Design* (Cambridge, MA: Harvard University Press, 1979).

[17]   See Hamilton McCubbin and Joan Patterson, 'The Family Stress Process: The Double ABCX Model of Adjustment and Adaptation', *Marriage and Family Review* 6 (1–2) (1983): 7–37.

negative stressors can nurture a belief in human control over life circumstances and a consequent belief that negative life events can be explained and understood solely or primarily in terms of human causes and effects. When tragic or traumatic events strike one's family, a deterministic or randomistic theodicy may become much more attractive and palatable – assigning cause could step closely toward assigning blame and responsibility, an uncomfortable position to take amongst one's kin.

Family Closeness

A counterpart to stability in family systems is closeness. Our primary indicator of family closeness was from teenagers' time use diaries from the 'experience sampling method'. Collections of data on 50–60 random waking moments during a week of each teenager's life gave us a sense of how they were spending their time, who they were with, and what their experiences were like to them. Out of these waking moments, the percentage of time spent with family provided indicators of how often they were with their families. Young adult theodicy was related to previous time with family during adolescent years (at least during the experience sampling): determinists as teenagers spent significantly more time than randomists with their families (24 per cent vs 14 per cent), with humanists between these two groups in their amount of family time (18 per cent). Figure 8.5 notes the strikingly different ways these three theodical groups spent their time as adolescents – humanists spent significantly more time alone, while randomists spent the most time with peers, and determinists spent more time than the other groups with their families.

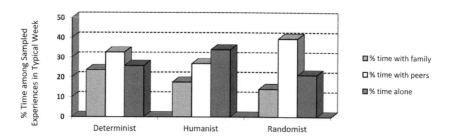

Figure 8.5   Differences in percentage of time with family as teenagers, according to young adult theodicy

Interestingly, no other facets of personal theology were related to the amount of time spent with family. But this relationship of theodicy to family time is worth further consideration – particularly in conjunction with family stress. Both randomists and determinists experienced more stress in their families than did humanists. But determinists spent more time with their families, while randomists spent less time with their families. These patterns fit well within the 'circumplex model' of family interaction: those raised in families that were more disconnected and more chaotic were more likely to adopt randomistic theodicies; those from families that were more connected but also more chaotic were most likely to develop deterministic theodicies, and those from more stable and somewhat connected families were most likely to construct humanistic theodicies.

Family Emotional and Motivational Environment

Two of the strongest family indicators of positive youth development from the *Youth and Social Development* (YSD) study were indicators of teenagers' perception of family support and family challenge – the degree to which they felt supported by their parents and families no matter what they faced, and the degree to which they felt challenged by their parents and families to excel in whatever they did. These robust measures, which gave clues to the emotional and motivational environment of teenagers' homes and were predictive of a number of positive outcomes in educational and vocational development, were also significant predictors of young adult life purpose and ultimate values. As teenagers, avoidant young adults had indicated the lowest sense of family support *and* family challenge. In contrast, young adults with higher affiliative values as teenagers indicated the highest sense of family support and family challenge – but those with higher eudaimonic values (and, as we shall see later, hedonistic values) indicated the lowest sense of family support.

The experience of family support and challenge in adolescence did not correlate in any significant way with young adult worldviews or theodicies.

Family Connection with Schools

What about the influence of parental connection with other important environments of adolescents? This is a developmental question rooted in ecological systems theory. Urie Bronfenbrenner described layered 'microsystems' of human life and experience that exert influence on development.[18] Bronfenbrenner also emphasized how the quality of connections and interactions ('mesosystems') between different microsystems exert important developmental influence. In the YSD study, teenagers answered questions about their sense of how parents sought information about, connected with and cooperated with their schools and peers. These included questions about parent-school consultations (attending school meetings and events, volunteering at school, direct calls to teachers or counsellors) as well as parent-child discussions about school, parental pressure on school performance and parental knowledge of peers and social time.

These measures were at best weakly related to some facets of young adults' personal theologies. None were related to worldviews. But parent-school consultations and parental pressure on school performance during adolescence were related to young adult theodicy and ultimate values. Randomists' parents had

---

[18]   Bronfenbrenner, *Ecology of Human Development.*

the fewest consultations and interactions with their children's schools, talked least frequently with their children about school, and put the least emphasis on their children's scholastic performance. These patterns are in keeping with other results that suggest randomists came from more disconnected and chaotic families.

A different pattern emerged in relation to life purpose. Engagers as adolescents saw their parents taking a balanced approach, equally concerned with encouraging their school performance and with direct consultation with their schools. In contrast, avoiders and role-observers as adolescents saw their parents were much more concerned with putting pressure on their school performance than with communication with teachers and school professionals. The parents of avoiders and role-observers were less likely, in other words, to model behaviour that demonstrated the value of broader social engagement. They did not make a standard practice of crossing borders and getting involved with their children's schools, and instead relied more on their capacity to apply pressure on their children. This may be related to financial and social capital: parents with less education (and income) did not interact as often with their children's schools.

Family Financial Capital

The last area of family life examined was that of financial capital. Family capital goods and parental financial support of college were directly related to young adults' worldviews. Young adults with positive worldviews grew up in homes with more capital goods than did young adults with negative or mixed worldviews. These worldview 'optimists' had significantly more non-intellectual capital goods in their parents' homes (for example, dishwashers, private bedrooms, VCRs) than worldview 'pessimists'. Interestingly, young adults with mixed or ambivalent worldviews came from homes with the fewest intellectual capital goods (for example, daily newspaper, dictionary, encyclopaedia), while young adults with a positive worldview came from homes with the most intellectual capital goods. The relationship between a positive worldview and family wealth extended to post-secondary financial funding of college, with worldview 'optimists' most often receiving parental funding of their post-secondary education.

Young adult theodicy was also affected, albeit weakly, by family financial capital during adolescence. Determinists reported as teenagers that their families had fewer household capital goods – and specifically, fewer intellectual possessions (for example, books, daily newspapers, magazines, typewriters, computers).

Ultimate values were also related to adolescent household goods. Adolescents with more household non-intellectual possessions (for example, televisions, DVD players) were more likely to give lower rankings as young adults to self-transcendent values. Those with more intellectual possessions tended to give lower rankings as young adults to affiliative values. These are patterns consistent with the patterns of 'affluenza' described by John de Graaf and colleagues[19] as afflicting American society, and by Oliver James[20] as a growing worldwide phenomenon. Moderation, control, or relative paucity in possession of goods may contribute to stronger spiritual and societal values – as well as greater affiliative values.

There was no relationship between household possessions during adolescence – intellectual or non-intellectual – and later life purpose.

Summary of Family Influences

Worldview

Family capital and family change during adolescence were the most predictive factors of later worldviews in early adulthood, accounting for 10 per cent of the variance in worldviews – particularly of the emergence of a positive or mixed worldview as an alternative to the dominant cultural pattern of a negative worldview. The absence of any relationships between worldview and family dynamics or parenting behaviour, combined with the significant relationships between worldview and both family capital and family stress, together suggest that young adults' worldviews are shaped more by their experiences of family financial capital than by their experiences of family psychological and developmental support. Additionally, the relationships of both distress and eustress in families to subsequent mixed or ambivalent worldviews suggest that increased family stress during adolescence – both positive and negative – can lead to young adult uncertainty or ambivalence about the world. Both distress and eustress can be understood as threats to stability in a family – and in many cases, threats to financial stability. Divorce, death, illness, remarriage, location changes, or job changes can significantly change a family's use of money and can unsettle a teenager's perception of how one's family fits within the social fabric of 'the world'. These results yield suggest two possibilities:

1. *Family goods shaping imagination* – Parent education level yields significant goods for children in terms of both financial and social benefits. A family's financial well-being, more than the family's interactive environment, contributes to the emergence of positive worldviews.
2. *Family stability shaping certainty* – Family stress and instability threaten the emergence of any clarity about the world and contribute to ambivalence about the world, as threats to stability retract teenagers' attention to their immediate experience, raise questions about certainty of anything in life,

---

[19]   John de Graaf, David Wann, Thomas Naylor and David Horsey, *Affluenza: The All-Consuming Epidemic* (San Francisco, CA: Berrett-Koehler, 2001).

[20]   Oliver James, *Affluenza* (London: Vermilion, 2007).

unsettle familial financial stability and shift adolescents' understanding of familial standing in society.[21]

Theodicy

The picture of familial impact is not the same with respect to theodicy. Here, familial closeness and parent-school connection contributed to later theodical perspectives. Determinists during adolescence spent the most time with their families and noted higher parental emphasis on their school performance. They also indicated the lowest number of household possessions (and the lowest parental financial support for college). In contrast, randomists as teenagers indicated the least amount of time with their families, and the least investment by parents in pushing their scholastic performance or in interacting with their schools (but also the highest parental financial support for college). Humanists as teenagers indicated the highest parental interaction with their schools, highest number of household possessions, and lowest number of family distressors. From these patterns, I would like to suggest the following as possible parental influences on later theodical orientations of young adults:

1. *Parent as Disciplinarian* – Familial discipline shapes ideas about control, cause and responsibility. Young adults with more disciplinary parents (who exercise more control over time use, assign more household chores and press children to perform well in school) seem more likely to form deterministic theodicies, while those with the least disciplinary parents seem more likely to develop randomistic theodicies.

2. *Parent as Mentor* – Parental interaction with their children's schools and teachers models an engagement that supports humanistic beliefs in self-determination and responsibility. Young adults with parents least involved in their children's school environments, regardless of financial support for their education, are more likely to adopt randomistic theodicies. In contrast, those with parents who interacted with schools and teachers may be more likely to develop humanistic theodicies.

---

[21]   Alternately, family stress may contribute to subsequent worldview ambivalence by reducing adolescent self-assurance and instead contributing to a sense of insecurity. This should be signalled by significantly lower self-esteem and self-efficacy. Or, family stress may contribute to subsequent worldview ambivalence by reducing parental attention to adolescents, leaving them to create their own lives. This should be signalled by significantly lower parental influence. But, while the pattern of scores suggests that parents of ambivalent young adults spent less time with them and exercised less control over their time use as adolescents, none of these patterns were significant predictors. In the larger *Transition* sample, family stressors were related to family capital goods, specifically to intellectual capital goods; but family stressors were not related to self-esteem or self-efficacy.

3. *Parent as Provider of Social Status* – Constraints and deprivation in financial capital contribute to theodicies that emphasize powers beyond oneself shaping destinies. Young adults from families who have the least household wealth seem more likely to adopt deterministic theodicies. Those from families with more household wealth become increasingly likely to adopt either humanistic or randomistic theodicies.

4. *Family as Signal of Stability* – Familial stability can foster assumptions about control and security that contribute to a more humanistic 'belief in a just world' theodicy. Young adults from households with the fewest significant distressors seem most likely to become theodical humanists; more family distressors might either reinforce the dominant deterministic orientation or shift young adults toward a more randomistic outlook – an outcome shaped by the level of familial connection or disconnection.

Life Purpose

Life purpose was not affected like worldview or theodicy by family financial capital. Of all family factors, parental engagement in children's schools and family dynamics of support and challenge had the most significant impact on later life purpose. Avoidant young adults experienced the least family support and challenge. Engaged young adults indicated higher involvement by parents in their schools combined with less pressure by parents on their personal scholastic performance, and they reported fewer negative family stressors. Family challenge, combined with family distressors and parental pressure on scholastic performance, accounted for only 6.9 per cent of the variance in life purpose.

Without sufficient emotional and motivational encouragement at home, adolescents may not develop a perception of themselves as strong and resourceful enough to contribute to others, either locally or more broadly. Perhaps the greater the support and challenge offered to teenagers in their process of exploring and becoming, the greater the likelihood that they will develop a sense of life purpose that includes the conception that 'I am here for others, and I have capacities to offer others.' In theological terms, the roots of vocation (*vocatus*: called, invoked, named) – whether more role-defined or more broadly committed – emerge at least in some part from the soil of familial explorations of potential, possibility and purpose.

But emotional and motivational support may only open the door for some sense of engagement of self in world. A greater sense of contribution to the world, beyond the defined parameters of immediate relationships and work, may not easily emerge without some role models. It may have been particularly important to engaged young adults to see their parents active on their behalf in their schools.

Ultimate Values

Values are indeed shaped in part by family experiences – but only in part. Different family factors influenced different sets of young adult ultimate values. Affiliative values were higher among young adults from two-parent families – and from homes with fewer household possessions (specifically, intellectual possessions). Self-transcendent values were higher among young adults from homes with fewer possessions (specifically, non-intellectual possessions). Eudaimonic values – and hedonistic values – were stronger among young adults who had not received as strong emotional and motivational support from their families.

The inverse relationship between household financial goods and later affiliative and spiritual/social values support the troubling conclusions of those documenting the phenomenon of 'affluenza' – the eroding of interpersonal and broader social concern as a result of increased consumption of goods in a consumer society. Fewer possessions during childhood and adolescence may indeed help young adults develop stronger goals and commitments to both their more local, tribal relationships and their larger connections to humanity – and more possessions may reduce commitments to these less self-focused ultimate values in early adulthood.

There is a psychodynamic interpretation to consider. Young adults who experienced less support from their families reported heightened eudaimonic values and hedonistic values. These young adults may have been seeking to fill a gap left in their lives – either through self-support and self-affirmation by emphasizing the pursuit of self-respect, freedom, accomplishment and wisdom, or through a substitution of extrinsic and soothing rewards of pleasure, excitement, beauty and a comfortable life. Both of these theological pathways may belie a yearning to fill a void in their own psychodynamic development of trust, autonomy and initiative.

In the same vein, it is interesting to note how it was relative deficit or paucity – whether in financial or emotional factors – in family life rather than relative plenitude that contributed to the formation of ultimate values. Indeed, values are not merely goals shaped by positive experiences. Values are also goals – strivings – constructed and sustained in part from unfulfilled desire.

In all of these circumstances, family factors accounted for little more than 10 per cent of the variance in worldview, theodicy, life purpose, or ultimate values. Parents and family do contribute to personal theologies – but they are by no means the sole contributors.

The Influence of Education

Education remains an extremely important gateway into adult employment, status and self-determinative power in America. Completion of high school is one critical benchmark. Evidence from the NELS study indicates that, even though as many as roughly 20 per cent of American youth dropped out of school before completion, over 90 per cent of these dropouts had subsequently earned a high school diploma within eight years.[22] Furthermore, 76 per cent of all NELS adolescents entered post-secondary education.

Educational experience turned out to be a stronger predictor of young adult personal theologies than any other social or developmental factor in adolescent life. School-related variables such as the intensity of education, student investment and performance, and school environment were consistently among the strongest predictors in any final regression equation predicting worldview, theodicy, life purpose and ultimate values.

Educational Intensity

The schools of teenagers in the YSD study offered a range of basic to advanced courses in mathematics, science, English and other disciplines. These teenagers accessed and (to the degree they could) selected widely different levels of education in their schools. The two most critical distinctions in educational intensity were in science and in mathematics. These two areas of educational intensity were directly related to worldview, theodicy and life purpose. The lowest intensity of science education in high school was among young adults with negative worldviews and deterministic theodicies. Determinists also had lower intensity math courses in high school. Randomists had the highest intensity of secondary science education among theodicy groups. Engaged young adults had the highest intensity of high school science and math education among life purpose groups. See Figure 8.6.

Looking just past high school, college attendance was also related to personal theologies. Those young adults who attended college indicated stronger affiliative values. Those who did not attend college, or who attended two-year vocational or community colleges, indicated stronger hedonistic values. Four-year college attendance was most common – and almost uniform – among young adults with positive worldview, humanistic theodicies, or engaged life purpose. Attendance at more prestigious colleges was also most common for these groups of young adults. Interestingly, randomists had most likely attended less prestigious four-year colleges – or had not attended any college. See Figure 8.7.

Student Investment and Performance

Students bring their own effort to the educational experience of schools, and so contribute to the impact of education on their later personal theologies. For young adults in *Making the Transition*, indicators of student effort and aptitude (grades, time put into homework and various school-based awards) were strongly related to later theodicies, senses of life purpose and ultimate values – but not to worldviews. Higher grades in high school were more common among young

---

22 See David Hurst, Dana Kelly and Daniel Princiatta, 'Educational Attainment of High School Dropouts 8 Years Later', National Center for Education Statistics, US Department of Education, NCES2005-026, November 2005.

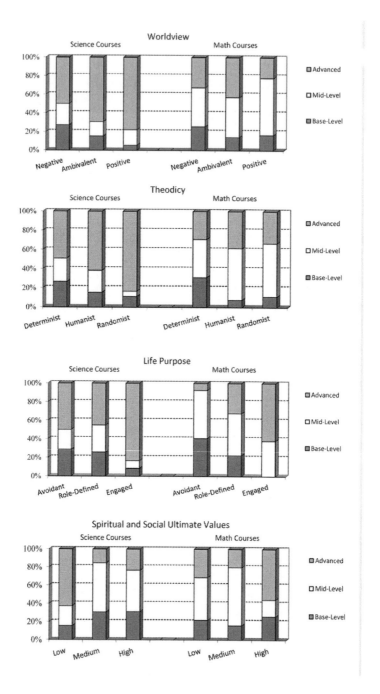

Figure 8.6   Academic intensity of science and math courses taken in high
school, by later young adult facets of personal theologies

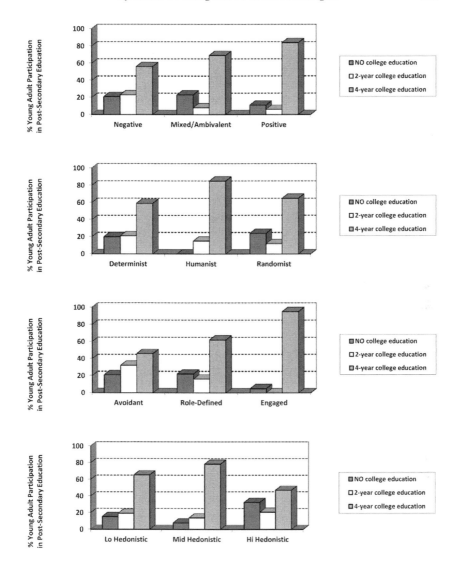

Figure 8.7   Post-collegiate education, by young adult facets of personal theologies

adults with humanistic theodicies, engaged life purpose and affiliative values – and less common among young adults with avoidant life purpose and hedonistic values. Engaged young adults were most likely to have received civic involvement awards from their schools, while those with stronger affiliative values were less likely to have received such awards. Oddly, humanistic young adults were less likely than deterministic or randomistic young adults to have received scholastic awards in high school. Time spent on high school homework was lowest among

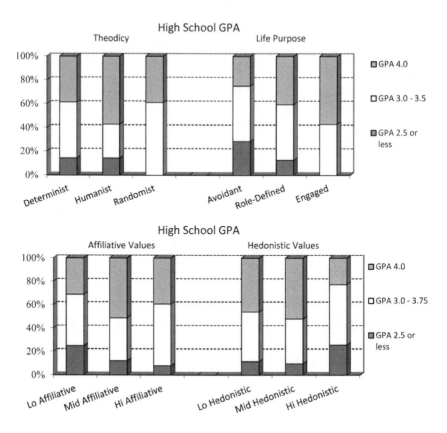

Figure 8.8   High school GPA, by later young adult facets of personal theology

young adults with deterministic theodicies, avoidant life purpose and stronger hedonistic values. See Figure 8.8.

School Environment

School is not only about scholastic intensity and performance. It is, in Bronfenbrenner's terms, a developmental environment – a microsystem with its own dynamics of emotion, support, interpersonal connection and distress. To examine how earlier school environment may have contributed to later personal theologies, I drew on young adults' prior adolescent YSD study ratings of school support, teacher support, distressors experienced in school, disruption by other youth and personal school problems.

It was not surprising that, in relation to life purpose, teenage ratings of school and teacher support were weakest among avoidant young adults and strongest among engaged young adults. Avoidant young adults also reported as teenagers the most schools distressors and personal school problems, while engaged young adults reported as teenagers the least school disruption by other youths. Also not surprising were relationships of school problems to theodicy: young adult humanists as teenagers reported the fewest school distressors and fewest personal school problems, while randomists reported the most.

But it was surprising that higher ratings of teacher support were also predictive later negative worldviews – a finding I will discuss later in relation to overall predictive models. Another intriguing pattern emerged in relation to ultimate values: looking just past high school, young adults with higher self-transcendent values reported fewer problems in college – while those with higher eudaimonic values reported more problems in college.

Summary of Education Influences

There were clear relationships between educational experiences in high school and later differences in worldview, theodicy and life purpose. But school factors alone, independent of other possible sources of influence, varied in predictive strength. Alone, school factors only accounted for 5.8 per cent of variance in worldviews and 7.0–8.4 per cent of variance in theodicies, but 19.9–30.6 per cent of variance in life purpose.

For worldviews, intensity of science education was the strongest predictive educational factor – young adults with positive worldviews had taken the most rigorous science courses in high school. Other school factors had less effect. However, when considered in co-variance with family factors, school factors became much more robust predictors: in predicting worldviews, teacher support joined science education as strong adolescent educational predictors – eclipsing the effects of parent educational attainment and marital status. (Oddly, adolescent ratings of teacher support were inversely predictive of worldview.)

Different school experiences contributed to different types of theodicies. As it was for worldview, science education was the strongest educational predictor for theodicy – a moderately strong predictor of determinism $(R=.084)$ and randomism $(R=.070)$. An immersion in science exposes individuals to alternative theologies from traditional religious stories, doctrines and beliefs. But for humanists, science education was not a significant predictor. Rather, higher grades – and, oddly, fewer academic awards – were the primary predictors of humanists' later theodical positions.

Both humanists and randomists tended to be stronger scholastic performers than determinists in high school. But in addition to receiving fewer scholastic honours, humanists tended to spend less time in school and experienced fewer school-related problems than randomists. It seems that humanistic young adults attained at least equivalent scholastic achievement as randomists in high school, but with somewhat less effort, less recognition and fewer problems. Perhaps those who developed humanistic theodicies possessed more 'natural' capacity for scholastic work than those who became randomists. Randomists also were immersed more in the most rigorous science education, contributing to diminished consideration of human choices, divine purposes, or future outcomes as ultimate causes. Determinists differed from both these groups: they received the lowest grades and had the least intensive math and science educations, despite spending equivalent time in school and on homework.

Scholastic investment and performance combined as particularly joint predictors of young adult life purpose. High school grades, time on homework and percentage of waking hours in school together accounted for 30.6 per cent of the variance in later life purpose, with homework time the strongest predictor. Scholastic intensity was also a strong combination of predictors: substitution of math and science intensity for grades resulted in similarly strong predictive equations that accounted for over 30 per cent of the variance. Other school-related factors were also somewhat strong predictors – and collectively more predictive than family factors. School support, school distressors and community service awards together comprised the next strongest set of school-related predictors, accounting for 19.9 per cent of the variance in life purpose. Higher indications of disruptive peers and school distress (more common in poorer communities) were predictive of a later avoidant life purpose orientation, while a higher frequency of community service awards (more common in wealthier communities where schools sponsored more community action projects) was predictive of an engagement orientation.

Scholastic performance and intensity opens adolescents up to stronger belief in the potential of people to have impact on the world. Across nearly all measures, engagers were top scholastic performers as teenagers. They were significantly stronger than both avoiders and role-observers in effort; they received significantly more awards in civic involvement, and they attained the highest grades. They stood out as teenagers who devoted themselves to their studies, challenged themselves with the most difficult math and science courses, and received superior grades – while at the same time getting involved in noteworthy ways in community activism, volunteering and student government. Avoiders were lowest of the three groups on nearly every indicator of academic performance and scholastic effort – but still attained average to above-average grades.

School environment also contribute in important ways to adolescents' sense of safety and personal power within a larger social milieu. Thus, experiences of safety and control in school environments may be essential ingredients in the formation of an engagement-oriented sense of life purpose. School settings in which teachers are not as supportive, where peers are more disruptive, and safety is not well-established may foster an avoidant orientation or (for more resilient students) a role-defined orientation, and not an engagement orientation. But schools with greater safety and discipline, where teachers provide strong student support, are much more likely to foster an engagement orientation in students. Of course, students within each school setting experience different degrees of teacher support and peer disruption, depending on their personal behaviour, peer group and curriculum level. But schools themselves also vary significantly depending on the socio-economic status of the community.[23]

Surprisingly, there were few relationships of adolescent academic intensity and educational investment with later ultimate values. Affiliative young adults as teenagers earned higher grades and had fewer incidents of delinquency, but received fewer community service awards. Hedonistic young adults as teenagers spent the least time on homework and had the lowest educational expectations of themselves. There were stronger relationships between ultimate values and the pursuit of post-secondary education: affiliative young adults were more likely to attend four-year colleges, while hedonistic young adults were more likely to go to two-year colleges or not pursue any post-secondary education. These were, at best, modest singular predictors of young adult values.

The Influence of Other Social Factors

In addition to family and school, I have considered the influence of adolescent employment, extracurricular activity, peer involvement and religion on personal theologies. Employment in typically low-skilled jobs, or working a high number of hours, might further instantiate the culturally dominant negative worldview and deterministic theodicy. More involvement in active extracurricular endeavours, whether in hobbies or school-related activities, might offer experiences that contribute to more positive worldviews, engaged life purpose and eudaimonic values. More time with peers could contribute to either negative or positive worldviews, depending on the values expressed by peers as important. And religion is understood in the sociological and anthropological literature as a primary contributor to worldview, theodicy and ultimate values. We will look at the relationships of each of these arenas of adolescent life and their relationship with the emerging personal theologies of our 82 young adults.

Extracurricular Activities

Personal theologies seemed to have very little to do with adolescent extracurricular involvement. Even though steady extracurricular participation among NELS adolescents was predictive of stronger early adult academic performance and interpersonal maturity,[24] there was little evidence of an impact of extracurricular

---

[23]   For the entire *Transition* sample of participants, SCC was significantly inversely correlated with adolescent reports of peer disruption, school distress and negative interactions with teachers and peers. Students from lower-class communities experienced significantly more negative school environments. Students from higher-class communities experienced higher teacher support.

[24]   See Jonathan Zaff, Kristin Moore, Angela Papillo and Stephanie Williams, 'Implications of Extracurricular Activity Participation during Adolescence on Positive

activity on personal theologies. There were no relationships of sports, hobbies, or overall extracurricular activities with theodicy or ultimate values. There was only a weak relationship between extracurricular hours and worldview – young adults with negative worldviews spent fewer hours in teenage extracurricular activities.

But there was an interesting relationship of extracurricular activities with life purpose: engaged young adults as teenagers reported *no* time in sports during a typical week, but indicated the *most* involvement in overall extracurricular activities. Perhaps an engagement-oriented life purpose is shaped not by sports but by other extracurricular activities – for instance, engagers as teens received more community involvement awards and participated more in student government and volunteer organizations. Interestingly, engagers also tended as teenagers to spend the most time in passive leisure – hanging out, watching television, or otherwise passing time without effort. This, combined with a lower frequency employment, suggests that at least some engagers may go through an adolescent 'incubation', during which ideas about greater human impact on the world could develop, untested.

Employment

During high school, one-fourth of NELS American tenth-graders and one-half of twelfth-graders worked for pay in some kind of job outside the home.[25] Among all *Transition* young adults, employment during high school was inversely related to community social class and parents' educational attainment. Teenagers from higher socio-economic communities and families worked fewer hours but for somewhat better pay. Among our 82 core young adults, teenage employment was also inversely related to their later life purpose and ultimate values. Over 90 per cent of avoidant young adults were employed as teenagers, compared with only about 70 per cent of role-defined and engaged young adults. Also, young adults who were employed in high school later gave lower emphasis to eudaimonic values. But adolescent employment was not related to later young adult worldview and theodicy.

Quality and duration of adolescent employment might make a minor difference in later personal theologies. Young adults with mixed or ambivalent worldviews, non-humanistic theodicies, avoidant life purpose, or higher hedonistic values and lower self-transcendent values were least likely to have had higher skilled jobs in health services, the arts, or business offices as teenagers. They were most likely to have worked instead in lower skilled manual and service jobs. Young adults who

---

Outcomes', *Journal of Adolescent Research* 18(6) (November 2003): 599–630.

[25]   See John Warren, Paul LePore and Robert Mare, 'Employment During High School: Consequences for Students' Grades in Reading and Mathematics' (CDE Working Paper No. 96-23, Madison, WI: Center for Demography and Ecology, University of Wisconsin-Madison, 1997), pp. 16, 36. Over 17 per cent of tenth-graders and 30 per cent of twelfth-graders worked more than 15 hours per week – and work hours were significantly higher among teenagers on a vocational track.

held longer-term teenage jobs reported higher self-transcendent values and lower eudaimonic values.

Work hours did not seem to contribute significantly to personal theologies – but wages may have. Young adults with negative worldviews earned significantly less per hour than those with other worldviews – and young adult randomists and engagers earned significantly higher wages. Engagers stood out distinctly: in spite of working fewer hours or being less likely to have a job, engagers were also most likely to earn higher wages in their employment. Teenage wages were not significantly correlated with later ultimate values (despite slightly higher teenage wages among those who later reported more hedonistic values).

Together, these results point to significant previous differences between personal theology groups in the nature, purpose and necessity of their teenage employment. They also provide further evidence of a critical relationship between socio-economic background and later personal theologies (particularly life purpose and ultimate values), mediated developmentally by the necessities, motivations and experiences of teenage employment. See Figure 8.9.

Peer Involvement

Peers and friends exerted influence on NELS adolescents – both for better and worse. Most NELS adolescents thought their friends considered academic performance more important than extracurricular social activity or than acting out.[26] What impact, then, do friends during high school have on later young adult beliefs and values?

The impact of friendship can be from the accumulation of contact (as indicated by the amount of time spent with friends), as well as from the type of activities shared and the nature of discourse (as indicated by teenagers' recognition of their friends' values). These two factors of peer relationships were related to later personal theologies – sometimes in surprising ways.

Young adult theodicy was related to the percentage of time spent with friends during a typical high school week (from experience sampling): randomists spent more time with their friends, while humanists spent more time alone, and determinists spent a higher percentage of time with their families. But there were no relationships between adolescent peers' values and later young adult theodicy.

Conversely, young adults' worldviews were correlated with their high school friends' values, but not with time spent with peers. Teenagers who considered their peers to give less value to contributing to society (and specifically, to religion, volunteering and holding a steady job) were more likely as young adults to hold positive worldviews – suggesting that, for some, a 'devil may care' set of

---

[26] See Xianglei Chen, 'Students' Peer Groups in High School: The Pattern and Relationship to Educational Outcomes' (Office of Educational Research and Improvement, US Department of Education, NCES97-055, 1997), pp. 2–4.

Teen Wages by Worldview

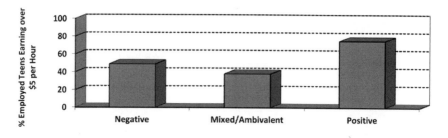

Teen Wages by Theodicy

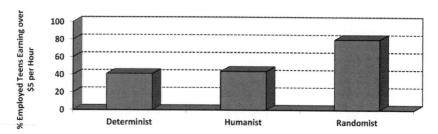

Teen Wages by Life Purpose

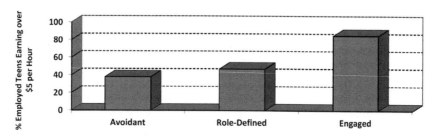

Figure 8.9   Wages among working adolescents, by later worldview and theodicy

assumptions about larger societal challenges might permeate the development of a more positive worldview.

Young adult life purpose was related to both time and quality in peer relationships. Role-defined young adults in high school spent the most time with their peers, while engaged young adults spent the least time with peers. In terms of friends' values, groups were also distinct. Engaged young adults during high school viewed their peers as having the highest academic performance values but the lowest values of having a steady job, while role-defined young adults viewed their peers as having the highest socializing values and religious involvement values.

Peer time and values correlated to ultimate values on the affiliative – self-image dimension, but not on the hedonistic–spiritual/social dimension. Young adults with higher eudaimonic values tended to spend less time in their adolescence with peers and spent significantly more time alone. Their adolescent peers were less oriented toward social contribution as important values – and particularly less oriented toward job stability and religious affiliation. Young adults with higher affiliative values spent less time alone in their adolescence, and tended as young adults to seek out affiliation more actively in both organized social groups and casual social venues.

Religion

Transition young adults were like other American young adults in their infrequent acknowledgement of conscious influences of religion on their beliefs and values – and, as we have seen, many of these young adults were prone to describe religiosity as zealotry and religious beliefs as dogmatism, adding to their tendency to deny any connection between religion and their personal theologies. However, using data from the preceding YSD study, I was able to explore direct influences of adolescent religious experience on personal theologies from three perspectives: familial and personal religious affiliation, perceived religious devotion (ranging from none to high), and frequency of actual attendance at religious services. These measures provided indications of basic religious enculturation, internalization of religious traditions, and behavioural commitment. Nearly half of NELS adolescents attended weekly religious services, while less than one-fifth did not attend any services in a year; but only 13 per cent considered themselves 'very religious', while over one-fourth considered themselves 'not at all religious'.[27] More religious NELS youth were more likely to participate in voluntary community work.

Comparably, most of the 82 core *Transition* young adults as teenagers had claimed some religious affiliation – 86 per cent total (70 per cent Christian, 16 per cent other religions, 14 per cent none). But teenage religious affiliation made no significant difference in later worldview or theodicy.[28] However, religious affiliation was directly related to life purpose and ultimate values. In terms of life purpose, engaged (90.5 per cent) as well as role-defined (87.5 per cent) young adults were

---

[27] Summarized by Laura Lippman, Erik Michelsen and Eugene Roehlekepartain, 'The Measurement of Family Religiosity and Spirituality' (paper prepared for *Indicators of Child, Family, and Community Connections,* HHS-100-01-0011 (05), Office of the Assistant Secretary for Planning and Evaluation, US Department of Health and Human Services, 2004).

[28] There were only minor, non-significant tendencies, such as non-religious teenagers later tending toward more positive worldviews and randomistic theodicies, but no differences emerged due to type of adolescent religious affiliation. Conservative or fundamentalist Christians did not differ from evangelical and Catholic Christians, liberal mainline Christians, non-religious and religious non-Christians.

much more likely than avoidant young adults (62 per cent) to have grown up with religion as some part of their lives. In terms of ultimate values, young adults with some religious affiliation during high school gave somewhat higher rankings to self-transcendent values (driven in part by higher ratings of 'salvation').

Young adults' teenage self-ratings of religiosity were also related to their later rankings of ultimate values. Those who placed higher emphasis on affiliative and self-transcendent values as teenagers saw themselves as more religious; but those who gave higher rankings to eudaimonic values previously saw themselves as less religious. There were no other noticeable relationships between teenage religious devotion and later young adult worldview, theodicy, or life purpose.

Behavioural investment in religion, in the form of frequency of attendance at religious services, may be one of the clearest indicators of familial and personal religious adherence. Christian Smith and colleagues found that this was a particularly important marker of divisions between teenagers in their explicitly religious beliefs and values.[29] We found a similar pattern in relation to three of the four facets of personal theology examined in the *Transition* study: attendance at religious services correlated significantly with later young adult worldview, theodicy and ultimate values – but not with life purpose. Young adults who as teenagers attended religious services less frequently were later more likely to claim positive worldviews, humanistic or randomistic theodicies, and somewhat lower affiliative values. Those reporting more frequent religious attendance during teenage years tended as young adults to claim negative or mixed/ambivalent worldviews, deterministic theodicies and somewhat higher affiliative values. See Figure 8.10.

Later religious attendance as young adults is also important to consider. For American college students as well as non-collegiate young adults, there is typically a marked drop-off in religious attendance during the first few years after the end of high school. In the early 2000s, just over 80 per cent of American college freshmen reported regular or occasional attendance at religious services upon entry into their first year of college (down from 92 per cent in 1968), but also continued the growing trend of 'no religious preference'.[30] Furthermore, over the span of the first year in college, non-attendance at religious services increased among American freshmen to over 40 per cent.[31] Overall, among the core 82

[29] See Phil Schwadel and Christian Smith, *Portraits of Protestant Teens: A Report on Teenagers in Major U.S. Denominations* (Chapel Hill, NC: National Study of Youth & Religion, 2005) <www.youthandreligion.org/sites/youthandreligion.org/files/imported/publications/docs/PortraitsProtTeens.pdf>.

[30] See Linda Sax, Alexander Astin, Jennifer Lindholm, William Korn, Victor Saenz and Kathryn Mahoney, *The American Freshman: National Norms for Fall 2003* (Los Angeles, CA: Higher Education Research Institute, UCLA Graduate School of Education & Information Studies).

[31] Alyssa Bryan, Jeung Yun Choi and Maiko Yasuno, 'Understanding the Religious and Spiritual Dimensions of Students' Lives in the First Year of College', *Journal of*

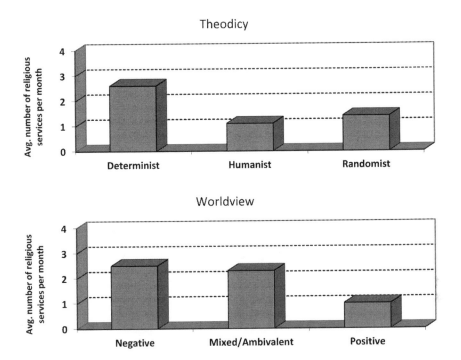

Figure 8.10 Adolescent monthly attendance at religious services, by later worldview and theodicy

Transition young adults, attendance declined only some, from an average of 2.1 services per month to an average of 1.7 per month.

Young adults' religious attendance was not related to their concurrent worldviews or life purpose – but was related to their theodicies and ultimate values. Infrequent attenders (about once every two months or less) were more likely to be randomists and more hedonistic in values, while frequent attenders (about twice a month or more) were most likely determinists and stronger in self-transcendent values.

Patterns in young adult religious beliefs (a marker of religiosity) tracked similarly to patterns in frequency of religious attendance. There were no significant differences by worldview or life purpose in endorsements of traditional, existential, or atheistic religious beliefs. But there were robust differences in these religious beliefs according with theodicy and ultimate values – mimicking the pattern described above for religious attendance.

Summary of Other Social Influences

In general, adolescent experiences in these social arenas – extracurricular activities, paid employment, peer interaction and religion – were not strongly predictive of later personal theologies in early adulthood. Neither religious experience nor experience in any other of these social arenas had any significant influence on later worldviews or later affiliative values. Work hours and peer performance-related values were the only adolescent experiences from these social arenas predictive of later life purpose, accounting for only 5 per cent of the variance, without any notable impact from religion. Likewise, adolescent work hours and peer values oriented toward social contribution accounted for almost 10 per cent of the variance in later eudaimonic values. In both cases, teenage work hours were negative predictors: more time in employment during high school was predictive of more avoidance-oriented life purpose and weaker eudaimonic values.

Religious commitment in the form of religiosity and regular attendance was a more consistent predictor from among these social arenas – specifically, in predicting theodicy and most ultimate values. Adolescent religious commitment and time with peers were both predictive of later deterministic and (in contrasting ways) randomistic theodicies, accounting for about 8 per cent of the variance in theodicies. Religious commitment also accounted for nearly 10 per cent of the variance in later hedonistic values and (in contrasting ways) for nearly 16 per cent of the variance in later self-transcendent values. As we shall see later in this chapter and in the following interlude, young adults' current religious attendance and beliefs were also strongly related to their theodicies and ultimate values.

Religion was not *directly* influential on young adult worldviews and life purpose. Religion's influence on worldview and life purpose may be mediated through young adults' earlier cultural, educational, familial and peer-related experiences. Peers' values during high school certainly seemed to contribute to later personal theology.

Theodicy was particularly strongly shaped in direct ways by religious experience. It might even be tempting to regard theodical beliefs simply as a mirror of religious identity. After all, anthropologist Clifford Geertz stated that a primary cultural function of religion is to guide people in how to suffer.[32] But theodicy as an account and explanatory system for unexpected or seemingly unjust human suffering can be either religious or non-religious.

The Influence of Psychological Attitudes and Dispositions

It is clear from the patterns discussed above that the environments of teenagers shaped their personal theologies as they entered early adulthood. It is not as clear how the inner qualities and dispositions of these teenagers shaped their

---

[32]   See Clifford Geertz, *The Interpretation of Cultures* (New York: Basic Books, 1973).

later emerging personal theologies. To what degree do personalities and personal theologies correlate? Do inner dispositions, attitudes and traits shape beliefs and values about the world, ultimate cause, life purpose and the good?

A common assumption among psychodynamically oriented theorists is that personal theology is simply an elaborate extension and externalization of the self. Self-perception and long-standing psychological dispositions and attitudes shape perceptions of the external environment and thus guide the formation of personal theologies as extensions of self-perception. From this view, worldview becomes simply a reflection of self-appraisals such as self-esteem and self-determination, and of habitual attitudes such as optimism. Theodicy simply becomes an extension of self-efficacy and locus of control. Life purpose becomes an externalized fantasy about a possible future self, shaped by habits of self-effacement, modesty, or grandiosity, or an extension of self-esteem mixed with introversion or extraversion. If such a position is tenable, then young adult personal theologies should be significantly related to – and predicted by – adolescent psychological attitudes and dispositions.

There are specific relationships between personality and personal theology that a traditional psychodynamic perspective might predict. In more 'cognitive' terms, teenagers who make more positive self-appraisals – that is, those with more positive self-esteem, a stronger sense of self-efficacy and a rosier outlook on the future – should have more positive worldviews, humanistic theodicies and less avoidant life purpose as young adults. In more 'affective' terms, teenagers who experience more positive mood states should be more prone to express positive worldviews and engaged life purpose as adults. Finally, in 'conative' or motivational terms, teenagers who are more motivated and conscientious in their daily activities should have more positive worldviews and engaged life purpose, and less deterministic theodicies and hedonistic values, later in early adulthood.

And indeed, there were measures of conative, cognitive and affective dispositions that correlated significantly with different facets of later personal theologies: the desire and intentionality toward achievement (motivation and conscientiousness), the sense of one's own power and capacity for influence (locus of control and self-efficacy), and sanguinity and buoyancy about one's life (optimism and future outlook). But other global measures such as self-esteem did not correlate at all with later personal theologies.

Measures of teenage conative, cognitive and affective dispositions and habits came from two sources in the YSD study. Surveys provided brief global indicators such as optimism, future outlook and locus of control. Self-ratings during a week of randomized experience sampling self-reports provided indicators of average moment-to-moment perceptions of mood, efficacy and motivation.

Motivation and Commitment to Achievement

Measures of motivation and commitment to achievement were drawn from ratings during random intervals of experience over one week, providing a picture of enduring dispositions and habits of mind. Average moment-to-moment motivation[33] was lowest among teenagers who later as young adults expressed negative worldviews or (surprisingly) an engaged life purpose. Average motivation was highest among those who as young adults expressed a role-defined sense of life purpose or who gave higher rankings to eudaimonic values.

Indicators of conscientiousness in daily life were also related to later young adult ultimate values. Teenagers who spent more of their time planning their futures and setting goals had higher eudaimonic values and lower affiliative values as young adults, and those who experienced greater challenge in their daily activities reported higher eudaimonic values as young adults. Average moment-to-moment concentration was highest among those who became young adult humanists and lowest among those who became determinists.

Power and Capacity for Influence

Adolescent sense of power and capacity for influence was not related to later worldview, but was related to other facets of later personal theology. Not surprisingly, young adults with humanistic theodicies and engaged life purpose expressed the highest general sense of self-efficacy as teenagers. In contrast, both deterministic and avoidant young adults indicated a lower sense of self-efficacy and were most likely as teenagers to agree that things in life happen due to chance. Teenagers with higher personal locus of control were more likely as young adults to give higher rankings to affiliative values, while those with higher external locus of control later gave higher rankings to eudaimonic values.

Sanguinity and Buoyancy

Finally, there was some impact of teenagers' personal sanguinity and buoyancy on their later theodicies, life purpose and ultimate values. Those with higher educational expectations were more likely to articulate an engagement-oriented life purpose as young adults, while those with less positive outlook on the future were more likely to express an avoidance-oriented life purpose or a randomistic theodicy. Interestingly, future outlook was most positive among those who later expressed deterministic theodicies and stronger affiliative values. Those with a more positive mood in their daily experiences as teenagers had stronger affiliative values as young adults, while those with lower overall daily mood later reported stronger eudaimonic values. Interestingly, there was no relationship between mood-related or outlook-related measures and later worldview. It is also worth noting that teenagers' global self-esteem was not related in any way to any facet of their later personal theologies.

One final difference related to sanguinity and buoyancy was intriguing: as teenagers, young adults with randomistic theodicies were most likely to view

---

[33]   Motivation, a factor-analytic variable derived from ESM items, provided an overall measure of individuals' level of interest, enjoyment and inclination during each activity.

more of their daily experiences as 'like play', and not to view their experiences as 'neither like play nor work' (that is, absent of interest). They also tended to enjoy themselves more across their daily experiences, and regarded their experiences more frequently as having lower importance. These patterns persisted even after controlling for the higher percentage of time they spent with peers. In general, randomists seemed to take a more cavalier, gleeful and somewhat dismissive approach to their daily activities – but they were not bored.

Summary of Psychological Attitudes and Dispositions

A few dispositions and attitudes were modest to moderately strong predictors of personal theology. Daily motivation was predictive of later worldview, accounting independently for 9.8 per cent of variance in worldviews. Stronger motivation in daily activities in adolescence pointed toward more positive worldviews in early adulthood.

The best predictors of life purpose – positive future outlook and self-efficacy – together accounted for 6.4 per cent of the variance in life purpose.[34] Teenagers' general sense of optimism and perception of capacity for self-determination

Regarding ultimate values, the picture was more mixed. *No* adolescent dispositions or attitudes were the least bit predictive of later hedonistic or self-transcendent values. But there were moderately strong psychological predictors of young adults' affiliative values (positive future outlook and more time devoted to goal-setting and making plans for the future, accounting for 10.6 per cent of the variance) and eudaimonic values (*less* time devoted to making plans and goals and *less* sense of personal power in the form of greater external locus of control, accounting for 9.2 per cent of the variance).

Psychological predictors of different theodicies were intriguing. A humanistic theodicy was modestly predicted by lower chance- or fate-related locus of control, lower daily sense of challenge and higher daily concentration, which together accounted for 6.8% per cent of the variance between humanists and non-humanists. Deterministic theodicies were a bit more strongly predicted by higher chance- or fate-related locus of control and lower concentration, along with a *more* positive future outlook; together, these three variables accounted for 11.6 per cent of the variance. Determinists' heightened external locus of control as teenagers coincided not with a diminishment in self-worth or future outlook, but with greater optimism about life ahead of them. Randomistic theodicies were predicted most strongly, with a heightened daily sense of challenge, more playful perspectives

---

[34] An analysis with three fewer young adults (due to missing data) showed an intriguing pattern: *higher* general self-efficacy and *lower* daily sense of power together were significant predictors of more engaged life purpose (Adj. R^2 = .133). This raises the possibility that teenagers who became engagement-oriented young adults recognized that their immediate sense of low control during high school would give way in the long term to greater control of their lives.

and higher enjoyment of daily experiences, less importance given to experiences each day, and a less generalized positive future outlook, together accounting for 19.9 per cent of the variance between randomists and non-randomists.

The Composite Picture: Predictors of Facets of Personal Theologies

Multiple social and developmental influences collude to shape each facet of personal theology. No single arena of adolescent life is singly responsible for the personal theologies of young adults. So, let us now look at the best composite predictions of each facet of young adult personal theology, drawing from the strongest related experiences in each arena of adolescent life. We will begin by looking at prediction of young adults' worldviews and senses of life purpose from their adolescent lives. The tables that accompany each discussion show results from a progressive set-wise approach to linear regression analysis, and provide examples of the iterative process used in this exploratory study of social and developmental influence on personal theologies. For each facet of personal theology, in order to arrive at the best composite predictive models, I proceeded by deriving the strongest predictors among variables from each arena of adolescent life correlated with personal theology, beginning with family experience and continuing through school experience, work, peer influences (if any), religion, and personal dispositions and attitudes.

Predictors of Worldview

Table 8.2 summarizes the strongest composite statistical relationships between specific adolescent experiences and later young adult worldviews. For simplicity in these exploratory analyses I have treated worldviews as if in a linear relationship, from negative (-1) to mixed/ambivalent (0) to positive (+1).[35] Analysis began with the first moderately strong statistical relationship discussed: parents' educational attainment. At each subsequent stage, I entered only those variables that were already identified as related to worldviews, excluding all others. Because parents' educational attainment signalled socio-economic status, at each new stage I also examined the impact of parents' educational attainment on the overall strength of the regression model. This approach allows us to see the cumulative effect of many life experiences in shaping worldview; it also allows us to see what predictors gain or lose statistical power in prediction of worldviews.

---

[35]   Even though there are indications of a more curvilinear relationship between worldviews, many of the relationships of worldview with prior longitudinal data are more linear. There are distinct markers and predictors of the 'middle' mixed/ambivalent worldview position, and future research should take a curvilinear approach to analysis.

Table 8.2 Regression models predicting worldview from adolescent environments and personal disposition

	Parent education (PE) Alone	Family		Family and school		Family and personal dispositions		School, family and personal dispositions	
		With PE	Without PE	With PE	Without PE	With PE	Without PE	With PE	Without PE
	β	β	β	β	β	β	β	β	β
Constant	-.72	-.86	-1.18	-1.28	-1.16	-2.44	-2.16	-2.05	-2.13
Parent educational attainment	.26*	.22†	—	.05	—	.22†	—	.08	—
Household capital goods (non-intellectual)		.15	.20†	.19†	.20†	.08	.14	.13	.15
Single-parent or divorce-parent family		-.15	-.18	-.13	-.14	-.16	-.19†	-.14	-.15
Family eustress		.18†	.19†	.18†	.19†	.18†	.18	.18†	.18†
Intensity of science education				.36***	.38***	—	—	.32**	.35***
Teacher support				-.22†	-.21†	—	—	-.17†	-.18†
Motivation in daily experiences						.30**	.28*	.25*	.24*
Number of cases◆	**78**	**76**	**76**	**74**	**74**	**76**	**76**	**74**	**74**
Adjusted R²	**.058**	**.103**	**.078**	**.191**	**.200**	**.179**	**.145**	**.234**	**.249**
Adjusted R², using **pairwise exclusion correlations** of all 315	**.058**	**.148**	**.115**	**.217**	**.203**	**.238**	**.194**	**.319**	**.297**

Transition Years 2 and 3 young adults◆

Notes: ◆ Number of cases decreased due to missing data; ◆ This method allows for embedding the model within the larger set of inter-item relationships of the combined Year 2 and Year 3 sample. † $p \leq .10$; * $p \leq .05$; ** $p \leq .01$; *** $p \leq .005$.

Parent education alone was only a modest predictor, accounting for 5.8 per cent of the variance in the worldviews of 78 young adults.[36] As seen in Table 8.2, each new regression model that joined new predictors with or replaced parent education accounted for progressively more variance in worldviews. Other factors of family life – household non-intellectual possessions, parental marital status and the number of positive stressors experienced by families – accounted for 7.8 per cent of worldview variance without parent education, and 10.3 per cent of the variance with parent education still in the equation. School experiences alone and personal dispositions alone also increased predictive accuracy (these are not shown in the table). Intensity of science education and teacher support accounted for 13 per cent of the variance alone, and the retention of parent education only improved prediction to 13.6 per cent. Motivation in daily life was the only dispositional predictor, but was moderately strong, accounting for 9.8 per cent of worldview variance without parent education and 14.8 per cent with parent education.

I then joined the strongest retained school variables to the strongest retained family variables as simultaneous predictors – with a marked increase in predictive accuracy. Together, these features of teenagers' school and family experiences accounted for 20 per cent of variance in later young adult worldviews. At this point, parent education was eclipsed as a predictor – and when added back into regression, decreased predictive accuracy overall. This reinforces my earlier claim, that teenagers' personal experiences in education overshadow the effects of parents' educational achievements and socio-economic status. It is also likely that the socio-economic influence on worldviews signalled by parent education was indirectly exerted through the disparate range of opportunities afforded by different school systems depending on the wealth of the community.

Most variables were positive predictors, with the exceptions of teacher support and of single or divorced parental marital status. Teacher support was a strong negative predictor of worldview, accounting for about 5 per cent of worldview variance alone. The negative relationship of teacher support to worldview is difficult to explain: in the larger *Transition*, YSD and NELS studies, teacher support was positively correlated with parent education, grades, hours of homework, and intensity of math and science courses – and negatively correlated with school-related distress or delinquency. Thus, it may have been students more capable of independent study and less reliant on teacher interaction who were more likely to develop positive or mixed worldviews.

Adding teenage daily motivation to family variables in regression analysis also yielded somewhat strong results, together accounting for 14.5 per cent of worldview variance (and 17.9 per cent when combined with parent education as an additional predictor). While daily motivation was a robust predictor, it did not eclipse the predictive strength of parent education. One might be tempted to assume a connection between adolescent motivation and parent education;

---

[36]   Recall from the previous chapter on worldview that four of the 82 young adults did not provide answers clear enough to categorize.

however, no such relationship was found among the core group of 82 young adults or in the larger sample of 315.

The final combination of family, school and dispositional predictors yielded a moderately strong regression model that accounted for 25.9 per cent of the variance in young adult worldviews. Including parent education as a predictor only reduced the model's predictive accuracy.

Thus, at the conclusion of these analyses, we can identify adolescent science education as the strongest predictor of young adult worldviews, followed by adolescent motivation in daily life, perceived teacher support and significant positive changes (positive stressors) in family life. The abundance of household possessions was also a steady predictor, especially when parental marital status was removed from the analysis. In summary, strong college-bound education and personal investment in achievement, combined with family financial and social capital, were the strongest contributors from young adults' teenage years to the worldviews they later declared.

Departures from culturally dominant negative worldviews become increasingly possible for young adults whose families benefited from positive changes and wealth sufficient to allow ownership of more possessions. More intensive science education also provides young people with a departure, by offering unique perspective on the nature of the world as a place of order rather than chaos, with known or knowable forces shaping events. Adolescent motivation and scholastic autonomy, both signals of direct engagement with the environment, are additional avenues to more positive worldviews. Thus, three forces from adolescence appear to contribute most significantly to the formation of more positive worldviews in young adulthood: family financial capital (fostering a cosmology of a 'world full of good things'), education in the natural sciences (providing an alternative cosmology from the predominant cultural cosmology, and contributing to a belief in a more ordered and less threatening world), and intrinsic motivation (reflecting each individual's unique degree of engagement with his or her external environments). These factors are far more predictive of worldview than family dynamics, general scholastic performance or employment activity, religious and extracurricular involvement, mood, or self-image.

Other factors undoubtedly contributed to young adults' worldviews – the analyses I pursued only begin to explore the possible impact on worldviews of different experiences from different arenas of life. It is intriguing to note the paucity of religious influence on worldviews, and the much stronger influence of socio-economic and educational factors. Motivation as a predictor may also signal that worldviews were already forming in the minds of adolescents, and possibly influencing their behaviours. After all, if the world is not such a good place, why try so hard? But if the world is good and rich with potential, then it might be a place in which personal interest and investment in life might lead to flourishing.

Predictors of Life Purpose

Table 8.3 charts the same kind of analytic path for life purpose that was used to generate predictive regression models for worldview – but with more careful attention to different ways that educational experience may have shaped later life purpose. I began again building the models with the strongest demographic predictor of life purpose – the overall social class of the community (SCC), which accounted for only 2.3 per cent of the variance. Like parent education, SCC was later overshadowed as a predictor by experiences in school.

Family circumstances and experiences were modest predictors of later life purpose. The best predictors from adolescent family life accounted for 8.5 per cent of the variance (and 12.4 per cent with the inclusion of SCC). This time, it was not household wealth that made a difference: rather, it was the motivational environment of a family. A familial environment of challenge to do one's best was predictive of later engaged life purpose, while parents' direct pressure on school performance predicted more avoidant life purpose.

School was by far the most powerfully influential arena of adolescent life on later young adult life purpose. Educational environment accounted for 14.6 per cent of variance in later life purpose (17.1 per cent with SCC added). More strongly supportive high school environments – and schools with fewer distressful situations, such as theft or fights – contributed to life purposes oriented more toward other people and the wider world. Educational intensity had an even stronger impact. Intensity of math courses taken by teenagers (as available) alone accounted for 24.2 per cent of variance in later life purpose (25.6 per cent including SCC). But the strongest education-related predictors of young adult life purpose were the students' own scholastic effort and investment – grades and average weekly time spent on homework together accounted for 31.5 per cent of variance in later life purpose, with stronger performance and more effort predicting later beliefs in contribution of self to the world. The effects of SCC were eclipsed by academic intensity and scholastic performance, but not by family dynamics or school environment. Academic achievement may mediate the effects of SCC in the development of young adults' life purpose.

Adolescent dispositions and attitudes were modest predictors of later life purpose. Teenagers' future outlook, combined with their sense of personal power in the events of their daily lives, accounted for 6.7 per cent of variance. Factoring in community social class, predictive power improved, accounting for 16.3 per cent of the variance. More positive future outlook – but weaker sense of personal power in daily circumstances – contributed to later engagement-oriented life purpose.

Adolescent religious non-affiliation was weakly predictive of later avoidant life purpose.[37] Adolescent work was also a moderately weak negative predictor – hours of paid work (including zero hours for those not employed) accounted for 4.4 per

---

[37]   Religious affiliation was not included in the final analyses because of too many cases missing data.

Table 8.3   Best regression models predicting life purpose from adolescent environments and personal disposition

	SCC alone‡	Family environment model		School climate model		Scholastic intensity model		Scholastic performance model		Best combined model	
		Without SCC	With SCC	Without SCC	With SCC	Without SCC	With SCC	Without SCC	With SCC	Without SCC	With SCC
	β	β	β	β	β	β	β	β	β	β	β
Constant	1.65***	1.71***	1.55***	0.84	.97†	.79***	.82***	-.08	-.05	-.88	-1.10
SCC – Upper class	.32***	—	.23*	—	.21†	—	.17	—	.05	—	-.03
Family challenge		.29**	.23*							.18*	.19†
Parents pushing school performance		-.20†	-.15								
School support				.26*	.19†					.13	.14
School distress				-.26*	-.23*						
Intensity of math education						.50***	.44***			.31***	.31***
High school grades								.30***	.29***		
Time on homework								.46***	.43***	.27*	.28*
Future outlook										.16†	.16†
Number of cases◆	**82**	**81**	**81**	**80**	**80**	**79**	**79**	**79**	**79**	**79**	**79**
Adjusted R²	**.094**	**.085**	**.124**	**.146**	**.171**	**.242**	**.256**	**.315**	**.308**	**.367**	**.358**
Adjusted R², using pairwise exclusion correlations of all 315	**.094**	**.100**	**.149**	**.157**	**.194**	**.242**	**.269**	**.311**	**.320**	**.386**	**.385**
Transition Years 2 and 3 young adults											

Notes: ‡ SCC = social class of the community; ◆ Number of cases decreased due to missing data; † p ≤ .10; * p ≤ .05; ** p ≤ .01; *** p ≤ .005.

cent of the variance (9.2 per cent with SCC), with more work hours predictive of a later belief in disengagement from and avoidance of the world. No peer-related experiences were significant predictors of life purpose.

The best final composite prediction of life purpose, together accounting for 36.7 per cent of the variance, included adolescent family challenge, school support, intensity of math courses taken, time on homework and positive future outlook. The strongest predictors were teenagers' intensity of scholastic courses and investment in scholastic work. Not surprisingly, this predictive model eclipsed any independent effect of community social class.

These regression analyses further clarify that young adults' belief in a life purpose oriented more towards the world beyond themselves was foreshadowed and fostered most directly by strong adolescent scholastic effort and performance, in concert with a familial environment encouraging personal challenge, fewer hours in adolescent employment, a less distressing school environment, and, dispositionally, a more positive future outlook.

It is possible that life purpose begins to germinate earlier in life, during adolescence or late childhood, as young people begin to formulate rudimentary life plans and vocational aspirations. Those with more academic ability and interest *and* with more altruistic intention may be more likely to develop broader life purpose goals, based on a stronger match between their advanced abilities and their values. Further, young people with an early engagement-oriented life purpose may be more likely to have stronger academic and career-related motivation, and may devote themselves to more intensive preparation for college and post-baccalaureate education.

This raises a potentially uncomfortable consideration. Perhaps belief in a more broadly engagement-oriented life purpose requires more strongly developed capacities for abstraction (particularly social abstraction) and empathy. Both avoidant and role-defined life purposes are more concrete – and certainly less grandiose – than more broadly engaged life purposes: the focus is more on the self or on people in one's immediate surroundings requiring more direct attention. As indicated in the cases above, engagement-oriented young adults tend to see beyond their immediate surroundings and personal experience, are able to imagine and express concern for difficulties and challenges faced by people with different experiences than their own, and are motivated by their empathic responses to these non-immediate difficulties and challenges. Higher abstraction scores on intelligence tests are strongly associated with academic achievement, scholastic interest and level of coursework.[38] It is disturbing to think that deeper altruistic intention and belief might be tied in some ways to intellectual capacity and the affordances of intellectual stimulation that come from communities with greater social capital. But as Dan McAdams has shown, altruism and generativity

---

[38]   See Barry Fraser, Herbert Walberg, Wayne Welch and John Hattie, 'Synthesis of Educational Productivity Research', *International Journal of Educational Research* 11(2) (1987): 145–252.

are higher among those who understand and appreciate the benefits they have experienced in their own lives, and who also have directly witnessed people in greater need than they themselves have experienced.[39]

This sounds a bit like a version of *noblesse oblige*, and carries with it a somewhat bitter aftertaste. I raise the question for the sake of further study. Let me offer two caveats:

1. Intention and belief are not the same as actual behaviour. Not all *Transition* young adults with engagement-oriented life purpose had actually embarked on mission or volunteer projects abroad or in the states (although many had).
2. Belief in broader engagement-oriented life purpose – or avoidant life purpose – may give way to more role-defined understandings of life purpose as young adults move into situations that set limits – getting married, having children, finding a reliable pattern of work in a particular career and connecting with a community.

Predictors of Theodicy

I was able to look at the preceding facets of personal theology, at least for initial exploratory purposes, as arranged linearly on a continuum – from negative positive worldviews, and from avoidant to broadly engaged life purpose. This approach is plausible for exploratory research of worldview and life purpose, and yields intriguing results. It is far less plausible to arrange the various theodical positions along a continuum. Each theodical orientation is unique and distinct from the others.

To examine the uniqueness of predictors for each theodical orientation, I used the same method as I did in the set-wise regression analyses of worldview and life purpose, extracting the strongest predictors from each arena of adolescent life – this time, independently for each type of theodicy. I arrived at a best combined set of predictors of deterministic theodicy, and another best set predicting humanistic theodicy, and a third best set predicting randomistic theodicy. I then forced regression of the same best predictors for one theodical orientation onto each of the other theodical orientations, to assess similarities and differences in how the same social and developmental experiences predicted contrasting theodicies. The final results, shown in Table 8.4, clearly reveal the distinct adolescent experiences that shape each type of theodical belief.

Predicting deterministic theodicy   The best set of adolescent circumstances and experiences predicting determinism accounted for 26.6 per cent of the variance.

---

[39]   Dan McAdams and Regina Logan outline some of the common threads in the narratives of generative people in Dan McAdams and Regina Logan, 'What is Generativity?' in Ed de St. Aubin, Dan McAdams and Tae-Chang Kim (eds), *The Generative Society: Caring for Future Generations* (Washington, DC: American Psychological Association, 2004), pp. 15–31.

Table 8.4   Best regression models predicting each theodical orientation and compared as predictive models of contrasting theodicies

	Determinism	Humanism	Randomism
Number of cases♦	75	75	75
	Best Model	Comparison	Comparison
Constant	-.756	.778†	.978†
Percentage time with family	.247*	-.125	-.184
Intensity of science education	-.231*	.010	.259*
Religiosity	.157	-.141	-.065
Chance locus of control	.221*	-.260*	-.041
Future outlook	.252*	-.072	-.233*
Adjusted R^2	**.266*** **	**.049**	**.139** **
Adjusted R^2 from pairwise exclusion correlations of all 315 Transition participants	**.277*** **	**.016**	**.183** **

	Comparison	**Best Model**	Comparison
Constant	1.18**	-.285	.107
Race (white/non-white)	-.178	.217*	.027
Percentage time alone	-.052	.302**	-.190
High school grades	-.187	.189†	.060
Academic awards	.024	-.192†	.132
Chance locus of control	.181	-.254*	.001
Adjusted R^2	**.060**	**.212*** **	**-.009**
Adjusted R^2, using pairwise exclusion correlations	**.046**	**.148** **	**-.012**

	Comparison	Comparison	**Best Model**
Constant	.755	.686	-.440
Age	-.119	-.107	.228*
Parents pushing school performance	.212†	.010	-.254*
Intensity of science courses	-.293**	.120	.242*
Future outlook	.211*	-.069	-.188†
Playful outlook on daily events	-.129	-.095	.228*
Adjusted R^2	**.218*** **	**-.031**	**.314*** **
Adjusted R^2, using pairwise exclusion correlations	**.182** **	**-.042**	**.296*** **

Notes: ♦ Cases restricted to those with complete data for all variables used across these nine regression models (n=75); † p ≤ .10; * p ≤ .05; ** p ≤ .01; *** p ≤ .005.

The strongest predictors were percentage of time with family, chance-oriented locus of control, future outlook, religiosity (all positively predictive of deterministic theodicy) and intensity of science education as a predictor of theodicies other than determinism.

These same social and developmental factors accounted for 13.9 per cent of the variance when predicting randomistic versus non-randomistic theodicies, with stronger science education and more pessimistic future outlook in adolescence predicting later randomism. But humanistic theodicy was predicted poorly using these social and developmental factors, which accounted for only 4.9 per cent of variance. Teenage chance-oriented locus of control was the only significant predictor: teens with the lowest chance-oriented locus of control later tended to report humanistic theodicies.

Predicting humanistic theodicy   Being white, spending a higher percentage of time alone, performing well in school but receiving fewer academic awards, and having a lower chance-oriented locus of control together predicted later humanistic theodicy. These demographic, social and developmental factors together accounted for 21.2 per cent of the variance between humanistic and non-humanistic theodicies. These same circumstances and experiences were poorly predictive of determinism alone (6 per cent of variance) and of randomism alone (0.9 per cent of variance).

Predicting randomistic theodicy   Randomism was the most strongly predicted theodical orientation, with age, science education and playful outlook as positive predictors, and with parental encouragement of school performance and future outlook as negative predictors, together accounting for nearly one-third (31.4 per cent) of the variance. These same social and developmental factors were also strongly predictive of determinism, accounting for 21.8 per cent of variance between deterministic and non-deterministic theodicies. Humanistic theodicy was again predicted poorly using these circumstances and experiences, accounting for only 3.1 per cent of the variance, with no variables as significant predictors.

These results suggest that, while determinism and randomism appear to be shaped in opposing ways by some of the same factors of adolescent experience (that is, science education, family involvement and personal future outlook), humanism is quite distinct as a theodical orientation and is shaped uniquely by different factors. In terms of external experiences, more intensive science education indeed led to increased likelihood of a later randomistic orientation and decreased likelihood of a deterministic position. This effect of science education was stronger than the countervalent effect of religious engagement. But a similarly contrasting effect of family involvement was strong in predicting both determinism and randomism: more time with family and more parental encouragement of school performance led to an increased likelihood of a later deterministic orientation and decreased likelihood of a randomistic outlook.

But science education, religious engagement and family involvement do not contribute significantly to the formation of a later humanistic orientation. Race was uniquely predictive of later humanism, and not predictive of the other two theodical orientations. Being white – that is, being part of the dominant racial group in the United States – was the primary demographic factor contributing to any likelihood of developing a humanistic orientation. A racially dominant group enjoys certain privileges and opportunities, and more importantly, is sheltered from certain limitations and lack of privileges among minorities. This social position may allow for the socio-political luxury of a theodicy that emphasizes personal responsibility for negative events in one's life.

Supporting this argument, the psychological qualities fostering a later humanistic outlook also are distinct from those qualities contributing to determinism or randomism. Young adult humanists as adolescents believed in personal responsibility and control of their own destinies. They also performed better in school, although they did not attain high academic honours as often as others. And they spent more time by themselves. These qualities suggest a high degree of self-sufficiency combined with personal responsibility among adolescents who later adopt a humanistic orientation. Together, these qualities contribute to an underlying script of either, 'God helps those who help themselves', or, 'You have to pull yourself up by your own bootstraps.'

In contrast, the psychological qualities contributing to randomism include less optimism about the future combined with a more playful outlook on immediate experiences, and a certain degree of autonomy from family. This set of psychological dispositions, together, suggest a different form of self-sufficiency in which enjoyment features prominently, contributing to an underlying script of 'enjoy life to the fullest, for who knows what tomorrow will bring.' Interestingly, determinism seems to be shaped by a lower degree of self-sufficiency (that is, more attributions to chance, and more reliance on family and institutional association such as religious affiliation) – but this is combined with more enthusiasm and optimism about the future. The underlying script may be something akin to the following: 'The world is ordered, I belong in that order, and nothing will happen to me that I am not meant to experience and learn from.'

Predictors of Ultimate Values

Like theodicy, ultimate values were differentially predicted. Each set of ultimate values – affiliative, eudaimonic, hedonistic and self-transcendent – was predicted uniquely by different adolescent circumstances and experiences. Following the same iterative set-wise procedure as before, I determined the most salient and robust predictors of each cluster of ultimate values. This time I also included prior adolescent values ratings as predictors. I also included several preceding young adult circumstances and experiences as key predictors: marital status (single vs married), collegiate education (yes or no), recent religious beliefs, and psychological maturation (as indicated by self-differentiation scales and locus of control). The best sets of predictors for each values-cluster, along with comparison models for remaining values-clusters, are presented in Table 8.5. The sample is larger, since it is comprised of young adults who completed the modified Rokeach values survey.

These regression models both verify and clarify the countervalent relationships between affiliative and eudaimonic values. The best adolescent experiences and circumstances predicting young adults' affiliative values also strongly predicted their eudaimonic values, but with inverted relationships with all predictors. Likewise, the best set predicting eudaimonic values was moderately but inversely predictive of affiliative values. Neither of these models was significantly predictive of either hedonistic or spiritual/social values. A similarly countervalent relationship was confirmed between hedonistic and spiritual/social values. Not only do affiliative values counter-compete with eudaimonic values, and hedonistic values with spiritual/social values (as seen previously in Chapter 7); personal experiences and dispositions cultivate clear preferences for either one or the other in these pairs of contrasting sets of values. Life events, behaviours and dispositions that contribute to strong affiliative values also tend to weaken eudaimonic values. And life experiences and dispositions that influence the emergence of strong hedonistic values also serve to diminish self-transcendent values.

Predicting affiliative values   An interesting set of adolescent and prior young adult circumstances and experiences together accounted for 25.5 per cent of the variance in rankings of young adults' affiliative values (true friendship, mature love, family stability and happiness). A stable family background with two parents, in which there were fewer books and other intellectual goods, combined with strong religious beliefs, a positive view of the future, and a more laid-back approach to the events of daily life during adolescence contributed to these young adults' heightened emphasis on affiliation as a core set of values. College education and marriage further foster young adults' emphasis on affiliative values. In general, young adults with higher affiliative values came from more secure family environments, were brought up with stronger commitments to religious beliefs, and were more positively disposed toward the future. Interestingly, these social and dispositional factors were also in inverse relationship with eudaimonic values, accounting for 17.3 per cent of variance – with inverse relationships from those indicated above. With the exception of adolescent religiosity, none of all these circumstances and experiences was predictive of young adults' self-transcendent values, and none were predictive of hedonistic values.

Predicting eudaimonic values   The best model predicting eudaimonic values (self-respect, freedom, accomplishment and wisdom) was quite strong, accounting for 31.5 per cent of variance in rankings – but its predictors suggest that this set of values was cultivated by experiences of deficit as much as by experiences of

Table 8.5   Best regression models predicting each values orientation, with comparative models

	Affiliative	Eudaimonic	Hedonistic	Self-transcendent
Number of cases	106	106	106	107
	Best model	Comparison	Comparison	Comparison
Constant	**.357**	1.12**	-.154	-.842†
Non-traditional family	**-.171†**	.162	-.007	-.020
Household intellectual capital goods	**-.161†**	.148	.017	-.023
Adolescent religiosity	**.193***	-.233*	-.082	.189†
Future outlook	**.291*****	-.185†	-.015	-.005
Percentage of time planning	**-.233****	.192*	.026	-.057
Percentage of activities like work	**-.192***	.086	.046	.080
College of any kind	**.226***	-.083	.155	.145
Married	**.215***	-.266***	.063	-.007
Adjusted R²	**.255*****	**.173****	**-.037**	**-.014**
Adjusted R², from pairwise correlations of all *Transition* participants	**.212*****	.134*	-.009	-.010

	Affiliative	Eudaimonic	Hedonistic	Self-transcendent
Number of cases	106	106	106	107
	Comparison	**Best model**	Comparison	Comparison
Constant	.812***	**.683**	.739**	-.843***
Family support	.187†	**-.274*****	-.002	-.016
Adolescent work hours	.099	**-.167***	-.034	.080
Percentage of time planning	-.219*	**.177***	-.005	-.035
Challenge in daily activities	-.068	**.200***	-.031	-.002
Adolescent religiosity	.181†	**-.198***	-.122	.206*
Adolescent hedonistic values	-.025	**-.195***	.128	-.008
'Powerful others' locus of control	.101	**-.262*****	.067	.027
Married	.177†	**-.280*****	.102	.015
Adjusted R²	**.115***	**.315*****	**-.030**	**-.027**
Adjusted R², from pairwise correlations of all *Transition* participants	.131*	**.301*****	-.015	-.017

	Affiliative	Eudaimonic	Hedonistic	Self-transcendent
Number of cases	103	103	103	104
	Comparison	Comparison	**Best model**	Comparison
Constant	.638*	.650*	**-.518***	-.077
Family support	.178†	-.249*	**.250****	-.161†
Adolescent hours spent on homework	-.176†	.094	**-.183***	.089
Adolescent autonomy values	.025	-.014	**-.137**	.039
Current religious attendance	-.009	-.044	**-.248****	.198†
Fusing with others (DSI subscale)	-.258*	-.013	**.325*****	-.205*
Current existential religious beliefs	.152	-.030	**.259****	-.342***
Adjusted R²	**.098***	**.002**	**.270*****	**.215****
Adjusted R², from pairwise correlations of all *Transition* Years 2 and 3 participants	.093*	-.012	.256***	.203***

	Affiliative	Eudaimonic	Hedonistic	Self-transcendent
Cases	102	102	102	103
	Comparison	Comparison	Comparison	**Best model**
Constant	.459	1.30***	.405	**-.977****
Household non-intellectual capital goods	.118	-.079	.015 -.176†	**-.189*** **.206***
Adolescent hours spent on homework	-.209†	.048	.087 -.015	**-.174†** **.158†**
Adolescent familial values	-.018	.162	.050	**-.184†**
Adolescent peer values: social contribution	-.037	-.190†	-.336*** -.142	**.233*** **.352****
Adolescent peer values: performance	.144	-.007	-.174†	**.152†**
Current religious attendance	-.028	-.022		
Current traditional religious beliefs	.058	-.128		
Current internal locus of control	.058	-.002		
Adjusted R²	**-.010**	**.007**	**.130****	**.288****
Adjusted R², from pairwise correlations of all *Transition* Years 2 and 3 participants	-.014	-.014	.122*	.264***

Note: † p ≤ .10; * p ≤ .05; ** p ≤ .01; *** p ≤ .005.

strength. Lower family support, less religiosity and fewer hours of employment as adolescents – and non-marriage during the years of emerging adulthood – contributed significantly to heightened young adult eudaimonic values. Along with these social factors were some important dispositional factors that heightened eudaimonic values: a stronger focus on challenge in daily activities, more planning and setting goals for the future, and less interest in hedonistic values during adolescence, as well as lower indications in early adulthood that other people had a direct impact on their lives.

Overall, young adults with a heightened emphasis on eudaimonic values felt less family support during their teenage years, and had less childhood connection with religion. Such experiences may have fostered a more isolationist approach to life, cultivated a less trusting stance toward other people, and contributed to an underlying ideal of the 'self-made man/woman' that encouraged a focus on seeking challenges and setting a course for the future, and de-emphasized their teenage interests in hedonistic values. As above, these experiences and dispositions were also moderately predictive of affiliative values, accounting for 11.5 per cent of the variance, but with inverse relationships. And, as above, none of these experiences and dispositions predicted young adult hedonistic values, and none aside from adolescent religiosity predicted later spiritual/social values.

Predicting hedonistic values Young adults' heightened hedonistic values (pleasure, comfortable life, excitement, and world of beauty) were predicted by several adolescent experiences and attitudes: stronger family support (but not challenge), fewer hours spent on homework, and less value given to future personal autonomy (for example, desire for future mobility and relocation). Several circumstances and dispositions from emerging adulthood were also predictive: lower religious attendance and stronger existentialist religious beliefs during the early adult years, along with a higher tendency toward psychological fusion with others during early adulthood, contributed to heightened rankings of hedonistic values. Together, these circumstances and dispositions account for 27 per cent of the variance in hedonistic values rankings.

Overall, young adult hedonists came from families that were highly supportive but not necessarily more challenging; they invested less effort in their adolescent educations, and were not as eager as other teens to leave the familiarity and ease of their homes and community environments in order to launch independent lives. They were unlikely to be involved in religious communities after high school, and favoured an existentialist rather than more traditional religious outlook, and they were less interpersonally mature or differentiated, tending as young adults to live more like psychological chameleons, taking on the feelings and thoughts of people around them.

These experiences and dispositions also accounted strongly (21.5 per cent) for variance in self-transcendent values, with countervalent relationships with all predictors. These factors were also somewhat predictive of affiliative values, accounting for 9.8 per cent of variance: stronger family support and fewer hours on homework as adolescents, and more interpersonal self-differentiation as young adults, contribute moderately to a stronger emphasis on affiliative values.

Predicting self-transcendent values   The best set of experiences and dispositions predicting self-transcendent values accounted for 28.8 per cent of the variance. The single strongest predictor of heightened self-transcendent values was traditional religious beliefs held during the early adult years. Adolescent predictors included fewer household non-intellectual capital goods, more hours spent on homework, lower familial values (for example, having children, getting married), and peers who more strongly valued social contribution and de-emphasizing academic performance. More frequent attendance at religious services and a stronger sense of internal locus of control during emerging adulthood were among the strongest predictors of self-transcendent values.

These circumstances and dispositions were also somewhat predictive of hedonistic values (accounting for 13 per cent of variance), with high school homework hours, and religious attendance and internal locus of control during early adulthood forming the strongest inverse relationships.

The results from predictions of ultimate values reinforce my earlier conclusion, that affiliative and eudaimonic values are contrasting choices in people's personal theologies. Likewise, hedonistic values are pitted against broader self-transcendent values. What in part pits these sets of values against each other are the life experiences that people encounter and the inner dispositions forming in people during their adolescence. More household possessions can indeed contribute to diminished affiliative and self-transcendent values – a finding consistent with the social patterns noted by scholars writing about 'affluenza'. Family stability – as well as stronger familial support and challenge – positively fosters further affiliative commitment and more positive consideration of the future, including willingness to marry at a younger age, which in turn further strengthens an emphasis on affiliative values. In contrast, lack of familial support can press teenagers and young adults, by way of deficit, toward greater desire to pursue eudaimonic values – almost an 'I'll show them what can become' position. But a family environment stressing support without accompanying challenge can contribute to less self-differentiation, which together contribute to stronger hedonistic values as ultimate ends.

Religion can amplify the differences between these competing sets of values – and may be the singularly strongest contributor to ultimate values. Religious involvement and devotion can reinforce the impact of stable and secure families in strengthening later affiliative and self-transcendent values. In contrast, lack of religious involvement can foster greater investment in eudaimonic and hedonistic values, by further contributing to a sense of individualism, isolation and alienation due to diminished regular connection with people who gather around a larger common purpose. Self-interest can take either more eudaimonic or more hedonistic directions – but it is still essentially atomistic.

Unlike the impact it has on other facets of personal theology, education may not have as strong a direct impact on ultimate values. Stronger scholastic investment and performance can nurture a higher emphasis on both self-transcendent and affiliative values, while weaker scholastic investment and performance can move individuals toward more hedonistic ultimate values. But the more robust predictors of religion and family experience overshadow education's impact.

Some Broad Conclusions

Overall, these analyses reveal how young adults' personal theologies are shaped by many more factors than religion. Teenagers' experiences of social and financial capital in their communities and families, stability and various forms of support and challenge in family environments, the educational resources available and their capacity to make the most of their educational experiences, and psychological dispositions such as sanguinity, conscientiousness, self-efficacy, intrinsic motivation and outlook on life together have some of the strongest impact on personal theologies – sometimes with and sometimes without any accompanying direct impact of religion. Experiences in education (in the forms of academic intensity, school climate, and academic effort and achievement) may have the strongest, widest reaching, and most enduring influence on personal theologies. In many ways, education mediated and even replaced the effects of community social class and familial socio-economic status. Religion did have significant impact on theodicy and ultimate values, in varying strength compared to the influence of education. But religion did not have any noticeable impact on worldview or life purpose, except perhaps as a social force that might reinforce culturally dominant beliefs.

The strength of schools and of teenagers' educational experiences are strongly related to the socio-economic strengths of communities and families. This relationship between educational quality and social class, side by side with the modest but frequent influence of family financial capital (as signalled by household possessions), suggests that the financial and social capital accessed and used by a community and family was a significant force shaping these young adults' personal theologies. As financial and social capital increase – and, consequently, educational resources increase as well – so does the likelihood that teenagers will begin to develop fundamental theological beliefs divergent from the dominant cultural scripts. But education's impact is not simply due to economics: the high school educational environment was also for adolescents the meeting place between intrinsic dispositions, attitudes and capacities on one hand, and the cultural limits and opportunities afforded them in their particular communities. And young adults' prior adolescent motivation and commitment to achievement, sense of personal power, and sanguinity and bouyancy were strongly influential in their own right on their later personal theologies.

Young Adults' Personal Theologies and Their Everyday Lives

In the research tour of this book, we have dug deeply into some of the beliefs and values constituting young adults' personal theologies. We have looked backward in time, examining the social and developmental experiences and the dispositional qualities during young adults' high school years that shape and contribute to their later personal theologies. But we have a remaining question: how do young adults' personal theologies intersect with their current lives, during this rapidly changing season of their lives known as emerging adulthood?

Young adults are fast-moving targets. Their lives develop, change course and shift at a rapid pace. Jason, whom I introduced at the beginning of the book, is just one example of this. We reconnected with Jason one last time during the *Transition* study, ten months after I interviewed him at his father's trailer home. In this lapse of time, Jason had left his job at the steakhouse and his father's home in the trailer park, and had taken to the road with a high school friend to work as contractors for Walmart, installing floors in their new stores across the country.

The following pages offer some brief sketches of the relationships that I found in this study of different facets of young adults' personal theologies with their concurrent educational, vocational, relational and religious experiences, and with their psychological dispositions and attitudes. All relationships presented are statistically significant. These sketches provide a picture of the ways in which personal theologies connect with the concurrent day-to-day experiences and attitudes of emerging adults in their quickly changing and developing lives.

Worldview

Young adults' worldviews were intertwined with their concurrent choices and experiences in learning and working, as well as in dating and dwellings – but not with their religion. Young adults' religious beliefs and level of participation did not vary with their worldviews. But young adults with different worldviews differed even in their basic choices and opportunities to pursue further education beyond high school. Those with negative worldviews – the dominant group – were least likely to attend four-year colleges, and were most likely to attend two-year colleges or no post-secondary education at all. Furthermore, those with negative worldviews were significantly more likely to experience challenges in college, in the form of delays, non-traditional transfers, or financial difficulties. In contrast, those with positive worldviews were most likely to attend more competitive four-year colleges,[1] and were most likely among college graduates to go to graduate school (see Figure Int.1).

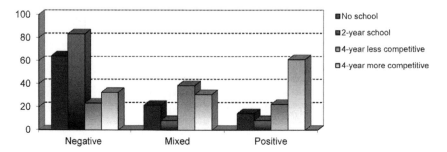

Figure Int.1   Worldviews and young adults' post-secondary educational choices and opportunities taken

It is important to note a pattern from the larger sample of 315 *Transition* study participants – that young adults attending more competitive four-year colleges were significantly more likely to receive full or partial payment of their educational expenses from their parents, while young adults attending two-year schools (and four-year less competitive colleges) were more likely to be paying their own way, through work, loans, and some grants. Social capital continued as a ubiquitous background force that shaped both worldview and educational opportunities and choices.

Dating and dwelling patterns were similar between young adults with negative and positive worldviews – but differed significantly for those with mixed or ambivalent worldviews (see Figure Int.2). Almost all those with mixed or ambivalent worldviews lived with their parents – quite different from young adults with negative or positive worldviews, who more frequently lived alone or with peers, lovers or spouses. Ambivalent young adults were also much less frequently involved in dating relationships over two years. These patterns corroborate the suggestive patterns from adolescence of less psychosocial maturity among young adults with ambivalent or mixed worldviews.

Employment patterns and experiences also varied with worldview (see Figure Int.3). Young adults with positive worldviews were least frequently employed, echoing the same pattern from high school. Among these non-employed young adults with positive worldviews, 89 per cent came from parents with college or graduate degrees. These were the young adults who received full financial support from their parents during their collegiate educations. In contrast, young adults with

---

[1]   College rankings in *Peterson's College and University Almanac* were used to categorize colleges and universities in each year of the study.

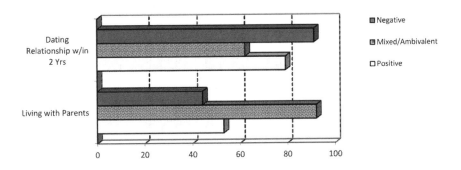

Figure Int.2 Worldviews and young adults' dating and dwelling

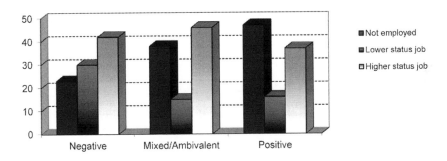

Figure Int.3 Worldview and young adults' work status

negative worldviews were most frequently employed, and a higher percentage of them were in lower-status jobs.

Among the employed young adults, those with positive worldviews reported more job responsibility and autonomy (for instance, making work-schedule and work-content decisions) than those with negative worldviews. They earned significantly higher wages than either negative or ambivalent young adults, reported the longest duration at their current jobs, and indicated a greater degree of work-life balance. They also felt most strongly that their work in their current jobs was related to their sense of life purpose. In contrast, employed young adults with negative worldviews least frequently saw their jobs as permanent, saw the least connection between their work and their prior education and training as well as their sense of life purpose, and reported the fewest extrinsic interests or 'perks' in their work (such as salary or location).

Finally, young adults with different worldviews also differed in some psychological dispositions such as motivation and self-efficacy. Young adults with more positive worldviews reported higher overall internal locus of control and a stronger sense of personal control in their day-to-day lives. They also indicated stronger motivation during their daily activities and experiences. Here, self-perception and world-perception clearly intermingle and likely reinforce each other.

Theodicy

For these young adults, theodicy intersected very clearly with religious life and belief, as well as with experiences in employment, relationships, and, to a lesser degree, education. Shaped so significantly from earlier religious experience and belief, young adults' theodical beliefs further pressed them toward continued religious involvement or disengagement. There was a linear relationship between young adults' level of religious participation (attendance) and theodical orientation, with determinists attending most frequently, followed by humanists, and with randomists attending infrequently (see Figure Int.4). Young adults with deterministic theodicies were more religiously active, prone to traditional religious beliefs, and least likely to hold existentialist or atheist religious beliefs.

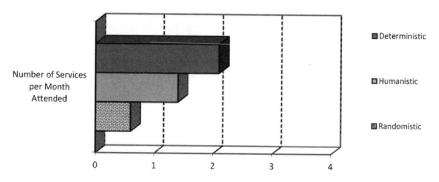

Figure Int.4   Theodicies and young adults' religious service attendance

In tension with the patterns of religiosity, it is intriguing that humanists reported the lowest sense of self-efficacy. Also unexpected, randomists and determinists were similar in their sense of self-efficacy, significantly higher than humanists. They were also distinct in their pursuit of further education. All humanists were engaged in post-secondary education, with 85 per cent at four-year colleges – a stronger showing than for determinists (59 per cent at four-year colleges and 20 per cent not enrolled in any school) and for randomists (65 per cent at four-year colleges and 24 per cent not in any post-secondary education) (see Figure Int.5).

There were no other clear differences in experience or performance in post-secondary education between young adults with different theodicies – except for college majors chosen (see Figure Int.6). While college majors for determinists were evenly split between humanities and sciences, humanists eschewed the sciences in favour of the humanities, and randomists favoured the sciences and completely avoided the humanities.

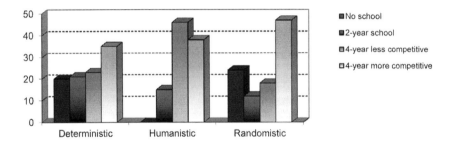

Figure Int.5 Theodicies and post-secondary education

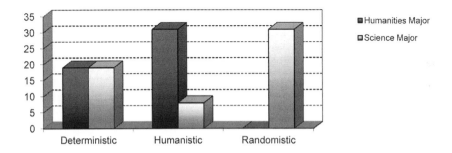

Figure Int.6 Young adults' theodicies and college major

Humanists were also the theodical group most frequently married during emerging adulthood. In contrast, no randomists were married, only one randomist had a child, and 71 per cent of randomists lived with their parents (compared to 54 per cent of humanists and 49 per cent of determinists). While randomists were still more likely to be living with their parents in emerging adulthood, they were less likely to be employed in lower-skilled jobs than determinists, and were most likely to be employed in higher-skilled occupations (53 per cent) (see Figure Int.7).

On most indicators of work performance and satisfaction, humanists had the lowest scores. Working humanists earned somewhat lower wages, worked fewer hours, indicated less advancement potential and reported less duration and permanence at their jobs than the other two theodical groups. They also indicated the least connection between their jobs and their prior education or training. This experience of work coincides with their weaker sense of self-efficacy.

But randomists consistently had the highest scores on these same measures: they were significantly more likely than either determinists or humanists to see their jobs as permanent, indicated significantly greater fit of their work with their education and training, and reported the highest degree of investment in their careers. Both humanists and randomists reported a higher degree of work-life balance than determinists.

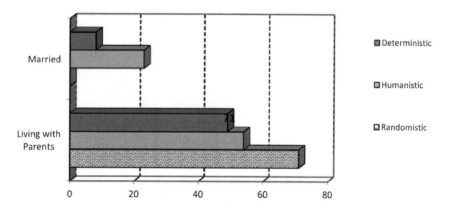

Figure Int.7   Theodicies and young adults' dating and dwelling

Life Purpose

Young adults' life purpose was strongly related to their engagement in post-secondary education. The relationship of life purpose to education was stronger than any relationship to early adult employment, habitation, or family formation status. As seen in Figure Int.8, young adults with an engaged sense of life purpose almost universally attended four-year colleges, with 75 per cent of them enrolled in or graduated from more competitive colleges. In contrast, young adults with an avoidant or role-defined sense of life purpose were roughly evenly distributed between no college enrolment, attendance at two-year colleges and attendance at both more and less competitive colleges. Avoidant young adults were most likely to have attended only two-year colleges

Life purpose also intersected with experiences in college. Young adults with an avoidant life purpose were significantly less satisfied with their post-secondary school experiences then were those with role-defined or engaged life purpose.

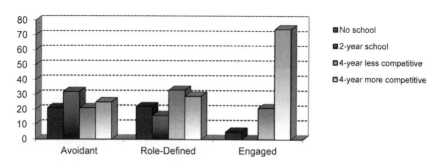

Figure Int.8   Life purpose and post-secondary education

Also, more avoiders experienced post-secondary school problems (38 per cent) than either role observers (18 per cent) or engagers (19 per cent).

Not surprisingly, young adults with role-defined life purpose were most likely to be married (16 per cent). In contrast, engagers were least likely to be married (0 per cent) and least likely to have children (see Figure Int.9).

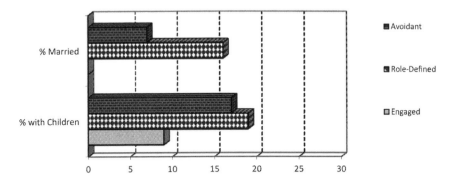

Figure Int.9   Life purpose and young adults' dating and dwelling

There were further indicators of difference in how avoiders, role observers and engagers allocated their time and energy in relationships, work and individual interests (see Figure Int.10). Investment in career did not differ across groups. But investment in relationships and in individual interests differed significantly. Engagers devoted less time and energy to their relationships than avoiders or role-observers. Avoiders devoted more of their time and energy to individual interests than did engagers or role-observers. In their daily experiences, they also gave higher importance ratings to their experiences of active leisure.

In terms of work, engagers were least likely to hold lower-skill jobs – they were either in higher-skill jobs or were in post-secondary schooling and not employed. Avoiders worked the longest hours, significantly more than role-observers or engagers, and they reported the longest current and anticipated duration at their jobs.

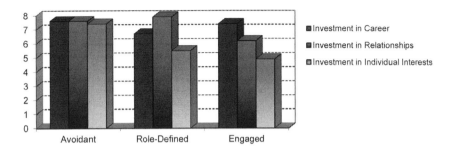

Figure Int.10   Life purpose and young adults' investment of time and energy

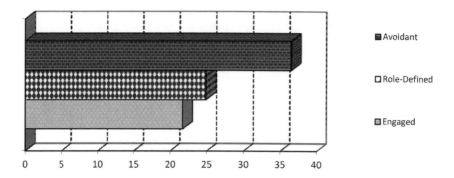

Figure Int.11   Life purpose and young adults' work hours

They reported significantly less interest in the social benefits of work than did engagers or role-observers (see Figure Int.11).

Day-to-day challenge and motivation also varied significantly in relation to life purpose (see Figure Int.12). Avoidant young adults reported significantly lower daily challenge, and their sense of challenge in daily life dropped dramatically from adolescence to early adulthood. Young adults with engaged life purpose had higher daily motivation, which increased from their adolescence. Role-defined young adults reported the lowest daily motivation, which decreased slightly from adolescence. These results suggest that engagers become increasingly invested in their daily experiences, while role-observers become less invested, in the transition from adolescence to adulthood. Additionally, avoiders experience less and less challenge in their daily lives during this transitional period.[2] Young adults' religious participation and beliefs were not related in any clear, statistically significant way to their concurrent sense of life purpose.

Ultimate Values

Young adults' ultimate values intertwined with their concurrent educational, marital, vocational and religious choices and experiences, and with their personal dispositions. In educational experience, young adults attending two-year colleges were more hedonistic, and young adults who did not engage in any post-secondary education were more hedonistic and less affiliative in their values. But hedonistic young adults who did attend college reported higher satisfaction with their school experience. Young adults who had more problems and delays in enrolling in or completing their college educations reported higher eudaimonic values and lower

---

[2]   These results were maintained when controlling for post-secondary college enrolment and age.

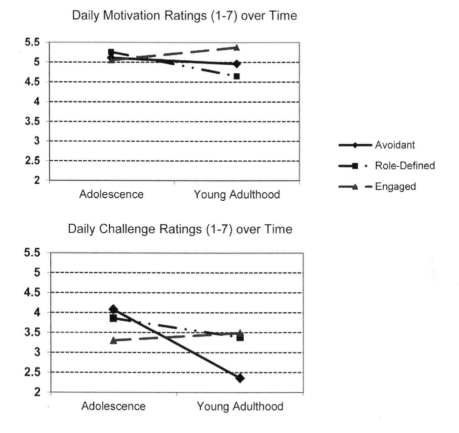

Figure Int.12   Changes in motivation and challenge, adolescence to young adulthood, by life purpose

self-transcendent values. And young adults enrolled in or completing graduate school held higher affiliative and lower eudaimonic values.

Marriage was more frequent among young adults with stronger affiliative values and less frequent among those with stronger eudaimonic values. Interestingly, none of the set of ultimate values – and, for that matter, none of the facets of personal theology – were significantly related to young adults' frequency of dating and sexual relationships within a two-year span. Across the range of beliefs and values, most young adults were involved in dating relationships that were monogamous, sexual and enduring for a period of one or more years. Emerging adults do seem to put dating relationships in a different category of relational values than the categories reserved for their friendships and anticipated or real marriages – with more emphasis placed on pleasure and less emphasis on commitment and trust. Young adults may actively prevent themselves from integrating their theological beliefs and values into their dating practices, placing a moratorium on such integration until they have chosen a mate or are in the process of evaluating the possibility of a long-term relationship with someone they are dating.

There was no direct relationship between ultimate values and employment status or work hours. But there were other differences in how young adults with different values experienced their work. Young adults with more highly ranked eudaimonic values earned higher wages and reported more intrinsic interests in their work – but also reported lower job satisfaction and less consideration of their current jobs as permanent. In contrast, young adults with stronger affiliative values earned lower wages and had less duration in their jobs – but were more satisfied with their jobs and saw them as more likely to be permanent. More hedonistic young adults reported more extrinsic interests (like pay and work hours) and fewer social interests in their work. In contrast, young adults with stronger self-transcendent values, expecting to be in their jobs for a longer duration of years, reported the most social interests in their work.

In terms of religion, young adults with more hedonistic values were noticeably less religious in both beliefs and participation. In contrast, young adults with stronger self-transcendent values were more religiously active, prone to traditional religious beliefs and least likely to hold existentialist or atheist religious beliefs.

Young adults' dispositions and attitudes intersected with their hedonistic and self-transcendent values in particular. More hedonistic young adults felt better about themselves in their day-to-day experiences and reported higher overall life satisfaction. They also attributed more control in their lives to chance. In contrast, young adults with stronger self-transcendent values reported lower overall life satisfaction, and those with stronger eudaimonic values attributed less control in their lives to other people. Values also intersected with indicators of maturity: young adults with more hedonistic, less affiliative, or less self-transcendent values showed signs of less self-differentiation, especially in their greater tendency to fuse psychologically with other people.

Chapter 9

Conclusions and Implications

It has now been over ten years since September 11, 2001. Life in the United States has not been the same, since that day when fundamentalist terrorists seized control of passenger airplanes and piloted them as missiles into the World Trade Center towers and the Pentagon. Since that time, the United States of America has gone to war in two Asian nations, struggled with a series of economic recessions, experienced increased disparity between wealthy and middle and working classes, contended with natural and ecological disasters, and borne witness to its own conflicted ideas about social and ecological responsibility versus individual and market freedom.

Shouldn't all of this change result in fundamental changes in personal theologies?

No. And yes.

If anything, these events together point to multiple theologies at work. The extremist Muslim terrorists that wreaked havoc and destruction in New York City operated from an extremely negative worldview as in a state of apostasy, and the ensuing wars and costs to veterans and communities increases a sense of the world as unbelievably chaotic and cruel. But the drivers of the market bubbles in the American economy operated from an unquestioned positive worldview. Arguments around social inequities, personal wealth and governmental roles in addressing social needs are laden with differing assumptions about theodicy, life purpose and ultimate values. Even when direct religious influence on individuals may be declining, personal and cultural theologies shape public actions, policies and politics.

Toward a Grounded Theory of Personal Theology

In a time of life – and, increasingly, in a period of history – when religion is considered less than relevant, when religious affiliation is declining, when people's knowledge of their own and other people's religions is rather weak, and when individuality in beliefs and values is upheld as a desirable standard, people must construct their own system of beliefs and values. In a time of post-institutional and extra-institutional spirituality, it is no longer adequate to examine gross differences in beliefs and values based on denominational or religious group membership. Many young American Catholics today are opposed to the institutional positions of the Roman Catholic Church on birth control, clergy celibacy, clergy gender limitations and hierarchical decision-making. Young American Buddhists do not always adhere strongly to the prayer disciplines and religious theodical beliefs of their parents. Many young American Jews are satisfied with periodic 'dipping' into the big traditions of their ancestors while leaving behind many day-to-day practices and beliefs. Some young American Evangelical Christians, increasingly disenchanted with limitations in the evangelical teachings they received in their youth, have shifted political parties, questioned biblical literalism on matters such as human sexuality, and been primary contributors to the emerging church movements.

Despite diversification of the beliefs and values that comprise personal theologies, certain foundational themes persist as undercurrents among people in the United States – even among young adults – binding many of them in varying degrees to a deep mythic tradition of this culture, across generations. Dominant cultural patterns in beliefs and values were an undercurrent shaping young adults' responses in the *Making the Transition* study – whether as assent to or refutation of assumed truths. Many of these beliefs and values have persisted across generations.

The close inspection of personal theology offers insights into the ways in which young adults perceive and approach the world, and the values that they pursue as ultimate goals for being in the world. Such study requires moving beyond gross differences based on group affiliation and begins to take a more careful, measured account of individual differences in perception, thought and motivation *vis-à-vis* 'the world'. Analyses that attend more closely to individual differences will become an increasingly important line of analysis in a historical and developmental period of increased institutional distantiation, multicultural pluralism and consumer-based ideologies.

The study of personal theology offers an antidote to constructivist perspectives that oversimplify the individual content of beliefs and values, and categorize personal theology according to preconceived notions of 'the ideal'. As moral and faith development theorists have learned, it is too easy to conflate 'is' with 'ought' and impose prescriptive ideals on what should first be descriptive studies. A simplified analysis of the content of people's expressed beliefs and values can provide a normative base from which theory that is more thoroughly descriptive of real, lived theologies may emerge.

The Imprint of Cultural Scripts

First, cultural imprints appear in the dominant patterns of young adults' beliefs and values. Recurrent among the core group of *Transition* young adults were negative views of the world, deterministic beliefs about ultimate causes for trauma and tragedy, and ultimate values stressing close familial and tribal affiliation but de-emphasizing broader national and social goods and spiritual well-being. If these young adults are any sign of the typical pattern of beliefs and values among emerging adults in the United States, then there are clear signs of culturally dominant beliefs and values undergirding the personal theologies of American young adults. A majority of emerging adults in America may indeed hold negative views of the world as chaotic and cruel. Even more may favour theodical perspectives that are deterministic, trusting the benevolence of a higher power or of the natural unfolding of fated purposes to bring order in the midst of chaos and sense to injustice. They may prefer those values more focused on affiliative bonds of kith and kin than on self-development, but also devalue broader spiritual and societal goals in comparison with hedonistic aims. They seem to understand at some fundamental level the Golden Rule as a principle for living, but also locate themselves between aversion to extreme self-absorption and extreme loyalties to any institutionalized or fundamentalist patterns of life.

Given that these dominant beliefs and values do not vary across genders, and only occasionally vary across races or age groups – and given that their dominance even carries through the variances related to community and familial social class – it seems likely that these beliefs and values reflect the imprinting of broader cultural theological scripts. Such cultural imprints carry enduring influences of religious and political scripts in the culture, even if specific dogmas and doctrines are not embraced personally.

But cultural imprint does not result in uniformity. Since individuals' experiences are diverse within a culture, in the widely varying contexts of communities, families, schools, work situations, leisure opportunities, peer groups and religion, theologies will diversify. To the degree that cultures are less homogenous and more complex in structures and practices, personal theologies will become more divergent from dominant cultural theological scripts. But cultural consistency and homogeneity are likely to engender greater personal conformity to culturally dominant beliefs and values.

Varieties and Divergences

However, culture is not the sole or force in shaping personal theologies. Otherwise, there would be nothing individual about these kinds of beliefs and values. Personal theologies among young adults in the United States are more complex and diversified – and this diversity alone argues against a ubiquitous cultural theological script. In the contemporary culture of the United States, among young adults, there is not one worldview. There is not one theodical orientation. There is not one values system.

This study has demonstrated – even with a relatively small sample – that none of the various aspects of personal theology are dipolar, either-or constructs. Using the very basic categorical scheme I developed from the interviews, I found young adults expressing at least three general but distinct categories of belief or value within each aspect of personal theology:

- Worldview is not expressed merely as negative or positive, but is also expressed as mixed or ambivalent – for young adults, a position rooted manifested particularly by uncertainty and lack of clarity.
- Theodicy is not merely expressed as an either-or continuum, either between absolute theistic determinism and assertions of random chance, or between determinism and belief in human will and action as ultimate causes. All

three are independent theodical positions, expressed along two dimensions of Aristotelian formulas for causation: efficient cause and final cause.

- Life purpose is not simply a chosen stance between polarities of withdrawal and engagement, but is also manifested as a role-limited form of clearly delineated engagement.
- Ultimate values are not reducible to a distinction only between more hedonistic pursuits focused on immediate gratification and more eudaimonistic or self-denying pursuits focused on the well-being of others and society. They are more complex, divided into a two-by-two matrix of value-sets.
- Affiliative or relational values (strongest among young adults) are in contrast and tension with eudaimonic values of self-improvement – and both of these value-sets are primary
- Hedonistic values are in juxtaposition with self-transcendent values of broader spiritual and societal concerns (weakest among young adults) – and both of these value-sets are secondary.

Even these general categories emerged only after significant reduction of more subtle variations found in people's interview responses. Further in-depth content analysis of people's beliefs and values, and their reasons for holding them, revealed an even more complex picture of variations in each facet of personal theology. For instance, not all negative worldviews are alike: a negative worldview can be expressed from least two quite discrete perspectives – the world as unpredictable (echoing the ancient chaos vs order myths) and the world as unjust (echoing later myths that focus on good vs evil and corruptibility of human nature). Not all deterministic theodicies are theistic, and even theistic determinist theodicies can differ in terms of what people perceive as a deity's benevolent, malevolent, or larger cosmic intentions. Even a role-defined sense of life purpose can vary dramatically, depending on whether the role is focused on family and relationships or on job and career, and depending on how individuals conceive of the impact of a particular role in lives beyond their own. Even at a more nuanced level, these varied beliefs or values occurred with sufficient frequency that they cannot be dismissed as rare curiosities. In any one of these facets of personal theology, it is likely that anywhere from 10 to 35 per cent of American young adults would express one of the culturally non-dominant patterns as their primary belief or value.

Regarding values: this analysis raises questions about some of the reductions proposed by MacIntyre in *After Virtue*, Bellah and colleagues in *Habits of the Heart*, and others in the social sciences and theology who have pitted hedonistic and individualistic values against the ideals of ultimate social goods. The American young adults in this study, at the turn of the twenty-first century, signalled that individualistic pleasure is not the sole alternative to more 'rational' social good. Rather, concern for broad social goods as the ideal is more readily supplanted by an individually defined and constructed 'tribalism', in which the ultimate good is found in one's closest and most secure relationships. Tribalism is not synonymous with the hedonisms and individualisms so often set up as the contrasts to ideals of ultimate social goods. Rather, tribalism focuses more on local affiliative bonds and consequent identities of belonging to a particular set of people. It is an ancient orienting sentiment that in Hebrew scripture stands as counterpoint to more nationalistic sentiments, drawing people toward a local focus of the ultimate good as identified by the prophet Micah: 'Nation shall not lift up sword against nation, neither shall they learn war any more; but they shall all sit under their own vines and under their own fig trees, and no one shall make them afraid.'[1] Some of the most riveting and pivotal narratives in the Hebrew scriptures are those involving close-knit bonds between friends and family members (such as between Jonathan and David, or Ruth and Naomi) that lead individuals into a 'community of souls'[2] whose importance overrides broader cultural or societal identities and expectations. Ecclesiastes gives voice to the depth of affiliative values:

> Two are better than one, because they have a good reward for their toil. For if they fall, one will lift up the other; but woe to one who is alone and falls and does not have another to help. Again, if two lie together, they keep warm; but how can one keep warm alone? And though one might prevail against another, two will withstand one. A threefold cord is not quickly broken.[3]

The cultural shift among young adults toward these more tribal values may indeed coincide with and signal a growing cynicism and distrust in anything institutional beyond the scope of what one knows most intimately – but this has not resulted in atomistic individualism, nor has it given way to a hedonism that overtakes their familial and affiliative interests, or their more eudaimonistic interests in self-development.

No Simple Theological Convergence

There is not any singularly dominant summative theology among American young adults. There is not any clear-cut logical or statistical coherence between worldview, theodicy, life purpose and ultimate values; rather, they vary independently. Thus, broad conclusions regarding cultural patterns of beliefs and values do not hold when examining the whole of personal theologies as expressed by American young adults. Holding a culturally dominant position in one facet of personal theology does not automatically place a young adult in the culturally dominant positions in the other facets of personal theology. Having a negative worldview does not

---

[1]   Micah 4:3–4 (NRSV).

[2]   Johannes Pedersen, *Israel: Its Life and Culture* (2 vols, London: Oxford, 1926), p. 279. Pederson also writes, 'Kinship is the nucleus of the psychic community. Every other kind of community must conform to it' (p. 285).

[3]   Ecclesiastes 4:9–12 (NRSV).

automatically predict that a young adult will hold a deterministic theodicy or regard social and spiritual values as relatively unimportant.

A presumptive error of theologians and social scientists alike is to assume logical coherence and individual consistency in endorsement of culturally dominant – or specific variant – beliefs and values. It is the error of sociologists who use aggregate patterns and trends in survey responses to individual questions to paint a picture of a coherent pattern, without examining individual coherence and variability from question to question. It is the error of theologians who extrapolate from a few statements a theological system presumed to be operating for a person (or a group the person represents), without exploring through further questions a person's internal theological map. For instance, Weber and MacIntyre have both assumed a logical coherence between dominant cultural theological constructs.[4] In her more nuanced examination of some of the same categories of beliefs and values in four American subcultures, Kluckhohn did not thoroughly examine the interrelationships between different sets and types of beliefs, but discussed her results of culturally dominant beliefs only in light of her specific analyses of each independent facet of subcultural theology.[5]

Results from this study draw such presumptions into question. The relationships between worldview, theodicy, life purpose and ultimate values are not simple or straightforward, and are only moderately interrelated – indeed, these four facets of personal theology may be orthogonal and distinct. This should not be surprising – certain facets of self-perception are also distinct from each other, even if somewhat related (for instance, as evidenced in the growing literature on the Five-Factor Model of personality – see below).

The diversity within each set of beliefs or values, as examined in this book, points to potential for even more striking diversity in summative personal theologies. Even though a majority of emerging adults expressed negative worldviews, and a majority expressed deterministic theodicies, the relationship between worldviews and theodicies was weak, and only 25 per cent of emerging adults held a combination of negative worldviews *and* deterministic theodicies. Across the four facets of personal theology, there was no clear convergent pattern. Even my simple identification of three worldviews, three theodical perspectives, three life purpose beliefs and two distinct sets of two polarized values systems yields a product of 108 possible combinations – that is, 108 distinct types of personal theology (see Figure 9.1).

Among the 82 young adults in *Making the Transition*, diversity in personal theologies exceeded any consistency, with 47 different types of the 108 possible

---

[4]   See M. Weber, *The Sociology of Religion*, trans. E. Fischoff (Boston, MA: Beacon Press, 1963); Alisdair MacIntyre, *After Virtue* (Notre Dame, IN: University of Notre Dame, 1981).

[5]   See Florence Kluckhohn, 'Dominant and variant value orientations', in C. Kluckhohn and H. Murray (eds), *Personality in Nature, Society, and Culture* (New York: Alfred A. Khopf, 1953), pp. 342–57.

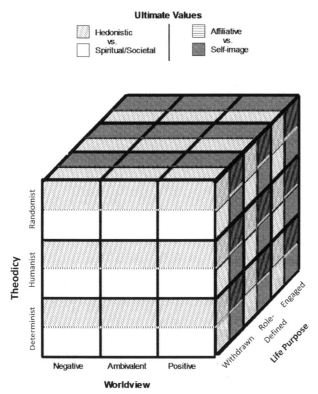

Ultimate Values

Hedonistic
vs.
Spiritual/Societal

Affiliative
vs.
Self-image

Figure 9.1   Three-dimensional representation of 108 possible personal theologies

belief/value combinations occupied by at least one young adult, and with no more than seven young adults (less than 10 per cent of the sample) occupying any single personal theology combination.

Some combinations of beliefs and values were so unlikely that they did not occur. For instance, a randomist theodicy and an engagement-oriented sense of life purpose did not occur together in any person, and a randomist theodicy was stated only rarely by young adults with stronger spiritual and societal values. But, in general, the spread of personal theologies points away from any universal pattern that coheres for the whole society. Coherence was no stronger among the larger sample of 192 young adults who answered standard survey questions about these four facets of personal theology: while some modest correlations indicated a few relationships (for instance, between worldviews and ultimate values), the relationships across the four facets of personal theology did not point to any clear, consistent, coherent, or culturally typical theology as a whole.

Despite hints of coherence in beliefs and values, this small sample points more to diversification of personal theologies than to a unity rooted in culturally dominant systematic theology or in a predictable logical coherence. Certainly, a much larger sample is needed to determine which cells in the figure above – if any – are dominant, and which – if any – are completely unlikely. But there is not a straightforward relationship between statistical likelihood and logical likelihood. And while there are certain dominant cultural patterns in beliefs and values among young adults in the United States, the relationships between worldview, theodicy, life purpose and ultimate values are complex and somewhat indeterminant. This alone raises questions about the legitimacy of the assumptions of 'logical coherence' by stage theorists in moral and spiritual development: a set of beliefs held at one level does not necessarily predict beliefs held at another level. In short, *A* does not always lead directly – or indirectly – to *C*. And personal theology is not equivalent to an idealized systematic theology, an assumed common cultural theology or *Weltenschauung*, or a philosophical system judged a priori by scholars as 'logically coherent'. Thus, the variety in personal theologies found in these young adults does not map neatly onto Christian Smith's now famous reductive interpretation of the 'de facto dominant religion among contemporary U.S. teenagers' as 'moralistic therapeutic deism',[6] – and the diversity in the arrangement of beliefs and values exceeds even what Smith claimed was the variation beginning to appear in emerging adulthood.[7]

Consequently, one may be tempted to suggest that personal theology is not meaningful or useful as a construct. It may seem a fruitless exercise to look for patterns in people's higher-order beliefs and values that comprise their supposed theological systems. But these objections are premature. To reflect adequately on the meaning of such diversity in personal theology, it may again be helpful to refer to the history of research in personality. No psychologist will deny that human personality is amazingly diverse and that subtle individual differences abound in people's dispositions, attitudes, self-images and habits of interpersonal interaction. And, at a certain point in the history of research and theory development in personality, there were so many different personality traits mentioned by different theorists (for instance, Raymond Cattell's 16 'source traits' of personality, when considered as 16 different dipolar possibilities, yields 2^{16}, or 65,536, possible personalities)[8] that it became difficult to make sense of any general overarching pattern. But since that time, clarity has emerged in the field, pointing to some general categories of consistent and enduring personality traits (such as McCrae's

---

[6]   Christian Smith, *Soul Searching* (New York, NY: Oxford University Press, 2005), p. 162.

[7]   Christian Smith, *Souls in Transition: The Religious and Spiritual Lives of Emerging Adults* (New York: Oxford University Press, 2009), p. 155. Smith and his colleagues offered this description cautiously as an interpretation of their data, 'less than a conclusive fact but more than mere conjecture'. Unfortunately, the indefinite quality of the claim has been forgotten by some practical theologians and replaced with certainty.

[8]   See Raymond Cattell, *Personality and Mood by Questionnaire* (San Francisco, CA: Jossey-Bass, 1973).

and Costa's well-known Five-Factor model of personality).[9] I am suggesting that the same path needs to be followed in the study and the development of theories about personal theology.

A Proposed Model of Personal Theological Development

The beliefs and values comprising personal theologies are not random bits of passing thought or motivation, any more than they are simple recitations of cultural theological scripts. They are mental constructs shaped by and built from heritage and experience.

Several social and psychological forces converge as important influences on personal theology development. Theologies diversify and individuate from the culturally dominant patterns as an outcome of these different forces. The social capital of communities and families collaborates with educational experiences and individual aptitudes and dispositions to shape the development and individual internalization of certain beliefs and values about the world, causal order, humanity and the good life.

The exploratory research presented in this book provides evidence of the following, at least for young adults in the United States at the turn of the twenty-first century:

1. Social class and race, familial socio-economic status and wealth, and the opportunities afforded by such social locations, directly affect personal theologies.
2. Family is not as influential as one might expect on personal theologies. Family deprivation and stress have some enduring impact.
3. Educational intensity and investment are among the most salient contributors to variation in personal theologies and departure from cultural scripts.
4. Religion tends to reinforce dominant cultural patterns in personal theologies, but otherwise is minimally influential in producing meaningful variations from dominant cultural patterns.
5. Generational differences are not as strong as might be expected, and cultural change, technological development and geopolitical action do not automatically change dominant cultural patterns in personal theologies.

---

[9]   Robert McCrae and Paul Costa, 'A Five-Factor theory of personality', in L.A. Pervin and O.P. John (eds), *Handbook of Personality: Theory and Research*, 2nd edn (New York: Guilford, 1999), pp. 139–53. Recent personality researchers have focused more on the qualities, developmental predictors and behavioural outcomes of the Big Five personality traits such as extroversion, neuroticism and conscientiousness, rather than attempting to develop such descriptive and predictive analyses for the multiple types of personality combinations (at least 32) that are possible from these five core traits.

6. Intrinsic motivation and conscientiousness are related to personal theologies at many levels.

A number of these findings may strike us as counter-intuitive. Most people would consider religion to be a primary direct influence on personal theologies. But Christian Smith's research already suggests that religion's influence is not as strong as one might think on the primary scripts of religious beliefs recited by adolescents and emerging adults – American culture may more significantly shape common theological ideas, and only those who grew up in the most adherent and consistent practicing religious environments differed markedly in their religious beliefs and values.[10] Most people would also consider the family to be a primary source of the beliefs and values comprising young adults' personal theologies. But young adults did not always situate their own beliefs and values in harmony with those of their parents, and teenage experiences of support and challenge in the family were not as directly influential as expected on later personal theologies. Finally, as discussed previously, generational differences were not as strong as people might expect.

More markedly influential on emerging adults' personal theologies were community or neighbourhood social class, parental socio-economic status, and household wealth. Furthermore, experiences and performance in adolescent education – themselves transmitters and enactors of social class distinctions – seem to be the singularly strongest influences on young adults' personal theologies. Education outweighed all other adolescent experiences such as work, extracurricular activity and time with peers in its impact on personal theologies. Work experience became more reinforcing of personal theologies during the early adult years. Religion was a less direct influence on personal theologies than wealth, education, employment and other forms of social capital.

Some life experiences serve to secure and further instantiate dominant cultural beliefs or values. These include the direct experience of – and adherence to – religion, as well as indirect infusions of religion through the dominant practices and mythic scripts of a culture (for instance, as experienced with peers). These also include familial closeness, parental protection and direct intervention in children's education, significant family stressors and lower socio-economic status in both community and family.

Other life experiences, in contrast, afford opportunities for divergence from dominant cultural patterns of belief or value. These include forms of social capital such as household wealth, community socio-economic status, educational opportunities and emphases, and employment motivated more by career interests than financial necessity. These also include familial factors such as family challenge, permissive support, stability, less direct intervention in children's

---

[10]   See Smith, *Soul Searching*, and Phil Schwadel, Christian Smith, Roxann Miller and Melinda Denton, *Portraits of Protestant Teens: A Report on Teenagers in Major U.S. Denominations* (Chapel Hill, NC: National Study of Youth and Religion, 2005).

education (which seemed to be expressed more as a Rousseauian trust in children finding their intrinsic motivation to learn and perform well). And dispositional factors such as personal challenge and motivation, self-efficacy and psychosocial maturity – which are also influenced by social and socio-economic factors – also contribute to individual divergence from culturally dominant beliefs and values.

Let me offer the following ideas, emerging from my interpretation of this research, as propositions moving toward a theory of how personal theologies arise and diversify.

Social Capital and Theology

Social capital is the first basic contributor to all facets of emerging personal theologies. Expansions of resources and opportunities for access to greater social and financial capital contribute to diversification of personal theologies. Greater social capital contributes to people's exposure to different experiences, learning opportunities and interactive interpretations of experiences that can call previously assumed and culturally dominant beliefs and values into question, leading to new theological frameworks. In contrast, restriction or limitation of social capital can contribute to closer adherence to the primary scripts for beliefs and values dominant in a culture.

Cultures, subcultures and social classes with less social capital (for example, poorer educational resources, less familial financial capital and fewer community resources) are more likely to develop theologies emphasizing the unpredictable and unfair nature of the world, a more cosmic or deity-based explanation for ultimate causes in the world, and a more survival-oriented sense of life purpose focused on oneself and one's closest relationships. As cultures, subcultures and social classes develop wealth and resources, they are likely to adapt and finesse their theological frameworks to incorporate more positive views of the world, a greater attribution of cause to human effort, and a bifurcation of interests in human engagement between making a difference in the world on one hand and self-indulgent hedonistic pursuits on the other hand. Cultures may shift theologically over history in accord with expansions and restrictions of social capital. Individuals may move theologically in similar ways, during their lifetime, as their access to social capital increases or decreases.

Social capital is afforded to communities, families and individuals through racial and ethnic dominance in a culture, relative economic wealth of communities, and the educational and consequent socio-economic attainments of parents. These affordances expand opportunities for children and youth. Being part of the racially or ethnically dominant subculture provides children and youth with political and economic clout – unbeknownst to them, but enacted on their behalf and on behalf of their parents in legislation, housing practices, and educational and workplace practices. in contrast, communities and families of racial and ethnic minority groups benefit less from a host of broader cultural assumptions, legislations and practices, having fewer resources for adequate government representation. For identity and mutual protection and care, they tend to stay together more in clustered communities, and are more likely to remain in conformity and solidarity with the general practices, beliefs and values of those groups. Communities with higher per capita income and a strong tax base can provide protective services, educational opportunities and leisure activities that poorer communities are unable to provide. Parents with higher educational attainment – most likely from more privileged communities themselves – are more likely to hold higher status and higher-paying jobs, which generate significantly more income for use by households, as well as better benefits, and a different kind of household discourse about the nature of work.

Social capital contributes to – but of course is not solely responsible for – family climate. Parents with higher educational attainment (college or beyond) are more likely to purchase intellectually stimulating goods for their households, are less likely to get divorced and experience fewer stressful changes that affect the family environment. Parents with higher education and in wealthier communities are more likely to emphasize strong educational performance with their children and advocate for expanded educational opportunities. They will also tend to emphasize autonomy and challenge children toward self-reliance, qualities and family experiences that are also associated with differences in personal theology.

Social capital also finds expression through the divergent educational opportunities found in different communities and emphasized in different families. Children from more wealthy families and communities tend to go to school in systems that have more resources and stronger pre-collegiate training – including particular attention to training in mathematics and the sciences. As young adults, they also matriculate to four-year colleges more frequently, and tend to go to the more competitive colleges. These colleges, often themselves resource-rich, are more expensive – but parents of these young adults more often pay completely or substantially for their children's post-secondary educations – leaving their children financially worry-free during college and relatively debt-free after graduation. Less pressure to work for a living means that young adults from wealthier communities and families can more deeply and fully explore a range of philosophies – and they may avail themselves of such philosophically rich courses, not feeling as much pressure to take courses that will have a direct and applicable pay-off in the workforce. In addition, college education provides a gateway to higher salaries, better jobs and greater career mobility.

And so it is not unexpected that various factors of social capital contribute consistently to diversification of the beliefs and values that comprise personal theologies. A childhood and adolescent experience of multiple opportunities created by stronger social and financial capital will introduce significantly more potential for a positive worldview, a belief in human purpose of broader social engagement, a non-deterministic theodicy, and ultimate values that emphasize a self-image of personal freedom and accomplishment. Surprisingly, the benefits of social capital alone do not seem to engender stronger hedonistic values or detract from broader spiritual and societal values – at least, not in any direct or consistent way.

In theological terms, social capital affects cosmology, theological anthropology and eschatology: it can foster a sense of a more benign, ordered and pleasant world, the possibility of human control and responsibility in controlling life's tragic and traumatic circumstances, and a positive developmental trajectory of emerging human history that supports a kind of 'functional grandiosity' and belief in human potential to right the wrongs of the ages. This is akin to the God and religion that Emile Durkheim described – the hopeful and positive religion that allows a society to worship an idealized image of itself and revel in its own effervescence.[11] It is the theological ground of a plutocratic deity and religion.

In contrast, the relative absence or dearth of social capital can perpetuate a sense of chaos, cruelty and injustice in the world, and of the impossibility for humans to control their own destinies, as well as a more cyclical or degenerative view of emerging human history, and a sense of the finitude and limited potential of individuals to make a difference much beyond their own immediate surroundings. This is akin to the God and religion described by Karl Marx – a salving religious confirmation and instantiation of the world as they have known it, as a vale of tears, with hope for protection in this world but change only in an afterlife or next life toward which a deity, deities, or ultimate truth urges the faithful. It is the theological ground of an apollonian deity and religion, most akin to Smith's 'moralistic therapeutic deism', and also bearing kinship with H. Richard Niebuhr's withdrawal-oriented 'Christ against culture'.[12] But, on occasion, it can also be the ground for the God and religion of movements of social agitation and intervention – most likely occurring in the meeting ground between these two theological perspectives and the resulting recognition of inequity and imbalance. Education may provide the most important space for this theological meeting ground.

The Power of Education

The influence of education is not merely a by-product of social capital. Independent of the shaping forces of social capital, education serves as a gateway to different ways of perceiving, experiencing and engaging in the world, contributing to diversification of personal theologies. As young people are exposed to different views of the world, humanity, causal order and the good life, they find themselves confronted with new choices in their personal theologies.

Intensity of education has a significant impact on personal theologies. The deeper the study in a discipline, the more profound the impact of its philosophy will be on a student. So, students of more intensive science curricula in high school gravitate toward more positive worldviews and non-deterministic theodicies; while in college, science majors and humanities majors develop differing theodical orientations, each divergent from the dominant cultural theodicy of determinism.

---

[11] See Emile Durkheim, *The Elementary Forms of Religious Life*, trans. K. E. Fields (New York: Free Press, 1995).

[12] H. Richard Niebuhr, *Christ and Culture* (New York: Harper & Row, 1951).

Through education, young people are exposed to systems of thought that were historically generated as alternatives to the religiously informed dominant beliefs and values in a culture – be they humanist, naturalist, positivist, or postmodernist philosophical systems. A historical tension between academy and religion can thus be perpetuated through the sciences and humanities. Because of its importance to future career and socio-economic status, education becomes a strong force that may compete with and at times contradict religion in its influence on shaping personal theologies. In short, curriculum matters to the shape of personal theologies – and intensity of exposure and immersion in a curriculum strengthens its impact.

Educational effort and attainment also contribute significantly to differences in personal theologies. Academic achievement and effort in part signal motivation and conscientiousness. They also are fruits of support and encouragement from family, teachers and peers. Those who make more effort and perform well will more likely develop more positive views of the world and more humanistic theodicies, and will tend to orient themselves more toward beliefs in engagement-oriented life purpose. Strong performance also opens up further possibilities for continuing education, career development and choice in vocational pursuits. So, stronger educational effort and achievement foster diversification of personal theologies from dominant cultural scripts – but weaker performance and effort further instantiate dominant cultural beliefs and values.

The environment in which education is offered makes a difference. Is it safe? Is it nurturing and supportive? Is it challenging? Is it encouraging? These qualities in a school's culture give young people a taste of the larger world beyond their families and neighbourhoods – for better or for worse. The way schools provide or fail to provide control, handle distress and disruption, and offer encouragement gives students a sense of how the world works – or fails to work – and what potential a person might possess to contribute to the lives of others.

Education is the singularly most powerful force in shaping personal theologies. It eclipses – or brings to fulfilment – the effects of social capital. It is supported by, but not easily overcome by, familial practices of support and challenge. It is young people's first major testing ground for perceptions of the world and self *vis-à-vis* the world. And it is a fundamental meeting ground for conflicting, contrasting and complementary views.

The Impact of Organized Religion?

While educational intensity and investment contribute to diversification of personal theologies, religion tends to reinforce more culturally conforming theological perspectives on the world. This is not always the case, and there are wide variations of effect, both between and within denominations in the Christian religion alone. But in the aggregate, religion's impact is not consistently strong or direct. It is a primary contributor to theodicy and also helps shape values. But its contribution to worldview and life purpose is weak in comparison to the effect of education. One may pause to consider the efficacy of religious education and the communication of theologies in various religious communities. Smith has noted how religion's effect on beliefs is clearest among adolescents who attend religious services quite regularly.[13] As the flip side, I and other religious leaders have noted the relative dearth of programmatic and pastoral attention in American Christianity to young adults – and their consequent atrophy of interest.[14]

However, in US culture, religion continues to have influence indirectly and ubiquitously, through its long reach into political and public discourse, folkways and basic cultural mythology and proverbial wisdom. Religious beliefs, affiliation and active involvement tend to reinforce culturally dominant beliefs and values such as a negative worldview, a deterministic theodicy and an emphasis on local affiliations and relationships – beliefs and values affirmed in American in some cultural myths and proverbs. While not all religions (nor all denominations within religions) teach or uphold these theological assumptions about the world, ultimate causes and the good, there is some consistency of religious perspective that the world is not as it should be, that there is an ordering of causes that makes sense beyond basic human understanding, and that care for those immediately around us is a fundamental and essential good. Religion in this sense gives voice to and responds to core human world-concepts and hopes. But it does not foster any singular, consistent sense of life purpose – not across religions, and not across Christian denominations.

While Smith points to the cultural triumph of liberal Protestantism in American civil and cultural theological scripts,[15] I would like to suggest that the prominence of negative worldviews, a cosmically deterministic understanding of causality, and a consequent value-emphasis on salvation and against hedonistic pursuits of pleasure and gratification are more direct cultural imprints from the evangelical and fundamentalist theologies emerging from the First and Second Great Awakenings and the survival-oriented 'soul theologies' of many African-American Christian traditions. These theologies, rooted in powerful American religious movements, treated this world as a 'vale of tears', focused on individual salvation and deliverance from present and future hell, and viewed the this-worldly life as something to endure and to prepare one for a future life directly with God. These theologies found and continue to find resonance with the naturally emerging beliefs and values of people in less privileged contexts. It is a religious message most implicitly attractive in a Marxian world of 'the masses' with less power, social capital, and patterns of assumed 'self-determination'.

---

[13]   See Schwadel, Smith, Miller and Denton, *Portraits of Protestant Teens*.

[14]   See Jacqueline Schmitt and David Gortner, 'The Episcopal Church Welcomes You?' in Sheryl Kujawa (ed.), *Disorganized Religion* (San Francisco, CA: Jossey-Bass, 1997); Kenda Creasy Dean, *Practicing Passion* (Grand Rapids, MI: Eerdmans, 2004), and Tom Beaudoin, *Virtual Faith: The Irreverent Spiritual Quest of Generation X* (San Francisco, CA: Jossey-Bass, 1998).

[15]   Smith, *Souls in Transition*, pp. 287–9.

Such beliefs and values have been questioned and stretched the most by theologians, religious leaders and laypeople in more liberal – and, not inconsequentially, typically more affluent – religious traditions (such as Unitarian, Jewish Reform, Presbyterian, Episcopal and Ismaili Muslim congregations[16]). Parallel stretching and questioning has also arisen within the more evangelical and fundamentalist traditions – often among those who have experienced the benefits of social capital and expansive education (for instance, the Emerging Church communities that have explored a wide range of Christian traditions and theologies are predominantly white middle- to upper-middle class). A more Durkheimian religious idealism emerges from these traditions – and the ensuing worldviews, theodicies, ultimate values and life purposes point toward an encounter with God and the good in life in this world. These beliefs and values support and encourage the experiences of self-efficacy, optimism about the future and the benefits of a world of lower risk and higher opportunity afforded to those who have more power, prestige and access to the benefits of society.

I realize that I am suggesting that differences in religion and its influence on personal theology are in no small part rooted in social class. Religion in America may be seen as a choice between theological assumptions that put religious communities more in line with Marx's critique of religion as appeasing the masses (more appealing to those who are poor or in the working and middle classes), or more in line with Durkheim's view of religion as society worshipping its own idealized image (more appealing to those who are in upper-middle and upper classes) – with rare choices for a third path that provides integration and challenge to differing assumptions about the world, theodicy, purpose in life and ultimate values and that offers a compelling vision transcending class.

Religion's comparatively weak and conflicted – but perhaps culturally ubiquitous – influence raises questions. Why is religion's effect weaker than that of education? And, what is religion's relationship with education, and vice versa?

Religious communities in most places do not have the same level of organization as schools to maximize impact and engagement with the world in demonstrable ways. The growth of service learning in schools, combined with the already higher percentage of contact time in the lives of children and adolescents allowing for deep exposure to varied traditions of knowledge and thought, give education a significant edge. In this light, Smith's finding noted above is not surprising – nor is the impact of other religious venues like camps and youth groups on beliefs and values.

The diversity of theologies within as well as between religions should not be underestimated. Religion's effect may not be weak – it may simply not be consistent enough from religious community to religious community, because of the variabilities in theological teachings in each community. Even within single religious communities, the core teachings by religious leaders may not be

---

[16]   See Rodney Stark and Charles Glock, *American Piety: The Nature of Religious Commitment* (Berkeley, CA: University of California Press, 1968); Niebuhr, *Christ and Culture*, and Farid Esack, *Qur'an Liberation and Pluralism* (London, UK: Oneworld, 1997).

embraced or endorsed by each person or family equally. Thus, families and peers become important mediators of the influence of religion on personal theologies.

Family, Peers, Mating and Work

Along with household financial capital, important family factors shaping personal theologies are experiences of constancy, stability, support and challenge. These experiences form the first world-experience for people, shaping their expectancies of others, their perceptions of the world and the good, and their conceptions of human purpose and potential for impact. Additionally, familial support and challenge – not in high-pressured forms – help to amplify the effects of education on personal theologies. Parents who emphasize time together as a family and who instil such a habit in their children contribute to a theodicy that emphasizes an unseen order in the 'household' of the universe. Such parenting practice may be related to a general American religious framework. Parents who involve themselves in their children's schools, through the PTA or other means, also contribute to young adults' formation of theodicies that emphasize some sense of order in life events.

These matters of family environment and climate cannot be divorced entirely from socio-economic status and social capital. Previous researchers have pointed to marked differences in parenting style that correspond with social class.

But familial instability due to divorce or other significant upheavals in the household can intrude significantly on the influence of other familial and educational factors, and shape personal theologies in limiting ways, including the more frequent occurrence of belief in a chaotic or unpredictable world.

Families are influential in other ways. Families are the primary basis for children's religious affiliation and educational trajectories. And family climate contributes to adolescent choices in peer relationships and leisure pursuits. Each of these different domains of school, work, religion, peer relationships and leisure may have a stronger direct impact on the formation of personal theologies – but family influence, along with overall socio-economic status, resides in the background as a first level of influence.

Other contributors to personal theologies are peer experiences, age at marriage and work experience. Some of these factors (that is, peer and work experience, age at marriage) are themselves strongly influenced by social capital, level of education, religion and family climate. For instance, ethnic and social class variations in peer relationships contribute to and stimulate teenagers' differing educational performance and plans.[17] Younger marriages are more common in middle-class or lower-class communities, among non-white ethnic and racial

---

[17]   See Wendy Hoglund, 'School Functioning in Early Adolescence: Gender-Linked Responses to Peer Victimization', *Journal of Educational Psychology* 99(4) (November 2007): 683–99, and Maureen Hallinan and Richard Williams, 'Students' Characteristics and the Peer-Influence Process', *Sociology of Education* 63(2) (April 1990): 122–32.

groups, and in strongly religious communities and families.[18] Work trajectories, beginning in adolescence, are influenced by familial and community social capital, continue beyond adolescence to be influenced by educational experience and by familial emphasis on education, and become embodied personal realities of socio-economic status. And thus these factors may function as mediating forces that can either further mitigate or attenuate the impact of the more fundamental influences on personal theology. They may also signal fledgling personal theologies at work: choices in affiliation and mating are likely related to ultimate values that are most central to people, as well as to beliefs about the world and about life purpose.

Most American young adults enter monogamous sexual relationships during their dating and pre-married lives. This practice of premarital sex does not seem to interact in any significant way with personal theologies. Differences in values around dating versus friendship and marriage raise questions about whether or not young adults engage in some kind of bracketing of their dating experience, quarantining it from influencing or being influenced by their personal theologies.

The Inner Person and Personal Theology

The person is not lost as a mere passive agent in the development of personal theologies. Individuals bring to bear on the world their own aptitudes, dispositions and maturity. Self-perceptions such as self-efficacy, and self-orientations to the world such as motivation and optimism, help shape personal theologies – and are likely also shaped by personal theologies. Indeed, self-perception and world-perception are likely mutually reinforcing, and form a source of influence on personal theologies independent of social capital and educational experience. Likewise, psychosocial maturation and clarity in personal theology may coincide.

Intrinsic motivation, conscientiousness, self-efficacy and optimistic orientation toward the future help shape personal theologies. They can either amplify or counteract the influences of social forces on personal theologies. Thus, individual dispositions and attitudes may function as moderating forces, as some individuals adopt personal theologies contrary to the general direction of social forces leading them toward either culturally dominant or divergent beliefs and values. But basic self-esteem seems to have little impact.

Ambivalence or lack of commitment in beliefs and values seems to correspond with under-developed psychosocial maturity. Psychosocial developmentalists refer to this as 'ideological identity diffusion', signalling individuals who have neither explored nor committed to any patterns in beliefs and values. Ambivalence is shaped in part by family instability and stress and is reinforced by a disposition toward minimal risk-taking. In attachment theory terms, people with ambivalent and uncertain beliefs may be caught in a mixed approach-avoidance orientation

---

[18]   See Frances Goldscheider and Calvin Goldscheider, *Leaving Home before Marriage: Ethnicity, Familism, and Generational Relationships* (Madison, WI: University of Wisconsin Press, 1993).

to the world as a whole, uncertain how to read signs and judge between the balances of good and bad, and unsure of their own capacity to make these kinds of judgements.

None of these social and developmental factors, alone or together, accounts for all of the variation in the personal theologies of young adults. The paths of individual construction of meaning are complex and emerge from a host of experiences and impressions that are processed uniquely by each person. Every day potentially brings new input, either to confirm or to alter one's operating beliefs and values. And beliefs and values already operating in people frame their perceptions, decisions and choices of experiences, further confirming or changing personal theologies.

Some Methodological Notes

A 'grounded-theory' approach is invaluable as a way to discover unexpected patterns and to generate new theories and ideas. It is by no means the end of research. Rather, it opens new doorways. It returns the scholar to the human roots of the questions being asked – and it may change the questions.

A focus on thick description of beliefs and values from each narrator's perspective helps to describe in tangible, everyday language how people interpret the world. The open-ended questions about different facets of personal theology were drawn from previous theoretical categories in theology, philosophy, sociology and psychology; but the open-ended questions allowed interviewees to respond as they wished, without directional cues that unfortunately are often embedded in Likert-scale questionnaires.

Asking people direct, open-ended questions about their personal theologies discloses an assumption that they are indeed capable of articulating and explaining their beliefs and values. This 'middle way' of research, between the poles of pre-designed questionnaires and unobtrusive observation, assumes more trust that people will be able to state their personal theologies without too much assistance and without excessive personal bias or self-enhancement. We found the young adults in *Making the Transition* to be remarkably straightforward about their anxieties and frustrations with the world, their widely varying sense of purpose, and their belief that things happen for a reason determined by personal or impersonal guiding forces in the universe. Since then, I have found young adults encountered in other research, pastoral work and student training to be similarly honest, thoughtful and direct. In the majority of cases, people are articulate about the beliefs and values comprising their personal theologies – or they struggle but become increasingly articulate as they talk.

Three factors may help in this process. First, I ask theological questions later in my interviews, after I have been able to establish some rapport, trust and confidence with the individuals I am interviewing. Secondly, in the research projects I have undertaken, I have entered these conversations with people who already have an established relationship with something I represent – ongoing participation in a longitudinal study, continuing connection with a school from which people graduated, or participation in religious community. Third, the simple practice of asking respondents for their own thoughts about some of the 'deep' questions of life, without being led by interviewers, communicates to respondents my implicit respect for their own intelligence and autonomy. The experience of answering similarly open-ended questions about their work, schooling, relationships, religious communities, or other experiences, and being met with respect and interest on the part of interviewers, fosters a general sense of acceptance and affirmation that eases the difficulty of answering the 'deep' questions of personal theology. Of course, the relative anonymity of a research interview also is helpful: the stranger-confessor effect has been recognized by interview researchers, pastoral counsellors and temporary confidants, such as hairdressers or bartenders. People are often willing to discuss quite intimate details of their lives with people who will guard their anonymity and are highly unlikely otherwise to invade their daily lives.

Two natural steps can proceed in the study of personal theologies: 1) further exploration, verification and expansion of the content of personal theologies through continued 'grounded-theory' research, and 2) testing the claims I have made from the patterns of beliefs and values – and the social and developmental factors contributing to them – that emerged from this small sample of young adults. The second process will necessarily involve the creation of surveys and questionnaires that allow people to respond to statements about worldview, theodicy, life purpose and ultimate values. But the questions on these surveys should be created from the native language of people interviewed. I am advocating the creation of 'grounded surveys', so to speak – surveys in which the items come from statements made by people in open-ended responses. In addition, it should be abundantly clear from the results of the qualitative analyses in previous chapters that simplistic dipolar questions pitting one belief against another along a scaled continuum are erroneous and presumptive – there is often at least a third alternative, quite distinct from two choices offered. Qualitative study must take the lead, allowing for the identification of a fuller range of beliefs and values as well as the generation of statements that can then become the basis for items in quantitative surveys. Appendix B offers a prototype questionnaire, drawn from the interviews of the young adults discussed in this book. I invite fellow scholars and religious leaders to join me in using this questionnaire in research and discussion groups with young adults.

The study of personal theologies is necessarily interdisciplinary. One cannot conduct research of sufficient depth on personal theologies without some grasp of philosophy and theology. One cannot easily resist the allure of the rush to prescriptive assessments or even conduct research of sufficient clarity and merit without some grasp of social scientific research methods. The pursuit of clarity and truth about people's theological beliefs and values will move forward only if theologians and religious leaders call social scientists to account for and question their assumptions, and only if social scientists call theologians and religious leaders to test their claims. In other words, the exploration and mapping of personal theologies will succeed only in an environment of interdisciplinary collaboration and sparring.

The same can be said for the study of psychology or sociology of religion, the study of religious and spiritual practices, and the study of local theologies in different cultures and subcultures. The fields of theology and religion require interdisciplinary sparring partners to question and test their claims about the impact of different religious beliefs, values, experiences, rituals, or relationships. The fields in the social sciences need interdisciplinary sparring partners to keep them honest about the nature of religion and spirituality, which are far more richly textured than is typically acknowledged. The best research moving forward in these different fields will involve interdisciplinary partnerships – and increasingly interdisciplinary scholars.

Directions for Future Research

Clearly, the sample in this study was limited – in both number and diversity of participants. Given the intense level of participation required of individuals, and the typical differential attrition rates that plague longitudinal studies, the limited sample was not surprising – and the benefits of longitudinal data outweighed the problems of sample restriction. However, future studies should include larger and more broad-based samples, with particular attention to stratified sampling, as well as specific ethnographic and small-sample studies within different racial, ethnic and social class groups.

The two methods – further 'grounded-theory' study and research using 'grounded surveys' – immediately raise possibilities for new directions in research. Here are some possibilities:

1. *An extended mapping of personal theologies* – What other beliefs and values should be explored as part of people's core philosophical theologies, and how do they relate to the other beliefs and values mapped in this study? Is epistemology, or beliefs about knowing and learning, another independent facet of personal theology?
2. *Verification of young adults' personal theologies* – Do young adults in a more widely representative sample state similar patterns of beliefs and values? Over a decade later, do young adults respond the same way? How do young adults respond to a questionnaire versus an open-ended interview in expressing their beliefs and values?
3. *Closer examination of differences in personal theologies* – How does theodicy change as people get older? What are similarities and differences across cultures, classes and communities in worldviews? In what ways do cultural scripts for worldview and theodicy differ? What are similarities and differences across religions and denominations, in these more nuanced,

philosophical facets of personal theology that are not explicitly about a deity?

4. *Correlational and predictive research* – Much future research could be devoted to more careful, hypothesis-driven studies of how family experience, social capital, education, religion, work experience and peers influence personal theologies – as well as the relationship between personality and identity on one hand and personal theology on the other. How do religion, education and class cohere and conflict in shaping personal theologies? What factors contribute to conformity or diversification of personal theologies in relation to cultural theological scripts? What are the relationships between the 'Big Five' factors of personality and the 'big four' facets of personal theology outlined in this book? Are there genetic predispositions as well as environmental experiences that contribute to personal theologies?

5. *The influences and impacts of personal theology* – What influence do personal theologies have on both day-to-day and long-term perceptions and interpretations, motivations, experiences and decisions? Do people who state an engagement-oriented life purpose actually devote themselves and their resources more to the common good? Are those with more hedonistic values and weaker social and spiritual values more likely to get divorced? Is worldview simply an epiphenomenal afterthought that has little impact on people's lives?

6. *Personal theology and religious belief and experience* – In what ways do religious beliefs and experiences amplify, verify, or alter people's personal theologies? How is God perceived in relation to a negative versus positive world? What do people's ultimate values have to do with their perception of the teachings of their religious scriptures?

Under all of these possible directions for further research is the question of how people construct meaning not just about themselves but about the cosmos they inhabit, not just about the figure but about the ground. How do figure and ground, or self-concept and world-concept, interact in people's narratives, perceptions and decisions?

Some Implications

So, what of young adults? At the turn of the twenty-first century, American young adults find themselves casting about in a sea of varied meaning-systems, a multiplicity of alternatives in worldviews, theodicies, life purposes and ultimate values. What might be offered to them as markers, signposts, Rosetta Stones along the way, so that their journeys of meaning-making are not so isolated?

Becoming Aware of the Impact of Social Capital

Resources matter when it comes to the theologies that emerge in a community and culture. More financial and social resources allow for a more positive theology to emerge, one that departs from dominant patterns of beliefs and values. This suggests that both religious leaders and educators need to be sensitive to the socio-economic status of the communities and families they serve, recognizing that world-perceptions might be very different depending on how resource-rich or resource-limited those communities and families are. Religious leaders and educators alike can help draw attention to the implicit theological assumptions that emerge from people's life circumstances, and offer them a space for encountering other possible ways of perceiving and interpreting the world and their place in it. Religious leaders and educators alike can also work to help people think about possibilities and means for accessing further resources and for distributing resources more widely.

Religious leaders trained in theology and pastoral care should beware that they avoid a scornful attitude toward families and communities with more 'primitive', less 'mature', or 'developed' theologies – or toward those with more 'privileged' or 'arrogant' theologies. For example, in some communities and families, a deterministic theodicy that stakes hope in a benevolent deity's final purposes may be the expected script for a religious leader to offer when unfortunate events beset those communities and families, and may actually function as a source of personal empowerment and self-efficacy. The religious leader must take this expected theodicy into account as valid, valuable and functional for those communities and families – even though such a theodicy may strike one as unsatisfying, theologically flawed, or psychologically 'unhealthy'. Similarly, a religious leader must be able to work with the randomistic or humanistic theodicies of some wealthier and more highly educated individuals, discerning their validity and functionality in people's lives. A religious leader may offer other theodical perspectives as alternatives in counselling and teaching, as well as invite discussion about the benefits and limitations of theodicies that arise out of differing circumstances of social class. But the effective religious leader will begin by listening to and respecting the theological frameworks which people in different socio-economic circumstances use to construct meaning in their worlds.

Likewise, educators would do well to take the theological frameworks of communities and families into account, if they wish to establish a helpful and minimally oppositional stance to the dominant beliefs and values among community and family members. People in racially, ethnically, or socio-economically bonded communities may share more consistency and adherence to religious and cultural scripts in their personal theologies, and may not be as receptive to brusque or erudite dismissals of their beliefs and values in the service of educational immersion in alternative theological frameworks implicit in the disciplines of the sciences and humanities.

Religion

It seems that religious institutions do not have significant direct influence on young adults' beliefs regarding worldview and sense of life purpose. But organized religion does have a direct influence on individuals' theodical orientations and on their ultimate value-orientations toward social and spiritual values and away from hedonistic values. And, for worldview and life purpose, organized religion's influence may be more systemic and indirect than personally direct, with Judaeo-Christian and generally religious assumptions about the world and human purpose operating in the background, embedded deeply in the cultural ethos.

For religions to have a more significant and direct influence on young adults' ideological development, religious communities and leaders must make a more personally direct effort. And the effort will require innovative strategies for a population that is increasingly dissociating itself from active involvement with and commitment to religious institutions. Traditional theologies, practices of religious organization, and forms of religious education may be more dissimilar than similar to experiences and emphases in other arenas of life, adding to an overall effect of religion seeming unfamiliar and somewhat odd. Not only will religious institutions need to re-evaluate and reinvent programmes of education and instantiation; they will also need to re-examine their own core philosophical and theological assumptions regarding worldview, theodicy, life purpose and core values, and the audiences to which those theological assumptions most readily speak.

As indicated by the young adults in *Making the Transition*, many young adults engage in this work of theological re-evaluation and reinvention – regardless of their affiliation or involvement with actual religious institutions. But they often embark on this work without much assistance, direction, or knowledge of resources that can assist them in their process of meaning-making. For instance, humanistic theodicies, positive worldviews and engagement-oriented senses of life purpose – each expressed by a significant minority of young adults – are positions in a wide variety of theologies expressed by religious scholars and leaders from many traditions. But young adults do not discover ready access to these resources. Parents are rarely prepared, themselves, to offer such resources to their children, any more than they are prepared to offer rich scientific or technological information. Conversations in the classroom in public education can be somewhat guarded about matters of meaning-making. So, where are young adults to engage in conversations that invite deeper reflection on meaning?

The choices made – and not made – by religious institutions regarding adolescent and young adult ministry and education may determine the place of religion in future generations in the United States. At different points in American history, religions have contributed significantly to the founding of colleges and universities, and to movements and organizations engaging young adults in commitments of their lives to higher purposes and to the common good – and these efforts have coincided with and contributed to efforts by the state in the same arenas of impact. The roles of college and university chaplains, campus ministers, youth ministers and groups of peers dedicated to forging lives of meaning and purpose – who help people more intentionally connect theology and daily life – deserve further attention and support.

More importantly, now may be a crucial time for religious leaders and theologians to take stock of their theological inheritances – and to reflect on how they have been shaped and reinforced by socio-economic situations. More negative worldviews and deterministic theodicies may have gained the greatest support as satiating cosmic explanations to real problems and challenges in people's daily lives – but they are not the only theological perspectives available within most religious traditions. Other perspectives have been offered throughout religious history – theologies that adhere to the expectations of orthodoxy, yet offer different worldviews, theodical understandings and orderings of ultimate values.

Education

In contrast to religion, education has a quite direct, powerful and consistent influence on the formation of young adults' beliefs and values. It seems that pre-collegiate education experiences are particularly powerful in shaping alternative belief patterns and systems of values. Intensity of investment in education foreshadows a more engagement-oriented sense of life purpose and worldviews and theodicies that are not simply the dominant beliefs.

Both science and the humanities continue to offer alternatives for how individuals construct personal theologies. Science education is a notably strong influence on personal theology. Deeper exposure to science fosters adaptations in basic ideological assumptions by introducing the possibilities of a more positive view of the world, a deeper and broader sense of life purpose, and an abandonment of a cosmic-deterministic theodical orientation. The oppositional effects of science education and religious involvement found in several parts of this study suggest that two different systems of meaning are competing – and that resolution and adaptation between the two systems are far from complete. Science's positioning *vis-à-vis* religion has especially been as an alternative rather than compatible view of reality, and its influence is exerted primarily in the culturally ubiquitous institutions of child and adolescent education. However, an immersion in science does not necessarily produce greater depth or clarity in beliefs and values. More scientifically oriented young adults who express randomistic theodicies can often be as philosophically thin in their thinking as more singularly religious young adults with deterministic theodicies, bordering on a kind of fatalism rooted in a folk-like assent to a 'law of probabilities'. This suggests that further exposure to critical thinking and to the implications of different beliefs and values would be helpful in strengthening young people's processes of meaning-making. Science educators who address issues of philosophical and theological meaning-making will have a marked effect on the clarity and depth of young adults' beliefs and values – particularly if they handle discussion with sensitivity and respect for the original theological orientations of the communities, families and religious heritages of individuals, and if they encourage continued conversation with others beyond the classroom on matters of meaning about the world, the good and humanity's place and purpose in the world.

Counselling

World-concepts are potentially as important as self-concepts of well-being and purposive life for young adults. To gain insight into how people order their priorities and interpret events in their lives, counsellors might ask questions about personal theologies that help illuminate how young adults see the nature of existence and its purposes and goods. These beliefs and values might be as important as self-perceptions to discuss and test in counselling sessions with people who seem trapped by the ways they make meaning – and with people who have struggled to find ways to construct meaning. In the absence of meaning about the world, meaning about oneself is at best atomistic and rootless. Counsellors of all sorts, both secular and religious, in schools and military and employment settings and private offices, can benefit from a wider picture of human *being* as encompassing both figure and ground – the formed and forming ideas about identity and place, self and world, who and where.

Citizenship

Personal theologies are important for how people see themselves as citizens of the world and of the nations, societies and communities in which they live. Do they contribute only as much as necessary, awaiting eventual deliverance to a better world? Do they take privilege as entitlement and view their lives as a series of inconsequential accidents, opting for paths of moment-to-moment pleasure, with little regard for the broader world? Do they become overwhelmed by problems too great for them and opt for withdrawal into a cocoon of localized relationships? Do they see potentials and barriers in conflict, and imagine and pursue ways of making the world better for others?

Places that provide significant venues for these kinds of reflections include service-learning initiatives of schools and universities, and social outreach and public religious engagement programmes of religious organizations and communities. Other places of public service, such as military service, longer-term volunteer work with, for example, Americorps or other such organizations, and domestic and foreign mission efforts can help young adults stretch and clarify their beliefs about the world, ultimate causes, life purpose and ultimate values. Leaders in government, business, social service, the arts and the military can collaborate with educational and religious organizations to create strong, high-impact experiences of action-reflection that help people discover and articulate their understanding of the connection between theology and citizenship, and of how their beliefs and values are intimately related to their use of resources and capacities for the sake of themselves and others.

Continuing the Conversation

In the face of all the upheavals faced from generation to generation, young adults' deepest beliefs and values shaping the philosophical foundations of personal theologies have been remarkably stable across generations in America. Major shifts in culture do not automatically produce changes in the personal theologies of different generational cohorts. For the most part, they did not change significantly across forty years among American young adults.

Nor do they appear to have changed dramatically since the turn of the millennium. Since 2000, I have continued interviewing young adults. In 2003, I visited two groups of Christian young adults – one a group of 50 African-American students involved together in a large campus ministry on a state university campus in the North-east, the other a group of 25 white and Latino volunteers living as interns in a Jesuit Volunteer Corps house in the Midwest. These were tightly knit groups, drawn together around common purposes of spiritual and psychological development, care for one another and contribution to society. I asked them the same questions I had asked young adults in the *Making the Transition* study – and heard surprisingly similar responses. These deeply religious young adults expressed similar worldviews, theodicies, values and senses of life purpose –this time, in relation to 9/11, Iraq, ecology and the traumas of life in American inner cities.

Since 2005, I have sent students out from my seminary classes and my religion and social science courses to talk to young adults in various American metropolitan neighbourhoods. I have asked them to listen for how young adults are constructing meaning not just about themselves but about the world in which they find themselves. The graduate students in my classes craft their own interview and conversation questions, but they also use the core questions I explored in *Making the Transition*, to see how young adults articulate their own deeper philosophical theologies. Consistently, student groups return from their brief ethnographic work to reveal a similar pattern of beliefs and values – whether among college students, young professionals, young service and blue-collar workers, or graduate students.

This simple exercise helps theology students and social science students learn that, in general, young adults willingly enter such conversations, show some depth of thought and struggle with questions of meaning-making, and are able, when invited, to express their beliefs and values about the world, ultimate causes, human place and purpose in the world, and the good. It helps students learn that people actually are theologians, or constructors of meaning about the ground of being. It exposes them to the variability in personal theologies, and the value of these personal theologies to the people expressing them. It gives them a capacity as rising scholars, teachers and religious leaders to do the work of listening for local theology in particular communities and personal theology among individuals. They join the practices encouraged by scholars – such as Robert Emmons and Kristen Monroe in their work on personal values and ethics, Robert Schreiter and Donald Sedmak who have spelled out the practices of discerning local theologies, David Heller and Rebecca Nye in their work learning about children's spirituality and personal theologies of God, and Joyce Mercer and Patricia Lyons in their careful interviews with youth about faith, ethic, and purpose – who all share a commitment to open-ended inquiry and an assumption that people – whether older adults, young adults, youth, or children – are capable of articulating deep philosophical and theological beliefs if given the opportunity and the right means to do so.

When young adults wrestle theologically, they encounter something beyond themselves and their known assumptions. If they come to know what they meet as the fates of time and probability, this has its own consequence for action. If they come to know what they meet as a God who creates order with benevolent purpose, this also has its own consequences. But once worlds have collided, life cannot easily be the same as it was. Whether in foxholes or in households, in classrooms, on the job or on the street, young adults come face to face with the limits of their own assumptions. They may find themselves lost. They may stop to listen. And then, theology becomes personal. The adventure of meeting and making meaning begins.

Appendix A
Adapted Life-Values Survey[1]

Please organize the following list of 18 values into 5 groups, based on how important the values are to you. Work slowly and think carefully, and use a pencil. Write each *italicized* word in one of the boxes below (there is one extra space). If you change your mind, feel free to change your answers. The end result should truly show how you really, honestly feel.

Most important	Quite important	Somewhat valuable	Not that important	Really not important

A *Comfortable* Life (a prosperous life)

A Sense of *Accomplishment* (lasting contribution)

A World of *Beauty* (beauty of nature and the arts)

Family *Security* (taking care of loved ones)

Happiness (contentedness)

Mature *Love* (sexual and spiritual intimacy)

Pleasure (an enjoyable, leisurely life)

Self-Respect (self-esteem)

True *Friendship* (close companionship)

An *Exciting* Life (a stimulating, active life)

A World at *Peace* (free of war and conflict)

Equality (brotherhood, equal opportunity)

Freedom (independence, free choice)

Inner *Harmony* (freedom from inner conflict)

National Security (*Protection* from attack)

Salvation (eternal life, security for one's soul)

Social *Recognition* (respect, admiration)

Wisdom (a mature understanding of life)

---

[1]   Milton Rokeach, *The Nature of Human Values* (New York: The Free Press, 1973), adapted for Q-sort methodology by David Gortner, 1999.

Below is another list of 18 values. Please arrange them in the table below, as you did for the list above.

Most important	Quite important	Somewhat valuable	Not that important	Really not important

Ambitious (hard-working, aspiring)
Capable (competent, effective)
Clean (neat, tidy)
Forgiving (willing to pardon others)
Honest (sincere, truthful)
Independent (self-reliant, self-sufficient)
Logical (consistent, rational)
Obedient (dutiful, respectful)
Responsible (dependable, reliable)

Broadminded (open-minded)
Cheerful (light-hearted, joyful)
Courageous (standing up for your beliefs)
Helpful (working for the welfare of others)
Imaginative (daring, creative)
Intellectual (intelligent, reflective)
Loving (affectionate, tender)
Polite (courteous, well-mannered)
Self-Controlled (restrained, self-disciplined)

Proposed Personal Theologies Questionnaire for Research and Development

Each section of the following questionnaire poses a 'big question' about the world, life and human purpose. Following each question are a series of responses that other people have stated. Please rate your level of agreement or disagreement with each response, indicating which responses are more or less in line with how you would respond to each 'big question'.

[Note to questionnaire administrators: It is expected that types of responses to each 'big question' will be shuffled, for instance, mixing negative and positive worldview responses.]

Worldview Optimism/Pessimism

Think for a minute about the world as you know it. How do you make sense of the world? What do you do to make sense of the world? What kind of a place is the world, in general?

Negative Worldview (32)	Disagree 1 2 3	Agree 4 5 6 7

The world is scary.

Sometimes when you just think about the world it's so depressing.

The world could be better.

The world is cluttered with people and they can't get along.

There are some horrible, horrible parts of the world.

The world is steadily getting worse.

People are massacring others, doing things that are totally inhumane.

I think there is, right now, more bad in this world than anything good.

Too many people are dying in this world.

When I think about the world, I think about disasters.

There are a lot of bad things happening in the world.

1 2 3 4 5 6 7

People act in their own best interest, and that leads to problems.

People's priorities are kind of mixed up.

People are working and looking out for themselves.

The world is a lonely place.

Human society is quite awful, in many respects.

There are intolerable amounts of unhappiness and despair in many parts of the world.

Parts of the world are economically very distressed.

There are always people who will try to stop you from moving forward.

The world is driven by money.

There are many places where people don't have freedom.

The world is steadily getting worse.

When I think about the world, I think about human cruelty.

It is a dog-eat-dog world.

It is an unjust world.

It is difficult to make people hear each other.

One should never underestimate the stupidity of humankind as a whole.

The world is going to shit.

The world is decaying.

It is hard to make sense of what is going on in the world.

It is hard for me to believe that people are inherently good.

The world is brutal.

Positive Worldview (27)	Disagree					Agree	
	1	2	3	4	5	6	7

The world is not really bad.

The world is beautiful.

You'll always find a way for yourself in this world.

The world is not as bad as it can seem.

There are some amazing parts of the world.

The small part of the world where I exist is a good place.

When I think about the world, I think of resorts and places of escape.

1 2 3 4 5 6 7

People have learned to look at other viewpoints than just their own.

A lot of people work for the betterment of society.

The world is a safe place.

The world is a very positive place.

The world is changing for the better.

When I think about the world, I think about experiences with friends.

I have faith in people.

People can make a difference in what the world is like.

A lot of people are working to make the world better.

When I think about the world, I think about people being fair and just.

It is a rational world.

I just find myself to be in a very lucky place in the world right now.

In most places in the world, you have a lot of freedom.

It is hard for me to believe that people are inherently bad.

In this world, you are generally rewarded for the work you do.

Never in any point in history has there been more potential for good.

Most people are normal.

There are many bright spots in this world.

Things are moving forward in the world.

The world is wonderful.

Theodicy

Say something bad – terrible, tragic, unexpected – happens in your life, or to someone you know. Think about that kind of event for a minute. How do you understand or make sense of life when things are going really badly?

Deterministic – Personal Deity (12)	Disagree Agree 1 2 3 4 5 6 7

I think that God has a plan.

God and Satan and angels and spiritual forces we can't see affect everybody's lives.

1 2 3 4 5 6 7

What happens is part of an ultimate divinely ordered plan.

There is a group of higher beings that manoeuvre events in our lives.

What happens in the material world is affected by what happens in the spiritual world.

God has a reason for what happens.

God doesn't put anything in our paths that we cannot handle.

When the path to something you have hoped for is blocked, God is showing you that it is not meant for you to have it.

Higher beings mess with our lives every now and then.

Bad things happen because of the Devil.

No particular force or deity is pushing all the events in life to happen. (reverse code)

In life, it seems like something, somewhere kind of rolls the dice for you.

Deterministic – Non-personal (20)

Disagree   Agree
1 2 3 4 5 6 7

I try to think of the reason that something has happened.

Everything out there is happening for a purpose.

There may be a reason, but it is unexplainable, for what has happened.

I try to learn from what happens.

Sometimes, you have numerous things happen to you that cause you to learn one lesson.

There is something out of every event that you need to learn.

I do wonder if certain things are predetermined or if there are certain variables that are preset.

Everything happens for a reason.

If it had not happened, then something else would not have happened.

We are on this earth to learn.

If you don't have challenges, then you will not be as strong a person.

Every bad experience makes me have a better perspective on life.

Some things happen for a reason.

Everything is interrelated - so, with everything that happens, something else happens because of it.

1 2 3 4 5 6 7

That which does not kill us makes us stronger.

Every event, whether it be good or tragic, is something where we
can learn and grow from it.

You become a better person with every bad experience.

For any event in my life, I can see how if it had not happened,
then something else would not have happened.

The idea that events in the future can in some way shape or
explain events that happen now, doesn't make sense to me.
[reverse code]

There are certain variables that are preset.

Humanistic (12)	Disagree Agree 1 2 3 4 5 6 7

Some things happen because people deserve them.

You have opportunities to make what you want of any situation
that comes your way.

Ultimately you can choose your own way, regardless of what
happens.

The way that you play the game is really the important part of
anything that happens.

I had some control over events and that's why they happened as
they did.

Every event has its own separate causes which you can trace to a
certain extent.

We were created with a choice in our individual lives.

We give purpose to things that happen.

Things that happen in life emerge from what has come before.

People set themselves up for the things that happen to them.

You have control over some event and situations that happen.

Even if some circumstances or qualities in your life are set, the
rest is up to you.

Randomistic (13)	Disagree Agree 1 2 3 4 5 6 7

People sometimes have bad luck.

I do not think that anything is totally predetermined – you just go
along with what happens.

                                                                    1 2 3 4 5 6 7

Some things happen randomly.

You are dealt whatever cards come your way.

You cannot justify or explain everything that happens.

Life follows the law of averages – things happen, and eventually
  they may happen to you.

Nothing causes things to happen – no one and nothing is in charge.

Some things are just coincidence.

For the most part, tragic events do not have any logic or sense to
  them.

There is no way to make sense of tragic events in life.

When shit happens, it is simply shit – shit is happening – and
  there is no explanation beyond that.

Bad things can happen at any time.

You consider yourself fortunate every day that tragedies or
  traumas do not happen to you.

Purpose/Place in World

What do you see as your place in the world? How do you 'fit' into the world?

Ignore the World (9)	**Disagree Agree** **1 2 3 4 5 6 7**

I've never actually thought about the world and my relationship
  to it.

I do not feel I have any great duty to the world for any purpose.

There is nothing you or I can do about the world.

I just live my life and do not think about the world much.

In the world, what happens, happens.

The world is just there, regardless of me and my life.

One person does not matter or make a difference.

I am the centre of my own world.

I am small in the scheme of things.

Retreat from the World (9)	**Disagree** **Agree**
	1 2 3 4 5 6 7

My main focus is to worry about myself and not about the world.

I am not involved personally in situations in the world, so I do not need to contribute time, money, or effort.

I play a passive role, and that is how I fit in the world.

We are to a large degree alienated from the world and each other.

My purpose in the world is to make what I want of myself.

I don't think that every person necessarily has to have some kind of purpose.

Generally, I live to do what is best for me.

I aim to be a hermit, to escape society.

I am nobody special, I am just here to get through the life.

Define Purpose through Close Relationships (9)	**Disagree** **Agree**
	1 2 3 4 5 6 7

I'm a people, people person, here for the people I know.

My primary place is being a role model for my children and family.

I try to be a friend, in a way that is mutually good.

My place in the world is in a network of personal relationships of family and friends today.

I find place and purpose with my family.

I dedicating myself to my family and friends more than to anything else.

I aim for positive relationships and for helping the people I know see the positive side of things.

As a parent, I'm shaping the future – at least for my own children.

I don't know that I want to sacrifice myself for humanity if it means taking myself away from love.

Define Purpose through Career, Job, or Societal Role (9)	**Disagree** **Agree**
	1 2 3 4 5 6 7

I'm a subordinate in society, no more than that.

I am a citizen of the United States *[or other country]*.

I coach or mentor others through my role at work.

I aim to offer my best at the job I do.

1 2 3 4 5 6 7

I find purpose primarily in work that I enjoy and that accomplishes something.

I find my purpose in trying to improve things or make things run more smoothly.

I am a cog, a small contributor, in the big machinery that makes this country run.

I dedicate myself through work that I like and can succeed at.

I find my sense of fitting into the world when I am making something that people use.

Engage Directly in the World (9)	Disagree Agree 1 2 3 4 5 6 7

I aim to make a difference in the quality of people's lives.

I dedicate myself to making a difference in the lives of younger people.

My place in the world is through active involvement in the work of charity, relief, or development.

I find purpose primarily by serving my community and giving something back to my community.

I seek to have an effect on this world that is greater than just because I exist.

As a human being, my purpose is to help other people beyond only my family and friends.

I aim to contribute actively to peace and good in the world, beyond only my family and friends.

I play an active role in the lives of others by setting a good example and being a role model.

A part of my place in the world is in leading others.

Index

Page references to illustrated matter are in **bold**.